Canadian Cases in Business Law

Deborah Meredith

University of British Columbia

Ellen McIntosh

University of British Columbia

Prentice Hall

Toronto

National Library of Canada Cataloguing in Publication

Meredith, Deborah Jean, 1950-
    Canadian Cases in business law / Deborah Meredith, Ellen McIntosh.

ISBN 0-13-093123-3

1. Commercial law—Canada—Cases. I. McIntosh, Ellen, 1960-
II. Title.

KE1388.5.M47 2003   346.7101   C2002-902883-3
KF1415.ZA2M49 2003

ISBN 0-13-093123-3

Vice President, Editorial Director: Michael J. Young
Senior Acquisitions Editor: Kelly Torrance
Marketing Manager: Deborah Meredith
Developmental Editor: Jennifer Murray
Production Editor: Judith Scott
Copy Editor: Bonnie DiMalta
Production Coordinator: Andrea Falkenberg
Page Layout: Heidi Palfrey
Cover and Interior Design: Anthony Leung
Cover Image: Digital Vision

1 2 3 4 5   07 06 05 04 03

Printed and bound in Canada.

Contents

Table of Cases

List of Citations

Caselaw Reporters

AC	Appeal Cases (British)
APR	Atlantic Provinces Reports
AR	Alberta Reports
BCAC	British Columbia Appeal Cases
BCLR	British Columbia Law Reports
BLR	Business Law Reports
CCC	Canadian Criminal Cases
CCEL	Canadian Cases on Employment Law
CCLI	Canadian Cases on the Law of Insurance
CCLT	Canadian Cases on the Law of Torts
CELR (NS)	Canadian Environmental Law Reports (New Series)
CECR	Canadian Environmental Law Reporter
CLR	Construction Law Reports
CPC	Carswell's Practice Cases
CPR	Canadian Patent Reporter
CR	Criminal Reports
CRR	Canadian Rights Reporter
DLR	Dominion Law Reports
DTC	Dominion Tax Cases
ER	English Reports
ETR	Estates and Trusts Reporter
FC	Canada Law Reports, Federal Court
FCA	Federal Court of Appeal Reports
ICR	Insurance Law Reporter
KB	King's Bench (British)
Man. R.	Manitoba Reports
MPLR	Municipal and Planning Law Reports
MVR	Motor Vehicle Reports
NBR	New Brunswick Reports
Nfld. and PEIR	Newfoundland and Prince Edward Island Reports
NR	National Reporter
OAC	Ontario Appeal Cases
OR	Ontario Reports
RPR	Real Property Reports
SCR	Supreme Court Reports
Sask. R.	Saskatchewan Reports
WAC	Western Appeal Cases
WWR	Western Weekly Reports

Alberta: http://www.albertacourts.ab.ca

British Columbia: http://www.courts.gov.bc.ca/

Ontario: http://www.ontariocourts.on.ca/

Supreme Court of Canada: http://www.lexum.umontreal.ca/

Federal Court: http://www.fja.gc.ca/

QUICKLAW Reporters

AJ	Alberta Judgments
BCJ	British Columbia Judgments
FCJ	Federal Court Judgments
MJ	Manitoba Judgments
NJ	Newfoundland Judgments
SCJ	Supreme Court Judgments
SJ	Saskatchewan Judgments

Edupage is a service of EDUCAUSE, an international nonprofit association dedicated to transforming education through information technologies.
LISTSERV@LISTSERV.EDUCAUSE.EDU

Tables of Correspondence

Preface

In a Common Law system such as ours, cases serve not just as an illustration of legal principles, but as a source. Judges enunciate the law based on particular facts, and the law is refined and developed relative to new cases with their own unique facts. In the classroom, reading court decisions is crucial to understanding where business law comes from and how it works. Reading decisions also serves to bring material to life and make it interesting.

In this book, we have assembled recent cases from all levels of courts across Canada. We have chosen these cases because they have engaging facts that business students should find relevant, and because they highlight key legal concepts applicable to business. Where feasible, the whole case has been reproduced, in order to give students as complete a picture as possible of the judge's legal reasoning and the specific facts on which it was based.

Undoubtedly, e-commerce will play a greater role in the way people do business. We have tried to include what useful cases are available to date in e-commerce areas. Some relate to timing and place of acceptance, place of the contract, and intellectual property issues such as protection of domain names. As e-commerce has its day in court, there will be cases in other areas, such as enforceability and scope of non-competition agreements where the Internet is used as a marketing tool. Some key questions for future courts will involve assessing authenticity of e-mail messages and validity of signatures. The response to many of these emerging issues will have to be addressed by our legislators.

We hope this book engages students in critical thinking and promotes the development of analytical tools that make their business law course not only intellectually stimulating, but one that they find directly relevant to their business studies and future careers.

About the Authors

Deborah J. Meredith has a BA (Hons) from McGill University and an LLB and LLM from the Faculty of Law at the University of British Columbia. She practised corporate-commercial and real estate law in Vancouver before becoming a member of the Faculty of Commerce at the University of British Columbia where she has, for many years, taught Commercial Law, Real Estate Law, and the Law and International Business Transactions to undergraduate and graduate students, as well as to executive and professional groups from Canada, China, Korea, and Liechtenstein.

Ellen J. McIntosh has a Bachelor of Laws degree from the University of British Columbia and a Master of Laws degree from the University of Alberta. She has recently completed the TAG Certificate Program on Teaching and Learning in Higher Education at the University of British Columbia. She practised corporate-commercial law and continues to practise law as a mediator. As a member of the Faculty of Commerce at the University of British Columbia, Ellen teaches Commercial Law, the Law of Business Associations, and Real Estate Law to undergraduate students, graduate students, and professional groups.

part one

The Law in its Social Context

chapter one

The Law and Society

Ramsden v. Peterborough (City)

[1993] 2 S.C.R. 1084, S.C.J. No. 87, 2 SCR 1084, 15 OR (3d) 548, 106 DLR (4th) 233, 156 NR 2, 66 OAC 10, 23 CR (4th) 391, 16 CRR (2d) 240, 16 MPLR (2d) 1

Supreme Court of Canada on appeal from the Court of Appeal for Ontario

June 1, 1993

Present: Lamer C.J. and La Forest, L'Heureux-Dube, Sponka, Gonthier, Cory, McLachlin, Iacobucci and Major JJ.

The following case shows how the Canadian Charter of Rights and Freedoms can operate to limit what municipal government can accomplish under a by-law. The extent and definition of the rights and freedoms established under the Charter is subjective and requires interpretation by the courts, so many cases involving the Charter have reached the Supreme Court of Canada.

The judgment of the Court was delivered by

1   **IACOBUCCI J.**:— This appeal concerns the constitutional validity of a municipal by-law prohibiting all postering on public property. The issue is whether the absolute ban on such postering infringes the Charter guarantee of freedom of expression, and if so whether that infringement is justified under s. 1 of the Canadian Charter of Rights and Freedoms.

I.   Background

2   As a means of advertising upcoming performances of his band, the respondent, on two occasions, affixed posters on hydro poles in contravention of By-law No. 3270 of the city of Peterborough. On both occasions, the respondent was charged under the Provincial Offences Act, R.S.O. 1980, c. 400, with an offence under the by-law. The respondent did not deny committing the offences but took the position that the by-law was unconstitutional because it was inconsistent with s. 2(b) of the Canadian Charter of Rights and Freedoms. The respondent was convicted by a Justice of the Peace who found that the by-law did not violate the Charter.

3   The respondent appealed to the Provincial Court on an agreed statement of facts. The parties agreed that postering on utility poles can constitute a safety hazard to workers climbing them and a traffic hazard if placed facing traffic. The parties also agreed that abandoned posters or those left for an unreasonable length of time may constitute visual and aesthetic blight and contribute to litter. The respondent's appeal to the Provincial Court was dismissed. His further appeal to the Court of Appeal was allowed by a majority of the members of the court who found that the by-law infringed the respondent's freedom of expression and was not justifiable under s. 1 of the Charter. Accordingly, the respondent's convictions were set aside and acquittals were entered.

4   On appeal to this Court, Chief Justice Lamer stated the following constitutional questions:

1.   Do ss. 1 and 2 of the Corporation of the City of Peterborough By-law 3270 (as amended by By-law 1982-147) limit the right guaranteed by s. 2(b) of the Canadian Charter of Rights and Freedoms?

2.   If the answer to question 1 is yes, are such limits demonstrably justified pursuant to s. 1 of the Charter?

II.   Relevant Legislative Provisions

5   In 1937, the city of Peterborough enacted By-Law No. 3270. In its original form, it read as follows:

1.   No bill, poster or other advertisement of any nature whatsoever shall be placed on or attached to or caused to be placed on or attached to any tree situate on any public street, highway or thoroughfare within the limits of the City of Peterborough or any pole, post, stanchion or other object which is used for the purpose of carrying the transmission lines of any telephone, telegraph or electric power company situate on any public street, highway or thoroughfare within the limits of the City of Peterborough.

6   In 1982, s. 1 of the by-law was amended by By-law No. 1982-147 as follows:

1.   No bill, poster, sign or other advertisement of any nature whatsoever shall be placed on or caused to be placed on any public property or placed on or attached to or caused to be placed or attached to any tree situate on any public property within the limits of the City of Peterborough or any pole, post, stanchion or other object which is used for the purpose of carrying the transmission lines of any telephone, telegraph or electric power company situate on any public property within the limits of the City of Peterborough.

7   Section 2 of the by-law reads as follows:

2.   *Every person who contravenes this by-law is guilty of an offence and liable upon summary conviction to a penalty not to exceed Two Thousand Dollars ($2,000.00) exclusive of costs for each and every such offence.*

III.   Canadian Charter of Rights and Freedoms

1.   *The Canadian Charter of Rights and Freedoms guarantees the rights and freedoms set out in it subject only to such reasonable limits prescribed by law as can be demonstrably justified in a free and democratic society.*

2.   *Everyone has the following fundamental freedoms:*

(b)   *freedom of thought, belief, opinion and expression, including freedom of the press and other media of communication;*

[Review of judgments in the courts below has been omitted].

IV.   Issues

18   The issues raised on this appeal are whether an absolute ban on postering on public property infringes freedom of expression, and if so whether that infringement is justified under s. 1.

V.   Analysis

A.   Section 2(b) of the Charter

19   Under *Irwin Toy* [[1989] 1 SCR 927] there are two basic steps in the s. 2(b) analysis. First, one must determine [page 1096] whether the activity at issue falls within the scope of s. 2(b). This first step is itself a two-part inquiry. Does postering constitute expression? If so, is postering on public property protected by s. 2(b)? Under the second step of the s. 2(b) analysis, one must determine whether the purpose or effect of the by-law is to restrict freedom of expression.

1. Does Postering Constitute Expression?

20   Under *Irwin Toy*, supra at pp. 968-69, the first question to be asked in a case involving s. 2(b) is whether the activity conveys or attempts to convey a meaning. This is an easy inquiry in the present case, and indeed the appellant city of Peterborough

has properly conceded that the respondent was engaging in expressive activity through the use of posters to convey a message. In the Court of Appeal, Krever J.A. held at pp. 291-92 that "[i]n informing the public, or those members of the public who read the [respondent's] posters, of a coming musical performance the posters conveyed a meaning". Postering has historically been an effective and relatively inexpensive means of communication. Posters have communicated political, cultural and social information for centuries. In *Ford v. Quebec* (Attorney General), [1988] 2 S.C.R. 712, this Court held that a law requiring public signs and posters to be printed only in French violated s. 2(b). Implicitly, this decision held that public signs and posters are a form of expression protected by s. 2(b). Regardless of whether the posters concerned constitute advertising, political speech or art, it is clear that they convey a meaning. Therefore, the first part of the s. 2(b) test is satisfied.

2. Is Postering on Public Property Protected by s. 2(b)?

21   The second question in the s. 2(b) inquiry is whether postering on public property falls within the scope of s. 2(b). In Committee for the Commonwealth [page 1097] of Canada there were three separate approaches articulated as to the appropriate standard to be applied to determine whether expressive activity falling prima facie within s. 2(b) and occurring on public property is constitutionally protected. While these approaches have been subject to some criticism, (see, for example, Michael Kanter, "Balancing Rights Under Section 2(b) of the Charter: Case Comment on Committee for the Commonwealth of Canada v. Canada" (1992), 17 Queen's L. J. 489; B. Jamie Cameron, "A Bumpy Landing: The Supreme Court of Canada and Access to Public Airports under Section 2(b) of the Charter" (1992), 2 Media & Communications L. Rev. 91), in my view it is neither necessary nor desirable to revisit Committee for the Commonwealth of Canada in the present case.

[Discussion of the different approaches taken by L'Heureux-Dube J., Chief Justice Lamer, and McLachlin J. in the Irwin Toy case have been omitted.]

32   In this case, one does not have to go further than the second value articulated in *Irwin Toy*, namely participation in social and political decision-making. As I noted above, posters have communicated political, cultural and social information for centuries. Postering on public property including utility poles increases the availability of these messages, and thereby fosters social and political decision-making. In *Re Forget*, supra, at pp. 557-58, McFadyen J. observed that

> after the invention of modern printing technology, posters have come to be generally used as an effective, inexpensive means of communication. Posters have been used by governments to publish notices dealing with health, immigration, voters' lists, recruitment of armies, etc. Posters have been used by political parties, private and charitable organizations and by individuals. They convey messages, give notice of meetings and fairs.... [I]n societies where the government tends to repress opposition ideas, posters are the only means of communicating opposition ideas to a large number of people.

33   In *Fink v. Saskatoon (City of)* (1986), 7 C.H.R.R. D/3431 at p. D/3440, a Saskatchewan [page 1102] Board of Inquiry found that a prohibition of postering in Saskatoon violated freedom of expression under the Saskatchewan Human Rights Code, S.S. 1979, c. S-24.1. In its decision, the Board referred to the evidence of the art historian Robert Stacey, author of *The Canadian Poster Book: 100 Years of the Poster in Canada* (at p. D/3440):

[Mr Stacey] testified it was early recognized that posters were an effective and inexpensive way of reaching a large number of persons. In order to be effective, posters of course must be affixed to a surface and publicly displayed. Posters are traditionally used by minority groups to publicize new ideas or causes. Posters are both a political weapon and an educational device. According to Mr. Stacey, one measure of the openness of a democratic society has been the willingness of the authorities to allow postering... . Posters are an economic way of spreading a message. Utility poles have become the preferred postering place since the inception of the telephone system... . Posters have always been a medium of communication of revolutionary and unpopular ideas. They have been called "the circulating libraries of the poor." They have been not only a political weapon but also a means of communicating artistic, cultural and commercial messages. Their modern day use for effectively and economically conveying a message testifies to their venerability through the ages.

34   I would adopt this characterization of the relationship between the message and the forum in the present case. In my view, it is clear that postering on public property, including utility poles, fosters political and social decision-making and thereby furthers at least one of the values underlying s. 2(b).

[Comments on the dissenting judgment of Galligan J.A. have been omitted.]

37   Therefore, I would conclude that, under any of the approaches proposed in Committee for the Commonwealth of Canada, the first step in the *Irwin Toy* analysis is satisfied. Postering on some public property, including the public property at issue in the present case, is protected under s. 2(b). [page 1104]. The focus then moves to the question of whether the purpose or effect of the by-law is to restrict freedom of expression.

3. The Purpose of the By-law

38   It seems evident that the by-law is aimed at the consequences of the particular conduct in question, and is not tied to content. On its face the by-law is content-neutral and prohibits all messages from being conveyed in a certain manner and at certain places. The by-law is directed at avoiding the consequences associated with postering, namely litter, aesthetic blight, traffic hazards and hazards to persons engaged in repair and maintenance. In *Irwin Toy Ltd.*, supra, at p. 975, Dickson C.J. noted that a rule against littering is not a restriction "tied to content". Rather, "[i]t aims to control the physical consequences of certain conduct regardless of whether that conduct attempts to convey meaning". The court below held that the purpose of the by-law is "meritorious" and not to restrict expression. I would agree.

4. The Effect of the By-law

39   In *Irwin Toy*, supra at pp. 976-77, Dickson C.J. discussed the burden on the individual seeking to establish that the effect of governmental action violates s. 2(b). After repeating the three principles and values underlying the protection of free expression in our society, he stated:

In showing that the effect of the government's action was to restrict her free expression, a plaintiff must demonstrate that her activity promotes at least one of these principles. It is not enough that shouting, for example, has an expressive element. If the plaintiff challenges the effect of government action to control noise, presuming that action to have a purpose neutral as to expression, she must show that her aim was to convey a meaning reflective of the principles underlying freedom of expression.

It is clear that the effect of the by-law is to limit expression. The absolute prohibition of postering [page 1105] on public property prevents the communication of political, cultural and artistic messages. The appellant did not dispute that the effect of the by-law is to restrict expression, but rather argued that postering on public property does not further any of the values underlying s. 2(b). As I have already concluded, the expression in question promotes political and social discourse, one of the underlying purposes of s. 2(b). Therefore, the respondent has established a violation of and the analysis now proceeds to s. 1.

B.   Section 1

40   The objective of the by-law is pressing and substantial. The by-law seeks to avoid littering, aesthetic blight, traffic hazards, and hazards to persons engaged in the repair and maintenance of utility poles. Similarly, the total ban is rationally connected to these objectives. By prohibiting posters entirely, litter, aesthetic blight and associated hazards are avoided.

41   The question therefore becomes whether the by-law restricts expression as little as is reasonably possible. The limitation at issue in the present case is a complete ban on postering on public property. In *Ford*, supra, at p. 772, the Court discussed the "distinction between the negation of a right or freedom and a limit on it". While the negation of a right or freedom does not necessarily require that such an infringement not be upheld under s. 1, "the distinction between a limit that permits no exercise of a guaranteed right or freedom in a limited area of its potential exercise and one that permits a qualified exercise of it may be relevant to the application of the test of proportionality under s. 1" (at p. 773). In *Ford*, the Court held that a complete prohibition on the use of languages other than French on commercial signs could not meet the requirements of the proportionality test, particularly the rational connection and minimal impairment branches. In contrast, in *Irwin Toy*, supra, the Court upheld substantial content-based restrictions [page 1106] (as opposed to a total ban) on advertising directed at children. It will therefore be more difficult to justify a complete ban on a form of expression than time, place or manner restrictions.

42   The U.S. Supreme Court considered a similar prohibition in Members of the City Council of *Los Angeles v. Taxpayers for Vincent*, 466 U.S. 789 (1984). Stevens J. for the majority of the court (Burger C.J. and White, Powell, Rehnquist and O'Connor JJ. concurring) accepted that the city's interest in avoiding visual clutter was sufficient to justify the complete prohibition on postering and that the ban curtailed speech no more than was necessary to accomplish its purpose. The majority rejected the argument that the public property concerned was a "public forum" protected by the First Amendment, or should be treated as a "public forum".

43   However, I find more helpful the dissent of Brennan J. (Marshall and Blackmun JJ. concurring) which discussed, at p. 830, less restrictive alternatives than a complete ban on postering:

> ... [the City] might actively create a particular type of environment; it might be especially vigilant in keeping the area clean; it might regulate the size and location of permanent signs; or it might reserve particular locations, such as kiosks, for the posting of temporary signs. Similarly, Los Angeles might be able to attack its visual clutter problem in more areas of the City by reducing the stringency of the ban, perhaps by regulating the density of temporary signs, and coupling that approach with additional measures designed to reduce other forms of visual clutter.

44   With regard to the objectives identified by the appellant in the present case, worker safety is only affected with posters attached to wooden utility poles. The by-law extends to trees, all types [page 1107] of poles, and all other public property. Traffic safety is only affected where posters are displayed facing roadways. The application of the by-law is not so restricted.

45   In *Re Forget*, supra, at p. 561, McFadyen J. suggested some alternatives to a total ban:

> ... such values might equally be preserved by regulating the location, size of posters, the length of time that a poster might remain in any location, the type of substance used to affix posters, and requiring that the posters be removed after a certain specified time. If necessary, a reasonable fee could be imposed to defray costs of administering such a system.

These kinds of alternatives could control the concerns of litter and aesthetic blight in a manner which is far less restrictive than the by-law. In my view, the total ban on postering public property does not impair the right as little as is reasonably possible—given the many alternatives to the appellant.

46   Moreover, the benefits of the by-law are limited while the abrogation of the freedom is total, thus proportionality between the effects and the objective has not been achieved. While the legislative goals are important, so is access to a historically and politically significant form of expression. I would agree with the majority of the Ontario Court of Appeal, at p. 294, on this point that "[a]s between a total restriction of this important right and some litter, surely some litter must be tolerated". Therefore, the by-law cannot be justified under s. 1.

VI.   Conclusion and Disposition

47   I would conclude, therefore, that under any of the approaches proposed in Committee for the Commonwealth of Canada, postering on some public property, including the public property at issue in the present case, is protected under s.2(b). Therefore the by-law is a limit on s. 2(b). This limit cannot be justified under s. 1 as it is overly broad and its impact on freedom of expression is disproportionate to its objectives.

48   For the foregoing reasons, I would therefore dismiss the appeal with costs, and answer the constitutional questions as follows:

1. Do ss. 1 and 2 of the Corporation of the City of Peterborough By-law 3270 (as amended by By-law 1982-147) limit the right guaranteed by s. 2(b) of the Canadian Charter of Rights and Freedoms?

Yes.

2. If the answer to question 1 is yes, are such limits demonstrably justified pursuant to s. 1 of the Charter?

No.

QUESTIONS

1. The court said that determination of whether or not there has been a violation of expression under s. 2 of the Charter is a two-step process. What are the two steps?
2. Did the court find that there had been a violation of s. 2 of the Charter? Explain.
3. How can s. 1 of the Charter operate to limit freedom of expression protected under s. 2?
4. Did the court find that the by-law could be justified under s. 1 of the Charter? Explain.
5. The objectives of the by-law were described as relating to safety and avoiding "aesthetic blight." Are there any ways in which the City of Peterborough could accomplish these objectives without infringing on s. 2 of the Charter? Explain.

R. v. Sharpe

[2001] 1 SCR 45, [2001] SCJ No.3, 2001 SCC 2, 194 DLR (4th) 1, 264 NR 201, [2001] 6 WWR 1, 146 BCAC 161, 88 BCLR (3d) 1, 150 CCC (3d) 321, 39 CR (5th) 72.

January 26, 2001

Supreme Court of Canada on appeal from the Court of Appeal for British Columbia

Present: McLachlin, C.J. and L'Heureux-Dube, Gonthier, Iacobucci, Major, Bastarache, Binnie, Arbour and LeBel JJ.

In this case, the Supreme Court of Canada decides that legislation that might be an unreasonable infringement on freedom of expression could be constitutional if the Court is prepared to infer that certain defences apply should the circumstances of the individual case warrant their application.

The judgment for the majority (McLachlin C.J., Iacobucci, Major, Binnie, Arbour and LeBel JJ.) was delivered by **MCLACHLIN C.J.** The following is a summary of her judgment.

In 1993 Parliament enacted new legislation relating to child pornography. Existing sections 163 and 172 in the Criminal Code had made it an offence to make, print, publish, distribute or circulate obscene material and to corrupt children. A new provision under section 163 (4) made it an offence to possess child pornography unless it had "artistic merit or an educational, scientific or medical purpose".

Mr. Sharpe was charged under section 163 (4). His defence was that the subsection was unconstitutional in that it infringed on section 2 of the Charter of Rights and Freedoms that protects freedom of expression. Mr. Sharpe's constitutional challenge was successful in both the Supreme Court of British Columbia and in the British Columbia Court of Appeal, but the crown appealed to the Supreme Court of Canada.

Six judges in the Supreme Court of Canada agreed that section 163 (4) does infringe on freedom of expression. They said that the real issue was whether the infringement could be justified under section 1 of the Charter as "a reasonable limit prescribed by law as can be demonstrably justified in a free and democratic society". Did society's interest in protecting children from the evils associated with the possession of child pornography justify the infringement?

Mr. Sharpe said no, because section 163 (4) catches material that poses no risk of harm to children. It could prohibit possession of drawings from the imagination, cartoons or computer generated material that does not involve actual children, and is produced solely for the use and enjoyment of the person who produced it. It could prohibit possession of pictures of real people taken for their own personal use.

The Court said that infringement of freedom of expression in the instances outlined by Mr. Sharpe would have to be justified under section 1 of the Charter as necessary to further the goal of preventing harm to children. To be justified under section 1, the goal, the Court said, must be "pressing and substantial, the law must be proportionate in the sense of furthering the goal, being carefully tailored to avoid excessive impairment of the right, and productive of benefits that outweigh the detriment to freedom of expression". The Court held that prevention of harm to children was indeed a pressing and substantial objective, and that in the vast majority of the law's applications the costs the law imposes on freedom of expression are outweighed by the risk of harm to children. However in the instances outlined by Mr. Sharpe, the infringement was found not to be justified because it could not be considered "proportionate in its effects".

The Court could have chosen to strike down the law, but questioned whether that would be appropriate where the law was substantially constitutional, but the accused could point to a hypothetical application far removed from his own case that might not be constitutional. As an alternative to that approach, the Court thought it should uphold the law because it would be constitutional in the vast majority of applications. It decided to read into the law an exclusion of problematic applications, namely self-created expressive material exclusively for the use of the creator, and private recordings of lawful sexual activity.

The case was referred back for trial on the charges.

QUESTIONS

1. What were the alternatives available to the Crown and government when the trial judge ruled that section 163 (4) was unconstitutional?

2. Do you think that the Crown and government made the right decision in pursuing an appeal? Can you see any drawbacks to this approach?

3. Do you agree with the majority decision in the Supreme Court of Canada?

4. Assume that the material Mr. Sharpe possessed consisted of:

    a. his own stories about sexual activity with children that he distributed using the Internet and

    b. pictures he possessed of real children involved in sexual activity that he kept for himself.

    Predict the outcome of the case after it was referred back for retrial.

Liebmann v. Canada (Minister of National Defence)

[2001] F.C.J. No. 1187, 2001 FCA 243

Federal Court of Appeal

July 31, 2001.

In the following case, it is s. 15 of the Charter that the appellant is using as the basis of his Charter challenge. His challenge is not to a law, but to a decision made by a representative of the Canadian Armed Forces.

1   **SEXTON J.A.:**— Lieutenant Andrew S. Liebmann was such a proven and accomplished member of the Canadian Forces' Naval Reserve that he was nominated for the important post of executive assistant to the Commander of the Canadian Forces Task Force in the Middle East during the Persian Gulf crisis. Nonetheless, he was not appointed to the position. The only objection taken to his nomination was his religion. He was Jewish. This appeal deals with his claim that the refusal to appoint him to the position to which he was nominated constituted discrimination contrary to s.15(1) of the Canadian Charter of Rights and Freedoms.

Facts

2   The appellant joined the Naval Reserve in 1983 and served in a variety of roles while completing a university degree and during subsequent employment as a public affairs specialist. By late 1990, he had attained the rank of Lieutenant and had qualified as a ship's officer of the watch and as a clearance diver. He was serving as an officer in HMCS Discovery, the Naval Reserve Division (or unit) in Vancouver. When the events giving rise to this litigation took place, he was employed by the government of British Columbia as a communications officer, serving his reserve commitment by attending at his unit several evenings a week.

3   On August 4, 1990, Iraq invaded and occupied Kuwait. During the weeks that followed, Canada commenced Operation Friction — the deployment of a contingent of military forces to the Persian Gulf region in order to enforce a number of resolutions passed by the United Nations Security Council pursuant to Chapter VII of the U.N. Charter. The contingent, known as Canadian Forces Middle East (CFME), was commanded by Commodore Kenneth Summers. His headquarters was in the Emirate of Bahrain. Part of the headquarters' establishment included an Executive Assistant (EA) on the commander's small personal staff.

4   At the time of CFME's deployment, Canada's commitment of forces was open-ended. As such, plans were developed to rotate personnel and units after a period of time so as to maintain the force at an optimum level of readiness. On December 24, 1990, the Commander of Maritime Command, who was responsible to the Chief of Defence Staff (CDS) for the generation of personnel to fill certain headquarters positions, caused a message to be sent to all Naval Reserve Divisions. A portion of that message called for nominations of officers qualified to fill the position of EA to the commander beginning in March 1991.

5   The appellant, who was highly motivated to participate in the Persian Gulf operation and who met all of the requirements set out in the message, was nominated for the EA position by his Commanding Officer. A message to that effect was sent on January 11, 1991.

6   The Maritime Command staff officers charged with recommending an officer for the EA position seem to have initially looked favourably upon the appellant's nomination. On January 21, 1991, they sent a message to the Directorate of Military Manning at National Defence Headquarters, recommending that the appellant be "hired" under a reserve force contract. The message indicated that he was being considered for the EA position. The Commanding Officer Naval Divisions (the commander of all naval reserve units) concurred in the recommendation. Upon receipt of a copy of this message, the appellant, with the assistance of the regular force Administration Officer at HMCS Discovery, began to make more specific preparations to deploy to Bahrain, following a set of "joining instructions" which had been faxed to him.

7   At some point during the same time period, the Maritime Command staff became aware that the appellant was Jewish.

8   At that time, the Canadian Forces had no formal policy regarding the consideration of personal characteristics such as religion in the selection of personnel for employment in non-peacekeeping operations. Several staff officers and their superiors at both Maritime Command and National Defence Headquarters allegedly dismissed the possibility that under the circumstances, the appellant's religion might have a detrimental impact upon his ability to effectively carry out the duties of the EA position and upon his personal safety. The result of these discussions was a decision that the appellant would not be selected for the position. In the end, the incumbent EA was not replaced.

9   The appellant was informed in late January or early February of 1991 that he had not been selected for the EA position. He was upset and disappointed. He contacted one of the staff officers who had participated in the decision-making process and was told that the superior officers had "decided that it was better not to send a Jew to the Middle East."

10   The appellant pursued several avenues of redress, finally bringing an action in the Trial Division of this Court. In his prayer for relief he sought a declaration that the process by which his nomination was considered had infringed his constitutional right to equality under the Canadian Charter of Rights and Freedoms as well as a number of statutory rights. He also sought declarations and injunctions relating to Canadian Forces Administrative Order (CFAO) 20-53, Policy for Employment of Canadian Forces Personnel on Peacekeeping Duty, which foresees the possibility that certain personnel may be restricted from participating in peacekeeping operations due to the "cultural, religious or other sensitivities of the parties or host country."

Decision Appealed From

11   Following a trial that covered eleven days of testimony and argument, the Trial Judge found that "[the appellant] more than adequately fulfilled the requirements for the posting," and that "the evidence clearly supports the [appellant's] allegation that he was not selected for the position of Executive Assistant because of his religion." He was "satisfied that Lieutenant Liebmann did have legitimate grievances with respect to the manner in which the defendants conducted themselves in the selection process." Despite these findings, he did not directly address the appellant's allegation that this conduct had infringed his right to equality.

12   The Trial Judge did give some consideration to the constitutionality of CFAO 20-53, finding that it was not contrary to the equality provisions of the Charter. However, he noted that since Operation Friction was not a peacekeeping mission, there was no basis for the application of either it or any other policy that preceded it to the appellant's situation. In the result, he dismissed the appellant's claim.

Issues

13   The appellant appeals to this Court, essentially repeating the claims made in the Court below. He is supported by two interveners who have focussed their submissions upon the constitutionality of CFAO 20-53 and the policies that preceded and succeeded it.

14   In my analysis, I will address the following issues:

    1. Should this Court inquire into the constitutionality of CFAO 20-53;

    2. Were the appellant's rights to equality under s. 15 of the Charter limited by the process by which his nomination for the EA position was considered; and

    3. If the appellant's equality rights were limited, were those limits "reasonable limits prescribed by law as can be demonstrably justified in a free and democratic society."

Relevant Constitutional Provisions

15   The Canadian Charter of Rights and Freedoms

1. The Canadian Charter of Rights and Freedoms guarantees the rights and freedoms set out in it subject only to such reasonable limits prescribed by law as can be demonstrably justified in a free and democratic society.

15.(1)   Every individual is equal before and under the law and has the right to the equal protection and equal benefit of the law without discrimination and, in particular, without discrimination based on race, national or ethnic origin, colour, religion, sex, age or mental or physical disability.

Analysis

Issue 1: CFAO 20-53, its Predecessors and Successors

16   The appellant and the interveners seek a declaration that CFAO 20-53, as it was amended, is unconstitutional. Further, they seek orders enjoining the Chief of

Defence Staff and his delegates from considering race, religion or ethnic origin in deciding whether a CF member will be deployed on an operational posting.

17   It is important to note that CFAO 20-53 was not applied to preclude the appellant from participating in Operation Friction. The order was not issued until March, 1991, over a month after the appellant's nomination for service with CFME was decided upon. Moreover, the policy set out in CFAO 20-53 applied only to the selection of personnel for peacekeeping operations. Operation Friction was not a peacekeeping operation. In fact, at the time the impugned decision was made, Canada was engaged in active hostilities against Iraq.

18   Thus, the order would not have applied to the selection of the appellant even if it had been in force in January and February of 1991. Similarly, screening policies contained in directives of the Deputy Chief of Defence Staff that were replaced with the promulgation of CFAO 20-53, all dealt expressly with peacekeeping operations and hence did not apply to the appellant's nomination. Indeed, the evidence of the decision-makers in the case at bar clearly demonstrates that they did not purport to apply any formal screening policy at all. The appellant and the respondents both concede this. Nonetheless, the appellants and interveners submit that the Court should hear and determine the constitutional challenge to CFAO 20-53.

[After analysis, which has been omitted, Sexton JA decided not to determine the constitutionality of CFAO 20-53 because it was not relevant to the outcome of this case.]

Issue 2:   The Appellant's Equality Rights

26   Section 15 of the Charter deals with a person's equality rights with respect to the "law". However, it is now well established that this term should not be given such a narrow meaning as to deprive individuals of protection from discrimination on the part of government actors. In *Slaight Communications Inc. v. Davidson*, [1989] 1 SCR 1038, the Supreme Court of Canada held that the Charter is applicable to administrative decisions made pursuant to statutory authority. Lamer J., as he then was, dissented in the result but wrote for a panel that was unanimous on this point:

> As the Constitution is the supreme law of Canada and any law that is inconsistent with its provisions is, to the extent of the inconsistency, of no force or effect, it is impossible to interpret legislation conferring discretion as conferring a power to infringe the Charter, unless, of course, that power is expressly conferred or necessarily implied. Such an interpretation would require us to declare the legislation to be of no force or effect, unless it could be justified under s. 1. Although this Court must not add anything to legislation or delete anything from it in order to make it consistent with the Charter, there is no doubt in my mind that it should also not interpret legislation that is open to more than one interpretation so as to make it inconsistent with the Charter and hence of no force or effect. Legislation conferring an imprecise discretion must therefore be interpreted as not allowing the Charter rights to be infringed. Accordingly, an adjudicator exercising delegated powers does not have the power to make an order that would result in an infringement of the Charter, and he exceeds his jurisdiction if he does so. (p. 1078).

27   In the more recent case of *Eldridge v. British Columbia (Attorney General)*, [1997] 3 SCR 624, the Supreme Court unanimously applied this approach to find that a decision made under a delegated statutory authority was contrary to s. 15.

28   In the case at bar, there was no selection policy to apply to the appellant's nomination and circumstances. However, the impugned decision was made under delegated statutory authority. The National Defence Act, RSC 1985, c. N-5, charges the CDS with the control and administration of all of the Canadian Forces:

> 18. (1) *The Governor in Council may appoint an officer to be the Chief of the Defence Staff, who shall hold such rank as the Governor in Council may prescribe and who shall, subject to the regulations and under the direction of the Minister, be charged with the control and administration of the Canadian Forces.*
>
> (2)   *Unless the Governor in Council otherwise directs, all orders and instructions to the Canadian Forces that are required to give effect to the decisions and to carry out the directions of the Government of Canada or the Minister shall be issued by or through the Chief of the Defence Staff.*

29   The Queen's Regulations and Orders provide a basis for the CDS's delegation of his authority to various officers. Thus, in this case, all of the officers involved in the process of considering the appellant's nomination were acting pursuant to the CDS's statutory authority to control and administer the Canadian Forces. As such, the decision to not appoint him to the EA position is subject to scrutiny under s. 15 of the Charter.

30   In the recent case of *Law v. Canada (Minister of Employment and Immigration)*, [1999] 1 SCR 497, the Supreme Court of Canada summarized the proper approach to a s. 15(1) analysis. Iacobucci J., writing for a unanimous Court, confirmed that the onus of establishing an infringement of a Charter right rests with the person claiming the right and outlined the following general approach:

> ... a court that is called upon to determine a discrimination claim under s. 15(1) should make the following three broad inquiries:
>
> (A) Does the impugned law (a) draw a formal distinction between the claimant and others on the basis of one or more personal characteristics, or (b) fail to take into account the claimant's already disadvantaged position within Canadian society resulting in substantively differential treatment between the claimant and others on the basis of one or more personal characteristics?
>
> (B) Is the claimant subject to differential treatment based on one or more enumerated and analogous grounds?
>
> (C) Does the differential treatment discriminate, by imposing a burden upon or withholding a benefit from the claimant in a manner which reflects the stereotypical application of presumed group or personal characteristics, or which otherwise has the effect of perpetuating or promoting the view that the individual is less capable or worthy of recognition or value as a human being or as a member of Canadian society, equally deserving of concern, respect, and consideration? (p. 548-549)

31   The Trial Judge's findings of fact establish that the appellant has made out the first two elements of the test. The decision-makers who considered the appellant's nomination drew a distinction between him and other members of the Canadian Forces, and subjected him to differential treatment on the basis of a personal characteristic – his religion. The respondents did not contest these findings before us.

32   There remains only to consider the final portion of the test: did the decision-makers' differential treatment of the appellant discriminate against him within the meaning of s. 15? In answering this question, the Court must bear in mind the purposes of the equality protection. These purposes were articulated by La Forest J. in *Andrews v. Law Society of British Columbia* [1989] 1 SCR 143 at 197 in a passage referred to by Iacobucci J. in Law:

> La Forest J. ... stated that the equality guarantee was designed to prevent the imposition of differential treatment that was likely to "inhibit the sense of those who are discriminated against that Canadian society is not free or democratic as far as they are concerned", and that was likely to decrease their "confidence that they can freely and without obstruction by the state pursue their and their families' hopes and expectations of vocational and personal development".

The inquiry into whether a person's dignity has been demeaned must be both subjective and objective, with the objective analysis considered from the perspective of a person in circumstances similar to those of the claimant.

33   In my opinion, the differential treatment of the appellant's nomination amounted to discrimination in the constitutional sense. The appellant testified that he had joined the Naval Reserve, in part :

> ... to do some national service and work with other Canadians from across Canada. I'm proud to be a Canadian citizen and Canada's been good to me and my family, and I wanted to give something back.

34   Through his seven years of training and professional development, the appellant acquired skills and knowledge that qualified him for the EA position for which he was nominated. However, by their actions, the decision-makers at Maritime Command and National Defence Headquarters denied the appellant the opportunity for professional and personal development that was presented by the position. He was also denied the benefit of applying his skills and knowledge in order to serve his country and the United Nations in an operational theatre.

35   There can be no doubt that the decision had a profound impact upon the appellant's human dignity, the very thing that s. 15(1) is meant to protect. The appellant testified that:

> ... up until that very point I thought that things were unlimited for me. ... and all of a sudden I found out that the really good jobs just weren't going to be open to me because I'm Jewish, because although I was good enough to join the forces and good enough to do jobs in Canada, I just wasn't Canadian enough to send overseas. ... I wasn't a good representative of my country.

> ... I was upset that I'd been selected for a job by the Navy and at the time and at that place I was the best person for the job.. but I [sic] was then overturned by somebody based only on hearing a German last name and checking out my religion. And so I was shattered in one way and angry in another.

36   On the basis of this evidence, the respondents concede that the appellant's dignity was demeaned in the subjective sense. However, while arguing that the objective portion of the analysis of the appellant's dignity had not been made out, counsel for the respondents was unable to point out how this could be so. Indeed, in my opinion, any reasonable observer in similar circumstances would conclude that the manner in which the appellant was treated did demean his dignity.

37   The record before the Court establishes that although the decision-makers allegedly felt that the appellant's religion might cause him to be less effective and less safe while carrying out his duties in an Arab state, they made little (if any) attempt to collect evidence that might validate or invalidate their concerns. There seems to have been no real consideration of the political climates of Bahrain or Saudi Arabia or the manner in which a Jewish Canadian officer might be perceived by military officials or citizens of those countries. In fact, one of the staff officers conducting an "appreciation" of the situation admitted to not having been aware of the politics of the region. No efforts were made to ascertain the views of any of the states in the Persian Gulf region. No attempt was made to determine the approaches being taken by other members of the coalition who were deploying forces to the region. In fact, the evidence shows that the United States had more Jewish personnel in the region than the total of all Canadian forces. In short, the analysis seems to have been conducted in a factual and evidentiary vacuum.

38   By confining whatever analysis they made to a simplistic "Jewish officer in an Arab state" model, the decision-making officers applied stereotypical thinking and based their decision upon presumed characteristics of both Jews and Arabs. This way of thinking had the effect, in essence, of imposing upon the appellant the burden of establishing that his religion would not have a detrimental impact upon either his safety or his ability to carry out his duties. It also had the effect of perpetuating the view that the appellant was a less worthy member of the Canadian Forces and, therefore, of Canadian society as a whole.

39   Therefore, I conclude that Chief of Defence Staff, through the actions of his delegates who considered the nomination of the appellant for the position of Executive Assistant to the Commander of CFME, limited his rights to equal treatment under the law and equal benefit of the law in a discriminatory manner, contrary to s. 15 of the Charter.

Issue 3:   Section 1

40   It only remains to determine whether the limitation of the appellant's equality rights imposed by the refusal to appoint him to the EA position because of his religion was a reasonable limit prescribed by law as can be demonstrably justified in a free and democratic society. At this stage of analysis, the burden falls upon the respondents to show, on the preponderance of probabilities, that the limitation was reasonable and demonstrably justified. [*R v. Oakes* [1986] 1 SCR 103 at 136]

41   In the case at bar, the respondents have failed to fulfill their burden. Their written submissions advanced no argument attempting to show that the impugned decision was reasonable or demonstrably justified. During the oral hearing, their counsel expressly told the Court that no such arguments would be advanced.

Conduct of the Respondents

42   There is one other aspect of the respondents' conduct that requires comment. Before the Trial Judge the respondents' evidence was that the appellant did not get the EA position because there was no position to fill. The respondents' pleadings were also to this effect. It appears that the respondents took the position that the decision not to send the appellant to the Gulf had nothing to do with his religion.

43   The Trial Judge did not believe the respondents' witnesses.

I am also satisfied that the evidence does not support the defendant's contention that the plaintiff did not get the position because there was no position to fill and that MARCOM was so advised some time on or about January 21, 1991. On the contrary, what the evidence demonstrates is that the extension of the current Executive Assistant's term of duty only arose after it became apparent that the defendants did not want to send Lieutenant Liebmann because of his religion but were concerned over the implications of letting the truth be known.

... Furthermore, the fact that the defendants continued processing [another nominee] for the position and advised him as late as February 4, 1991 that he would be going to the Middle East, negates their contention that the decision not to replace the current Executive Assistant was made during the third week of January 1991.

... Even the three people directly involved in the selection process for the position of Executive Assistant had no records or files of any kind, in spite of the plaintiff's stated intention of filing a grievance. The conduct of the respondents described by the Trial Judge calls for the disapproval of this Court.

44   It should go without saying that when the respondents are faced with a complaint of discrimination under section 15, the proper course of action is to face the issue squarely, make an honest assessment of whether the action taken was discriminatory and if it appears to be, whether it can be justified. Pleadings, evidence and argument must then be addressed to these issues.

Conclusion

45   I would allow that part of the appeal dealing with the process by which the respondents considered his nomination for the EA position. The appellant is entitled to a declaration that the refusal to select him for duty with CFME because of his religion was unconstitutional, being contrary to his rights to equality under the Canadian Charter of Rights and Freedoms. I would dismiss the other parts of the appeal.

46   I would order the respondents to pay the appellant's costs both at trial and in this appeal.

ROTHSTEIN J.A.:— I agree.

EVANS J.A.:— I agree.

QUESTIONS

1. Does the Charter apply to decisions of the Canadian Forces? Explain.
2. Which section of the Charter did Mr. Liebmann use to challenge the decision? What did he have to prove to show infringement of his Charter rights?
3. Why did the judge say that the "conduct of the respondents...calls for the disapproval of this Court"?
4. Assume that the appellant had been prevented from participating in a peacekeeping mission because of CFAO 20-53. Do you think that the appellant could show CFAO 20-53 to be invalid because it infringed the Charter?

chapter two

The Machinery of Justice

Hollick v. Toronto (City)

[2001] SCC 68, [2001] SCJ No. 67, 205 DLR (4th) 19, 277 NR 51, 24 MPLR (3d) 9, 13 CPC (5th) 1, 1530 AC 279, 42 CELR (NS) 26.

Supreme Court of Canada on appeal from the Court of Appeal for Ontario

October 18, 2001

Present: McLachlin C.J. and Gonthier, Iacobucci, Major, Bastarache, Binnie and Arbour JJ.

Class proceedings are a relatively recent innovation in many jurisdictions. Class proceedings allow a plaintiff to represent a class with the same cause of action against a defendant, and thereby minimize costs and the necessity for a multiplicity of court proceedings. In order to represent the class, the plaintiff must apply to court for permission.

The judgment of the Court was delivered by **MCLACHLIN C.J.** The following is a summary of the case and her judgment.

Hollick applied to be certified under Ontario's Class Proceedings Act 1992 SO 1992 c.6, as representative of 30,000 other residents living in Toronto in the vicinity of a landfill owned and operated by the City. He said the Keele Valley landfill had been unlawfully emitting onto his own land and the land of other class members large quantities of methane and other pollutants, loud noises and strong vibrations. He said that the class members form a well-defined group with a common interest and that the suit would best be prosecuted as a class action. As support, he said that in 1996 139 complaints were registered on Toronto's telephone complaint system. He sought on behalf of the class an injunction, $500 million in compensatory damages and $100 million in punitive damages.

The relevant sections of the Ontario Class Proceedings Act state as follows:

Section 5 (1) The court shall certify a class proceeding on a motion under section 2,3 or 4 if,

a) *the pleadings or the notice of application discloses a cause of action;*

b) *there is an identifiable class of two or more persons that would be represented by the representative plaintiff or defendant;*

c) *the claims or defences of the class members raise common issues;*

d) *a class proceeding would be the preferable procedure for the resolution of the common issues; and*

e) *there is a representative plaintiff or defendant who,*

   i) *would fairly and adequately represent the interests of the class,*

   ii) *has produced a plan for the proceeding that sets out a workable method of advancing the proceeding on behalf of the class and of notifying class members of the proceeding, and*

   iii) *does not have, on the common issues for the class, an interest in conflict with the interests of the other class members.*

Section 6 The court shall not refuse to certify a proceeding as a class proceeding solely on any of the following grounds:

1. *the relief claimed includes a claim for damages that would require individual assessment after determination of the common issues.*

2. *The relief claimed relates to separate contracts involving different class members.*

3. *Different remedies are sought for different class members.*

4. *The number of class members or the identity of each class member is not known.*

5. *The class includes a subclass whose members have claims or defences that raise common issues not shared by all class members.*

The motions judge found that Hollick had satisfied the certification requirement set out in the Act, and that he should be allowed to pursue his action as representative of the stated class. The Ontario Divisional Court overturned the certification order because it said that to satisfy the requirement that there be an identifiable class. He had to show that there was a class that could all pursue the same cause of action, meaning they must have suffered the interference with use and enjoyment of property Hollick complained of. The court concluded that even though 150 or so people had complained, it was unlikely that 30,000 members had the enjoyment of their properties interfered with. The court also said that there were no apparent common issues relating to the members of the class. Hollick appealed, but the Ontario Court of Appeal agreed with the Divisional Court that commonality had not been established.

Hollick then appealed to the Supreme Court of Canada. McLachlin C.J., delivering judgment for the Court, said that Hollick had disclosed a cause of action, and that he had defined a class by reference to objective criteria - a person is a member of the class if he or she owned or occupied property inside a specified area within a specified period of time. The class was bounded, and not unlimited. There was no doubt, she said, that if each of the class members had a claim against Toronto, they would have some aspect of the issue of liability in common. There was also evidence of some factual basis to support the cause of action.

What was not as clear, according to McLachlin C.J., was that a class procedure would be a preferable procedure for the resolution of common issues. The representative must show that the class action would be a preferable means of resolving claims over use of individual proceedings. To assess this, the Court must consider judicial economy, access to justice and behaviour modification. It was unlikely, she said, that pollution would be evenly distributed over a geographical area or time period. It was difficult to say that resolution of the common issue would significantly advance the legal action. Individual class members with substantial claims against Toronto would likely be willing to prosecute the claims individually, and if the claims were small, compensation could be available through Ontario's Small Claim Trust Fund. No claims had been made against that fund. Behaviour modification would not be advanced by a class action here.

McLachlin C.J. emphasized that although Hollick had not met the certification requirements here, that did not mean that the class action requirements could never be met in an environmental tort case. The question of whether an action should be permitted to be prosecuted as a class action turns on the facts of the individual case. The Court dismissed the appeal.

QUESTIONS

1.   What would the cause of action be in this case, and what would the plaintiffs have to prove?

2.   Why did the Court refuse to certify Hollick as representative of the class?

3.   Would someone seeking to represent a class bringing an action against the manufacturer of faulty breast implants, or victims of an air crash, be successful? Explain.

part two

Torts

chapter three

The Law of Torts

Poirier v. Murphy

[1986] B.C.J. No. 2374 , 36 CCLT 160.
British Columbia Supreme Court
February 17, 1986

Once the plaintiff has established that the defendant owed a duty to be careful to the plaintiff, that the defendant's conduct fell below the standard of care required in the situation, and that the conduct complained of caused some injury or loss to the plaintiff, negligence is established. Still, there may be some matters the defendant can raise in defense. *Poirier v. Murphy* examines some of these defenses.

MacKINNON J.:— On June 24, 1982 the plaintiff Peter Albert Poirier (Poirier) and the defendant John Anthony Murphy (Murphy), each 18 years of age, agreed to perform and in fact did carry out a "stunt" which resulted in Poirier being injured by the car driven by Murphy. With Poirier and Murphy, as passengers, were three girls and two boys, all around 17 years of age. They had been driving around with no particular destination and were looking for something to do. A conversation took place between Poirier and Murphy about doing a "stunt." The passengers were unaware of what this meant. However, they did hear Murphy asking Poirier to do it and Poirier refusing twice and then agreeing. The stunt was done in an underground parking lot of the Lougheed Mall in Coquitlam where Poirier would stand underneath a water sprinkler pipe and Murphy, as the driver of the car, from a position about 100 feet away, would drive towards Poirier and at the last moment Poirier would jump up, grab the pipe, do a chin-up, and swerve his hips and legs to one side, and thereby allow the car to pass under him. The expected clearance between Poirier's body and the car would be approximately four to six inches. It was intended to be thrilling to the participants and anybody watching. It was certainly a dangerous act. In the past, and on the occasion of the accident, the signal indicating that Poirier was ready for the stunt to commence was a slight nod by Poirier. It was to be seen only by Murphy. On observing the signal (the slight nod by Poirier) Murphy would drive the car toward Poirier and expect him to escape any impact.

At the outset it should be said that drinking was not involved in this accident. On the occasion of the accident the first stunt narrowly succeeded; the second did not. The car struck Poirier and he was thrown to the concrete floor and sustained a serious brain injury. He testified at trial but was unable to recall the circumstances immediately preceding the accident. However, Murphy and four of the passengers testified as to what occurred. The following is a short summary of what these witnesses testified as to how the accident occurred.

Murphy said he believed he asked if Poirier wanted to do the stunt, and that he agreed. He said that when the plaintiff gave him a nod, he proceeded at 20-23 miles per hour and, after he passed under him, he saw in his rear-view mirror that Poirier was standing facing him. He said that he backed the car up and proceeded to do the stunt again. On the second run, Poirier was standing in the same spot and when the car was about 20 feet away he jumped up and, as the car passed under the pipe, some part of his body hit the windshield. Murphy said he cannot explain why Poirier did not complete the jump so as to escape an impact.

In cross-examination Murphy testified that after the first stunt he backed the car up to where the plaintiff was standing. He and Poirier had a conversation, and then he backed the car to the original spot from whence he had commenced the first run. He said that it was not a matter of making a U-turn because you could not make a U-turn in the underground parking lot. He said that during the second run he looked at the speedometer to see that he was not going over 23 m.p.h. He has no recollection of anybody saying that Poirier was not ready. He said Poirier was standing facing him when he started the second run. Poirier was standing in front of the car, so he assumed that he knew the stunt was going to take place a second time. Murphy said that Poirier gave the signal (the nodding) on both the first and second run.

Mark Anderson testified that Murphy asked Poirier to do this stunt and Poirier refused on two occasions. He said that he and the others did not know anything about the stunt itself. Nothing was said between them about the stunt being done twice. On the first occasion Murphy drove at 20-25 m.p.h., and just before hitting Poirier he pulled himself up and the car passed underneath. Then Murphy made a 180° turn. "Poirier had his back to us, and the second time the defendant was going faster and Poirier couldn't pull himself up." This witness testified that on the first run he heard Poirier's shoes or sneakers hit the top of the roof. He was worried about this and, as Murphy started the second run, he told him to stop. He felt Poirier was not ready for the second stunt. As Murphy completed the U-turn, Poirier was swinging back and forth from the pipe with his back to them.

Linda Vogt, 17 years at the date of the accident, said that Murphy suggested a trick be done and Poirier said he didn't want to do it, but he was persuaded to go along with it. She described that the car was driven towards Poirier and he jumped and the car went underneath him. Then Murphy turned the car around and Poirier was standing on the ground and Murphy drove toward him again. She said that Poirier was not ready for this and, as a result, he hit the windshield and rolled over the back. She heard Mark say something about Poirier not being ready. In cross-examination she stated that she does not remember Mark saying that Pete was not ready, but she had that impression herself. She said that when the car started back on the second occasion Poirier was standing and she does not remember if he was facing them or not. She testified that Poirier tried to grab the pipe and he did not try to step aside.

Shelley Kennedy, 17 years at the time of the accident, testified that Murphy asked Poirier to do the stunt for the people and he refused to do so and was then persuaded to go along. There was no discussion as to how many times the stunt was to be done. After they got to the underground parking lot Poirier got out of the car, went to the pipe, jumped up and he was hanging onto it as Murphy drove at him at about 30 m.p.h. Poirier then pulled himself up. After the first run, Murphy did a U-turn and drove at Poirier — he was partly turned and did not pull up in time. She testified that Poirier was not ready for the second stunt, and he was just turning around as Murphy started coming toward him. She had seen the trick done by the two of them about a week before the accident. She testified that Poirier's back was towards Murphy but he could have been facing Murphy.

Chris Poirier, the brother of the plaintiff, age 16, testified the plaintiff did not want to do the trick but finally agreed. On the first run he estimated the speed at 20-30 m.p.h. but he does not recall any signal or anything said about being ready. There was nothing said about doing the stunt twice. He testified the car passed under the first time, and he said he heard something that could have been his brother's foot. Mark Anderson said something after they made the turn about his brother not being ready. He said that his brother's back was facing towards him as the second run was commenced. He does not recall if anything was said between the first and the second run.

Thus, on the first run, it would appear the stunt performance went as planned with one exception. It almost failed. Even though Poirier signalled to Murphy his readiness for the commencement he was not able to completely escape contact with the car. His foot or part of his body was hit by the car. That impact did not release his grip on the pipes so as to cause a fall but it was of a sufficient force to be perceived by two of the passengers.

On the second run there are different stories as to what occurred. I do not accept Murphy's evidence that on the second run he backed up and performed the second stunt in the same way as the first. Other witnesses testified that he made a U-turn, headed at Poirier with his back facing Murphy. I have concluded that, after completing his first run, Murphy turned the car around in some manner and immediately commenced his run from the opposite direction. At this time Poirier was still hanging from the pipe. I find Poirier did not signal his readiness for Murphy to start the second run. Notwithstanding Mark Anderson's cry to stop, Murphy proceeded ahead in the belief that Poirier would pull himself up and avoid the impact.

The issues

1. Does the maxim of volenti non fit injuria apply to the circumstances of this case?
2. If not, was there contributory negligence?
3. Damages.

Volenti non fit injuria

The defendant submits the plaintiff knew, or ought to have known, the real risk involved in carrying out the stunt and that, when he agreed to do it, he impliedly exempted the defendant from liability. The defendant says that Poirier consented to assume the risk without compensation, and he absolved Murphy from the duty to take care.

Cartwright J., in delivering the majority judgment of the Supreme Court of Canada in *Lehnert v. Stein,* (1962-63), 40 W.W.R. 616 said, at p. 620:

> The decision of this court in *Seymour v. Maloney;* Car and Gen. Insur. Corpn. (Third Party) [1956] S.C.R. 322, affirming (1955) 36 M.P.R. 337, renders it unnecessary to make any lengthy examination of the authorities, which were fully considered in the judgments delivered in that case, particularly in that of Doull, J. in the Supreme Court of Nova Scotia, in Banco (1955) 36 M.P.R. 337, at 360. That decision establishes that where a driver of a motor vehicle invokes the maxim volenti non fit injuria as a defence to an action for damages for injuries caused by his negligence to a passenger, the burden lies upon the defendant of proving that the plaintiff, expressly or by necessary implication, agreed to exempt the defendant from liability for any damage suffered by the plaintiff occasioned by that negligence, and that, as stated in Salmond on Torts, 13th ed., p. 44:
>
> "The true question in every case is: did the plaintiff give a real consent to the assumption of the risk without compensation; did the consent really absolve the defendant from the duty to take care?"

In *Lackner v. Neath* (1966) 57 W.W.R. 496 (Sask. C.A.) Culliton, C.J.S., quoted the excerpt from *Lehnert v. Stein* (supra) and then stated at 499:

> Clearly, then, to admit the defence of volenti non fit injuria there must be established, either by direct evidence or by inference, that the plaintiff: (a) Voluntarily assumed the physical risk; and (b) Agreed to give up his right for negligence, or, to put it more briefly, that the plaintiff accepted both the physical and legal risk.

Although the principles of the maxim of volens are now clearly set out, their application to the facts are not without difficulty.

In circumstances where the plaintiff is a willing passenger in the defendant's car and each had consumed excessive alcohol, it was found the plaintiff had assumed the physical but not the legal risk: *Pottage v. Patterson et al. and Insurance Corporation of British Columbia* (1980), 24 B.C.L.R. 43.

In *Kinney v. Haveman* [1977] 1 W.W.R. 405 the plaintiff was a passenger in a jeep doing some off-road driving and agreed with the defendant to take a hazardous route. Ruttan J. found the plaintiff by implication consented to the physical and the legal risk of injury and applied the maxim of volens in dismissing the plaintiff's claim.

In *Deskau et al. v. Dziama* (1973), 3 O.R. 101 the plaintiff agreed to assume the risk of riding with the defendant driver whom he knew was driving the car over hills at high speeds so that the car would fly from the crest of the hill with all four wheels off the ground. Keith J. found the nature of the risk voluntarily assumed by the plaintiff was unlimited. He said at p. 106:

I respectfully agree with the following statement from Fleming, Law of Torts, 4th ed. (1971), pp. 243-4:

> "Formerly it mattered nothing whether a plaintiff was defeated on the ground of voluntary assumption of risk or contributory negligence. Now, however, the distinction has become critical, since the relevant legislation does not purport to extend apportionment to voluntary assumption of risk. All the more reason therefore for the courts to have taken an ever more restrictive view of the defence (sic "volenti no fit injuria") in order to avoid the distasteful consequence of having to deny the plaintiff all recovery instead of merely reducing his award. In the result, the defence is nowadays but rarely invoked with success."

In *Lucas v. Antoniak et al.* (1978), 7 C.C.L.T. 209 Callaghan J. stated, at p. 219:

> Defences of volenti non fit injuria and contributory negligence were pleaded in the alternative by the defendant, Antoniak. In order to support a defence of volenti, the defendant must prove that the plaintiff, either expressly or by necessary implication, agreed to exempt the defendant from liability for any damages suffered by the defendant's negligence. *Car & Gen. Ins. Corpn. v. Seymour,* [1956] S.C.R. 322, 2 D.L.R. (2d) 369, and *Miller v. Decker,* [1957] S.C.R. 624, 9 D.L.R. (2d) 1. The defendant must satisfy two distinct requirements before availing himself of volenti; knowledge of the risk and some sort of acceptance which relates to that risk (*Eid v. Dumas,* [1969] S.C.R. 668, 1 N.B.R. (2d) 445, 5 D.L.R. (3d) 561).
>
> The defendant, in raising the defence of contributory negligence, need only establish that the plaintiff did not, in his own interest, take reasonable care of himself and contributed by that want of care to his own injury. *Nance v. B.C. Elec. Ry. Co.,* [1951] A.C.601, [1951] 2 All E.R. 448 (P.C.). Thus, it is only necessary that the defendant show the plaintiff did not observe ordinary prudence (*Car & Gen. Ins. Corpn. v. Seymour,* supra). Although there was some evidence of drinking (five beer over a period of six or seven hours and reading of 40 milligrams of alcohol in 100 millilitres of blood), there was, in my view, insufficient evidence to satisfy the requirements enunciated in *Eid v. Dumas,* supra, and consequently, the defence of volenti must fail. Again, for lack of evidence, the defence of contributory negligence has not been established.

The defendant submits, and I agree, that had Poirier been injured in the first run the authorities would support the application of the doctrine of volens, and his claim would be dismissed. The risk knowingly assumed by Poirier was in my view a much greater one than the passengers in *Deskau* (supra) and in *Kinney v. Haveman* (supra).

However, the second run by the defendant was not done as the first. Poirier assumed a known risk in the first run. In the second I am satisfied he was not ready. It may be that in the test runs on previous occasions Murphy did back the vehicle up and do his second run from the same position as he commenced the first. It may be that Poirier on the day of the accident was expecting Murphy to return to that position. Poirier did not assume a risk until he nodded his approval. He did not give such approval on the second run. Unlike the first stunt, Poirier was not ready for the second. He did not expect Murphy from that direction. After the first run he may have remained swinging from the water pipes so as to stay out of the way as Murphy was to (but did not) return to the starting position for the second stunt. Had Murphy done so, Poirier could have indicated or withheld his signal to commence the second stunt.

Accordingly, I have concluded that Poirier had not assumed the physical risk of the second stunt and the defence of volens does not succeed.

Contributory negligence

Murphy was negligent. As the driver of a motor vehicle, he owed a duty to drive it in a manner different than he did in the underground parking lot where the accident occurred. He was negligent in doing the stunt. He was negligent in failing to hear the noise in the first stunt (Poirier's foot), in failing to pay heed to the passenger's cry to stop, and in failing to recognize that Poirier was not ready for the second stunt. His negligence caused or contributed to the damages suffered by Poirier.

Poirier contributed to his own fate. He failed to take reasonable care for himself. He clearly was negligent in agreeing to the stunt. Though he may not have agreed to the second stunt being done in the manner it was, he placed himself in a hazardous position and failed to remove himself from the risk.

In my view Poirier and Murphy were equally negligent in the first run, and both were negligent in the second. In the second run I attach more blame to Murphy. I apportion the liability two-thirds on the shoulders of Murphy and one-third on Poirier.

Damages

Poirier was rendered unconscious when struck by Murphy's car. He was immediately admitted to the Royal Columbian Hospital and found to have a brain injury. He was unconscious for several days and remained in the hospital for 23 days. He was declared fit for work by July 1982. In August he returned to vocational training and completed a course by December 1982. He then returned to work as a longshoreman where he remains today.

Counsel for the plaintiff asks that damages be fixed on the basis of a significant brain injury that has seriously affected his personality and emotions, and will substantially impair his earning ability.

Counsel for the defendant and third party acknowledges the plaintiff suffered a moderately severe head injury. It is submitted, however, that the intellectual and emotional impairment are not significant and that the plaintiff's loss of income is of a modest nature. Both the plaintiff and the defendants produced neurological, psychiatric and psychological opinions. There were extensive psychological tests as to whether or not there was intellectual impairment. The findings made by the respective psychologists were very similar; the opinions were not. Dr. Crockett for the plaintiff rendered the opinion based on his tests and examination of pre-accident I.Q. tests and on his clinical examinations, that the plaintiff manifested symptoms that showed left front brain damage with permanent residual impairment.

Dr. Klonoff for the defendant had about the same test results as Dr. Crockett. As to the intellectual impairment, he concluded the loss was marginal or minimal and would not appreciably affect the plaintiff's vocational functioning.

A neurologist testified that the plaintiff made a good recovery from a severe head injury and there were no emotional problems.

A psychiatrist found no evidence of depression.

The plaintiff's performance at grade school showed he was functioning at less than his appropriate grade level. He had failed grades 2 and 7. He went to remedial school. It was mainly in verbal functioning that he was deficient. In other matters he was above average.

Thus, the defendants contend that the intellectual deficits post-accident also preceded it. Counsel for the plaintiff submits that Dr. Crockett's psychological opinion shows a marked disparity in the verbal performance of the plaintiff before and after the accident. It was much poorer after the accident. He concludes the diminished intellectual functioning was caused by the accident.

In addition there was evidence as to behaviour and personality changes since the accident. He now has some memory problems. He speaks slower and with less clarity. He is easily frustrated and angers quickly. He no longer has girl friends. He shows an inordinate affection for his mother by kissing and hugging her in private and in public, and referring to her as "mummy." He is not now involved with his friends to any great extent.

I accept that evidence and find there are changes in the plaintiff. The family members testified Poirier looks as he did before the accident but he is now a completely different person. I assess his damages on the basis of his having suffered a serious head injury that caused brain damage giving rise to permanent residual problems. This includes personality and emotional changes. They may diminish over the years but they exist today some four years after the accident. He is, however, able to function in practically all aspects of life (albeit in a less satisfying manner) including vocational, social and athletic activities.

The plaintiff submits the following cases should be of assistance in making the award for non-pecuniary damages:

- *Harrison v. Brown,* Campbell River Registry No. 830077, May 22, 1985, Finch J., not yet reported.
- *Dayton v. Uppal and Gill,* [1985] B.C.J. No. 236, Vancouver Registry No. B830380, September 4, 1985, Gould J.
- *Tomljenovic v. Laliberte,* [1985] B.C.J. No. 1287, Vancouver Registry No. C825236, February 1, 1985, Hinds J.

Counsel for the third party submits the injuries in each of those cases were much more serious than those suffered by the plaintiff. I agree.

As solace for loss of amenities and pain and suffering I fix $40,000 as an appropriate sum.

Loss of income

There is wide disparity in the submissions on this issue. As to the plaintiff's loss to the date of trial, the defendants contend it should be restricted to a period of eight months. He was said to be ready in August of 1982 to resume his vocational training and therefore was ready to commence employment. In a similar period in 1981 he earned $4,289 as a longshoreman. It is submitted that sum represents fairly his loss of wages occasioned by the accident.

The plaintiff submits his loss to the date of trial was $39,728. His prospective loss of income is said to be $71,202 as a longshoreman. In addition, however, it is claimed that the brain impairment occasioned by the accident will prevent him from achieving the position of a foreman and that, as a consequence, he will suffer a loss over his working career of $295,000.

The plaintiff's claim for lost wages to the date of trial is based on the premise that, but for the accident, he would have worked the same or more hours than a certain fellow-worker Ashikian who, at the time of the accident, had less seniority than the plaintiff. Ashikian now has more seniority than the plaintiff. Evidence was led that Ashikian's income during 1981 before the accident was a little less than that earned by the plaintiff. Since the accident, however, he earned $39,728 in excess of that of the plaintiff.

The claim for loss of income is not based on the usual considerations. Ordinarily a claim is made on the basis of inability to perform services to earn a livelihood. If that inability arose from the negligence of the tortfeasor, the party would be entitled to recover damages.

Here, as a direct result of the accident, the plaintiff was unable to work for a period of eight months following the accident. In the year preceding the accident he earned during an eight-month period the sum of $4,289. I consider a proper award for this loss should be $5,000.

The evidence shows there is no physical impairment preventing the plaintiff from doing the work he did before the accident. Indeed there is little evidence supporting a claim for loss of wages arising out of any mental impairment.

However, counsel for the plaintiff submits a claim, not on the grounds the plaintiff is unable to perform services, but rather that the accident caused a loss of seniority which will reduce his income. The loss of seniority arose during the eight-month disabling period and thereafter. The plaintiff says it will result in substantial losses over the years.

Counsel for the third party submits the evidence clearly demonstrates that Ashikian made himself available for work to a much greater extent than the plaintiff and, as a result, he worked much longer hours. I agree. The plaintiff has not established, as is contended by his counsel, that his loss of seniority brought about the loss of income claimed. Seniority in his work as a longshoreman is determined on the basis of hours worked. However, persons on the same despatch board should over the period of a year get approximately the same work, providing they make themselves available. Seniority determines movement to a higher board which gives a worker a preference in earning income. Through the accident the plaintiff would have lost some seniority that may have delayed his advancement to a preferential board. A comparison to Ashikian's income does not establish the loss the plaintiff may have suffered through loss of seniority. Ashikian earned income in excess of the plaintiff not because of more seniority but because he worked longer hours than the plaintiff.

As to the prospective loss of income, the plaintiff submits it has proven lost income attributed to loss of seniority amounting to $71,202. It takes 9 to 11 years for a worker to emerge from the casual despatch boards and qualify as a member of the Union. Once there, one can be assured of greater working hours. For instance, in 1984 a casual worker with a mechanic's rating on Board "E" was likely to get 87 hours' work in a year. That happened to be the plaintiff's board at the date of the accident. The higher boards were likely to have the following annual hours of work:

Board "D" - 138 hours with an income of $2,422

Board "C" - 580 hours with an income of $10,179

Board "B" -1198 hours with an income of $21,025

Board "A" -1532 hours with an income of $26,887

In the same year an average union member was making approximately $51,000.

The plaintiff says this loss of seniority caused by the accident will result in losses amounting to $71,000.

That loss does not arise exclusively from the accident. The plaintiff probably suffered something from loss of seniority. However, I am satisfied the loss cannot be determined by simply comparing the income of Ashikian and the plaintiff. Furthermore, I am of the view the loss occasioned by the loss of seniority is not substantial.

As to his claim for lost income in not being able to assume the responsibilities in the future as foreman, there is some, though very little, evidence to support the proposition that the intellectual impairment suffered from the accident will deprive him of the opportunity to become a foreman.

Taking all these factors into consideration, I allow the sum of $20,000 as damages for loss of income from August 1982 and for any prospective loss of income.

In the result the damages are as follows:

Non-pecuniary damages	$40,000
Loss of income to August 1982	5,000
Loss of income after August 1982, including prospective loss of income	20,000

The plaintiff is entitled to two-thirds of the damages together with Court Order Interest. Judgment accordingly.

QUESTIONS

1. Explain the defences of *volenti non fit injuria* and contributory negligence. In what ways do these defences differ?
2. Are these defences complete defences? Explain.
3. If Poirier had been injured in the first run, would the court have held that the *volenti* defence would apply? Would the *volenti* defence also apply in the second run?
4. Explain how the effect of the presence of contributory negligence has been modified by statute in recent years.

Campbell Estate v. Pederson

[1991] B.C.J. No. 2819, (1991) 35 MVR (2d) 278, Skeena Disposal Co. Ltd. and Universal Handling Equipment Co. Ltd.

British Columbia Supreme Court

Judgment: September 24, 1991

It is seldom easy to predict the outcome of a negligence case, but it is clear that certain elements must be established for a plaintiff to prove the case. When a defendant is sued in negligence, the defendant will usually try to establish a complete or partial defence based on negligence of a third party, or even of the plaintiff. In this case, with the permission of the court, the trucker joined the manufacturer as a third party in the action in an attempt to shift all or part of the responsibility for the accident to the manufacturer.

LOW J.:— Peter Alexander Campbell and his wife, Edith Mitchell Campbell, died in a tragic highway accident on Highway 16 near McBride, B.C. on April 27, 1988. This action was brought for the benefit of their two infant children one of whom, Alison Campbell, was a passenger in their car at the time of the accident. Damages are claimed under the Family Compensation Act and for personal injuries sustained by Alison Campbell. The parties have settled the quantum of damages (subject to approval by the Public Trustee and by the court) and the plaintiffs, with the agreement of all other parties, have not appeared at trial. It remains to determine liability for the accident as between the defendants.

The defendant Matthew Robert Pederson is the sole owner of the defendant Skeena Disposal Co. Ltd. ("Skeena"). That company is in the waste disposal business in Prince Rupert, B.C. It uses large metal bins that are manufactured in Red Deer, Alberta by the defendant Universal Handling Equipment Company Ltd. ("Universal"). Mr. Pederson was returning from Red Deer to Prince Rupert with some new bins on his company's large truck and trailer when the accident occurred. The forty cubic foot bin on the back of the truck came off and fell into the oncoming lane where the Campbell vehicle ran into it. No party alleges negligence on the part of the driver of the Campbell vehicle.

It is common ground that Universal made an error in the manufacture of the bin by placing certain lugs on the underside of the bin in the wrong place. This error prevented the lugs from hooking onto two plates on the truck deck, thereby eliminating the critical part of the mechanism that normally gives stability to the bin on the truck deck. Skeena says the manufacturing error was the sole cause of the accident. Universal says Mr. Pederson should have conducted an inspection to see if the lugs and plates were engaging, that he undertook to do so in any event and that the accident was partly caused by him driving negligently.

Mr. Pederson began his business in 1980. Skeena purchased metal bins from Universal since 1982 or 1983. There are two types of bins - front end loading and roll-off. Each type has various sizes. It was a roll-off type that came off the truck at the time of the accident. Skeena has a 1981 Mack truck properly equipped to handle that type of bin and Mr. Pederson was driving that truck when the accident happened.

On January 15, 1988 Skeena ordered two new 40 cubic yard roll-off bins from Universal. In February, Mr. Pederson took the Mack truck and a trailer to Universal's factory in Red Deer. He left them there for repair of cylinders on the bin hoist apparatus and for certain modifications to the trailer. At some point he also ordered a new 30 cubic yard roll-off bin.

Mr. Pederson returned to Red Deer in April expecting his equipment to be ready, but Universal was behind schedule and he had to wait a couple of days. On the morning of April 26th he took possession of the truck and loaded one of the 40 cubic yard bins onto it. Then he drove the truck, perhaps with the trailer attached, to a nearby tire shop to get new tires for one or the other. As he left Universal's yard the truck's tires went into a depression in the ground. He felt and heard the bin slide to one side for one inch or less. He attributed that to the design of the bin and I accept his evidence that this movement was nothing like the movement he felt just before the accident. I do not find that this incident should have put him on notice that there was something wrong with the security of the bin on the truck.

This is a good place to attempt to describe the configuration of the truck and the bin and the mechanics of loading the one onto the other. The deck of the truck consists of two large parallel steel rails each running from the back of the cab to beyond the rear axle. At the forward end of each rail is welded a vertical wide steel block. These blocks are known as "stops".

The 40 cubic yard bin is 6.25 meters long, 2.32 meters wide and 2.28 meters high. It is made of sheet steel. The bottom of the bin is articulated in a complicated way that I need not describe, except to say that there are parallel lengthwise flanges which slide over the outsides of the rails on the truck deck. To load the bin the operator backs the truck to the front end of the bin after tilting the front end of the truck rails to about a 45 degree angle by means of an hydraulic mechanism operated from inside the cab of the truck. Then he gets out of the truck and, by means of a u-bolt, hooks a cable onto an eye on the bottom of the bin front. The cable runs between the rails from the front to the rear. From inside the cab he then operates another hydraulic system which pulls the cable forward drawing the bin over the rails. As he draws the bin forward he also tilts the truck deck rails forward until the bin is parallel to the ground and is against the front stops previously described. The bin is then in its proper position for transport. The operator need do nothing further to secure it.

The bin is secured laterally by the bin flanges sitting over the truck rails. I would think that the cable at the front of the bin would give it some security both laterally and vertically. But it is obvious that additional vertical security is needed over the length of the bin as it sits on the truck rails. The lugs and plates mentioned earlier in these reasons are designed to meet this safety need. Without them the bin would eventually come off the rails and fall to the side given a certain degree of lateral force as the truck takes corners.

The lugs are pieces of steel welded to the underside of the bin, one inside each flange. They are square-u-shaped, with the open ends toward the front of the bin. The throat of each lug is three inches deep. When the bin is drawn fully forward by the cable, the lugs are supposed to hook over flat steel plates welded inside the truck rails on each side. Photographs in evidence appear to show the plates to be located between and above the rear tandem axles, perhaps closer to or even above the rear axle. This is a standard and very simple method of achieving the necessary stability.

Universal has factories in Red Deer and Hamilton, Ontario with a total of about 200 employees. It has been in the business of manufacturing waste disposal equipment since the 1960's. In the Red Deer plant quality control is the responsibility of the foremen in the metal preparation department and the assembly department. It is their duty to inspect the work as it is produced.

Roll-off containers are built to order by Universal. Each one must properly fit the truck that is to haul it and the trucks decks are likely to have differing dimensions. Skeena's truck was a common type within the industry and used the common method of loading and unloading bins that I have already attempted to describe. Universal had provided bins for Skeena's truck for several years and had its particular and unchanged deck and rail dimensions on file. It also had the truck in its possession as it manufactured the bin and in fact attached (or reattached) the front stops to the rails as part of the work it did for Skeena. If I correctly understand the examination for discovery evidence of Carson Dyson, Universal's plant manager in Red Deer, Universal also welded (or rewelded) the plates onto the rails.

The fatal error occurred because the assembly department did not follow drawings for the bin supplied by the engineering department. The drawings called for a three inch recess on each side of the front end of the bin where the bin, when loaded, abuts the front stops on the rails. Employees in the assembly department arbitrarily decided to eliminate the recesses and they made the front end of the bin flush right across. They did not also place the lugs on the bottom of the bin a corresponding three inches forward of the place called for by the drawings. Nor did they move the plates inside the rails three inches back. The result of this negligent assembly was that the lugs could not engage the plates, except marginally, once the bin was fully loaded on the truck rails.

It seems that no employee of Universal took the obvious safety step of simply measuring the finished bin and perhaps the truck deck to ensure that the lugs and the plates were properly positioned. If measurements were done, they were done negligently.

Universal turned over to Mr. Pederson a faulty bin that, given its size and weight and the likelihood it would eventually come off the truck, presented a very serious danger to the driving public, including Mr. Pederson and anybody else operating the unit. Universal accepts that it was negligent, but seeks to have a greater portion of the blame for the accident imposed on Mr. Pederson and Skeena.

Mr. Pederson had a duty to drive with his load secure. This common law duty is codified by several Motor Vehicle Act regulations [Division (35) Securement of Vehicle Loads, May 31, 1987]. After the accident, Mr. Pederson was charged with and later convicted of driving with his load not tied down as required according to a table set out in Regulation 35.04. There was no necessity to tie or chain the bin to the truck if the lugs properly engaged the plates. However, two other regulations better describe the duty more applicable to the circumstances of this case. Regulations 35.03 and 35.ll(2) read as follows:

> 35.03   No person shall drive or operate on a highway a vehicle or combination of vehicles carrying a load unless the load is secured in a manner which ensures that
>
> (a)   the load or a portion of the load will not escape from the vehicle or
>
> (b)   the load or a portion of the load will not shift or sway in a manner that may affect the operation of the vehicle or combination of vehicles.
>
> 35.11(2) No person shall drive or operate on a highway a self-loading commercial vehicle transporting a refuse container unless the refuse container is located and secured to the hoist frame by a means which is of adequate strength to prevent movement between the container, the hoist frame and the truck frame.

Mr. Pederson had a duty to drive with the bin secure and the issue is whether he took all reasonable steps to discharge that duty before leaving Red Deer. Once the bin is fully loaded on the truck one cannot see if the lugs are engaging the plates. There are two ways to check; the first, by crawling underneath the vehicle and up through various attached pieces of equipment; the second, by operating the hydraulic control inside the cab to lift the deck up until the lugs and plates are visible. The first way is awkward and inconvenient. The second way is more convenient. Mr. Pederson did neither. He limited his inspection to observing from the rear that the bin was properly over the rails and observing that the front of the bin was against the front stops. He assumed that the lugs would have to be engaging the plates properly because the bin was properly against the front stops. The one thing would normally follow the other. It did not occur to Mr. Pederson that Universal might have put the lugs or the plates in a wrong place.

As I have already said, Mr. Pederson felt a slight sideways movement of the bin when he drove through the depression. He attributed this to the bin being built without being recessed where it abuts the front stops. He knew that Universal made the bins both ways. Although he raised it in a conversation with Mr. Dyson after his return to Universal's yard from the tire shop, neither of them had any ongoing concern about the absence of the recesses. Each of them must have assumed that the bin was designed that way.

Mr. Dyson testified that it is not common for Universal's customers to take delivery of bins at the plant. Universal usually ships them to the customers on flat bed trucks. He said that Universal's employees are not qualified to load the bins onto the trucks and the customer does the loading when delivery is taken at the plant. He added that "most often" the trucker tilts back the loaded bin to visually ensure that the lugs and the plates are engaged and to be sure that the bin's features are as ordered. I view this evidence with scepticism and do not accept the practice he described as a safety check expected by the manufacturer. The most that can be said of Mr. Dyson's evidence on this point is that he knew that a trucker taking delivery of a new bin might or might not do the visual inspection. This could hardly give Universal comfort that any error it made in manufacturing the bin would be detected before the bin was put to its intended use.

Mr. Dyson recalled that Mr. Pederson mentioned the load shift caused by driving through the depression in the ground. He said that Mr. Pederson told him that he would check the stops. Mr. Dyson took this to mean the lugs, which are often referred to as "container stops." Mr. Pederson did not recall this part of their conversation.

I do not accept Universal's assertion that Mr. Pederson undertook to Mr. Dyson to check the lugs. Mr. Pederson's mind was not then directed to them. He had already assumed they were engaged because the bin was against the front stops. Mr. Dyson's subsequent evidence is inconsistent with Universal's position on this point. Mr. Dyson said that Mr. Pederson, after their conversation, looked under the truck toward the lugs and plates and said something to the effect that the stops were okay. This does not make sense because it is not possible to visually inspect the engagement of the lugs and plates in this manner. Mr. Dyson knew that. If he was relying on Mr. Pederson to visually ensure engagement, he would have made sure Mr. Pederson did so by tilting the rails up and would not have accepted his assurance from an inspection Mr. Dyson knew to be inadequate. I do not accept Mr. Dyson's evidence on this point.

Hans Idzes gave expert evidence for Universal as to the practice employed by operators of waste disposal equipment to ensure lug engagement. He is a service manager of a large waste disposal company in Vancouver and has many years experience in the operation of such equipment. He testified that it is not standard practice for an operator to assume engagement unless he is loading a bin he has loaded before on the truck he is using at the time. The way to check is to raise the rails after loading and get out of the cab to visually see if there is engagement. Mr. Idzes said he would expect an operator to check the lugs of a container with which he is not familiar.

Counsel argues that Mr. Pederson was, in effect, familiar with this truck and bin combination because the bin was standard in the industry, he had purchased numerous similar bins from Universal with no problems and he had left his truck with Universal for two months for proper fitting. Counsel says it was reasonable for Mr. Pederson to assume lug engagement when he saw that the bin was properly on the rails and there was abutment with the front stops.

It is easy to see why Mr. Pederson made the assumption he did. However, in order to fully discharge his statutory duty it would have been prudent for him to make a visual check for lug engagement after raising the rails. His failure to take this step amounts to negligence on his part.

Mr. Pederson left Red Deer late in the evening of April 26th. Inside the bin on the truck were a 30 cubic yard bin on its side, about six front-end loader bins and some additional small items. The other forty cubic yard bin was strapped to the trailer with smaller bins tied inside it. On the neck of the trailer Mr. Pederson had strapped four small bins, two side by side with another on top of each. Everything inside the large bins was properly tied down. Apart from the lack of engagement of the lugs, there can be no suggestion that the size of the load, the weight of the load, the combination of vehicles or the method of loading was illegal, unsafe or in any way causative of the accident.

From a road map in evidence I have attempted to determine the distance from Red Deer to the accident scene some 52 kilometres west of McBride. The driving distances on the map are difficult to follow, but I would estimate the distance at 700 kilometres. Mr. Pederson drove through the night, having had some sleep during the previous day. Along the way he stopped for additional rest. I find that he was fit to drive at all times. The accident occurred around noon.

Until just before the accident occurred, Mr. Pederson had no difficulty with the load or with handling the truck. He had no reason to believe the bin on the truck to be vertically unsecure. I find that he drove at ordinary highway speeds.

Victor Baker, an accident reconstruction expert, tested the speed capacity of Skeena's truck two years after the accident. I accept his opinion that with the load Mr. Pederson transported from Red Deer, the vehicle could not exceed a speed of 100 k.p.h. on a slight downgrade and would then drop to its governed speed of 88 k.p.h. on a level surface. For reasons which should become apparent, I find that excessive speed was not a factor in the accident.

Approaching the accident scene, Mr. Pederson drove down a fairly long hill. The two-lane highway then levelled out for a short distance before starting uphill and into a right hand curve. Where the hill started there was also the beginning of a passing lane for westbound traffic. Therefore, as he started up the hill Mr. Pederson had a choice of two lanes. On his right was a solid white line known as a "fog line" marking the commencement of the paved shoulder. The two westbound lanes were divided by a dotted white line. There were two yellow solid centre lines and there was another fog line marking the commencement of the paved shoulder on the south side of the highway. The posted speed limit was 90 k.p.h.

Mr. Pederson testified that he went down the first hill at 55 to 60 m.p.h. (88 to 96 k.p.h.); that he slowed down by 5 to 8 m.p.h. (8 to 13 k.p.h.) as he started up the second hill and before he got to the start of the right hand curve; that he shifted to a lower gear as he started uphill; that he proceeded up the hill in the right hand or slow lane; that when he got into the curve he felt the bin on the truck to be unsteady; that he moved into the passing lane in an attempt "to get my truck back under the load"; that he had to continue to his left until he was straddling the yellow centre lines; and that he then saw the oncoming Campbell vehicle to which he reacted by turning hard to his right to get out of its way. At this point the bin came off the truck and fell into the eastbound lane where the Campbell vehicle ran directly into it.

The bin on the truck initially became unstable because the lugs did not engage the plates. Mr. Pederson's subsequent corrective and evasive actions were all taken in the agony of the moment and he cannot be faulted for those actions. However, Universal contends that Mr. Pederson caused the initial instability by taking the corner too sharply. I find this position difficult to maintain.

Both sides called accident reconstruction experts; Mr. Baker by Skeena and Peter Keith by Universal. Their opinions as to what caused the bin initially to become unsteady are not very different.

On the application of strict principles of physics together with assumptions about the weight distribution of the load, an expert can perhaps come close to measuring the combination of speed and sharpness of turning that would set up the lateral force necessary to make the bin start to tip. Mr. Baker attempted to do this. He did some theoretical reconstruction of the load and made some assumptions about its distribution. He used a radius of the curve as determined by Cpl. R. S. Sanderson, a qualified R.C.M.P. traffic analyst who attended the scene of the accident. He concluded that a normal turn into the particular curve at 93 k.p.h. or slightly less would likely set up the lateral force necessary to cause the bin to tip. He further concluded that with the lugs engaged properly the speed would have to be 124 k.p.h., far beyond the capacity of the truck.

Universal employed a surveyor, Ronald Johns, to measure the radius of the curve. Cpl. Sanderson measured the curve of the north side fog line. Mr. Johns' crew measured the curve of the shoulder of the pavement because when they were at the site this year the road was being re-coated and there were no traffic control lines. Mr. Johns' crew used modern technical equipment to measure the radius, and it is his opinion that such measurement is more reliable than Cpl. Sanderson's geometric method based as it is on physical measurement and a fundamental equation. Mr. Johns determined that the curve was less sharp than the corporal's measurements indicate, but not substantially so.

It is Mr. Keith's opinion that Mr. Pederson must have swerved sharply from the passing lane to his right because otherwise the radius of the curve as measured by Mr. Johns could not have caused the load as calculated by Mr. Baker to become unsteady at the speed the vehicle was capable of going and must have been going. To me that is purely theoretical analysis and I think the technical answer to it is in Mr. Baker's detailed report of April 27, 1988 (p. 9):

There are other factors which contribute to a reduction in the dynamic stability of the vehicle compared to the idealized rigid vehicle analysis. The percentage of weight distributed to the front axle of the vehicle, if increased, serves to reduce the roll stability since front axle suspensions are typically less stiff than the rear axle suspensions. Any degree of freedom of movement of the cargo can induce dynamic forces which could contribute to a rollover accident. In this load there may have been some degree of movement of the smaller containers within the 30 cubic yard container. This would likely reduce the dynamic rollover stability of the vehicle assuming the 40 cubic yard container was secure. In the case where the 40 cubic yard container was not secured, the load would only need to rotate about the left frame rail 10 degrees before the right side rail of the container disengaged the truck frame. Sudden lateral shift of the container would cause the load to roll off the truck frame.

I believe that precise reconstruction of this accident is impossible and Mr. Baker says as much. I generally accept Mr. Pederson's evidence as to his manner of driving and the events leading up to the collision. I find that he went into the curve as he was slowing down and that his speed when the instability began was likely below 80 k.p.h., a reasonable speed in the circumstances.

Universal argues that Mr. Pederson must have misjudged the curve and cut sharply to his right to correct his error, thereby causing the bin to tilt to the left and necessitating the emergency recovery action he attempted. That is a submission without a future. Even if the chain of events did commence with Mr. Pederson making a corrective move to his right, that does not amount to negligence unless Universal establishes that the manoeuvre, with the lugs properly engaged, would have affected the stability of the load or Mr. Pederson's control of his vehicle in such a way as to present a hazard to other traffic. It is not possible to reconstruct the accident that way and neither expert has attempted to do so.

The lack of engagement of the lugs was the direct cause of the accident. Universal has not proved that any negligent driving on the part of Mr. Pederson contributed to the accident.

Apportionment of liability remains. The risk that Universal's faulty construction of the bin would not be detected before use on the highway was substantially greater than the risk taken by Mr. Pederson in assuming, without visual confirmation, that the lugs properly engaged the plates. I assign responsibility at 80% to Universal and 20% to Mr. Pederson and Skeena.

Counsel may speak to the appropriate order to follow and disposition of the third party proceedings. The same applies to costs.

QUESTIONS

1. Explain how the elements of an action in negligence applied to lead the court to find Universal Handling Equipment Company Ltd. liable.

2. Explain how the elements of an action in negligence applied to lead the court to find Mr. Pederson liable.

3. What did Mr. Dyson expect the trucker to do when the bins were loaded on his truck? Was this a reasonable expectation? Explain.

4. Would Universal Handling equipment Company Ltd. have successfully defended this claim if it had been shown that Mr. Pederson had been driving at excessive speed? Explain.

Chase v. Goodyear Tire & Rubber Co. and Goodyear Canada Inc.

[1991] N.B.J. No. 305, 291 A.P.R. 18,115 N.B.R. (2d) 181
New Brunswick Court of Queen's Bench
April 12, 1991

The increasing complexity and sophistication of many products and the resultant inability of consumers to detect dangers in these products places manufacturers in a position of having a growing responsibility for the safety of consumers.

TURNBULL J.:— On February 14, 1986 the plaintiff John Chase was working at his brother's service station in Minto, New Brunswick. He was in the process of inflating a large truck tire for a Mr. Cameron Fulton when the tire exploded. Mr. Chase intended to inflate the tire to 100 lbs. per square inch. It had been stored at the garage and Mr. Fulton used it as a spare. John Chase bent over it and held the compressed air chuck against the tire valve. The compressor had been set at 100 lbs. per square inch and he gauged the pressure before putting in any air. It was at 30 lbs. After putting some air in he paused and gauged it at that time. It read that the pressure was at 60 lbs. He put some more air in again and stopped and gauged the tire and it was at 80 lbs. He had just started to put more air in and has no recollection of what happened after that.

The tire split along the sidewall breaking many of the radial cords in what is known as a zipper tear. The explosion caught the plaintiff presumably in the chest area, knocked him back ten or twelve feet, ripping his vest and shirt in the process. He was knocked unconscious and obviously badly injured. He was rushed to the Minto hospital and later that day transferred to the Fredericton hospital where he remained in intensive care for several weeks. He suffered a collapsed lung and major damage to his heart which has led to a severe psychological problem.

The tire itself is a Model G186. It is 10 inches in width between the sidewall casings and the rim has a diameter of 20 inches. It is made with steel radial wires for strength and is intended for use both off and on paved highways. Goodyear specifically advertises that these tires are suitable for heavy loads and may be retreaded using the original casing and should be good for two, three or maybe more retreads (exhibit No. 17, tab 16). When manufactured there is 22/32 of an inch of tread on the tire. The tire was manufactured by Goodyear Tire & Rubber Company in 1983. It was sold to an unknown party who returned it and received a credit. It was inspected by Goodyear Canada Inc. who determined that it was suitable for retreading. This was done and the tire eventually sold to Keith Chase who in turn sold it to Fulton in February of 1985. The accident happened February 14, 1986. Prior to the accident it had been in Chase's garage for repair and was used by Mr. Fulton as a spare tire after that. It had been used after the repair and had been returned to the garage for some reason. It had lost some air as it only had 30 lbs. of pressure in it when John Chase retrieved it and was in the process of inflating it when this explosion occurred. After the accident the tire remained in a shed behind the garage and was only retrieved and inspected by experts perhaps twenty months later. The inner tube was not found.

Three experts testified at trial as to what in their opinion happened with this tire. Hill Cunliffe and Frank Garey were both called by the plaintiff. They are friends living in Whitby, Ontario who spent their adult lives in the tire industry and they collaborated on their opinions. Briefly put they were of the opinion that the use to which Mr. Fulton had put the tire was not sufficient to have caused the zipper tear which resulted from metal fatigue in the radial cords and were of the opinion that this fatigue must have been caused in the tire's first life. Both were again called on rebuttal and I had the impression that Mr. Garey modified his opinion somewhat to the effect that the overdeflection causing the metal fatigue in the radial cords was probably progressive over the first and second life.

Tom Baker testified on behalf of the defendants. He also had excellent credentials. A brief summary of his opinion is to the effect that the overdeflection of the tire which caused the fatigue in the radial cords must have been immediately prior to this tire being returned to the garage. If Mr. Fulton had a flat tire and drove for eight or ten miles the filaments would buckle and the sidewall of the tire would become permanently weakened. He believed this was the only explanation as to why the tire exploded with just over 80 lbs. of pressure in it. While there is a considerable amount of logic to his opinion I prefer the opinions of Mr. Cunliffe and Mr. Garey. From examining the tire they were of the opinion that they would have seen some evidence on the tire if the cord failure was from recent abuse as envisaged by Mr. Baker. They were unable to see any such evidence.

In its retreaded condition Mr. Fulton used the tire as one of eight on the rear of his truck. He hauled coal with it. There was a considerable amount of evidence given at trial as to what would happen if the truck was overloaded but basically I accept the evidence of Mr. Garey in particular that overloading on occasion would not cause the fatigue in these cords and I accept the evidence of both experts called by the plaintiff that a constant overload condition would have shown up as evidence of wear on the tire and the rim which was not present. I do not however accept their opinions that the tire was abused during its first life as again there is no evidence of this shown in the wear on the rim or by the cords themselves becoming loose inside the rubber of the tire. I believe this portion of their opinion was a deduction which may logically follow but I am not prepared to take this final step.

There are too many unknowns in this case. I do not know what use was made of the tire in its first life. I do not know what happened to its mate. I do not know the condition of the four supporting tires while in its retreaded life when it was being used by Mr. Fulton. I do not accept the evidence of Mr. Fulton and Mr. Keith Chase on the particular care that Mr. Fulton took with his tires. The fact is he was using this tire as a spare when he should not have. Even if one ignores the weakened cord condition it was in an obviously dangerous condition with a hole in the tread that had been improperly patched and the tire was at the end of its retreaded life having only 3/32 of an inch of tread left. Mr. Fulton was of the opinion that the tire still had six months of life in it, but I accept the evidence of Mr. Garey that it should not have been on the road. The tire was obviously at the end of its life. All experts were of the opinion that if it were not for the puncture in the tread and the zipper tear the remainder of the sidewall and the interior of the tire looked in excellent condition and would have passed inspection to be retreaded.

Based on the evidence of Anderson, Wilson, Cunliffe and Garey that there was no flaw in manufacture of the original tire or indeed the retreading job, I am of the opinion that the tire has been overdeflected at various periods of time during its life which caused the filaments in the cords to break. I believe the deterioration was progressive in both its first and second life. The final inflation to 80 lbs. psi was just the "straw that broke the camel's back", to use Mr. Garey's words.

If the claim were one solely for a breach of warranty I would dismiss it because I do not believe the plaintiff has proved such a case. Counsel for the plaintiff has properly stressed in my opinion the claim as one for failing to warn the plaintiff that the radial cords may have gradually weakened through overdeflection while the tire has been in use, that the sidewalls may explode while being inflated and that anybody inflating the tire should use the clip-on air chuck and stand well away when the tire is being inflated.

Goodyear Tire & Rubber Company have about 1500 zipper breaks a year reported to it. Goodyear Canada Inc. has recently opened a retreading plant in Fredericton. It produces about eighty-eight tires a day of the medium truck size. Mr. Fanjoy has been the manager of the Fredericton plant for two years and he sees or knows of about twenty-five zipper breaks per year in their shop. Both companies know that there is a risk that the tires can be overdeflected and the radial cords damaged and that such damage cannot be detected. This was readily admitted by the witness Paul Wilson under cross-examination by Mr. Gilbert. To me, after hearing all of the evidence, it is common sense that the failure and consequent explosion can occur either on the road or during inflation and will occur along this line of the casing. I am of the opinion this possibility should have been anticipated by the defendants' engineering departments.

The company's warnings did not specifically point to this latent problem, rather the warnings to stand clear were directed to using a tire cage or chains so that the lock ring would not pop out during the early part of inflation. At thirty lbs. the danger from the lock ring is over. The cage will not protect the person inflating the tire from the possibility of a latent weakness in the radial cords.

The law on this subject has been well summarized by Holland, J. of the Ontario High Court in the case of *Buchan v. Ortho Pharmaceutical (Canada) Ltd.* (1984) 28 C.C.L.T. 233 at pp. 253-254:

> The duty to warn can best be described in relation to the thing that is being warned against, of which in product liability cases three categories exist: (1) warning about dangers resulting from negligent design or manufacture; (2) warnings about dangers involved in using the product in certain circumstances or in certain ways; and (3) warnings about inherent, unavoidable risks to the unusually susceptible consumer ("thinskulled") of the generally safe product.

The first category of cases turns on negligence in the design or manufacture of the product. There is a duty to take reasonable care in design and manufacture and a separate duty to warn of dangers caused by defects in design or manufacture. See *Rivtow Marine Ltd. v. Washington Iron Works,* [1974] S.C.R. 1189, [1973] 6 W.W.R. 692, 40 D.L.R. (3d) 530. The second category of cases involves breach of a duty to warn about the dangers resulting from use of the product in certain circumstances or in a certain way.

In *Lambert v. Lastoplex Chems. Co.,* [1972] S.C.R. 569, 25 D.L.R. (3d) 121, the plaintiff applied a fast-drying lacquer to the floor of his recreation room. Fumes were ignited by a pilot light in an adjoining room, causing an explosion. At p. 125 [D.L.R.] Laskin J. (as he then was) said this:

> "Where manufactured products are put on the market for ultimate purchase and use by the general public and carry danger (in this case, by reason of high inflammability), although put to the use for which they are intended, the manufacturer, knowing of their hazardous nature, has a duty to specify the attendant dangers, which it must be taken to appreciate in a detail not known to the ordinary consumer or user. A general warning, as for example, that the product is inflammable, will not suffice where the likelihood of fire may be increased according to the surroundings in which it may reasonably be expected that the product will be used. The required explicitness of the warning will, of course, vary with the danger likely to be encountered in the ordinary use of the product."

For other examples of a duty to warn falling into the second category see *Pack v. Warner County* (1964), 46 W.W.R. 422, 44 D.L.R. (2d) 215 (Alta. C.A.); *Labrecque v. Sask. Wheat Pool,* [1977] 6 W.W.R. 122, 78 D.L.R. (3d) 289 (Sask Q.B.) [reversed in part [1980] 3 W.W.R. 558, 110 D.L.R. (3d) 686, 3 Sask. R. 322 (sub nom. *Labareque v. Eli Lilly (Can.) Ltd.*) (C.A.)]; and *Stewart v. Lepage's Inc.,* [1955] O.R. 937 (H.C.). I am of the opinion that both defendants are liable to the plaintiff under both of these categories. In its new condition Goodyear Tire advertised the tire as being reusable several times as a retread.

Goodyear Canada must also have anticipated that a significant number of retreaded tires will have a latent defect in that the cords will break because the tires may have already been overdeflated and that the tire may burst in its sidewall. For this reason anybody who inflates the tire must use a clip-on chuck and stand well away.

The defendants pleaded contributory negligence. The only evidence before me relating to contributory negligence was the evidence of John Chase and his brother Keith Chase and of course the written warnings which I find related to the lock rings. The plaintiff and his brother have each had many years of experience in handling tire for cars, trucks and inflating same and never heard of a tire exploding through such a zipper break. On the basis of such evidence as is before me I am not prepared to hold that the plaintiff was contributorily negligent.

On the question of injury and damages I accept the evidence of Dr. Robert Anderson. The plaintiff has suffered 21% damage to his heart. To put this in perspective the heart needs 50% efficacy to function and a heart transplant is considered a possibility for anyone who has over 20% damage. Mr. Chase has suffered damage to "a relatively major degree". Dr. Anderson does not believe that the damage has increased after the first three months after the initial trauma. The plaintiff will be restricted from doing any moderate work for a prolonged period of time. He is suffering post trauma stress disorder which has been pronounced and prolonged. Dr. Anderson was pessimistic about the plaintiff's employment prospects. He did not feel he was likely to be retrained and at present he is unable to cope with anything other than trivial matters. He was examined by Dr. Eugene LeBlanc who is a clinical psychologist and his opinion was that Mr. Chase's ability to learn new skills is below average and his employment prospects bleak. I do not believe the plaintiff will be gainfully employed again.

There was considerable evidence led on the plaintiff's loss of his earning capacity. For several years there was a pattern of work followed by periods on unemployment insurance. Plaintiff's counsel stressed that the plaintiff earned a considerable amount through a "hobby" namely buying old cars, fixing them up and reselling them at a profit. I will not allow any claim under this heading as I believe the plaintiff was cheating on his reports of taxable income. I do not believe there were as many sales as Mr. Chase now claims there were. To me it was obvious that this was not a hobby. Mr. Chase made these purchases and sales regularly in a clandestine manner to avoid paying taxes on this income. Some purchases were made in his girlfriend's name (now his wife). Some were made in other relatives' names. All expenditures for parts were made in cash. No records were kept. No receipts were kept.

Mr. Gilbert argues that while the law does not allow damages for past earnings not reported I should be looking at future earning capacity. I am of the opinion that public policy operates both as to past earnings and to future earnings. I will not allow anything for the plaintiff's loss of income from the sale of automobiles.

There was evidence that Mr. Chase could have obtained a higher paying job at Knox Contracting or Bailey Construction prior to the accident, but the fact is that he did not apply for such jobs. I am of the opinion that the pattern that had developed of working part time and going on UIC part time would have continued.

I accept the evidence of John Tarrel that based on the plaintiff's tax returns his loss is $245,000.00. This figure included past and future loss, and interest on past loss to the date of trial.

The plaintiff will continue to suffer post trauma stress disorder for the foreseeable future. He has been through a terrible ordeal and his heart is severely damaged. He is only 42 years of age. I will allow general damages in the amount of $65,000.00. I allow Medicare at $20,025.16 and Workers' Compensation Board at $1,716.67. The plaintiff claims long distance phone call charges in the amount of $1,450.50. I think this claim is exaggerated and will allow $1,000.00. The plaintiff claims $410.00 for prescription drugs; I will allow this. Mrs. Chase claims living expenses in Fredericton of $1,365.00 immediately after the accident. I will allow $1,000.00. There is claim for loss of clothing, i.e. the wool shirt and green and red type of hunting vest that the plaintiff was wearing at the time of the explosion and I will allow $60.00 for this. The plaintiff claims $600.00 for going on a Nutri-System diet and I will not allow this claim. It is too remote. There is a claim for $450.00 for the children's travelling, and meals in Fredericton and I will allow $250.00. The plaintiff claims for clothing because of weight gain and loss. To me that is also too remote and I will not allow it. The plaintiff claims over $2,000.00 for special foods and diets from Nutri-System; again I am not going to allow any of this. The plaintiff claims $1,000.00 for travel to hospitals in Fredericton and Minto. There is no breakdown of this and I believe it is exaggerated. I will allow $200.00. I will allow babysitting expenses of $500.00 and I will allow $520.00 for two trips to Halifax to see Dr. Anderson at the Victoria General Hospital in 1986 and again in 1990. This is over and above $807.05 that was advanced by Workers' Compensation Board. For the loss of valuable services I will allow $600.00 per year and capitalize that at 15.59 for a loss of say $9,350.00. The plaintiff will need professional investment counselling over the years. I do not accept Mr. Tarrel's evidence expressed at 5% to be added to the multiplier. The plaintiff testified he would like to be in some sedentary business and with his stress disorder I do not believe he will solely rely on market investments. I will allow a lump sum of $5,000.00 under this heading.

John Chase will have judgment for $349,781.83 jointly and severally against the defendants.

I allow interest on general damages and the personal out of pocket expenses at 10% per annum not compounded from the date action was commenced and interest on past and future earnings at 12% not compounded from January 1, 1991.

The plaintiff is entitled to costs on an amount involved of $355,000.00 on Scale 3 and I will allow $1,000.00 extra due to the necessity of having to recall and re-brief Messrs. Cunliffe and Garey.

TURNBULL J.

QUESTIONS

1. In order to establish liability in negligence, a plaintiff must establish a duty of care owed by the defendant. What is the nature of that duty in this case?
2. When is a manufacturer under a duty to warn?
3. Why was the use of expert testimony important in this case?
4. What is meant by economic loss? What are the two types of economic loss?

Hollis v. Dow Corning Corp.

[1995] 4 SCR 634, [1995] SCJ No. 104, 127 DLR 94th) 609, 190 NR 241, [1996] 2 WWR 77, 14 BCLR (3d) 1, 26 BLR (2d) 169, 27 CCLT (2d) 1.

Supreme Court of Canada on appeal from the Court of Appeal for British Columbia

December 21, 1995

Present: La Forest, L'Heureux-Dube, Sopinka, Gonthier, Cory, McLachlin and Iacobucci JJ.

One of the most important cases in manufacturers' liability in recent decades was the action brought against Dow Corning for injuries arising from silicone breast implants. The case established what responsibility rests on a manufacturer where warnings are unlikely to reach a consumer directly.

Judgment for La Forest, L'Heureux-Dube, Gonthier, Cory and Iacobucci JJ. was delivered by **LA FOREST J.** The following is a summary of the case and his judgment.

Dow Corning is a U.S. corporation that developed silicone breast implants during the 1970's and 1980's. Ms. Hollis had congenital breast deformity and her family physician suggested that she consult Dr. John Birch, an experienced plastic surgeon. Dr. Birch told Ms. Hollis that surgery and implants could correct the shape of her breasts. Dr. Birch explained the surgical implantation procedure, but did not warn Ms. Hollis of the risks of post-surgical complications, or the possibility that the implants could rupture. On the basis of Dr. Birch's advice, Ms Hollis consented to surgery, and in 1983 Dr. Birch modified Ms. Hollis' breasts with two silicone breast implants manufactured by Dow Corning.

About a year after surgery, Ms. Hollis experienced problems including a lump in one breast and pain in her side. Dr. Quayle, another plastic surgeon, removed the implants. He discovered that the right implant had ruptured and its silicone envelope was missing. For the next two years Ms. Hollis experienced severe pain in her right breast. Dr. Courtemanche, another surgeon, performed a subcutaneous mastectomy on both breasts and implanted different implants. The surgery was successful and Ms. Hollis had no problems afterwards, but has scarring, depression and was worried about the missing silicone envelope and the possibility that the new implants might rupture.

Ms. Hollis sued Dow Corning, Dow's Canadian agent Dow Canada, Dr. Birch and Dr. Quayle in the Supreme Court of British Columbia. She sued Dow Corning for negligence in the manufacture of the implant placed in her right breast, and sued Dow Corning and Dow Canada for failing to warn doctors or the public of the possibility that the implants could rupture. She sued Dr. Birch for negligent advice and negligent surgery, and for breach of the Sale of Goods Act. She sued Dr. Quayle for negligence in failing to remove the implants promptly and for failing to remove remnants of gel in her right breast.

The trial judge found Dow Corning liable for negligent manufacture of the implants because he could not find any other cause for the rupture of the implant. He drew an inference of negligence from the fact that Dow Corning had ceased to manufacture the type of implant that Ms. Hollis originally received, and replaced the original implants with a new model. He dismissed the actions against Dow Canada, Dr. Birch and Dr. Quayle. Dow Corning appealed liability to the British Columbia Court of Appeal.

The majority in the British Columbia Court of Appeal found that the trial judge was wrong in holding Dow Corning liable for manufacturing the implant negligently. He should not have concluded that Dow Corning was negligent just because he could find no other cause for the rupture, and he should not have inferred negligence from the fact that the implants had been replaced with a new model. The majority in the Court of Appeal did find, however, that Dow Corning breached its duty to warn Ms. Hollis and Dr. Birch of the risk of post-surgical implant rupture.

Dow Corning appealed to the Supreme Court of Canada, saying that the British Columbia Court of Appeal erred in finding Dow Corning liable for failing to give adequate warnings. La Forest J. wrote the judgment for the majority, dismissing the appeal, and holding Dow Corning liable for failing to warn. He said that it was well established in Canadian law that a manufacturer of a product has a duty in tort to warn consumers of dangers inherent in use of its product which it has knowledge of, or ought to have knowledge of, and that the duty to warn is a continuing duty, requiring manufacturers to warn not only of dangers known at the time of sale, but also of dangers discovered after the product has been sold and delivered. All warnings must be reasonably communicated, and must clearly describe any specific dangers that arise from ordinary use of the product.

With medical products, the majority decided, the standard of care to be met by manufacturers in ensuring that consumers are properly warned is necessarily high, given the intimate relationship between medical products and the consumer's body. The lack of dialogue between manufacturer and consumer creates a relationship of complete dependency between manufacturer and patient. It is reasonable to expect manufacturers to make clear, complete and current information known to consumers about the risks inherent in ordinary use of the product.

In a case where the consumer will not realistically receive direct warning, warning the ultimate consumer may not be necessary, and the manufacturer may satisfy its duty to warn by warning a "learned intermediary" of risks. This does not, however, alleviate the duty on the manufacturer; it discharges its duty to warn by ensuring the intermediary's knowledge approximates that of the manufacturer. In the case of breast implants, where the product is not sold directly to patients, it is appropriate to warn the surgeon.

Although Dow did warn, the version of the warning in 1976 and 1979 related to "abnormal squeezing or trauma" and not of the danger of rupture from normal squeezing or non-traumatic everyday activity. In 1985, Dow began to warn physicians of the possibility of rupture due to normal, non-traumatic activity. If Ms. Hollis had received a more explicit warning, the court held, she might have chosen a job other than baker, which involves vigorous upper-body movement. The important question was whether Dow Corning knew or should have known earlier of the risk referred to in the 1985 warning. The Court referred to field complaints of doctors communicated to Dow Corning, which showed Dow knew of problems encountered from unexplained rupture earlier. It would not have been onerous for Dow Corning to have mentioned unexplained ruptures, and have listed possible side-effects earlier.

Dow would only be liable, the Court pointed out, if a more comprehensive warning would have prevented Ms. Hollis' injury. Would Ms. Hollis have consented to the surgery if she had properly been informed of the risks? There was ample evidence, the Court said, that if Ms. Hollis had been properly warned, she would not have consented to the surgery. She was not "pre-sold", and before she saw Dr. Birch, had no desire to have breast surgery. Dow Corning said, however, that Dr. Birch did not usually give patients warning of the risk of implant ruptures and relied more on medical journals than on manufacturers' warnings. The Court said that in 1983 the average plastic surgeon did not know there was a significant risk of rupture, and that after the 1985 warning knowledge became more prevalent. By 1989, Dr. Birch was warning all patients of the risk of rupture.

In any event, Ms. Hollis should not be required to prove that had Dow Corning warned Dr. Birch, he would have warned her. That would call on her to prove a hypothetical situation. Ms. Hollis' right to an informed consent was not respected. To hold otherwise would mean that the doctor could escape liability because he was not properly warned by the manufacturer, and the manufacturer to escape liability because the doctor would not have warned the patient. The manufacturer can discharge its duty to the patient by giving adequate information of risks to a learned intermediary, but if it fails to do so, cannot raise as a defence that the intermediary could have ignored this information.

QUESTIONS

1. A case that reaches the Supreme Court of Canada will involve huge legal costs. How might the plaintiff have been able to afford this legal action?

2. Usually the Supreme Court of Canada will grant leave to appeal only in the most important civil cases. Why might the Supreme Court of Canada have considered this such an important civil case?

3. Why did the British Columbia Court of Appeal consider the trial judge erred in holding Dow Corning liable for negligent manufacture of the breast implants? Do you agree?

4. Explain why the Supreme Court said that if it did not hold Dow Corning liable for failing to give adequate warning, Ms. Hollis would probably not have been able to sue anyone successfully.

5. What legal principle regarding manufacturers' liability is established by this case?

Waldick v. Malcolm

[1991] 2 SCR 456, [1991] SCJ No. 55, 83 DLR (4th) 114, 125 NR 372, 47 OAC 241, 8 CCLT (2d) 1.

Supreme Court of Canada on Appeal from the Court of Appeal for Ontario

June 27, 1991

Present: La Forest, Sopinka, Gonthier, Cory, McLachlin, Stevenson and Iacobucci

This case confirms that modern legislation in the area of occupier's liability has extinguished the common law distinctions between different categories of people who might be injured on property, and established "reasonable care" as the appropriate standard to apply.

The judgment of the Court was delivered by **IACOBUCCI, J.** The following is a summary of the case and his judgment.

Mr. Waldick suffered a fractured skull when he fell on the icy parking area outside the Malcolm's rented farmhouse. Mr. Waldock was Mrs. Malcolm's brother. The owners of the farmhouse were Ms. Stainback and Mr. Hill.

Four days before the accident, there had been an ice storm that made the laneway slippery. Mr. Waldick was aware of the condition of the laneway and was very cautious driving up it. Upon arriving at the Malcolm's house, Mr. Waldick proceeded from his car to the house carefully because of the ice.

Later Mr. Waldick left the Malcolm's house to get something out of his car. Before doing so, he put on his winter boots and turned on the porch light. As he was walking back to the house from the car, he slipped on the ice, fell backwards, and fractured his skull. Mr. Waldick sued the Malcolms for negligence and won at the trial level.

The trial judge applied sections of the *Ontario Occupiers' Liability Act.*

> *Section 2*
> *Subject to section 9, the provisions of this Act apply in place of the rules of the common law that determine the care that the occupier of premises at common law is required to show for the purpose of determining his liability in law in respect of dangers to persons entering on the premises or the property brought on the premises by those persons.*
>
> *Section 3 (1)*
> *An occupier of premises owes a duty to take such care as in all the circumstances of the case is reasonable to see that persons entering on the premises, and the property brought on the premises by those persons are reasonably safe while on the premises.*

> *Section 4 (1)*
> *The duty of care provided for in subsection 3 (1) does not apply in respect of risks will-*
> *ingly assumed by the person who enters on the premises, but in that case the occupier*
> *owes a duty to the person to not create a danger with the deliberate intent of doing*
> *harm or damage to the person or his property and to not act with reckless disregard of*
> *the presence of the person or his property.*
>
> *Section 9 (3)*
> *The provisions of the Negligence Act apply with respect to the causes of action to*
> *which this Act applies.*

According to these provisions he considered that the duty towards invitees, licencees and trespassers was one of reasonable care. He found the Malcolms liable because they should have anticipated the dangerous condition of the parking area because of weather conditions, and did nothing to make it safer. He suggested that the Malcolms should have cleared, sanded or salted part of the parking area to serve as an entrance to the house. The fact that Mr. Waldick was aware of the conditions did not serve as a defence under section 4 (1), and the trial judge rejected the Malcolm's contention that Mr. Waldick should be held contributorily negligent.

In the Supreme Court of Canada the Malcolms argued that local custom or community standards should be taken into account in determining what constituted reasonable care, and that rural standards are different from those that apply in urban areas. Apparently Mr. Waldick, who lived nearby, had not salted or sanded his own driveway. Speaking for the Court, Iacobucci J. rejected this argument, stating that the existence of customary practices that are unreasonable in themselves do not lower what will be considered reasonable care.

The Court said that while section 4 of the *Occupiers' Liability Act* establishes a defence based on "volenti" or consent, for that defence to apply the plaintiff must not only have knowledge of the risk, but also have shown a willingness to accept the entire risk of injury and have expected the defendant to take no care. This would be a very narrow exception. Mr. Waldick, the Court held, had not shown that he intended to accept all risk and waive his legal rights. The Court also rejected the Malcolm's argument that Mr. Waldick had been contributorily negligent.

QUESTIONS

1. Why would Mr. Waldick be suing his close relatives, the Malcolms? Why would the Malcolms defend this legal action up to the Supreme Court of Canada level?

2. Why would the legal action against the owners of the farmhouse have been dismissed with consent?

3. What is the effect of section 9 (3) of the *Ontario Occupier's Liability Act*, which says that the provisions of the Negligence Act apply ?

4. What should an occupier do to ensure that the occupier does not risk financial ruin as a result of an occupier's liability claim?

chapter four

Professional Liability

Rangen Inc. v. Deloitte & Touche

[1994] B.C.J. No. 1910, [1994] 10 WWR 55, 48 BCAC 17, 95 BCLR (2d) 182, 21 CCLT (2d) 92.

British Columbia Court of Appeal

Judgment: filed August 26, 1994.

Because the range of people that have access to audited financial statements is broad, the potential for claims against auditors for negligent misstatement is huge. To whom should auditors be expected to be responsible when they audit statements for a client? This is an issue with which many courts have grappled, and most have been careful to limit the scope of an auditor's duty of care.

1   **GOLDIE J.A.:**— This appeal raises again the question of recovery for economic loss.

2   The plaintiff Rangen, Inc. ("Rangen") supplied aqua culture products on credit to a company operating a fish farm. Rangen says it extended credit in reliance on the company's audited financial statements. It suffered loss when the company failed. The defendants are chartered accountants of which a predecessor firm were the auditors of the failed company. I shall refer compendiously to the defendants as "Deloitte".

3   In the court below Rangen's statement of claim was struck out under Rule 19(24)(a) of the Rules of the Supreme Court of British Columbia because it disclosed no reasonable cause of action. This may be done only when it is plain and obvious the pleading contains that kind of radical defect ranking with the others listed in Rule 19(24)(a).

4   In a reasoned judgment, now reported at (1993), 79 B.C.L.R. (2d) 31, Mr. Justice Blair, after referring to *Hunt v. Carey Can. Inc.*, [1990] 2 S.C.R. 959 and to the relevant authorities, concluded this action would fail if it went to trial. From his judgment, pronounced January 22, 1993, Rangen appeals. But for the appellant's submission that the law has enlarged Rangen's right of recovery since the date of Mr. Justice Blair's judgment I would be content to adopt his reasons for judgment and to dismiss this appeal.

Facts

5   The facts alleged in the statement of claim are assumed, for the purpose of an application under Rule 19(24)(a), to be true. The relevant facts so alleged are as follows:

1. Rangen supplied salmon feed to Royal Pacific Sea Farms, Inc. (the "Company") in August, September and October of 1989. The Company failed on October 27, 1989 and Rangen incurred a loss of $300,493.38 (U.S.).

2. The Company was a public corporation whose shares were listed on the Vancouver Stock Exchange. Deloitte were the auditors in 1987, 1988 and 1989 who were responsible, in the words of the allegation, "... for the preparation of audited financial statements and making financial reports of the company."

3. These statements and reports were, to Deloitte's actual or constructive knowledge, available to the public and Deloitte knew or ought to have known that the Company intended to and did present these audited statements and financial reports to its suppliers for credit purposes.

4. It was reasonably foreseeable that trade suppliers would rely upon these statements and reports in deciding whether and how far to extend credit.

5. As a supplier of salmon feed to the Company Rangen was of a class of persons, again in the words of the allegation, "... likely to rely upon the skill and care of [Deloitte] in the preparation of audited financial reports of the company".

6. Rangen examined these reports and statements at the request of the Company and in reliance upon them extended credit and incurred the loss claimed.

7. The reports and statements were negligently and carelessly prepared, misleading and likely to cause economic loss to persons doing business with the company who relied upon them.

6   Recent judgments of this Court have considered in one aspect or another the issues raised in this appeal. I refer in particular to the following: *Kripps v. Touche Ross* (1992), 69 B.C.L.R. (2d) 62; *Dixon v. Deacon Morgan McEwen Esson* (1993), 102 D.L.R. (4th) 1; *The Queen v. RBO Architecture Inc.* et al., [1994] B.C.J. No. 1297 (9 June 1994), Vancouver CA016637 and CA016661 and *D'Amato v. Badger,* [1994] B.C.J. No. 1678 (18 July 1994), Vancouver CA017086. I note also that the Ontario Court of Appeal has dismissed the plaintiff's appeal in *Canadian Commercial Bank v. Crawford, Smith & Swallow.* The trial judgment is reported at (1993), 15 C.C.L.T. (2d) 273. The Court of Appeal's judgment, released March 29, 1994, is at [1994] O.J. No. 632. In that case the plaintiff bank failed to establish a duty of care on the part of accountants to a successor bank where the accountants were unaware of the impending change of banks.

7   Rangen's principal submission in this Court is that the following allegations support a cause of action that is distinguishable from those referred to in the above cases and from those relied upon by Mr. Justice Blair:

8.   The Defendant knew or ought to have known that the Company in the normal and ordinary course of its business intended to and did present the financial reports and audited statements prepared by the Defendant to its suppliers for the purposes of negotiating credit terms in the operation of its business.

9.   It was reasonably foreseeable that trade suppliers of the Company would rely on the work of the Defendant in deciding whether and how far to extend credit terms and take other risks of financial consequence in the ordinary course of doing business with the Company.

10.   Being a supplier of salmon feed to the company, the plaintiff was of a class of persons likely to rely on the skill and care of the defendant in the preparation of audited financial reports of the company.

11.   The plaintiff did actually examine the audited financial reports of the defendant at the specific request of the company, and did actually rely on the information and statements contained therein, extending short term credit to the company in August, September, and October of 1989.

8   The question here is whether these allegations, taken to be capable of proof, establish the proximity necessary to create a duty of care on the part of the respondent in respect of its role in the preparation of audited financial statements and financial reports of the Company.

Issues

9   Broadly speaking, the question raised is whether the appellant is entitled to recover in circumstances referred to by Mr. Justice Taylor in *Kripps v. Touche Ross & Co.,* supra, at p. 65:

> ... the scope of recovery in negligence for what may be called "pure economic loss simpliciter" - loss suffered in circumstances in which there is no personal injury or physical property damage, nor any risk that anyone would suffer either, but loss only to pocket or estate.

10   The circumstances giving rise to the present claim here were considered by Mr. Justice Blair who concluded his judgment at p. 39 with these words:

> On the material before me in the statement of claim I find that even if the allegations are proven, they do not disclose a reasonable cause of action against the defendant. The radical defect in the plaintiff's claim lies in the lack of proximity between the plaintiff trade creditor and the defendant accountant. The relationship is not one that falls within the umbrella of proximity such as to call upon the defendant to exercise a duty of care to the plaintiff.

11   The appellant maintains in this Court that the subsequent judgment of the Supreme Court of Canada in *Edgeworth Construction Ltd. v. N.D. Lea & Associates*, [1993] 3 S.C.R. 206 (S.C.C.) requires acceptance of a broader basis of recovery under the principles of *Hedley Byrne & Co. v. Heller & Partners Ltd.,* [1963] 2 All E.R. 575 (H.L.) than was recognized by the chambers judge.

12   Reliance is placed on passages in the judgments of Madam Justice McLachlin and Mr. Justice La Forest that, in the submission of the appellant, support this conclusion.

13   I would frame the issue in these terms:

> Do the allegations of actual and constructive knowledge of the appellant as set out in paragraphs 8 and 9 of the statement of claim, when taken with other relevant allegations, state a cause of action which entitles the plaintiff to a trial of this cause?

Discussion

14   Some consideration of juridical history is called for. Fifteen years before the judgment of the House of Lords in *McAlister (or Donoghue) v. Stevenson*, [1932] A.C. 562 (H.L.), then Judge Cardozo delivered the majority judgment for the New York Court of Appeals in *MacPherson v. Buick Motor Co.* (1916) 217 N.Y. 382, 11 N.E. 1050. Of it, Lord Atkin said at p. 598 in *Donoghue*:

> The mouse had emerged from the ginger-beer bottle in the United States before it appeared in Scotland, but there it brought a liability upon the manufacturer. I must not in this long judgment do more than refer to the illuminating judgment of Cardozo J. in *MacPherson v. Buick Motor Co.* in the New York Court of Appeals (2), in which he states the principles of the law as I should desire to state them, and reviews the authorities in other States than his own.

15   As would be done in *Donoghue*, the long-standing notion that lack of privity was a bar to recovery by a third party who alleged loss as a result of negligence of another was replaced in MacPherson by the concept of proximity.

16   MacPherson was the first of three judgments by the same judge to which I will refer. In *Glanzer v. Shepard* (1922), 233 N.Y. 236, 135 N.E. 275 the Court of Appeals held that the buyer of goods by weight could recover loss resulting from the weigher's negligence, although the latter was instructed and paid by the seller. The weigher had actual knowledge of the purpose for which its certificate was supplied to the buyer. Of this case Lord Reid said at p. 583-4 in *Hedley Byrne & Co. Ltd. v. Heller & Partners Ltd.*, supra:

... there was a direct relationship between the weigher who gave a certificate and the purchaser of the goods weighed, who the weigher knew was relying on his certificate: there the weigher was held to owe a duty to the purchaser with whom he had no contract.

17   Lord Reid was contrasting Glanzer with the result in the third of these cases: *Ultramares Corporation v. Touche* (1932), 255 N.Y. 170, 174 N.E. 441. In *Ultramares* Chief Judge Cardozo (as he had by then become) denied liability for negligent misstatement. In the course of his judgment the bounds of proximity were sketched in words which have been repeated numerous times in common law jurisdictions. As was said recently in *Al Saudi Banque v. Clark Pixley*, [1989] 3 All E.R. 362 (Chan.Div.) at p. 366:

> Claims for damages for economic loss resulting from negligent misstatements, however, are very different. There is a potential for foreseeable but indeterminate and possibly ruinous loss by a large and indeterminate class of plaintiffs. Foreseeability of reliance by itself is not an adequate limiting factor. Ever since the celebrated case of *Ultramares Corp v. Touche* (1931) 255 NY 170, courts in the common law jurisdictions have been concerned to avoid, in the well-known words of Cardozo CJ, 'liability in an indeterminate amount for an indeterminate time to an indeterminate class' (at 179). (emphasis added)

18   The circumstances in *Ultramares* were closely similar to those which we are to assume in the case at bar. Accountants were employed by a client to prepare and to certify the year-end balance sheet. The client's importing business required extensive credit. This was known to the accountants who prepared some 32 copies of the financial statements as counterpart originals. There was nothing said to them as to the persons to whom these counterparts would be shown or of the transactions in which they would be used.

[A discussion of the Ultramares case follows but has been omitted here...]

25   It will have been already apparent from what I have quoted above that the reluctance of Cardozo C.J. to impose a duty of care in favour of the trade creditor was based on the impossibility of determining at what point the consequences of this could or would stop. As he succinctly stated at N.E. p. 442:

> The range of the transactions in which a certificate of audit might be expected to play a part was as indefinite and wide as the possibilities of the business ...

28   In my view that background demonstrates that neither actual reliance nor the foreseeability of reliance alone constitutes proximity.

29   In *Haig v. Bamford* [1977] 1 S.C.R. 466 Mr. Justice Dickson, as he then was, considered the facts in that case closer to Glanzer's case than to Ultramares. He spoke for himself and five members of the court at p. 483:

> The statements were for benefit and guidance in a business transaction, the nature of which was known to the accountants. The accountants were aware that the company intended to supply the statements to members of a very limited class. Haig was a member of the class. It is true the accountants did not know his name but, as I have indicated earlier, I do not think that is of importance. I can see no good reason for distinguishing between the case in which a defendant accountant delivers information directly to the plaintiff at the request of his

employer, (Candler's case and Glanzer's case) and the case in which the information is handed to the employer who, to the knowledge of the accountant, passes it to members of a limited class (whose identity is unknown to the accountant) in furtherance of a transaction the nature of which is known to the accountant. I would accordingly hold that the accountants owed Haig a duty to use reasonable care in the preparation of the accounts.

30   The actual knowledge of the accountants was held to include knowledge of the furtherance of a specific transaction respecting a limited class of potential investors. In the case at bar there is no allegation of actual knowledge on the part of the accountants of a comparable particularity when they performed their work.

31   Three members of the Court concurred in the result on the basis of findings of fact in the trial court:

> I [Martland J.] agree with the conclusion reached by my brother Dickson that, based upon the finding of the learned trial judge, which was not disturbed by the Court of Appeal, that the respondents knew, prior to the completion of the financial statement, that it would be used by Sedco, by the bank with which the company was doing business and by a potential investor in equity capital, the respondents owed a duty of care, in the preparation of that financial statement, to that potential investor (the appellant), even though they were not aware of his actual identity. - p.484

32   The appellant, relying on the first sentence of Madam Justice McLachlin's judgment, says *Edgeworth*, supra, stands for the proposition that liability for negligent misrepresentation arises when a person makes a representation knowing that another may rely on it, and where the plaintiff in fact relies on the representation to its detriment.

33   I think, with respect, that the ultimate basis for the duty of care held to arise in *Edgeworth* lies in the court's finding that the engineering firm had actual knowledge that the immediate purpose of its work was to elicit bids from a limited class of contractors.

34   For the majority Madam Justice McLachlin said at p. 214:

> The facts alleged in this case meet this test, leaving the contract between the contractor and the province to one side. The engineers undertook to provide information (the "tender package") for use by a definable group of persons with whom it did not have any contractual relationship. The purpose of supplying the information was to allow tenderers to prepare a price to be submitted. The engineers knew this. The plaintiff contractor was one of the tenderers. It relied on the information prepared by the engineers in preparing its bid. Its reliance upon the engineers' work was reasonable. It alleges it suffered loss as a consequence. These facts establish a prima facie cause of action against the engineering firm.

35   Only in this way can *Edgeworth* be reconciled with *Haig v. Bamford*, supra. It will be recalled in the latter case the accountants prepared the statements in question in the knowledge that the purpose, indeed the only purpose, was to meet a requirement of a lender from whom the client was seeking additional capital.

36   It is important at this point to bear in mind just what the respondents in the case at bar were doing. It was conceded Deloitte was performing its statutory function as described in s.212 of the *Company Act* of this province, R.S.B.C. 1979, c. 59, as amended: [*the text of s. 212 has been omitted...*]

37   The material before the chambers judge and in this Court does not disclose the date of the Company's year end. It was assumed in argument that the reports and statements that were in question were in fact the year-end statements and that the opinions of Deloitte with respect to them were not qualified.

38   As has been so for many years, the auditor's report under s. 212 of the Company Act is made to the members of the company. The remuneration of the auditor is a matter for the members at the company's annual general meeting. Other provisions of the Company Act carry forward established principles with respect to the purpose of the auditor's opinion.

39   The uses to which a client may put the audited statements prepared for the purpose of complying with the requirements of the *Company Act* are legion. In addition to demonstrating to suppliers, present and potential, that the client is creditworthy, copies of the statements may be lodged with term lenders, used by appraisers and others in a variety of legal proceedings, filed with regulatory agencies to support licence applications or with stock exchanges for listing purposes. The principals of a company may use them as the basis for determining the value of family assets and so on. All these, and many more, are reasonably foreseeable uses. But none constitutes the purpose for which the statements were prepared by an accountant performing the task referred to in s-s. 212(2) of the *Company Act*. In my view a duty of care does not arise upon reliance for any of the extraneous purposes I have referred to unless the maker of the statements knew, not only of the intended reliance, but accepted the potential risk of reliance. I think, with respect, that this is all that Mr. Justice La Forest may be taken as saying at p. 212 of *Edgeworth*:

> The appellant here was quite reasonably relying on the skills of the engineering firm and the firm in turn must be taken to have recognized that persons in the position of the respondents would rely on their work and act accordingly. I have cast the relationship in terms of reliance but it may also be seen as a matter of voluntary assumption of risk. As Professor Fleming put it in The Law of Torts, 8th ed. (1992), at p. 641, "the recipient must have had reasonable grounds for believing the speaker expected to be trusted".

40   There is no allegation that Deloitte in the case at bar distributed the statements in question to the public or to anyone other than the Company whose directors were under the statutory obligation of sending the statements, together with the auditor's report, to the members prior to each annual general meeting and of placing those statements before the members at the meeting. I can find no basis in Edgeworth for questioning the conclusion stated by Mr. Justice Blair at p. 39 of his judgment:

> The relationship is not one that falls within the umbrella of proximity such as to call upon the defendant to exercise a duty of care to the plaintiff.

41   This conclusion is not one that would be uniformly accepted in all jurisdictions in the United States. In matters of state common law the Supreme Court of the United States, unlike the Supreme Court of Canada, has no general appellate jurisdiction. Thus there are both legislative and judicial variations to be found from the Cardozo judgments.

42   This is exemplified in a recent judgment of the Supreme Court of California in *Bily v. Arthur Young & Co.* (1992) 834 P. (2d) 745 (Sup. Ct. Cal.). At p. 754 the majority refer to the present New York rule as requiring certain prerequisites to be sat-

isfied before allowing recovery to non-contractual parties who rely to their detriment on inaccurate financial reports:

(1) the accountant must have been aware that the financial reports were to be used for a particular purpose or purposes; (2) in the furtherance of which a known party or parties was intended to rely; and (3) there must have been some conduct on the part of the accountants linking them to that party or parties, which evinces the accountants' understanding of that party or parties' reliance.

43   This amounts to a modern restatement of *Ultramares*.

44   Without deciding whether the New York rule described in *Bily*, supra, has been or should be adopted in Canada, it is self-evident that the granting or withholding of credit permeates the commercial life of modern society.

45   Accountants know as a matter of ordinary commercial life that their clients utilize credit in the normal course of business. But unless expressly advised, accountants performing functions as in the case at bar have no way of knowing, and no reason to anticipate, how, when or why any one or more trade creditors will be relying upon financial statements which the accountants have audited.

46   There are good reasons why foreseeability and unilateral reliance are unacceptable as controlling considerations in cases of pure economic loss, simpliciter. One is that an auditor's certificate expresses an opinion with respect to historical records and it would be a distortion of commercial reality to suggest as a general proposition that the terms of trade are determined or even significantly affected by the previous year's financial results which are often out of date by the time they are made known. Whether an enterprise pays its accounts when they fall due is of greater current importance to suppliers of goods and services than the last or previous years' results. Credit reporting and rating agencies flourish for this purpose.

47   The Plaintiff has not pleaded Deloitte was forewarned of its intention to use Rangen's financial statements to regulate future credit terms in its dealings with Rangen. Nor is it pleaded Deloitte had an opportunity of protecting itself against such use. It will be recalled the defendant's disclaimer in Hedley, Byrne was proof against liability. Nor has Rangen pleaded it was reasonable for it to rely upon the financial statements in the circumstances. In my view, for the reasons already stated, the Plaintiff cannot possibly succeed in establishing that it would be reasonable for the trade creditors to rely upon such statements or for "indeterminate" liability to be imposed in the circumstances of this case.

48   In short, it is difficult to imagine a clearer case where the imposition of liability would extend in an indeterminate amount for an indeterminate time to an indeterminate class.

Conclusion

49   I think Mr. Justice Blair reached the correct conclusion and in my view no change in the substantive law extending the duty of care has been effected since his judgment. I would dismiss the appeal.

MCEACHERN C.J.B.C.:— I AGREE.

TAGGART J.A.:— I AGREE.

QUESTIONS

1. The plaintiff claimed that the auditors owed the plaintiff a duty of care because it was reasonable for the auditors to foresee that trade suppliers would rely on the audit. Did the court consider that this fact created a sufficiently close relationship to create a duty of care? Explain.

2. What kind of relationship must exist between the auditors and a party relying on an audit for it to be found that the auditors owed the party relying on the audit a duty of care?

3. The court referred to a decision of the Supreme Court of Canada in *Haig v. Bamford.*, in which the Supreme Court of Canada held that the auditors owed an investor a duty of care. Why did the auditors owe the investor a duty of care in that case? How did the relationship between the auditors and the investors in the Haig case differ from the relationship between the auditors and the plaintiff in this case?

4. How does the court justify the conclusion that there was a duty of care owed in the *Edgeworth* case?

Hercules Managements Ltd. v. Ernst & Young

[1997] 2 SCR 165, [1997] SCJ No. 51, 146 DLR (4th) 577, [1997] 8 WWR 80, 115 Man. R. (2d) 241, 31 BLR (2d) 147, 35 CCLT (2d) 115, 211 NR 352.

May 22, 1997

Supreme Court of Canada on appeal from the Court of Appeal for Manitoba

Present: La Forest, Sopinka, Gonthier, Cory, McLachlin, Iacobucci and Major JJ.

Shareholders would seem to be the group with the closest connection to auditors, but this case illustrates that in some circumstances, the courts are reluctant to even extend protection from auditors' negligence to shareholders.

The judgment of the Court was delivered by **LA FOREST J.** The following is a summary of the case and his judgment.

Northguard Acceptance Ltd. (NGA) and Northguard Holdings Ltd. (NGH) were in the business of lending and investing money on the security of real property mortgages. Hercules Managements Ltd. (Hercules) and Max Freed were shareholders in NGA. Ernst & Young had been engaged since 1971 to perform annual audits of NGAS and NGH. In 1984 the corporations went into receivership.

Several investors in NGA brought action against the auditors alleging that audit reports for 1980, 1981 and 1982 were negligently prepared. They claimed that they used the audit for the purpose of monitoring their equity, and that owing to the negligent audits, they failed to extract their investment before NGA and NGH collapsed. Hercules was seeking damages for advances of $600,000 that it made to NGA in 1983, and Freed sought damages for money he added to an investment account in NGH in 1982. The plaintiffs also alleged that there was a contract between themselves and the auditors under which the auditors undertook to protect the individual interests of the shareholders in the audit. The claims of the investors were dismissed both at the trial court and by the Manitoba Court of Appeal. Hercules and Max Freed appealed to the Supreme Court of Canada.

The Supreme Court of Canada held that there was no evidence of a contract between the shareholders and the auditors. The only contracts were between NGA and NGH and the auditors. It then considered whether the auditors owed Hercules and Max Freed a duty of care. The Court said that although special considerations might stem from the fact that recovery was being sought for pure economic loss as opposed to physical damage, in both cases the same general framework should be used to determine if a duty of care was owed. The questions that a court must ask are:

1. Where a prima facie duty of care is owed—is there a sufficiently close relationship between the parties so that, in the reasonable contemplation of the parties, carelessness of one might cause damage to the other?

2. Whether that duty, if it exists, is negatived, or limited by, policy considerations.

A requirement that the defendant know the identity of the plaintiff (or class of plaintiffs), and that the plaintiff use the statements for the specific purpose for which they are prepared, is consistent with those requirements and serves as a policy-based limiting function with respect to the ambit of the duty of care.

The Court acknowledged the significant negative repercussions of exposing auditors to "indeterminate" liability. Writing for the Court, Mr. Justice La Forest concluded that the auditors owed Hercules and Max Freed a prima facie duty of care because it was reasonably foreseeable that Hercules and Max Freed would rely on the audit in conducting their affairs, and that harm to them from a negligent audit was reasonably foreseeable.

As for the second branch of the test, policy considerations, the auditors knew the specific identity of Hercules and Max Freed through their engagement over the ten years preceding the negligent audits. The limiting factor was that the auditors were not aware of the purpose for which Hercules and Max Freed would use the audit. The standard purpose of an audit is to guide shareholders, as a group, in making decisions as to how the corporation should be managed, to assess the performance of the directors and officers, and to decide whether or not to retain existing management. Where shareholders use audits as guidance to make personal investment decisions, they are using the audit for a purpose for which it was not prepared. The Court held that to extend an auditor's duty of care to investors in the position of Hercules and Max Freed would be an unacceptably broad expansion of the bounds of liability, and dismissed the appeal.

QUESTIONS

1. Commentators have argued that imposing broad duties of care on auditors would provide economic and social benefits in that it would act as an incentive to auditors to produce accurate reports. Do you agree? What are the disadvantages of imposing broader duties of care on auditors?

2. Are there any means available other than imposing tort liability on auditors to produce more accurate audit reports?

Coldunn Holding Ltd. v. Montreal Trust Co. of Canada and Josef Sutej

[1993] O.J. No. 625, 30 RPR (2d) 263

Ontario Court of Justice - General Division

March 18, 1993.

Professionals owe their clients a fiduciary duty because their relationship of trust results in vulnerability of the client. Remedies can involve not only compensation for damage suffered by the client, but also the professional can be deprived of any benefit derived from the impugned transaction.

ROBERTS J.:— The plaintiffs bring this action to recover $37,500.00 in real estate commissions from the defendants. The real estate commissions arose out of the sale of 2 properties municipally known as 585 Jane Street in the City of York and 152 Priscilla Avenue in the City of York. The plaintiff claims a return of its commission in the amount of $25,000.00 paid to the defendant Montreal Trust as a result of a sale of the said properties to Grieve. The plaintiffs further claim the right to the disgorgement up of a further commission in the amount of $12,500.00 paid to Montreal Trust in a transaction of sale pertaining to the two properties when the purchaser, Grieve, sold the properties to third parties prior to the closing of the first transaction.

The Facts

585 Jane Street was at all material times a multi-unit apartment building owned by the plaintiff. The plaintiff's sole shareholder was Lillian Kastner whose father owned the property at 152 Priscilla Avenue which property abutted the 585 Jane Street apartment building. The

property at 152 Priscilla Avenue had been used for parking for the Jane Street apartment building. Some time in early 1986 Lillian Kastner and her father decided to sell the two properties as a package. The properties were offered for sale through Royal LePage Realty Company. The listing agreement with Royal LePage expired at the end of November, 1986.

In early December, 1986 a representative of Montreal Trust contacted Lillian Kastner, the sole shareholder and president of the plaintiff company, and advised her that they had a potential purchaser for the two properties. They requested a two day exclusive listing agreement which Lillian Kastner agreed to execute in her capacity as an officer of the plaintiff. The listing agreement was executed but expired after the presentation of an offer which was not accepted by the plaintiff.

On December 31, 1986 Joseph Sutej, one of the defendants and a real estate sales representative for Montreal Trust together with another sales representative attended on Lillian Kastner with a new offer to purchase for the two properties, naming D. Grieve (in trust) as purchaser. Lillian Kastner received that offer without comment and took it to her solicitor Mr. Fine for review on January 2, 1987. The agreement of purchase and sale as presented was varied on the advice of Mr. Fine and signed back to the purchaser. D. Grieve (in trust) accepted the sign back on January 5, 1987. The agreement called for a closing date of April 30, 1987.

The price in the accepted agreement of purchase and sale was the asking price, the same price as that which had been contained in the Royal LePage Listing earlier in 1986. The evidence from Mrs. Lillian Kastner was that at the time she was satisfied with the deal and satisfied with the price. There was no evidence led at trial at any time to indicate that Mrs. Kastner was not satisfied with that price.

The agreement of purchase and sale contained a clause as follows:

"3. The purchaser shall have the right to assign this agreement, at any time or times, on or before closing to any person, company, or corporation, and upon such an assignment all liability, if any, of the purchaser herein shall cease . . .".

When the accepted agreement of purchase and sale was returned to Lillian Kastner, the agents for Montreal Trust requested that an exclusive listing agreement be signed for each property. They wanted that agreement to protect their commission. Lillian Kastner agreed to execute those agreements and did so on January 5, 1987. The deal called for a commission of $25,000.00 to be paid by the plaintiff to Montreal Trust upon the completion of the transaction. The plaintiff had agreed with Lillian Kastner's father to pay the entire commission on the two sales and in fact when the transaction closed on April 30, 1987 the plaintiff paid the $25,000.00 commission as required.

The plaintiff makes no complaint with respect to the behaviour of Montreal Trust until on or about the 6th of April, 1987.

The evidence establishes that on or about the 6th of April, 1987 the purchaser Grieve was contacted by a real estate agent from another real estate firm known as Realty View with an offer to purchase the two properties. Some time on April 6th or April 7th Mr. Grieve advised the representative of Montreal Trust of this transaction. Neither Montreal Trust nor any of its agents advised the plaintiff at any time of this second sale or "flip".

There was some evidence led during the cross-examination of the defendant Josef Sutej which indicates that Montreal Trust on April 7th took part in the final negotiations which resulted in the sale by Grieve of the property to the third parties. The evidence clearly establishes that Montreal Trust did not introduce the third party purchaser to Grieve nor did Montreal Trust or any of its agents have any knowledge of the second transaction prior to April 6th, 1987.

The evidence also establishes that Montreal Trust shared in the commission earned the second sale to the extent of $12,500.00 which, upon the closing of that transaction, was paid to Montreal Trust.

The evidence further establishes that some time after the 7th of April, 1987 the solicitor for the plaintiff Mr. Fine, became aware of the assignment to the new purchaser by Grieve. The evidence established that Mr. Fine considered such information pertaining to the assignment to be in the normal course and that there was nothing untoward about that assignment in his mind. He further stated that on the 28th of April he discussed the assignment with the Kastners. The Kastners took no steps at that time. The only evidence that the Kastners had at that time was that there had in fact been an assignment and of course there had been an assignment contemplated in the agreement of purchase and sale. There was no evidence that the Kastners had been advised that there had been a resale at a profit or that Montreal Trust had earned any commission on that resale.

On the basis of these facts the plaintiff brings this action claiming a return of its commission on the first sale in the amount of $25,000.00 and a disgorgement up to it of the $12,500.00 secret commission obtained by Montreal Trust on the second transaction. In addition the plaintiff claims punitive damages.

The Law

The case of *Hennessy v. Martens* (1990), 15 R.P.R. (2d) 293 a decision of Mr. Justice Hollingworth of the Ontario Court (General Division) states as follows at page 296:

> "As to general principles of fiduciary duty I cite first Mr. Justice Galligan, as he then was, in *D'Atri v. Chilcott* (1975), 7 O.R. (2d) 249 . . . His Lordship points out a real estate agent's obligation and duties as follows. First, the relationship between the real estate agent and the person who has retained him to sell his property is a fiduciary and confidential one. Second, that there is a duty upon such an agent to make full disclosure of all facts within the knowledge of the agent which might affect the value of the property. Three, that not only must the price paid be adequate but the transaction must be a righteous one and the price obtained must be as advantageous to the principal as any other price that the agent could by exercise of diligence on his principal's behalf have obtained from a third person and, four, the onus is upon the agent to prove that those duties have been complied with."

Further, at page 260:

> "It is in the interest of equity that persons upon whom members of the public rely for advice, knowledge and trust must act with the best good faith and if any dispute arises must be able to demonstrate unequivocally that they did so act. Any doubt must be resolved in favour of the person who relies upon them."

At page 298, Hollingworth, J. states quoting from Mr. Justice Holland in the Yorkland *Real Estate Limited v. Dale* (1987) 60 O.R (2d) 460 as follows at page 467 of that report:

> "We are all agreed that the fiduciary duty cast upon the plaintiffs by the listing agreement continued notwithstanding the acceptance of Quaranta (subsequent) offer and that duty continued up to the completion of the sale or the expiration of the listing agreement [once again this was a sale to a third party and the question of the commission was in issue] . . . The fiduciary relationship required that the plaintiffs advise the defendants of the interest expressed by [the third party] and their participation in the arrangement of the second sale. . . .Accordingly, the plaintiffs being in breach of their fiduciary duty to the defendant . . . it is appropriate that they be disentitled to any commission on the sale.

In the *Hennessy* case the court held that the commission on the first transaction should be retained by the agents but that they should disgorge the commission on the second undisclosed transaction.

In *Yorkland Real Estate v. Dale* (1987) 60 O.R. (2d) 460 the Divisional Court held as follows at page 467:

> "It is trite that the obligation cast upon a fiduciary is very high and is to be strictly enforced as a matter of public policy."

Disposition

The law pertaining to the fiduciary duty owed by a real estate agent to its principal, in this case the vendor, is that the real estate agent's obligations are very high and must be strictly enforced. The two cases of *Yorkland Real Estate Limited* and *Hennessy v. Martens* set out what that duty is.

In the case before me the duty of the fiduciary, the real estate agent, was, upon being advised of the second sale by Grieve to the third parties, to immediately inform the vendor of this second sale and of Montreal Trust's involvement in that sale with respect to a further commission.

The evidence discloses that Montreal Trust did not take any such steps to advise the plaintiff. The plaintiff was therefore deprived of exercising any options it might have had up to the closing of the transaction.

It is my opinion that nothing that Montreal Trust did affected its entitlement to the commission of $25,000.00 earned by it in the sale from the plaintiff to Grieve. The plaintiff's evidence was that it was satisfied with the price and that transaction.

Montreal Trust and the defendant Josef Sutej however are in breach of their strict fiduciary obligations to inform the plaintiff with respect to the second transaction.

This is not a case for punitive damages.

Accordingly, an order will go directing Montreal Trust and Josef Sutej to disgorge up the commission earned in the second transaction in the amount of $12,500.00, to the plaintiff.

In my opinion on the facts of this case there should be no pre-judgment interest on the said $12,500.00.

The plaintiff shall have its costs on a party and party scale to be paid by the defendants to the plaintiff forthwith after assessment thereof.

QUESTIONS

1. Did the Montreal Trust agents have a duty to advise the plaintiff what would be an appropriate price for the property?

2. Why did the court order the Montreal Trust agents to disgorge the $12,500 commission on the second sale?

3. The judge says that because the Montreal Trust agents did not advise the plaintiff of the second sale, the plaintiff was deprived of exercising any options it might have had up to the time the transaction closed. What might those options have been?

4. Why do you think the court said that this was not a case for punitive damages?

Hodgkinson v. Simms and Waldman

[1994] 3 SCR 377, [1994] SCJ/ACS 84, 117 DLR (4th) 161, 171 NR 245, [1994]
9 WWR 609, 97 BCLR (2d) 1, 16 BLR (2d) 1, 6 CCLS 1, 22 CCLT (2d) 1, 57
CPR (3d) 1, 95 DTC 5135, 5 ETR (2d) 1.

Supreme Court of Canada on appeal from the Court of Appeal for British Columbia

September 30, 1994

Present: La Forest, L'Heureux-Dube, Sopinka, Gonthier, McLachlin, Iacobucci
and Major JJ.

The majority allowed the appeal, Sopinka, McLachlin and Major JJ. dissenting.

Advisers run the risk of liability where they try to marry the interests of two clients, as the adviser did in this case.

Judgment for La Forest, L'Heureux-Dube and Gonthier JJ. was delivered by **LA FOREST J.**
The following is a summary of the case and his judgment.

Hodgkinson was a 30-year old stockbroker with fairly limited investment experience. He
sought advice from Simms, a chartered accountant with the firm of Simms & Waldman, about
accounting and how to shelter his income from taxation. In choosing Simms, Hodgkinson considered the fact that Simms was not part of the high-risk world of promoters, and would be
someone who could be relied on for independent analysis in the area of tax sheltered investments. He wanted primarily to minimize his exposure to income tax and acquire stable long-
term investments.

Simms suggested that Hodgkinson invest in MURBs, projects to construct apartment units,
under which investors could deduct costs such as financing from their personal incomes.
Hodgkinson did not ask many questions about the investments and relied on Simms to do the
analysis. As a result of Simms' advice, Hodgkinson invested in four MURBs. When the real
estate market crashed in 1981, Hodgkinson lost substantially on all the MURBs. The evidence
was that Hodgkinson had paid fair market value for them.

Hodgkinson's complaint was that Simms acted for the developer of the MURBs in structuring
the projects and did not disclose this to Hodgkinson. In fact, business with the developer represented 1/6 of Simms' firm's billables for 1980 and 1981. The developer paid Simms & Waldman
bonuses depending on the extent to which Simms & Waldman clients purchased the projects.

Hodgkinson sued Simms in the Supreme Court of British Columbia for breach of fiduciary
duty and breach of contract and was awarded damages of $350,507.62 calculated on what
Hodgkinson lost on the MURBs because of the downturn in the real estate market. Prowse J.
said there was a fiduciary duty because Simms agreed to act on behalf of Hodgkinson and was

)sition to affect his interests. She said that a fiduciary duty is marked by vulnerability, in
e fiduciary can abuse power to the detriment of the other party.

Prowse J. found that Simms knew that Hodgkinson was relying on him to apply Hodgkinson's
income towards stable tax sheltered investments. Hodgkinson's interests were in real or potential
conflict with the developer's and with Simms', and Simms did not disclose this to Hodgkinson. If
Simms had disclosed his conflict of interest to Hodgkinson, Hodgkinson would not have invested
in the MURBs. Simms appealed to the British Columbia Court of Appeal.

Speaking for the Court of Appeal, McEachern C.J. found that there was no fiduciary duty
because the required degree of vulnerability had not been proved, and that Hodgkinson was
fully acquainted with questions of risk. The Court did hold, however, that there had been a duty
of disclosure because of the implied retainer between the parties, but held that Hodgkinson's
losses were due to the unforeseeable collapse of the real estate market, rather than on the failure
of Simms to disclose. Damages should be limited to a prorated share of the amounts paid by the
developers to Simms. Hodgkinson appealed to the Supreme Court of Canada.

La Forest wrote the majority judgment in the Supreme Court of Canada. He said that vulnerability is common to breach of fiduciary duty, undue influence, unconscionability and negligent misrepresentation. Inequality of bargaining power triggers unconscionability, but need
not be present for a fiduciary duty to exist.

To determine whether a fiduciary duty exists, one must ask whether, given all the surrounding circumstances, one party could reasonably have expected that the other party would act in
the former's best interests. Where a broker is just a conduit of information or an order taker, no
fiduciary duty exists. Whether or not one should be considered vulnerable in a situation
depends not just on whether that person is capable of protecting himself from harm.
Vulnerability can exist because a person has reasonable expectations that the other party will
act in the person's best interests, and that makes the person vulnerable to an abuse of power.
One should not focus on a narrow class of "power-dependency" relationships. The essence of
professional advisory relationships is trust, confidence and independence.

According to the evidence, Simms went out of his way to represent himself as independent.
He made a conscious decision not to disclose his fee arrangement with the developers because
it might interfere with his practice. The Court referred to many cases where fiduciary duty was
affirmed without regard to the level of sophistication of the client. The Court also cited policy
reasons to enforce duties of honesty and good faith in the case of financial advisors, and the fact
that the principles that underlie fiduciary duty are reflected in Codes and directives of many
professional bodies. What vulnerability really means in the context of fiduciary duty is suscep-
tibility to harm.

In addition, the Court said, there must also be reliance. The evidence in this case was that
Hodgkinson did meet with the developer independently, but that without Simms' stamp of
approval, he was not willing to invest in the MURBs. Hodgkinson's trust in Simms was based
on his assumption that Simms was independent, and Simms knew that.

Regarding the issue of damages, Simms said that Hodgkinson's loss was caused by the general economic recession that hit the British Columbia real estate market in the early 1980's, and
not by Simms' advice. The Court rejected that argument, saying that because of Simms' advice,
Hodgkinson was induced into investments he would not otherwise have made, and that his failure
to disclose caused Hodgkinson to be exposed to the risk of those investments. The breach of fiduciary duty initiated the chain of events that led to Hodgkinson's loss, and therefore it was right that
the advisor should be liable for the investor's loss. The Court also said that from a policy perspec-

tive it would be unjust to place the risk of market fluctuations on a plaintiff who would not have entered into a given transaction but for the defendant's wrongful conduct. The Court agreed with the trial judge that Hodgkinson should recover losses on his investment due to the fall in the real estate market, as well as consequential losses such as legal and accounting fees.

QUESTIONS

1. Why did the Court hold that there had been a breach of fiduciary duty in this case?
2. How do the circumstances that create:

   a) undue influence

   b) unconscionability

   differ from the circumstances that create a fiduciary duty?
3. Would the result have been the same if, before buying MURB investements, Hodgkinson had had them evaluated by an independent investment adviser unrelated to Simms? Explain.
4. Compare this case with a previous case brought in British Columbia in which an investment adviser had received an undisclosed finder's fee from a seller of real estate investments. The Court held in that case that there had been a breach of fiduciary duty, but refused to award market losses on the investment to the investor, and limited damages to the amount of the finder's fee that the adviser had received. Is there any way you could reconcile the decision in that case with the decision in *Hodgkinson v. Simms*?

part three

Contracts

chapter five

Formation of a Contract

Montane Ventures Ltd. v. Schroeder

[2000] B.C.J. No. 679, 200 BCSC 532.
British Columbia Supreme Court
March 27, 2000

The essence of a contract is, at least in theory, the meeting of the minds of the contracting parties. The two parties must have a common will in relation to the subject matter of their negotiations and must have struck an agreement. Sometimes it is difficult to tell what constitutes a rejection or a counter-offer. When the offeree is merely requesting information or clarification, that does not constitute a counter-offer or a rejection and the offer remains in force.

1   **BLAIR J.**:— The plaintiff, Montane Ventures Ltd. ("Montane"), pursuant to R. 18A of the Rules of Court, seeks an order of specific performance directing the defendant, Frank Schroeder, to complete an agreement to sell real property located at 100 Mile House.

2   Montane and Mr. Schroeder on September 3 and 4, 1999, negotiated a contract of purchase and sale ("the agreement") which provided that Montane would purchase from Mr. Schroeder property described as Lot 1, District Lot 2136, Plan 29717 ("the property") at a price of $215,000, with the sale to be completed on November 30, 1999. The agreement addressed the issue of the leasehold interest in the property held by the Internet Cafe, with the parties making the completion of the agreement pursuant to the following term:

> Subject to the purchasers receiving copy of the above lease and being satisfied with such by 10th Sep 99.

> This condition is for the sole benefit of the purchasers.

3   Montane's realtor, Mike Jeves, subsequently communicated directly with Mr. Schroeder regarding the lease. Mr. Schroeder was experienced in the real estate business, having formerly been the owner of Caldwell Banker Cariboo Lone Butte Realty of 100 Mile House, the listing company for the property.

4   Mr. Schroeder, on September 8, 1999, faxed Mr. Jeves information regarding the lease and requested that he have Montane initial and return a copy of the fax. Mr. Schroeder also asked Mr. Jeves to telephone him directly and during the ensuing conversation the two discussed the alterations done to the property which had been performed for the leased premises. Mr. Jeves asked Mr. Schroeder whether the municipality had completed a final inspection on the alterations and he deposed that Mr. Schroeder advised that he had not asked for the final inspection permit, but indicated it was no problem and he would do so straightaway.

5   On September 9, 1999, Mr. Jeves forwarded to Mr. Schroeder an addendum to the agreement ("the addendum") removing the subject to clause regarding the lease with the Internet Cafe. At the bottom of the addendum, Mr. Jeves included the following sentence which led to this action:

> Seller agrees to provide final inspection certificates for alterations re above lease by Sep 22nd 1999.

Mr. Schroeder responded in the following terms:

> As a result of receiving your addendum dated Sept. 10, 1999, but received on Sept. 9, 1999 at 12:13 p.m. via fax the seller takes the position that the buyer either repudiated the original contract or made a counter offer and either way the seller is not prepared to complete pursuant to terms of the original contract.

6   Mr. Schroeder added he was still prepared to sell the property, but for $225,000, a $10,000 increase in the price from that contained in the parties' earlier agreement.

7   The issue is whether the addendum constitutes a repudiation or a counter-offer which amounts to a rejection of the agreement. In Cheshire, Fifoot and Furmston's Law of Contract, 3d ed., (Butterworths 1996) at p. 41 the authors note:

> The task of the courts is to extract the intention of the parties both from the terms of their correspondence and from the circumstances which surround and follow

it, and the question of interpretation may thus be stated. Is the preparation of a further document a condition precedent to the creation of a contract or is it an incident in the performance of an already binding obligation?

8   In *Singh v. Chung* (1995), 8 B.C.L.R. (3d) 279, a case involving the interpretation of a real estate transaction, Cumming J.A. noted at para. 24:

> It is common ground that, as a general rule, a counter-offer may, and indeed generally does, constitute a rejection of the offer and terminate it so that it is not longer open for acceptance. See Chitty on Contracts, 27th ed., para. 2-063 [vol. 1, p. 128]:

And Cumming J.A. continued at para. 25:

> But not every inquiry or request for information is to be construed as a counter-offer; it may be a mere inquiry. In Chitty the learned authors continue, in para 2-064 [pp. 128-29]:
>
>> 2-064 Inquiries and requests for information. A communication from the offeree may be construed as a counter-offer (and hence as a rejection) even through it takes the form of a question as to the offeror's willingness to vary the terms of the offer. But such a communication is not necessarily a counter-offer: it may be a mere inquiry or request for information made without any intention of rejecting the terms of the offer. Whether the communication is a counter-offer or a request for information depends on the intention, objectively ascertained, with which it was made.

9   The inclusion by Mr. Jeves in the addendum of the sentence regarding the inspection certificates follows from the condition precedent that Montane must be satisfied with the lease arrangement with the Internet Cafe. After reviewing the lease, Montane sought further information regarding the lease from Mr. Schroeder, with some of the details being provided by Mr. Schroeder in his fax to Mr. Jeves of September 8, 1999, which included a request that Mr. Jeves telephone him directly. During that telephone conversation the two men discussed the inspection certificates.

10   Mr. Jeves deposed that following his September 8, 1999, discussion with Mr. Schroeder he arranged for Montane's principal, Ian Briggs, to sign the September 9, 1999, addendum removing the subject to clause from the agreement and he included the sentence regarding the inspection certificates merely to confirm his conversation with Mr. Schroeder the previous day, September 8, 1999, not in any way to put forward a counter offer.

11   In reviewing the material relating to the lease, I find that there were ongoing communications with Mr. Schroeder as Mr. Jeves sought information regarding the lease arrangement with the Internet Cafe. As a result of inquiries and information provided by Mr. Schroeder, Montane removed the subject-to clause regarding the lease from the agreement. The sentence regarding the inspection certificates merely confirmed the conversation that Mr. Schroeder would provide the inspection certificates. Had the sentence been a counter-offer or new term of the agreement, then Mr. Schroeder would have been required to sign the September 9, 1999, addendum: See Waddams S.M., The Law of Contracts, 3rd ed. (Canada Law Book Inc., 1993) at pp. 40-41. There is no suggestion in the addendum or attached material that Montane sought Mr. Schroeder's signature on the September 9, 1999, addendum. The subject-to clause regarding the lease was included for the sole benefit of Montane and its removal needed only Montane's signature.

12   I conclude, based on the peculiar factual context of this case, that the sentence in the addendum relating to the inspection certificates was neither a counter-offer nor repudiation, but merely confirmed Mr. Schroeder's earlier response to Mr. Jeves' inquiries regarding the lease. Mr. Schroeder's response came during the September 8, 1999, telephone conversation between Mr. Jeves and Mr. Schroeder, which conversation had been initiated by Mr. Schroeder in his September 8, 1999, request that Mr. Jeves telephone him. Neither Montane nor its agent, Mr. Jeves, had any intention of putting forward a counter-offer or repudiating the agreement. If the sentence regarding the inspection certificates were to constitute a counter-offer, then it would have required Mr. Schroeder's written acceptance of the term. Neither Montane nor Mr. Jeves made such a request.

13   Montane will have judgment and relief in the form of an order for specific performance. Counsel advise that the details can be worked out by agreement, but they have leave to apply for directions if difficulties occur. Montane will have its costs at scale three, as I see no justification for awarding special costs.

QUESTIONS

1. How did the court in this case determine whether a counter-offer or a mere inquiry was made? Why is the distinction important?
2. If the offeree rejects a counter-offer, is the original offer revived?
3. When the offeree merely inquires whether the terms are the best he/she can expect, does this amount to a rejection?

Alcon Electric Ltd. v. Maksymchuk

[1995] B.C.J. No. 3018
British Columbia Supreme Court
December 14, 1995

At the heart of contract law is the concept of consensus and mutual commitment. The contract is formed and the parties are bound by it at the point of acceptance. The key to understanding acceptance is that the commitment must be total.

1   **ARKELL J.** (orally):— The Plaintiff company, Alcon Electric Limited Ltd., seeks damages for breach of a contract. The Defendants deny any contract or breach of contract between the parties.

2   Al Jee, the operating mind of the Plaintiff company, is an electrical contractor. He had worked with the Defendant Larry Maksymchuk, a general contractor, for approximately two years, from 1991 he estimated on approximately 26 different contracts with a value in the vicinity of $125,000.

3   Prior to January of '94 Mr. Jee had notice of a potential contract for the construction of ten houses on the Okanagan Indian Band lands. Mr. Jee notified Mr. Maksymchuk of this opportunity. The Plaintiff company then, as operated by Mr. Jee, at the request of Mr. Maksymchuk, then prepared a bid for the electrical contract on the Okanagan Indian Band housing project and he presented a separate contract proposal to Mr. Maksymchuk which was dated January the 13th, 1994, for each of the ten houses in a total amount of $34,600.

4   On each contract proposal the Plaintiff, Mr. Jee, signed a note stating, and I will read the note:

"Any changes in the work and the price to be charged for same shall be made in writing. This proposal is made on the basis of current material and labor costs. A delay in acceptance of more than ten days will require review of the proposal and re-dating before the agreement becomes binding."

5   There was also an acceptance at the bottom of this contract proposal which was signed by Mr. Jee which said:

"You are hereby authorized to furnish all materials and labor to complete the work mentioned in the above proposal, for which the undersigned agrees to pay the amount mentioned in the said proposal, and according to the terms thereof."

6   The date was blank and the place for Mr. Maksymchuk's signature was also blank.

7   In the budget prepared by Mr. Maksymchuk for the main contract to the Okanagan Indian Band, which was entitled "Scope of Work" and dated January the 19th, 1994, Mr. Maksymchuk indicated the cost of electric wiring in the subcontract at $39,790, which was the sum of 34,600, being Mr. Jee's bid, plus a 15 percent markup. Mr. Maksymchuk also on the schedule of subcontractors, which was dated January the 25th, 1994, listed the Plaintiff company, Alcon Electric, as the electrical subcontractor. Mr. Maksymchuk used the Plaintiff's bid price because, as he stated in his evidence, he knew that Mr. Jee was quite thorough.

8   Mr. Maksymchuk was notified that he was the lowest bidder on January the 26th, 1994. On that date Mr. Jee spoke to Mr. Maksymchuk on the telephone and Mr. Jee testified that Mr. Maksymchuk stated, "I couldn't do it without you. It's your job." However, in February of '94 the Defendant notified Mr. Jee that he would have to reduce his bid for the electrical subcontract by $8,000 in order to get the job, as another subcontractor for the electrical work had entered a lower bid.

9   Mr. Jee refused to lower his bid price and the Defendant then awarded the electrical subcontract to another electrical subcontractor, Bates Electric, who had filed a contract proposal for the electrical work in the amount of $28,518.44.

10   The Defendant had to obtain bonding for the main and prime contract. On February the 22nd, 1994, after receiving his bond, he was awarded the prime contract as the general contractor to build the ten houses for the Okanagan Indian Band. The final contract price was in the sum of $714,514, with extras in the amount of $38,814. Bates, the other electrical subcontractor, was awarded, and in fact completed, the electrical subcontract for the bid price of $28,518.44, although the Defendant had bid and in fact was awarded the prime contract based upon Mr. Jee's bid of $39,790.

11   The Plaintiff company now claims that it lost anticipated profits when the Defendants breached the subcontract for the electrical work which they had granted on January 26, 1994.

12   The Defendants deny any breach of contract, and in fact Mr. Maksymchuk denied the conversation in which Mr. Jee stated that he had been advised by Mr. Maksymchuk that, "It's your job." Mr. Maksymchuk, however, did admit that Mr. Jee had told him of the main contract originally. Mr. Maksymchuk also stated that he did tell Mr. Jee, "I couldn't do it without you."

13   In the original contract documents from the Okanagan Indian Band project, which were dated December the 7th, '93, and was in fact the basis upon which the bid by Mr. Maksymchuk was based, did contain a clause which was clause 9 under the heading "Subcontractors", and it stated this:

> "I/We submit here with a Schedule of Subcontractors whom we propose to employ for the performance of certain portions of the work as indicated. All portions of the work that are not identified on the said Schedule of Subcontractors for completion by a subcontractor shall be completed by our own forces.

> "We have investigated the subcontractors and confirm that they are reliable and competent to carry out the work satisfactorily. It is agreed that there will be no substitution of contractors or additional subcontracting of portions of the work without the prior, written approval of the project manager."

14   It was Mr. Maksymchuk's evidence that he carried out an investigation with regard to Mr. Bates after January the 26th, and then pursuant to clause 9, after the prime contract was awarded, the Defendant submitted a change for the electrical subcontractor as named from the Plaintiff company to Ted Bates Contracting and they obtained the approval of the owner in that regard.

15   The main question in this litigation is whether there was a contract between the parties.

16   The Defendants deny any contract or subcontract with the Plaintiffs and they submit that there was no formal tendering process and that the Defendants always had the right to choose or change the subcontractor with the owner's approval.

17   The Defendants deny that there was any acceptance of the Plaintiff's bid offer, since the Plaintiff did have a ten-day escape clause in his contract proposal and the Defendants never signed the acceptance on the Plaintiff's contract proposal.

18   The Defendant has directed my attention to two decisions. The first is a decision by Mr. Justice Hamilton in this Court in *Brown v. Johanson,* Vernon Registry Number 337/87, dated August the 10th, 1990.

19   In *Brown v. Johanson* Mr. Brown was a mechanical subcontractor and he put in a bid to Johanson, who was the main contractor. Mr. Brown had the lowest bid price that was submitted to Mr. Johanson, but Johanson did not hire Brown. Johanson, after he used the information he obtained from Brown, then did the mechanical work with his own crew. As a result Mr. Brown brought the action against Mr. Johanson. The Court in that case found that Brown had failed to prove any express or implied agreement with Johanson and the claim in contract was dismissed. However, at page 6 in the judgment the Court stated had Johanson nominated Brown in his tender he could have been forced to hire Brown.

20   The judge at that time referred to *Peddlesden Ltd. v. Liddell Construction Ltd.* (1981), 32 B.C.L.R. 392, as well as *Northern Construction v. Gloge* (1986), 27 D.L.R. (4th) 264. One of the leading cases in this regard is the case of Regina, or sometimes referred to as the *Province of Ontario v. Ron Engineering*, a decision of the Supreme Court of Canada cited in [1981] 1 S.C.R. 111.

21   In the *Brown v. Johanson* decision the Court on the question of damages at page 10 in the judgment stated that:

"Brown's damages would have been the profit that he might reasonably have expected to make had Johanson hired him to do the work."

22   The Defendants also rely on a decision in the Ontario Divisional Court in *Scott Steel v. R.J. Nicol Construction,* which is cited in 15 C.L.R. (2d) 10. In this decision the Court also referred to the *Northern Construction v. Gloge,* the *Peddlesden* and also the *Regina v. Ron Engineering* decisions.

23   In Scott the Defendant general contract Nicol had requested quotes for structural steel for construction of a new school. The Plaintiff Scott had put in a bid by telephone. The Defendant Nicol used Scott's bid price and included the name of Scott in the list of subcontractors. The Defendant Nicol was awarded the main contract, but he then awarded the subcontract to another firm. The Defendant Nicol claimed that Scott could not perform the work according to the required schedule. Scott then sued for loss of profits.

24   The trial judge rejected the Plaintiff's claim and the Divisional Court on appeal also dismissed the Plaintiff's claim. The Divisional Court held that there was a contract between Scott and Nicol, but the use of the Plaintiff's name on the list of subcontractors did not constitute acceptance by Nicol and therefore the Scott tender was never accepted by Nicol and therefore did not give rise to contractual obligations and it was open for Nicol to change subtrades with the consent of the owner.

25   The Divisional Court in Scott reviewed the Supreme Court of Canada decision in *Ron Engineering* in which it was held by the Supreme Court of Canada that a call for tenders can constitute an offer and the submission of a tender can constitute acceptance giving rise to a contractual relationship. The Supreme Court referred to this contract as contract "A", being a unilateral contract that arose as a result of the submission of the tender in response to the call for tenders. The Supreme Court of Canada referred to the contract between the principal general contractor and the owner as contract "B".

26   In *Scott* the Court concluded that contract "A" was formed upon Scott making his phone bid to Nicol, but there was nothing to require Nicol to accept Scott's bid and an obligation could arise upon proper acceptance and communication of the acceptance of Scott's bid. The Court, however, held that the fact that Nicol used the Scott bid price or his name in the subcontract list was not an acceptance. The Court then held that Scott's tender was never accepted by the Defendant Nicol so as to give rise to contractual obligations between them.

27   In the *Scott* decision, however, the Divisional Court accepted the findings of fact by the trial court judge and stated this at page 132. This is the trial court judge's findings of fact.

> "I find that there is no evidence of bid shopping; rather it would appear that the contrary is true by the fact that the general contractor paid $7,800 more for the services of the subcontractor, Trenton. Nor do I find that there was a promise made by the general contractor that Trenton would get the contract or do I find any other improper motive on the part of the Defendant for not proceeding with the Plaintiff as subcontractor. I do find that the scheduling of the project was of the utmost importance and the timing of fabricating and erection of the steel structure was crucial to a timely completion of the project. I further find that the Plaintiff was relatively new in the business and that the Defendant found the Plaintiff's attitude and schedule unacceptable."

28   Those are not the facts in this case that is now before the Court.

29   In this case I must say that where there is a conflict between the evidence of Mr. Jee and the evidence of Mr. Maksymchuk, I accept the evidence of Mr. Jee.

30   I am satisfied that Mr. Maksymchuk was pleased with Mr. Jee's quality of work from his previous experience and he was also extremely pleased with the fact that Mr. Jee had notified him of the main contract, and that in this telephone conversation on January the 26th I am satisfied that Mr. Maksymchuk did state to Mr. Jee and advise him that it was his job. That was with reference to the electrical subcontract.

31   That was an acceptance. It was communicated to Mr. Jee by Mr. Maksymchuk and it did give rise to a contractual obligation and relationship. The terms of the resulting contract could then have easily been determined from the tendered documents.

32   However, after this acceptance and the contract had been established Mr. Maksymchuk entered into what is referred to as bid shopping when he attempted to have the Plaintiff lower his bid price by $8,000 to meet the bid by Bates. The Defendant was motivated by the fact that on the Bates price he would obtain excess monies in the sum of $11,000, being the difference between the Plaintiff's bid of 39,000 and the Bates' bid of 28,000. This was the improper motive on the part of the Defendant for not proceeding with the Plaintiff as the subcontractor.

33   I am satisfied the Defendant knew from experience that Mr. Jee was a quality electrical contractor and that the Plaintiff's company tender was complete in its terms and there was a basis for a contract between them, that he could use and did use in his contract with the owner.

34   Therefore there was a contract, it was breached by the Defendant and the Plaintiff is entitled to damages in the amount of the profit he might reasonably have expected to earn from this contract.

35   Mr. Jee, in his evidence, estimated that he would have earned a profit of $5,500 on materials and approximately $5,500 on labor. I accept his evidence in that regard also as to the anticipated loss of profits.

36   Therefore I am prepared to award judgment to the Plaintiff in the sum of $11,000. He is also entitled to his costs on Scale 3 and prejudgment interest at 6 percent from October the 30th, 1994, when this project was completed.

QUESTIONS

1. What qualities must an acceptance demonstrate to be effective? What constituted acceptance in this case?
2. If Mr. Maksymchuk had wanted to accept a bid other than Mr. Jee's, what should he have (or not have) done?
3. Is bid shopping improper? Explain.

chapter six

Consideration

Hongkong Bank of Canada v. New Age Graphic Design Inc., Margaret Chronister and David Cran

[1996] B.C.J. No. 907
British Columbia Supreme Court
April 22, 1996

Central to contract law is the bargaining process in which the parties to a contract exchange a promise for another promise or a promise in exchange for an act or service. The exchange is called consideration. Consideration is not restricted to the exchange of money. A bargain may involve the exchange of anything the parties to the contract think is of value.

1   **B.M. DAVIES J.C.:** The plaintiff's application for judgment pursuant to Rule 18A against the defendant, New Age Graphic Design Inc., and the defendant, Margaret Chronister, came on for hearing before me on March 12, 1996. New Age Graphic Design Inc. was not represented. The plaintiff proved the debt owing by New Age Graphic Design Inc. and I awarded judgment against it in the amount of $24,133.26, together with interest at the plaintiff's prime rate of interest, plus 3% per annum per month from October 2, 1995 to March 12, 1995.

2   Prior to the hearing of the application by me on March 12, 1996, the defendant, David Cran, had made an assignment into bankruptcy and accordingly the only matter requiring further consideration by me was the plaintiff's claim against the defendant, Margaret Chronister, pursuant to a guarantee (the "Guarantee") of the debts of the defendant, New Age Graphic Design Inc., executed by her and the defendant, David Cran, on October 6, 1991.

3   The Guarantee provided, amongst other things, that:

"no sum in excess of $20,000 and interest thereon as herein provided calculated from the date demand is made under this Guarantee and accruing both before and after judgment (the "Limited Amount"), shall be recoverable from the undersigned hereunder".

4   Demand was made upon the defendant, Margaret Chronister, on October 3, 1995.

5   The Guarantee also contained a provision in bold face type immediately above the signature of the defendant, Margaret Chronister, stating that:

"Each of the undersigned hereby acknowledges that he or she has read the contents of this Guarantee and understands that the signing of this Guarantee involves joint and several financial liability on the part of the undersigned."

6   Various defences as to the enforceability of the Guarantee against the defendant, Margaret Chronister, were raised by the pleadings but most were abandoned on the plaintiff's judgment application before me so that on this application, counsel for the defendant, Margaret Chronister, only defended on the basis that the Guarantee was not enforceable against her by reason of lack of consideration.

7   Counsel for the defendant, Margaret Chronister, advised me that he believed there was a decision which would support an argument that because Margaret Chronister was not a shareholder or officer of the company to whom the funds had been advanced, she could not be liable on the Guarantee in the absence of consideration flowing directly to her. I was aware of no such authority and so advised counsel.

8   Counsel for the plaintiff suggested that even if such a principle did exist, which he did not concede, the issue of consideration was in any event governed by the fact that the Guarantee was executed by the defendant, Margaret Chronister, under a statement which provided that the Guarantee was "Given under seal at Vancouver, B.C. this 6th day of October, 1991" (emphasis added).

9   The Guarantee did not, however, have wafer seals affixed to it and since neither counsel was in a position to fully address all of the consideration matters raised before me, I adjourned the matter pending receipt of written submissions.

10   I have now received those submissions, reviewed them and read the authorities to which I was referred by both counsel.

11   I am persuaded by the submissions made by Mr. Shatford, on behalf of the plaintiff, that the statement that the Guarantee was "given under seal" and nothwithstanding that no wafer seals were affixed, is effective to preclude further consideration being necessary. I specifically refer to and adopt the analysis of Mr. Justice de Weerdt of the Northwest Territories Supreme Court (as he then was) in *Canadian Imperial Bank of Commerce v. Dene Mat Construction Ltd.* and others, [1988] 4 W.W.R. 344.

12   If I am wrong in my assessment of the Guarantee being a contract made "under seal" and thereby requiring no further consideration, I have also determined that the defendant, Margaret Chronister, is in any event liable to the plaintiff pursuant to the Guarantee.

13   Counsel for the defendant, Margaret Chronister, was unable to locate the case which he had advised me he believed supported her position that she could not be liable in the absence of specific consideration because she was not a shareholder, officer or director of the principal debtor.

14   Mr. Cran did, however, refer me to *Bank of Nova Scotia v. Hallgarth* et al (1986) 32 D.L.R. (4th) 158 (D.C.C.A.) and submitted that on the facts of that case, the defendant, Margaret Chronister, should not be held liable under the Guarantee. I do not agree.

15   In *Bank of Nova Scotia v. Hallgarth*, Madam Justice McLachlin speaking for the court stated (at page 160) that:

"It is clear from the authorities cited by the appellant that consideration may consist either in a benefit to the maker, in this case Mr. Hallgarth, in a detriment to the promissee, in this case the bank, or in a benefit to a third person provided that the promissee, in this case the bank, would not otherwise have entered into the alleged contract. It seems to me that under all of these headings consideration is established in the case at bar."

16   Madam Justice McLachlin also went on to say (also at page 160) that:

"It is apparent that the new financial arrangements which culminated in the promissory note of June 8, 1984, relieved the pressure on the wife and thus relieved the pressure in the family and improved household finances."

17   As to these issues, in her affidavit dated March 11, 1996 (in paragraph 9), the defendant, Margaret Chronister, deposed:

"I recall that the bank manager came down to the New Age Graphic's office some time in late July or early August 1991. I was probably told his name, but I cannot recall it. My husband and him had a discussion in which he offered to increase line of credit to New Age from $10,000 to $20,000. I do recall that the bank manager told me that I would have to sign a guarantee for my husband's company, but that I had nothing to worry about as the bank would file a lien on all the equipment of New Age."

and also deposed (in paragraph 10) that:

"I did not want to sign the guarantee document, but did so as I was very scared that my husband's business would go under and I would have no means of support for my baby."

18   The evidence establishes that the plaintiff did obtain security over the assets of New Age Graphic Design Inc. and as I indicated above, the only defence which the defendant, Margaret Chronister, advanced before me was that of lack of consideration.

19   In my judgment, based upon the affidavit material and the principles of Hallgarth, consideration has been proven.

20   The plaintiff is therefore entitled to judgment against the defendant, Margaret Chronister, in the sum of $20,000 plus interest thereon at the plaintiff's rate of interest plus 3% from October 3, 1995 to today's date. The plaintiff is also entitled to its costs against the defendant, Margaret Chronister, on scale 3 with inclusion of Item 26 set at 5 units.

QUESTIONS

1. While the consideration given in return for an act or promise must have some value in the eyes of the law, will a court inquire whether the promisor made a "good" bargain? When will the court examine the adequacy of consideration?

2. What did the court determine constituted "good" consideration in this case?

3. How does the presence of a seal affect the requirement that consideration must be present in a contract?

4. Does a guarantee "given under seal" without a wafer seal being affixed constitute good consideration? Does the use of a seal answer for failure to satisfy all the essentials of a binding contract?

5. A promisor usually bargains for a benefit to him/herself. Must the consideration bargained for necessarily be directly for the promisor's own benefit? Explain.

Saskatchewan River Bungalows Ltd. v. Maritime Life Assurance Co.

[1992] A.J. No. 512, 10 C.C.L.I. (2d) 278, 20 W.A.C. 43, 92 D.L.R. (4th) 372, 127 A.R. 43

Alberta Court of Appeal

June 4, 1992

When an acceptance is mailed and the use of the postal service is a reasonable means of communication in the circumstances, that acceptance is effective when and where it is deposited in the mailbox. The effect of the postal acceptance rule may be that for a period of time after the acceptance is mailed, the offeror is bound in contract without being aware of it until the acceptance is actually received. If this uncertainty poses a problem, the offeree is free to stipulate another means of acceptance.

HARRADENCE J.A.:—

I.   Background

Maritime Life Assurance Company (Maritime) issued an insurance policy on the life of Mr. Fikowski in July 1978. The ownership of this policy was eventually transferred to Mrs. Fikowski, at which time she became the beneficiary under the policy.

The policy provided that the agreements contained therein were conditional upon payment of the premiums as they became due, the said payments to be made on or before the specified due date. According to the policy there was a grace period of 31 days following the due date during which the policy holder could make the overdue payment and maintain policy coverage.

According to the policy if the premium was not paid by the end of the grace period, the policy lapsed or terminated automatically. It was possible for the policy holder to reinstate the policy upon written application to the company, subject to certain conditions. One condition was that the life insured was in good health and insurable.

However, it was the practice of Maritime that if payment was not made during the grace period, a late payment offer was sent (by ordinary mail) to the owner of the policy. While an application for reinstatement was not required, the offer was subject to several conditions.

In the present case a premium payment was due from Mrs. Fikowski by July 26, 1984. Saskatchewan River Bungalows Ltd. (S.R.B.), more specifically the general manager Mr. Fikowski Jr., and the administrator Mr. Thomas, thereof, acted on behalf of Mrs. Fikowski. S.R.B. sent a cheque by ordinary mail in the amount of $1316.00 and dated July 24, 1984 to pay this premium. The cheque was never received by Maritime and was not returned to S.R.B. The cheque amount was never deducted from the company's account.

A premium due notice, ordinarily sent by the company to policy holders three weeks before the due date, was received by Mr. Thomas on August 13, 1984. Return envelopes were enclosed with these notices and they were sent by ordinary mail. The notice required payment in the amount of $1361.00 but Mr. Thomas, believing he had already made payment in the amount of $1316.00, remitted a cheque to Maritime for the amount of $45.00.

The grace period expired without Maritime receiving payment. Thereafter Maritime sent a late payment offer in accordance with its general practice. The late payment offer read as follows:

"IMPORTANT
If a premium is not paid within the days of grace stated in the policy, the policy lapses. . . .

LATE PAYMENT OFFER
The premium shown on the front of this notice being unpaid, the policy has terminated . . . . This special voluntary offer to accept late payment, without interest, is subject to the following conditions

1.   Payment must be

(a) made during the lifetime of the life insured

(b) postmarked or, if not mailed, received in the Head Office at Halifax, K.S. on or before the date on which this offer ends.

2.   This offer applies only to this premium.

3.   The grace period provided in the policy is not extended by this offer.

4.   Any remittance not in cash is accepted subject to actual cash payment.

5. The company reserves the right to request evidence of insurability.

6. This offer expires Forty-Five days after the Due Date shown on the front and is subject to the important conditions above.

If payment has just been made, please disregard this Late Payment Offer."

Subsequently, Maritime wrote a letter, dated November 28, 1984 advising Mrs. Fikowski that the premium due on July 26, 1984 remained unpaid. The letter stated that the policy was "technically out of force" and that immediate payment was required. It was not suggested that an application for reinstatement was required.

Finally, on February 2, 1985, Maritime sent a lapse notice (to a Vancouver address) stating unequivocally that the policy had lapsed for non-payment of the 1984 premium. It invited Mrs. Fikowski to apply for reinstatement of the policy but by the time the lapse notice came to the attention of Mr. Fikowski, Jr. or Mr. Thomas in April 1985, Mr. Fikowski was neither in good health or insurable.

The premium due notice, the late payment offer, and the November 28, 1984 letter were sent to the address specified in the transfer of ownership registered with Maritime, which was also the address of S.R.B. However, like the lapse notice, the late payment offer and the November 28, 1984 letter did not come to the attention of Mr. Fikowski, Jr. or Mr. Thomas until April, 1985.

According to the evidence at trial, mail was picked up by the Appellants from the S.R.B. address on an infrequent basis during the fall and winter months of 1984 and 1985, and some mail received during this period was not opened or read until April, 1985.

After receiving notice of the correspondence in April, 1985 Mr. Fikowski, Jr. and Mr. Thomas attempted to ascertain the location of the cheque they had sent to pay the 1984 premium. The cheque was never found. Subsequently, in July of 1985, S.R.B. submitted a cheque for the 1984 premium to Maritime's agent. The payment was refused by Maritime. In August of 1985, Mr. Fikowski the life insured, passed away. A claim was presented by the Appellants under the Maritime Life policy for death benefits but it was refused by Maritime on the ground that the policy was no longer in force.

II.   Issues

1. Does the Postal Acceptance Rule apply?

2. Is the doctrine of equitable estoppel applicable?

3. If yes to 1 or 2 above, was the policy in force when Mr. Fikowski, the life insured, died?

4. If the policy was not in force, does the Court have jurisdiction to relieve against forfeiture?

III.   Postal Acceptance Rule

I concur with the conclusion of Hetherington, J.A. on the applicability of the postal acceptance rule, but with the following additional comments.

As Hetherington, J.A. indicates, the policy provided that premium payments had to be made at Maritime's head office in Halifax. The policy provided that any alteration to the terms therein had to be in writing and have the signature of the president or vice-president of the company. There was no such alteration here.

The policy did not, however, provide the method or manner by which payment could be made at the head office in Halifax. Relevant in this regard is the conduct of Maritime in encouraging premium payments to be made by ordinary mail. The Premium due notice received by the Appellants on August 13, 1984 contained an envelope addressed to Maritime's head office. As well, the premium due notice, the late payment offer, the November 28, 1984 letter and the lapse notice were all sent to the Appellants by ordinary mail. Finally, both the premium due notice and the late payment offer stated:

"(1) Payments must be

    (a) made during the lifetime of the insured;

    (b) post-marked or, if not mailed, received in the Head Office at Halifax, N.S. on or before the date on which this offer ends."

To reiterate, though, the premium payment provision in the policy stipulated that "each premium is payable on or before its due date at the Head Office of the Company". Throughout the aforementioned correspondence Maritime required that payment be made in accordance with the policy. The premium due notice stated that:

"If a premium is not paid within the days of grace stated in the Policy, the Policy lapses."

Thus, Maritime, by consistently relying on the terms of payment contained in the policy, did not vary the policy requirement that payment be made at its head office. By encouraging policyholders to use the post, Maritime identified one potentially acceptable method that could be utilized by policyholders when attempting to comply with the premium payment provisions in the policy. I would emphasize that this was only one potential method, for compliance was not attained when the premium payment was mailed, but only when it was received by Maritime.

I would conclude by referring to the decision of Lawton, L.J. in *Holwell Securities Ltd. v. Hughes,* [1974] 1 All E.R. 161 (C.A.) where he commented upon the postal acceptance rule in the following manner at p. 166:

"Does the rule apply in all the circumstances where one party makes an offer which both he and the person with whom he was dealing must have expected the post to be used as a means of accepting it? In my judgment, it does not. First, it does not apply when the express terms of the offer specify that the acceptance must reach the offeror."

The postal acceptance rule does not apply here. An express term in the policy required that premium payments be made at Maritime's head office in Halifax.

IV.   Estoppel

In view of Maritime's policy of encouraging payment by mail, a discussion of the doctrine of promissory estoppel is required. According to C. Brown & J. Menezes, Insurance Law in Canada, 2nd ed. (Scarborough: Carswell, 1991) at pp. 290-291, the doctrine may be stated as follows:

" . . . . if one party by his conduct leads another to believe that the strict rights arising under the contract will not be insisted on, intending that the other should act on that belief, and he does act on it, then the first party will not afterwards be allowed to insist on the strict rights when it would be inequitable for him so to do . . . ."

While it is true that Maritime never altered the policy requirement that payment be made at the head office in Halifax, Maritime represented to the Appellants that premium payments could be made by mail and in fact encouraged this practice. This indicated to the Appellants that the strict rights arising under the policy with respect to payment of premiums would not be insisted upon by Maritime. The Appellants relied on Maritime's representation to their detriment, for the 1984 premium payment mailed by S.R.B. was never received by Maritime. Maritime is therefore estopped from demanding strict compliance with the time requirements for premium payment under the policy.

(Other portions of this decision have been omitted. Maritime appealed to the Supreme Court of Canada. The appeal raised two issues: 1) did Maritime waive its rights to compel timely payment in accordance with the terms of the policy? and 2) if there was no waiver, are the respondents entitled to relief against forfeiture under the Judicature Act, RSA 1980 c.J-1., s.10? The Court concluded that the respondents were not entitled to any of the benefits under the policy. The demand for payment in the November letter was a clear and unequivocal expression of Maritime's intention to continue coverage upon payment of the July premium and as such constituted a waiver of time required for payment of the policy. The waiver was not still in effect however when SRB tendered payment of the missing premium in July '85. Relief against forfeiture is an equitable remedy and is purely discretionary. The respondents were barred by their conduct from recovering)

QUESTIONS

1. How do courts determine when the postal acceptance rule should be applied?
2. Can acceptance be effective from the moment a letter of acceptance is mailed even though the offer was not made by mail?
3. Why was it that the postal acceptance rule did not apply in this case? What effect did this finding have for the parties? Explain.

chapter seven

Capacity and Legality

Collins (Re)

[1991] B.C.J. No. 2914
British Columbia Supreme Court
October 21, 1991

The age of majority or the age at which a person was considered to be an adult was 21 at Common Law. Also, the Common Law rule was that a contract made by a minor was unenforceable against the minor but enforceable by the minor against the other party. Today, the age at which a person becomes an adult in Canada is controlled by statute and varies from province to province, and in some jurisdictions, such as British Columbia, the protection provided to minors is governed by a special statute. In some situations, it will be necessary or desirable that a minor be bound in contract so jurisdictions have made provision for a process for approval of minors' contracts. The criteria that a court should apply in approving a contract made by a minor came under consideration in the following case.

HOLMES J.:— The Petitioner Andrea Collins ("Ms. Collins") is the mother of the Petitioner Simon Philip Nando Collins ("Simon"), an infant aged 15. Simon and his sister Joely Meri Collins, 19 years of age, are parties to a contract dated December 11, 1989 with Ms. Collins the subject matter of which involves the infants interest in a residential property in Vancouver which is owned by a trust created irrevocably by their father Philip Collins. The contract was unenforceable from inception as both Simon and Joely (collectively hereafter referred to as "the children") were minors at that date. A letter of August 9, 1991 purportedly affirming the contract and stated to be pursuant to Section 16.2 (1) (b) of the Infants Act was signed by Joely the day after she reached the age of majority. As Simon remains an infant the contract is unenforceable against him and the purpose of the Petition is to make the contract enforceable by obtaining an Order under Section 16.4 (1) (b) of the Infants Act granting to Simon: "capacity to enter into a contract....specified in the order".

Counsel for Philip Collins and the Public Trustee both are opposed to the Court granting the Order. Counsel for the Petitioners requested that James Martin, a barrister and solicitor, be appointed Guardian Ad Litem for Simon due to the conflict of interest of Ms. Collins who is also a petitioner. The request was unopposed, Mr. Martin signed a Consent to Act, and an Order for his appointment was given.

Facts

Ms. Collins married Philip Collins in England in September 1975, they separated in 1979, and were divorced in August 1980. Prior to their marriage Ms. Collins had a brief common-law relationship with another person during the course of which she became pregnant with Joely, who was born August 8, 1972. That relationship was terminated prior to Joely's birth, and Philip Collins adopted Joely. Simon was born September 14, 1976. Philip Collins is a person of considerable financial means and has always paid a significant amount of maintenance in respect of Simon and Joely. The amount of maintenance has been varied upward by Order of the High Court in England following application on different occasions and since 1989 $9,926 per month per child has been paid, and is to be paid, until each child is 17 years of age or completes full time education if that is a later date. Philip Collins deposed that he believes Joely has completed full time education, however he has no present intention of ceasing the payment he makes on her behalf. Counsel advised Joely is attending a school. It appears evident that whether legally obligated or not Philip Collins is paying over $238,000 a year maintenance in respect of the two children. Philip Collins obviously loves his children and intends they benefit from his wealth. He is obviously capable of meeting his financial obligations with indication he will be generous beyond the bounds of his strict legal obligation.

As a consequence of her divorce from Philip Collins the Petitioner received a lump sum settlement of 100,000 and spousal support of 8,000 per annum. Spousal support was forfeited in September 1982 when she married a Mr. Fleming. Ms. Collins, Mr. Fleming, Joely and Simon moved to Richmond B.C. and lived in a house the Petitioner purchased with her separate funds. In May 1986 Ms. Collins and Mr. Fleming separated and he moved from her house. They divorced in March 1988.

Ms. Collins wished to move to Vancouver as she had concern as to the quality of schooling in Richmond and "other lifestyle considerations". The cost of houses the Petitioner considered suitable were beyond her means and she was "...also concerned about the lack of financial security afforded her by the terms of the previous Orders". Discussions ensued with Philip Collins regarding his possible contribution towards the purchase of a residential property. The Petitioner located a suitable house and Philip Collins paid the $750,000 purchase price and created an irrevocable trust "Collins Childrens' Trust" to hold title with the Canada Trust Company as Trustee. The purpose of the Trust was to provide a home for Joely, Simon and Ms. Collins until Simon (the youngest child) reached age 20 at which time Simon and Joely would receive the property absolutely as tenants in common. Ms. Collins signed a Licence Agreement requiring her to pay property taxes and cost of maintenance repairs.

Ms. Collins was apparently under the impression during the course of the property acquisition that she would be sharing in the ownership. She believed that she and the children would hold title. In fact she receive no ownership interest and her right of occupation was subject to the Licence Agreement. The reality of the trust arrangement was not known to her until after completion of the purchase and just prior to taking possession. She learned of the arrangement when given documents by Philip Collins' lawyer which included the Licence Agreement which she was required to sign before being given occupancy. The Petitioner felt she had no alternative but to sign because she was aware Philip Collins had no legal obligation to pay her either spousal maintenance or support for her own benefit.

Ms. Collins and the children moved into the house in September 1987 and Ms. Collins remains unhappy about what she considers was a misunderstanding as to the ownership interest she felt was promised in the house. Negotiations since 1987 with Philip Collins did not resolve the matter. The trust was intended by him to be irrevocable and it is. Ms. Collins deposes that she has expended in excess of $91,000 since September 1987 for repairs, renovations, and furnishings to make the house a home. I have perused the accounts provided and the vast majority was spent on furniture, or other items of moveable personal property which do not form any part of the trust property and if paid for by Ms. Collins remain her property. I note Philip Collins in addition to the purchase funds deposes he has paid $102,000 for legal costs of purchase, the trust costs, house improvements, repairs and insurance premiums.

The unhappiness and insecurity of Ms. Collins in respect of the property became known to Joely and Simon. I am uncertain precisely how that occurred but assume she told them and the three of them discussed the matter. Joely and Simon felt their mother had been treated unfairly and wished her "...to have a secure future without having to worry about having a house...". The decision by the children to help rectify the problem was apparently made before July 12, 1989 because on that date Joely and Simon saw Michael Elterman, a Clinical and Consulting Psychologist "...to assess the children's state of mind, the influences on their decision, and the cogency of their reasoning". In essence the children told Dr. Elterman that the Petitioner was a good mother, had always looked after them, and deserved the security of having a house. Dr. Elterman's opinion was that Joely had "...thought her way through the personal and family consequences of this and that her thinking is lucid and reasoned". In respect of Simon Dr. Elterman's opinion was that "He is obviously close to Joely and has followed her lead in the way he thinks of and articulates the issues but I believe that his willingness to enter into this contract is his own. His reasons are clear and seem deeply felt".

The children were referred to James Martin, a barrister, for legal advice. He saw them September 12, 1989, November 1, 1989 and December 11, 1989 when they signed the contract. He was of the view by their second meeting that "...the children understand the nature and legal consequences of the agreement" and that they "...were solidly in support of (it)...".

In preparation for this hearing an appraisal of the value of the property was obtained and filed by counsel for Philip Collins. The approximate market value was given as $1.4 million. Simon filed an affidavit that knowledge of the increased value of the property did not change his wish to have the contract made binding upon him.

The contract of December 11, 1989 provides that the children transfer their beneficial interest in the Collins Childrens' Trust to Ms. Collins when their interest vests. In return Ms. Collins agrees to provide financial support for their reasonable maintenance, care, education and benefit until they are age 25 (extended to age 28 if still completing their education). Ms. Collins also agrees to create a trust in favour of the children which will see the property, or its remainder, returned to them if she should remarry or die. Ms. Collins is Trustee under the Agreement with extremely wide and unfettered powers, including a power:

> 3.01 (b)   "Until the Material Date (her death or remarriage)...in her absolute discretion, encroach upon the capital of the Trust Property and pay or transfer any amount or amounts of the capital...to or for the benefit of ANDREA COLLINS...as the Trustee, in her absolute discretion, shall determine.
>
> (c)   Notwithstanding the generality of clause 3.01 (b), the Trustee may encroach upon the Trust Property to such an extent that the Trust Property is completely distributed and used up.

The Law

The relevant provision of the Infants Act is Section 16.4 (1)(b) and (2):

> *"The court may, on an application on behalf of an infant, make an order granting to the infant...capacity to enter into a contract...(but the Court must be) satisfied that it is for the benefit of the infant and that having regard to the circumstances of the infant, he is not in need of the protection offered by law to infants in matters relating to contracts."*

It is obvious that the court's power is discretionary, but to grant the infant capacity to contract it is mandatory that:

> (a)   the contract be for his benefit, and
>
> (b)   considering the infant's circumstances does not need the protection accorded by the law to infants relating to contracts.

Counsel advised that they knew of no case law concerning this section which would be of assistance. Counsel also agree that the phrase "...for the benefit of the infant..." is to be given the same meaning at law as "...in the best interests of the infant...". Counsel for the Public Trustee argues there is a presumption in law that an infant is under the influence of a parent or guardian. I agree there is such a presumption however I concur with Petitioner's counsel that is a rebuttable presumption, and the opinion evidence of Dr. Elterman and Mr. Martin supports the view there was no undue influence or pressure by Ms. Collins and both children fully understood the agreement and wished to enter into it.

I accept Simon is an intelligent young man who does understand the legal implication of his intended contract. He is not under direct compulsion, duress, or undue influence in respect of his agreement to sign. It is my view however that it was Ms. Collins who set a chain of events in motion by in some manner making it known to Simon and Joely how unhappy and insecure she felt because Philip Collins had not given her an ownership interest in the property. The inference has to be that in some manner the children received what she was promised and entitled to. I have no concern as to whether she is right in a moral context, I do have concern that the remedy for her insecurity has involved the children.

I view the contract of December 11, 1989 as a thinly disguised attempt to vary the trust set up by Philip Collins. In fact Dr. Elterman's understanding was that "The children and Ms. Collins now wish to vary the trust...". I was advised in general, without knowledge of specifics, that this unenforceable agreement of December 11, 1989, lay dormant until now, without application for a request of court approval of capacity for the infants, because certain negotiations were ongoing between Mr. and Ms. Collins. In my view the Court's discretionary power should not be exercised on a pretext of being for the benefit of the infants when in essence it is to have Ms. Collins achieve financial security.

The consequence of the agreement of December 11, 1989 is essentially that Simon would be giving up to Ms. Collins an interest in property which will vest in him within 5 years that has a present market value in excess of $700,000. Ms. Collins would have the ability to encroach upon that property for her exclusive benefit so there might be no reversion to him at all. Simon's father is currently providing close to $10,000 per month for his maintenance, and that will continue through completion of his education. Indeed there is every reason to believe maintenance would be continued so long as a proper reason or need existed. I do not accept that Philip Collins will see Simon in need. The stated consideration to be given by Ms. Collins for the contract is not needed by Simon, and in relation to what he would be giving up is totally inadequate. In my view it is in the circumstances here insulting to suggest that this contract is of any financial benefit to Simon.

It is suggested that the emotional well being of Simon is best served by Ms. Collins being happy and secure, and that he genuinely wishes that to be so. I am sure that is true, as it would be in any family relationship. I cannot justify Simon giving away his interest in the trust to purchase that feeling of security for Ms. Collins. I see no benefit to Simon in the contract in question. I am of the opinion it is not in his best interest.

The decision to give up as substantial an asset as his interest in this trust is one to be reserved until he reaches the age of majority. Should he feel then, as he does now, he is free to make that gift. If his views, or the circumstances, change in the next five years he is not bound to an improvident contract.

The Petition is dismissed with costs to opposing parties represented by counsel on scale 3.

QUESTIONS

1. Who has the legal capacity to form contracts?

2. Explain the circumstances in which an infant or minor may escape liability for a contract and the circumstances in which an infant is bound by a contract.

3. In what circumstances may a court in British Columbia make an order granting an infant capacity to enter into a contract?

4. Why, in this case, did the court refuse to approve the contract on behalf of the infant?

Maksymetz v. Kostyk

[1992] M.J. No. 7, 4 B.L.R. (2d) 129, [1992] 2 W.W.R. 354

Manitoba Court of Queen's Bench

January 20, 1992

The object of a contract must be legal. This means that in order for a contract to be binding, it cannot be contrary to public interest nor can it violate any law. Statutes that restrict the right of parties to contract often contain provisions setting out the rights of the parties in the event of a violation. Unfortunately, many statutes do not, and in such cases the courts are left to apply the Common Law provisions with respect to illegal contracts.

MONNIN J.:— The plaintiff seeks an accounting from the defendants of his share of the partnership L.J.S. Ventures. The plaintiff had originally sued the defendants to obtain this remedy but on the morning the trial was to commence along with another action which had been consolidated, the parties arrived at a settlement of this action. In my written reasons in the second of the consolidated actions, *Gateway Hotel (1985) Ltd. v. Schur et al.* (1990), 66 Man. R. (2d) 305, at 308 (Q.B.), I set out the terms of the settlement that the parties had reached:

> "(1) That Maksymetz's share of a partnership he had formed along with Schur and Kostyk to manage the hotel in The Pas, Manitoba was 41%.
>
> (2) That if the partnership is found to have an option to purchase the hotel, Maksymetz's share of that option is 37%.
>
> (3) That there are to be no costs payable by any party in the lawsuit."

In the Gateway matter, I made the following findings which have some bearing in this action:

> "[12] During the course of the summer and early fall, meetings took place between Brooks, on the one side, and Schur, Kostyk and Maksymetz, on the other side, with a view of entering into an agreement, whereby Schur, Kostyk and Maksymetz would invest some money into the hotel and make extensive refurbishing and repairs to standards acceptable to the Manitoba Liquor Control Commission and the Health and Fire Departments, and eventually manage the operation of the hotel.
>
> [15] In accordance with Regulations made pursuant to the Liquor Control Act, R.S.M. 1988, c. L-160, the agreement was submitted for approval to the Manitoba Liquor Control Commission. This approval was denied on October 13, 1987 for the following reasons:

'The agreement as submitted is unacceptable and cannot be approved. Commission Policy states:

> "Where a premises is managed by an individual or corporation other than the licensee, who is to receive a percentage of the profits from the sale of liquor, that percentage must not exceed 10 percent."

The ownership and control of the hotel must remain the responsibility of the licensee.'

[31]   As to Maksymetz, I find he became truthful and believable only when, during the course of his cross-examination, the discrepancies between his evidence and the facts were put to him by the plaintiff's counsel. To his credit, when it became clear that he was not being completely truthful, Maksymetz admitted it. I find, therefore, that I can place a limited amount of reliance on his evidence.

[32]   Kostyk and especially Schur, I find, purposefully attempted to deceive the court and failed miserably in their attempt due in no small part to the thoroughness of the counsel for the plaintiff's cross-examination. Schur and Kostyk are liars and frauds and their conduct throughout this matter and in the witness stand was despicable. I place absolutely no reliance or faith in their evidence.

[36]   Clearly, the parties intended that the agreement of September, 1987 required approval by the Manitoba Liquor Control Commission, but it was just as clearly evident to anyone who had experience with the Commission that the terms of the contract would never be approved. If Schur and Kostyk did not know this, and I suspect they did, I find that Schur was told by his then solicitor, Don Bjornsson, who drafted the agreement, that the terms would not be acceptable to the Manitoba Liquor Control Commission.

[37]   I am satisfied that the agreement contained in exhibit no. 15 was an illegal contract and was in fact void ab initio. In the event that I am in error on this finding, I then find that the performance of the contract was done in an illegal manner and therefore is also rendered void.

[55]   If it appears in these reasons that I am unduly harsh against Schur, it is by design. I consider him to be the key link and the engineer of this sordid affair, and I would not want him to be in a position to profit whatsoever any more than his co-defendants."

The defendants have since the date of settlement refused to honour it and the plaintiff now seeks this accounting as the first step in enforcing the settlement.

The defendants now come before this court asserting that it is contrary to law for a court to order an accounting of a partnership engaged in an illegal act as I found L.J.S. Ventures to be doing in the *Gateway* decision. The defendants also assert that the settlement, if based on an illegal contract, cannot be made legal and is therefore unenforceable. In support of their position, the defendants rely on *Munroe v. Clarke* (1977), 1 B.L.R. 137 (N.S. T.D.), an action for a declaration that a partnership existed between the parties. The trial judge found that a partnership existed but found, after an extensive review of authorities, that it could not be enforced because it was performing illegally by operating a bar without the approval of the Nova Scotia Liquor Control Board. The trial judge cites them following passages from 28 Halsbury's Laws of England (3rd), paras. 949-950, at 495-496:

"A partnership formed for making profits by a business which is contrary to public policy, or which cannot be carried on without a breach of the common or statute law, is illegal. Thus, a partnership in the profits of a crime is illegal, but a joint venture for blockade running is not illegal at common law.

... An agreement for an illegal partnership will not be specifically enforced, even though partly performed, nor can damages be recovered for breach of it, and, if the whole purpose of the partnership is illegal, the court will not recognise it, or enforce any rights which the supposed partners would otherwise have, especially where the parties have agreed to enter, as partners, into a transaction which they know to be illegal. Therefore an action will not lie for an account of profits of illegal underwriting, even though defendant does not plead the illegality, if it is brought to the notice of the court; and if the plaintiff's case discloses the illegality of the transaction the court will not help him. Where partners are engaged in illegal contracts and one of them pays the whole of partnership debt in respect of the illegal transaction, he cannot enforce the duty of the court to aid either in carrying out an illegal contract or in dividing the proceeds arising from an illegal contract between the parties to that illegal contract; and no action can be maintained either for the one purpose or for the other; but, if a partnership is not illegal in itself, the fact that the partners have evaded a statute is not a bar to an action by one of them against the others for an account."

Munroe was followed with approval by the Appeal Division of the Nova Scotia Supreme Court in *Tara Lounge Ltd. v. McVicar Resorts Ltd.* (1978), 5 B.L.R. 206.

The plaintiff takes the position that he is not attempting to enforce an illegal agreement but a valid and binding settlement. If that were the only issue or if a consent judgment had been filed prior to this application, I would have less difficulty with the request for the accounting because the courts will clearly enforce a settlement arrived at between parties or an order of the court.

The question still remains, however, whether a court has the right to enforce such a settlement when it clearly flows from the conduct of the parties in an illegal undertaking such as running the Gateway Hotel by the parties to this action in clear breach of The Liquor Control Act, R.S.M. 1988, c. L160 and the regulations that flow from it.

My sympathies lie with the plaintiff because the defendants cannot be prevented from benefiting from their illegally obtained bounty but the law, I am afraid, does not support his request. If one associates oneself with thieves and participates in illegality, one cannot come later before the court and ask that the thieves be punished even if on the face of it the request appears to be reasonable. The plaintiff, even though his hands are less dirty than those of his two other partners, still is not before the court with clean hands himself and therefore cannot avail himself of the remedies of the court. With marked reluctance, I find that I must deny the plaintiff's request for an accounting.

QUESTIONS

1. Will an agreement for an illegal partnership be enforced? Explain.

2. Why might it be important for a party to a dispute to show that a void contract is not also illegal?

3. In order to obtain a remedy from a court of law, must the parties have "clean hands"? Explain.

Rhino Freight Systems Ltd. v. McTaggart

[1999] B.C.J. No. 1390
British Columbia Supreme Court
May 18, 1999

Business people often enter into contracts that contain provisions prohibiting certain types of activities. If such a provision is reasonable and necessary to protect the interests of the parties, it is enforceable. However, if the provision is unreasonably restrictive or against the public interest, it may be void for illegality.

1   **STROMBERG-STEIN J.**:— The application of the plaintiff, Rhino Freight Systems Ltd., to enforce a restrictive covenant in an employment contract against the defendant, Daniel F. McTaggart, was granted in chambers on May 18, 1999. These are my reasons for granting the application.

2   The defendant entered into an employment agreement with the plaintiff on April 20, 1998. The defendant was employed as the general manager for a term of five years, commencing March 1, 1998.

3   The plaintiff was a new company engaged in a highly competitive industry. The defendant was well known and respected in the freight industry. The defendant ran the business and had direct contact with the plaintiff's customers. He was apprised of confidential business information respecting the operation of the plaintiff.

4   To compensate the defendant for committing himself to the terms of the employment agreement, the agreement provided for a bonus of $50,000 of which he was prepaid $35,000 at the time of termination. In addition, he was allocated 20 shares of the plaintiff with an option to purchase more shares. He was permitted to spend $1,000 a month on promotional activities.

5   In the event the defendant did not meet the stated sales goals listed in the agreement, the plaintiff could terminate the employment of the defendant. The consequences of early termination, addressed in the agreement, were that the defendant was required to re-pay the bonus and return the allocated shares.

6   The agreement provided the following restrictive covenant at clauses 21 and 23:

   21.   In the event this Agreement is terminated under the provisions of paragraph 18 by the Employee or by the Company under the provisions of paragraph 19, the Employee covenants and agrees with the Company that following such termination of his employment with the Company he will not, for a period of one year:

(a) solicit business from any person, firm or corporation which was or had been a customer of the Company in the year preceding termination of his employment;

(b) within a One Hundred (100) mile radius of Greater Vancouver, either individually or in partnership or jointly or in conjunction with any person or persons including without limitation, any individual, firm, association, syndicate, corporation or other business enterprise, as a principal, agent, shareholder, officer, employee or in any manner whatsoever: carry on or be engaged in or be concerned with or interested in or advise, lend money to a business carrying on a business in British Columbia similar to the business of the Company. ...

23. The Employee agrees that, because of the position he will hold with the Company and the information which will be made available to him, the restrictions set forth in this agreement are reasonable and necessary and fundamental to the protection of the business of the Company and that the compensation he will be receiving from the Company compensates him for agreeing to such restrictions.

7 The plaintiff terminated the agreement on December 1, 1998 due to the failure of the defendant to meet sales goals. When the defendant left the plaintiff company, the plaintiff lost most of its customers. Since his termination, the defendant has engaged in employment with two competitors of the plaintiff: Street Hawk Express, located in Langley, and Kel-Mac Cartage, located in Delta. He has also solicited customers of the plaintiff.

8 The position of the plaintiff is that the covenant not to compete is a fundamental term of the agreement entered into in good faith. The defendant was compensated by means of a pre-paid bonus, approximately equal to one year's salary, which he has not repaid. The bonus is now the subject of a default judgment and since the defendant has made an assignment in bankruptcy this bonus will never be repaid.

9 The position of the defendant is that he stupidly signed the agreement on the assurance of the President of the plaintiff company, Allan Eng, that he did not have to worry about the "I's" being dotted and the "T's" being crossed. He now says the agreement was very one-sided, not allowing for any error on his part. He describes Mr. Eng as a cruel and tyrannical silent partner. He tried to buy the company from Mr. Eng upon termination without success. He denies soliciting the plaintiff's customers, but acknowledges sending faxes to four friends to let them know where he was currently employed.

10 The principles of law respecting covenants against competition in employment contracts are found in: *Elsley v. J.G. Collins Insurance Agencies Ltd.* (1978), 83 D.L.R. (3d) 1 (S.C.C.). Having regard to those principles, I conclude the covenant against competition is enforceable. It is reasonable and not contrary to the public interest. It is limited to the Greater Vancouver area where the majority of the plaintiff's customers are located. It is for only a one year term of which five and one half months remain.

11 The defendant has special knowledge of confidential information of the company and its customers. He acknowledged this in Clause 23 of the agreement. He was amply compensated for agreeing to the restrictions set out in the agreement. He acknowledged in Clause 23 that these restrictions were reasonable, necessary and fundamental to the protection of the business of the plaintiff company.

12   It is for these reasons that I made the following Order in chambers:

That the defendant is restrained, for a period of one year commencing December 1, 1998, within a 100 mile radius of Greater Vancouver, either individually, or in a partnership, or jointly, or in conjunction with any person or persons including, without limitation, any individual firm, association, syndicate, corporation or other business enterprise as principle, agent, shareholder, officer, employee or in any manner whatsoever from carrying on, or being engaged in, or being concerned with, or interested in, or advising, or lending money to a business carrying on a business in British Columbia similar to the business of the plaintiff.

QUESTIONS

1. Are all contracts in restraint of trade unlawful?

2. If the courts presume that any term in restraint of trade is against public policy, which party to the contract has the burden of rebutting this presumption? Which of the parties in this case had the burden of proof? What must the party seeking to enforce the covenant prove in order to demonstrate that the covenant is not void?

3. Do you think that a court would be more or less likely to uphold a restrictive covenant where the employee has special knowledge of confidential information about the employer and its customers? Explain.

4. Would the restrictive covenant, in this case, have been considered void if the restricted geographical area had been British Columbia? Explain.

Imperial Oil Ltd. (c.o.b. Imperial Oil) v. Westlake Fuel Ltd.

[2001] M.J. No. 337, 2001 MBCA 130, 203 DLR (4th) 604, [2001] 9 WWR 28, 156 Man. R. (2d) 296, 16 BLR (3d) 1, 8 CPC (5th) 213, 15 CPR (4th) 85.

Manitoba Court of Appeal

Judgment: July 27, 2001.

This case illustrates how carefully restrictive covenants must be drafted to ensure that they have the desired effect. In drafting such clauses, one must consider not only the nature of the activities covered by the restriction, but also the parties who will be affected by it.

PHILP J.A.:—

Introduction

1   This is an appeal by the defendants against the order of Keyser J. granting the application of the plaintiff (Imperial) for interim injunctive relief against them. The validity of a restrictive covenant in an agency agreement made between Imperial and the corporate defendant, and its application to the personal defendants (the corporate defendant's controlling shareholder and his wife), are the questions that are raised.

Facts

2   By an agreement dated March 1, 1996 (the agency agreement), Imperial appointed the defendant Westlake Fuel Ltd. (Westlake) its agent for the sale of its products to its customers in, a defined market area (the Amaranth Agency) in the Langruth/Amaranth, district of Manitoba. The personal defendants, Kevin Jonas Johnson (Johnson) and his wife, signed the agreement as guarantors, guaranteeing amongst other things:

> ... [T]he due payment by the Agent of all monies payable under the said Agreements [sic] by the Agent to IMPERIAL at the time or times appointed therefor, and the due observance and performance by the Agent of all the covenants, terms, provisions, stipulations and conditions contained in the said Agreement and on the part of the Agent to be observed and performed.

3   The agency agreement superseded an agreement in similar terms executed in November 1995, pursuant to which Imperial had appointed Johnson as its agent for the Amaranth Agency. Specifically, any restrictive covenant in the November 1995 agreement that may have bound Johnson personally "expired and terminated" upon the execution of the agency agreement.

4   In September 1995, Johnson had learned that Imperial's agent for the Amaranth Agency had left the business, and he applied to Imperial for the position. He brought with him qualities that were attractive to Imperial. He had graduated from the University of Manitoba with a bachelor degree in agriculture, with a major in economics, and he was computer literate. He lived in the area, and he had a farm background. Robert Strachan, Imperial's territory manager at the time, observed that - "Mr. Johnson seemed to have the ability to adapt to changes that were taking place in the plaintiff's business and grow with the plaintiff's business long term."

5   But that was not to be. An accounting irregularity was uncovered during a routine audit of Westlake in February 1998, some months after Westlake had purchased a service station in Langruth, and Johnson "was put on probation." In January 2001, Imperial received information from Westlake's financial institution that raised concerns about the correctness of Westlake's accounting records. After discussions with Johnson, Imperial launched an internal investigation. That investigation confirmed that there were serious concerns with the accounts of particular customers. Following a meeting with Johnson on March 19, 2001, during which, Imperial says, Johnson acknowledged the inaccuracy of Westlake's accounts, Imperial terminated the agreement.

6   During cross-examination on his affidavit, Johnson admitted, amongst other things, that Westlake's accounts receivable had been "re-aged" to avoid its responsibility to pay down its line of credit with its financial institution; that in order to inflate the accounts receivable, customers were not credited with payments they had made; that accounts receivable were created for fuel that had not been delivered to customers; and that fuel delivered to Westlake's Langruth service station had been shown on the Amaranth Agency weekly inventory reconciliation and, as well, had been invoiced to other customers of Imperial. He acknowledged that the indebtedness of three particular customers that totalled $424,265 in Westlake's accounts receivable ledger was only approximately $86,400.

7   Finally, Johnson was unable to explain the "short fall on the accounts of some $531,000."

8   The defendants say that break-ins and thefts at the Amaranth Agency depot and the failure of Imperial to provide adequate training and support in the Agency's accounting and record-keeping systems are the cause of the irregularities. Johnson says that computer equipment and customer and accounting records were stolen in the break-ins. Whether these allegations will provide the defendants with a defence to the claims Imperial has brought against them is a question that remains to be determined on the evidence adduced at trial.

9   Shortly after the termination of the agency agreement, Johnson registered the business name Westshore Fuel and Oil (Westshore) and began the delivery of fuel and oil products in the Langruth/Amaranth district using that business name. In their statement of defence, the defendants say that a corporation, 4367635 Manitoba Ltd. (4367635), has since assumed the Westshore business name and carries on the business. Details of the ownership of 4367635 have not been put before the court, and the corporation has not been added as a party to the proceedings.

10   Johnson (or 4367635) now operates the business out of Westlake's service station premises in Langruth and makes use of Westlake's trucks and equipment. Johnson has advertised the Westshore business in the market area by a flyer, by radio advertisements, and by an advertisement in a local weekly newspaper. He denies that he has "approached or otherwise solicited any of the customers of Imperial to whom product was sold in the 12 month period prior to the termination of my Agreement." He says that a number of Imperial's customers have approached him, and he has put before the court a number of letters from former customers attesting to that fact.

11   Section 9.08 of the agency agreement, upon which Imperial's application for injunctive relief is founded, provides:

> Agent agrees that he will not for a period of twelve (12) months after the expiration or other termination of this Agreement, directly or indirectly, as principal, agent, partner, employee or otherwise howsoever, solicit orders for or supply within the market area any products then being sold by IMPERIAL within the market area, to any person, firm or corporation who purchased such products within the market area either as an assigned or as an unassigned customer within the period of twelve (12) months preceding the date of expiration or termination of this Agreement.

The Motions Court Decision

12   In granting an interim injunction, the motions judge, in brief oral reasons, identified the principal issues put before the court; namely, the validity of the restrictive covenant and whether it binds Johnson and his wife. In concluding that the covenant was both reasonable and binding upon Johnson and his wife, she applied the reasoning in *Imperial Oil Ltd. v. Frank R. Scott Ltd.* (1993), 51 C.P.R. (3d) 488 (Ont. Gen. Div.). In that decision, a virtually identical covenant in a similar agency agreement was enforced by an interlocutory injunction against - the agent, its controlling shareholder, and a long-time employee of the agent (the son of the controlling shareholder). The motions judge distinguished *Imperial Oil Limited v. Neufeld Holdings Ltd.* et al. (7 March 1997) Docket No. 960325887 (Alta. Q.B.), in which the same covenant was again judicially considered. In that decision, interlocutory relief was denied.

13   The motions judge found evidence of irreparable harm - Imperial's loss of its goodwill and the difficulty of quantifying that loss; and the fact that the defendants had "little expectation of satisfying a judgment in the event that the litigation goes against them." The fact that "[t]he defendants are not precluded from general advertising nor from competing with the plaintiff nor from supplying other customers," the motions judge concluded, tipped the balance of convenience in favour of granting an injunction.

Analysis

14   In these proceedings Imperial seeks interlocutory relief. They ask the court to enforce the restrictive covenant in the agency agreement before the validity of the covenant and the breadth of its reach have been determined after a full and thorough examination of all of the circumstances at trial. Imperial's entitlement to this relief will be determined by the application of the test laid down in *Manitoba (Attorney General) v. Metropolitan Stores Ltd.*, [1987] 1 S.C.R. 110, and reviewed and applied in *RJR - MacDonald Inc. v. Canada (Attorney General)*, [1994] 1 S.C.R. 311. The threshold test, as we will see, is whether on a preliminary assessment of the merits of the case there is a serious question to be tried.

Is the Restrictive Covenant Enforceable?

15   In the leading Canadian case of *Elsley v. J.G. Collins Ins. Agencies Ltd.*, [1978] 2 S.C.R. 916, Dickson J. (as he then was), delivering the judgment of the court, observed at p. 924:

> The validity, or otherwise, of a restrictive covenant can be determined only upon an overall assessment, of the clause, the agreement within which it is found, and all of the surrounding circumstances.

16   This court had the opportunity recently to review the law relating to restrictive covenants in *Winnipeg Livestock Sales Ltd. v. Plewman et al.* (2000), 150 Man.R. (2d) 82, 2000 MBCA 60. In that decision, Scott C.J.M., writing for a unanimous court, referred to the Elsley decision and at para. 25 summarized the three principal questions that Dickson J. had reasoned should be asked in assessing the reasonableness of a restrictive covenant:

(1)   Does the party seeking to enforce the covenant have a proprietary or legitimate interest entitled to protection?

(2)   Are the temporal and spatial features of the covenant reasonable, or too broad?

(3)   Does the covenant prevent competition generally, and if so, is this restriction reasonably required for the protection of the covenantee in the circumstances?

17   In this case, the defendants do not challenge the temporal or spatial limits of the restrictive covenant. They argue, however, that there was no "legitimate proprietary interest that justified the imposition of a restrictive covenant in the Agency Agreement." They argue, as well, that the covenant "is void for attempting to prevent competition."

18   I disagree. The evidence before the court establishes that Imperial provided Johnson and Westlake with an established list of identified customers. Some of the letters filed by Johnson to establish that he was not soliciting former customers illustrate, as well, that there was a longstanding loyalty by those customers (and perhaps by others) to Imperial. The experience of Johnson in the bulk fuel business began with his appointment as Imperial's agent and continued with the subsequent appointment of Westlake. It was as Imperial's agent that Johnson gained the skill and knowledge that now enables him to be a competitor of Imperial in the bulk fuel business. However, it is not on this ground that the courts have upheld restrictive covenants. See *Routh v. Jones*, [1947] 1 All E.R. 179 at 181 (Ch.D.), aff'd [1947] 1 All E.R. 758 (C.A.).

19   Rather, it is on the ground that "he might obtain such personal knowledge of and influence over the customers of [Imperial], ... as would enable him, if competition were allowed, to take advantage of [Imperial's] trade connection."' The customer letters Johnson has filed, in my view, confirm that he has acquired that knowledge and influence.

20   The restrictive covenant in this case is not one against competition generally. As the motions judge observed, "[t]he defendants are not precluded from general advertising nor from competing with the plaintiff nor from supplying other customers." Assuming without deciding the point that the third question applies to the circumstances of this case, I am of the view that the covenant meets that test. The covenant goes no further than addressing a legitimate proprietary interest that arose from the nature of the relationship that was contemplated by the agency agreement. It is obvious that when the agency agreement was executed, it was known that Johnson would acquire a special and intimate knowledge of Imperial's customers as he carried out his responsibilities of supplying product and rendering services to them.

21   A covenant proscribing only solicitation would not have met Imperial's proprietary interest. A paraphrase of the reasoning of Dickson J. in *Elsley* at p. 928 illustrates the point:

> Does an advertisement which comes to the attention of Imperial's customers amount to solicitation? Was there solicitation by Johnson? I need not attempt to answer those questions. The point is that a non-solicitation covenant, in the circumstances here found, would have been meaningless.

Johnson and Westlake's Post-termination Activities

22   Johnson concedes that he is carrying on business under the Westshore business name and is supplying bulk fuel products to customers who had purchased the same kind of products from Imperial within the period of 12 months preceding the termination of Westlake's agency agreement. There is no evidence that Johnson has solicited those orders.

23   The only evidence before the court is that Westlake discontinued its business operations at the time that the agency agreement was terminated and that its only employee, a truck driver, was hired by Imperial's St. Rose agency. There is no evidence that Westlake has solicited orders for or supplied the kind of products that are the subject of the agency agreement to Imperial's customers since the termination of the agreement. However, Johnson acknowledges that Westlake's trucks and equipment are being used by him in his Westshore business and that he operates that business out of Westlake's service station premises in Langruth.

24   Johnson's concessions raise two questions that are at the crux of this appeal: firstly, has Westlake breached its covenant; and secondly, is Westlake's covenant binding upon Johnson (and his wife)?

Has Westlake Violated the Restrictive Covenant?

25   The facts in *Imperial Oil Limited v. Neufeld Holdings Ltd.* et al. bear some resemblance to those before the court. Neufeld Holdings Ltd. had been appointed in 1986 as agent for Imperial Oil, and Abe Neufeld, its sole shareholder, was shown as a guarantor in the agency agreement. The agreement was similar to the agreement that is before the court on this appeal and contained a virtually identical restrictive covenant. The agreement was terminated in 1996, and immediately thereafter a company in which Abe Neufeld's wife was the sole shareholder, Neufeld Propane and Petroleum Ltd., began operating as a Petro-Canada agent in activities competitive with Imperial Oil. Murray J. found at para. 29 that "[t]he evidence does not disclose a breach [of the restrictive covenant] by Holdings beyond allowing Propane to use its equipment." It is implicit in that finding that Murray J. thought that by allowing Neufeld Propane and Petroleum Ltd. to use its trucks, Neufeld Holdings Ltd. had violated the restrictive covenant in the agency agreement. However, Murray J. appears to have resiled somewhat from that conclusion later in his reasons. In para. 30 he ponders:

> The only evidence before the Court that Holdings is or has done anything with respect to Propane is that it has allowed its trucks to be used by Propane either by leasing them or simply making them available. Can it be said that by doing so Holdings is "supplying" product? Simply delivering a product would not likely constitute "soliciting".

26   In the result, he concluded at para. 43 that "there is not a clear cut breach of covenant."

27   The same uncertainty, in my view, applies to the circumstances of this case. Can it be said that by allowing Johnson to use its trucks and equipment and to operate his business out of its service station, Westlake is soliciting orders for or supplying product within the market area to Imperial's customers, even indirectly?

Is the Covenant Binding upon Johnson and his Wife?

28   Johnson and his wife signed the agency agreement as guarantors. Their guarantee was directed in the main to the due observance and performance by Westlake of the covenants, terms, provisions, stipulations, and conditions in the agreement. The agreement did not bind Johnson and his wife, in their personal capacities, within the terms of the restrictive covenant. Nor did they enter into a restrictive covenant running collateral to the agency agreement.

29   It would have been a simple matter for Imperial to have the personal covenants of Johnson and his wife included in the agency agreement or in a collateral agreement. See, for example, the standard clause often found in franchise agreements that is reproduced in *Frank Zaid, Canadian Franchise Guide, looseleaf* (Toronto: Carswell, 1993), and *Big Iron Drilling Ltd. v. Standard Holdings Ltd.,* [1981] 1 W.W.R. 599 at 602 (Sask. Q.B.). But Imperial did not do so.

30   The courts have shown a willingness to "pierce the corporate veil" in order to prevent parties from avoiding their personal liabilities and obligations. *Sask. Econ. Dev. Corp. v. Patterson-Boyd Mfg. Corpn.,* [1981] 2 W.W.R. 40 (Sask. C.A.), and *Colonial & Home Fuel Distributors Ltd. v. Skinners' Ltd.* (1963), 39 D.L.R. (2d) 579 (Man. Q.B.), aff'd (1963), 46 D.L.R. (2d) 695 (Man. C.A.), are examples involving restrictive covenants. In the latter case, the trial judge, Nitikman J., observed at p. 585:

> It would indeed be a travesty of justice if Ignat were permitted to employ that artificial creature of statute, the corporation, to circumvent and avoid the very restrictions which he; the controller of that corporation, has bound himself to observe.

31   But those are not the circumstances in this case. Johnson and his wife have simply not covenanted, in their personal capacities, to be bound by any restrictive covenant. In signing the agency agreement as guarantors they did not agree that they would not, either directly or indirectly, solicit or supply Imperial's customers after the termination of the agreement. The covenant in the agency agreement binds Westlake alone.

32   It might be argued that Johnson and his wife, as the controlling minds of Westlake, have caused Westlake to allow its trucks and equipment and its service station to be used by Johnson in his Westshore operations; and that in doing so they have breached their guarantee in the agency agreement. As considered above (see para. 26), however, it is far from clear that Westlake's conduct since the termination of the agency agreement amounts to a violation of the covenant.

33   In *Imperial Oil Ltd. v. Frank R. Scott Ltd.,* the corporate defendant was the plaintiff's agent pursuant to an agency agreement, and F. R. Scott, its controlling shareholder, was the guarantor of the covenants and obligations of the corporate defendant. After the termination of the agreement by the plaintiff, F.R Scott's son Bradley, a longtime employee of the corporate defendant, commenced business in competition with the plaintiff and solicited and supplied the plaintiff's customers: The plaintiff's application for interlocutory - injunctive relief against the corporate defendant, F. R. Scott, and Bradley Scott was granted, and in doing so, Sills J. reasoned at pp. 492-93:

> In the event that the termination of the agency agreement is found to be valid, then it is likely that the restrictive covenant in art. 9-08 of the agency agreement will stand and Frank R. Scott and Frank R. Scott Limited will almost certainly be subjected to the terms of that covenant. It is also likely that Bradley Scott, because of his close personal relationship with the customers of the plaintiff

(through the agency agreement) and because of his unique knowledge of the business of Frank R. Scott Limited, will be found to be in a fiduciary relationship to the plaintiff and subject to a duty of confidence to the plaintiff with respect to solicitation of and supply to customers of the products of the plaintiff with respect to the products as defined in the agency agreement.

34   The record does not indicate that F. R. Scott, in his personal capacity, had bound himself by the restrictive covenant in the agency agreement. Sills J. does not explain why F. R. Scott "will almost certainly be subjected to the terms of that covenant." No authority is given for that conclusion.

35   Alternatively, Imperial argues that Johnson and his wife "owe a fiduciary obligation to [Imperial] to refrain from soliciting orders for or supplying fuel to [Imperial's] customers within the Market Area for the minimum of one year." Imperial relies upon the finding of such an obligation in *Imperial Oil Ltd. v. Frank R. Scott Ltd.* and the comment of Murray J. in *Imperial Oil Limited v. Neufeld Holdings Ltd.* et al. at para. 42 that "there may be a finding of a fiduciary relationship and there may be certain obligations imposed upon both Holdings and Abe Neufeld."

36   Sills J. found in *Imperial-Oil Ltd. v. Frank R Scott Ltd.* at p. 494 that Bradley Scott owed a fiduciary obligation to the plaintiff arising "out of the influence he has on the customers: *Gerrard v. Century 21 Armour Real Estate Inc.* [(1991), 4 O.R. (3d) 191 at 200 (Gen. Div.)]."

37   The law recognizes that a fiduciary obligation may be owed by a director or senior officer of a corporation to the corporation and that the obligation may persist after a formal employment relationship has ended. See *Canadian Aero Service Ltd. v. O'Malley*, [1974] S.C.R. 592, and *Alberts et al. v. Mountjoy et al.* (1977), 16 O.R. (2d) 682 (H.C.J.). That principle has been extended to prevent an employee from acting "in an unfair way to a former employer." See, for example, *Barton Insurance Brokers Ltd. v. Irwin et al.* (1999), 119 B.C.A.C. 109 at para. 17. In *Gerrard v. Century 21 Armour Real Estate Inc.*, the decision cited by Sills J. in *Imperial Oil Ltd. v. Frank R. Scott Ltd.*, the principle was applied to a former employee who had been the sales manager at an office of the defendant real estate company.

38   With respect, however, *Gerrard v. Century 21 Armour Real Estate Inc.* does not support the conclusion that an employee of a corporation (or even an officer, director, or controlling shareholder of the corporation) may owe a fiduciary obligation to a party with whom the corporation has contracted. That is the position Imperial asserts... in its alternative argument. It finds no support in the case law.

39   The comment of Murray J. in *Imperial Oil Limited v. Neufeld Holdings Ltd.* et al. at para. 42 that "there may be a finding of a fiduciary relationship and there may be certain obligations imposed upon both Holdings and Abe Neufeld" cannot be taken as support for that position. The remark followed his review of *Lac Minerals Ltd. v. International Corona Resources Ltd.*, [1989] 2 S.C.R. 574, *Hodgkinson v. Simms*, [1994] 3 S.C.R. 377, and *Trophy Foods Inc. v. Scott* (1995), 123 D.L.R. (4th) 509 (N.S.C.A.), and his conclusion at para. 40:

[The relationship in this case] was purely a commercial arrangement and in my view falls within the purview of the Lac Minerals class of case.

40   I share that view. In *Lac Minerals Ltd. v. International Corona Resources Ltd.,* the court adopted the indicia of fiduciary duty that Wilson J. had identified in her minority reasons in *Frame v. Smith,* [1987] 2 S.C.R. 99 at 137-38:

> The third characteristic of relationships in which a fiduciary duty has been imposed is the element of vulnerability. This vulnerability arises from the inability of the beneficiary (despite his or her best efforts) to prevent the injurious exercise of the power or discretion combined with the grave inadequacy or absence of other legal or practical remedies to redress the wrongful exercise of the discretion or power. Because of the requirement of vulnerability of the beneficiary at the hands of the fiduciary, fiduciary obligations are seldom present in the dealings of experienced businessmen of similar bargaining strength acting at arm's length: see, for example, *Jirna Ltd. v. Mister Donut of Canada Ltd.* (1971), 22 D.L.R. (3d) 639 (Ont. C.A.), aff'd [1975] 1 S.C.R. 2. The law takes the position that such individuals are perfectly capable of agreeing as to the scope of the discretion or power to be exercised, i.e., any "vulnerability" could have been prevented through the more prudent exercise of their bargaining power and the remedies for the wrongful exercise or abuse of that discretion or power, namely damages, are adequate in such a case.

41   The one feature that is indispensable to the existence of a fiduciary relationship is that of dependency or vulnerability. 'That feature is absent in the circumstances of this case. Imperial is Canada's largest integrated oil company and largest marketer of petroleum products. It is owned by Exxon Mobil Corporation, a multi-national corporation with annual sales in the billions of dollars. Imperial serves the Canadian farm, residential heating, and small commercial markets through about 295 sales facilities.' The Amaranth Agency is one of them. Imperial contracted initially with Johnson when he was 23 years of age and inexperienced in business. Imperial appointed Johnson and later Westlake as its agent pursuant to its standard form of agency agreement. Any vulnerability Imperial now asserts could have been prevented through the more prudent exercise of the superior bargaining power it enjoyed.

Conclusion

42   In my view, *Imperial Oil Ltd. v. Frank R. Scott Ltd.* was wrongly decided. The motions judge followed that decision, and in doing so, she fell into error. Her conclusion that the restrictive covenant binds Johnson and his wife finds no support in the case law. As well, although she referred briefly to Imperial Oil Limited v. Neufeld Holdings Ltd.et al., she does not appear to have put her mind to the fact that Westlake has discontinued its business operations. She did not consider whether Westlake was violating the restrictive covenant by allowing Johnson to use its trucks and equipment and to operate his business out of its service station.

43   I turn to the three-stage test courts are directed to apply when considering an application for either a stay or an interlocutory injunction. The first test is to determine whether there is "a serious question to be tried": *RJR - MacDonald Inc. v. Canada (Attorney General)* at pp. 335—40. The threshold is a low one, but even so, a preliminary assessment of the merits of Imperial's case leads me to the conclusion that the test has not been met. This is particularly so with respect to the issue as to whether the restrictive covenant binds Johnson and his wife, in their personal capacities. No binding or even persuasive authority has been advanced to support such a finding in the circumstances that have been put before the court in this interlocutory proceeding.

44   The second test is "whether the litigant who seeks the interlocutory injunction would, unless the injunction is granted, suffer irreparable harm": RJR - MacDonald Inc. v. Canada (Attorney General) at pp. 340-42. If it were necessary to apply that test, I would have no difficulty in concluding that Imperial would not suffer irreparable harm. I reach that conclusion even if it is assumed that Westlake has violated the covenant by allowing its trucks and equipment and its service station to be used by Johnson in his Westshore operations. There is no evidence to support directly or by inference the conclusion that Westshore's use of Westlake's trucks and equipment and its service station would have any effect on Imperial's apprehended damages or that Imperial would, unless the injunction is granted, harm.

45   Assuming again for the moment that Westlake has violated the covenant, Johnson and his wife might be enjoined from causing Westlake to allow its trucks and equipment and its service station to be used in the Westshore operation. In my view, that is the limit of the injunction that could possibly be granted against them personally. Again, there is no evidence that such an injunction would curtail Westshore's solicitation of and supplying to Imperial's customers or that Imperial would, unless the injunction is granted, suffer irreparable harm.

46   The final test is "a determination of which of the two parties will suffer the greater harm from the granting or refusal of an interlocutory injunction, pending a decision on the merits": Manitoba (Attorney General) v. Metropolitan Stores Ltd. at p. 129. If it were necessary to apply this test to the circumstances of this case, it would be answered by the weakness in Imperial's case for injunctive relief. At this preliminary stage in the action, Imperial's claim for an accounting and payment of monies due to it appears to be a formidable one. That cannot be said of its application for interlocutory relief. The defendants would clearly suffer greater harm by the granting of an interlocutory injunction than Imperial would suffer by its refusal.

Disposition

47   The defendants' appeal is allowed, and the order of Keyser J. is set aside. The defendants are entitled to their costs in this court and in the Court of Queen's Bench.

KROFT J.A.:— I agree.

STEEL J.A.:— I agree.

QUESTIONS

1. What was the "legitimate proprietary interest" that justified imposition of a restrictive covenant by Imperial Oil in the agency agreement?

2. Why was Johnson found not to be personally bound by the restrictive covenant in spite of the personal guarantee he signed? What should Imperial Oil have done to ensure that Johnson was bound?

3. Might there have been a more effective way to word the restrictive covenant?

4. Why did the Court of Appeal find that Johnson did not owe Imperial Oil a fiduciary duty?

chapter eight

Mistake

Credit Foncier Trust Co. v. Glimjem Holdings Ltd.

[1994] O.J. No. 2931, 770 AC 34
Ontario Court of Appeal
December 19, 1994

Generally, the courts will not interfere with a contract unless it can be demonstrated that the mistake claimed is a very serious one. It must be a factual mistake as to the subject matter of the contract or the identity of the parties or a misunderstanding of the agreement that is so fundamental, it destroys the element of consent. If the written contract does not reflect the common intention of the parties to the contract, the courts are willing to correct or rectify the document. However, there must be the clearest evidence that both parties agreed to something other than what was embodied in the written contract to obtain rectification by the courts.

1   **THE COURT** (endorsement):— This appeal does not turn on findings of credibility. The essential facts are not in issue. Rather, this appeal is based on the appellant's submission that the trial judge erred in how he interpreted them. We agree. The two main issues on this appeal, are whether the trial judge erred in finding (1) that the parties had not negotiated a final settlement of the amount owing on the mortgage arrears in May 1987; and (2) that there was a common mistake in the settlement entitling Credit Foncier to rectification.

2   The chronology of this dispute started in March 1984 when Credit Foncier's wraparound mortgage with Glimjem matured and Credit Foncier discovered that it had made a $57,000 error in calculating the tax instalment account two years earlier when Glimjem had purchased the property and assumed the mortgage. Credit Foncier attempted to recover this amount from Glimjem. Glimjem denied liability and said that any recovery should be from the vendor.

3   In the course of the multiple negotiations which followed between Credit Foncier and Glimjem, Glimjem found itself waiting for months to get responses from Credit Foncier about the resolution of the tax issue; about the amount required to renew the mortgage; and then, having decided not to renew the mortgage, about the amount required to discharge it. The replies from Credit Foncier when they came, were consistently inaccurate, including a dozen erroneous mortgage statements. Glimjem spent more than a year waiting for the necessary accurate information.

4   In May 1985, 14 months after the mortgage had matured, the two parties were able to agree on the terms upon which they were prepared to sign a Mortgage Amending Agreement discharging the mortgage. The terms of this agreement included not only the usual discharge provisions, they included as well a complete release of all outstanding matters between the parties including the tax issue.

5   Two months after the mortgage was discharged Credit Foncier noticed yet another mistake in its calculations and, as a result, demanded payment of a shortfall of $72,587.36 from Glimjem to correct the error. It also sought rectification of the mortgage amending agreement.

6   Five years later, a few days before trial, Credit Foncier produced a new statement by a new accountant with a new set of figures. This revised statement indicated that the proper amount still owing under the mortgage was $61,958.36. The trial judge accepted this figure as the appropriate amount owing and rectified the Mortgage Amending Agreement accordingly. The basis for his decision to rectify the agreement was common mistake, in accordance with the decision of Grange J. in Stepps *Investments Limited v. Security Capital Corporation* (1976), 73 D.L.R. (3d) 351.

7   The first issue raised on this appeal is whether or not the parties were in fact settling all outstanding matters between them in signing the mortgage amending agreement. In our view that is precisely what the agreement represented. After more than one year of incomprehensible delays and errors, everyone of which was due to Credit Foncier, Glimjem, as the voluminous correspondence reveals, was increasingly frustrated. This dispute started with Credit Foncier's mistaken calculations over the tax instalment account, then proceeded through Credit Foncier's mistaken calculations over the mortgage accounts, and concluded, after an agreement had been signed and registered, with one final major error over the amount due under the mortgage.

8   It is quite possible that Glimjem "ought to have known", in the words of Stepps, that the amount they would ultimately be required to pay to discharge the mortgage would be based on some mistake or other in the underlying calculation, since every calculation Glimjem had been given my Credit Foncier had contained some kind of error. Glimjem would have been perfectly and reasonable entitled, given this history of unreliable and inaccurate calculations, to assume that it might never be able to get a truly accurate amount. But this is very different from the principle of common mistake, where one determinative error reveals itself upon proper scrutiny.

9   This pattern of error is also the very reason Glimjem wanted and thought it had received a final settlement and release. Glimjem was anxious to discharge the mortgage. It was not obliged to wait indefinitely until Credit Foncier had accurate information. It waited until it thought Credit Foncier had information as accurate as it and Credit Foncier were prepared to accept.

10   The evidence discloses Credit Foncier's increasing embarrassment over the negligence of its calculations and the inconclusiveness of its responses to Glimjem's request for accurate information. When, for instance, Glimjem challenged a figure of approximately $9,300, Credit Foncier conceded the point and deducted this amount. As Mr. Chong, Manager of Administration for Credit Foncier, stated in chief:

> Q. Please take a look at that memorandum, and could you advise the court whether or not that assists you in including the reason for the $9,329.27 adjustment from the discharge statement.
>
> A. I, I got a request — it could have been from Mr. [sic] Silverstein or it could have been from Mr. Goldlist — I don't recall at this point — but I got a request, and they said that the interest was overstated by 9,329.27 at that point in time. I took that information and I spoke to Mr. Anderssen and I asked how he wished to proceed with this matter, and he told me that if this meant this entire trans-action could be closed he was willing to forego the 9,329.27. This was although we could not come up with the figure anywhere—-

And then in cross-examination, Mr. Chong was asked the following questions and gave the following answers:

> Q. The final figure reflected in 9,300 reduction?
> A. Correct.
>
> Q. And it was a bargained figure?
> A. Yes.
>
> Q. It wasn't the exact sum that you believed Foncier was entitled to under the mortgage?
> A. Correct.
>
> Q. In other words, Foncier was prepared to accept less than one hundred percent of its claim?
> A. At this point in time.
>
> Q. To clean this up?
> A. Correct.
>
> Q. And that was communicated directly or indirectly by you to a representative of Glimjem?
> A. Yes, that is correct.

11   The evidence also discloses Glimjem's wish to resolve the matter conclusively. This, in our view, was what both parties thought they were doing, when after months of discussions and negotiations, they signed the Mortgage Amending Agreement on May 7, 1985, namely, settle all issues between them once and for all even if the figures turned out to be, inaccurate as they had consistently been in the past.

12   It was therefore not open to Credit Foncier to revisit the settlement notwithstanding that yet again its negligence had resulted in an error in the calculations. There is no doubt in our view that there was a final settlement of all claims, including any claim arising out of the very real possibility that Credit Foncier had yet again, somehow erred in calculating the amount required to discharge the mortgage.

13   Although, given our decision about the effect of the agreement, it is not necessary to make any finding about common mistake, it is, in our view, difficult to see how the doctrine of common mistake can apply in the circumstances of this case. However, in view of our conclusion on the matter of settlement, we need express no definite opinion on this point. In any event, it would be inequitable for Credit Foncier to be able to recover the shortfall it discovered after signing the agreement, given its extraordinary carelessness and lassitude in dealing with Glimjem.

14   Accordingly, we would allow the appeal, set aside the order of Farley J. and dismiss Credit Foncier's claim with costs both of the appeal and at trial. The dismissal of the counterclaim without costs will stand.

HOULDEN J.A.

GRIFFITHS J.A.

ABELLA J.A.

QUESTIONS

1. Why is the use of mistake to avoid legal obligations strictly limited by the courts?

2. How does the concept of a legal mistake differ from its ordinary meaning?

3. What conditions must be satisfied before a court will order rectification? Under what circumstances is a court unlikely to order such a remedy? Why, in this case, did the court deny the appellant this remedy?

4. In this case, what is the difference between the principle of common mistake and negligence? What effect did this finding have for the appellant?

5. In this case, at what point in time had the parties resolved the matter of the mortgage conclusively? Explain. Was it open for Credit Foncier to revisit the agreement later? Explain.

Performance Industries Ltd. v. Sylvan Lake Golf & Tennis Club Ltd.

[2002] SCJ No. 20, [2001] SCCA No. 260

Supreme Court of Canada on Appeal from the Court of Appeal for Alberta

February 22, 2002

Present: McLachlin C.J. and L'Heureux-Dube, Gonthier, Major, Binnie, Arbour and LeBel JJ.

The courts will not usually allow rectification of a contract where there has been unilateral mistake, but in this case, the Supreme Court of Canada outlined the circumstances that would justify a court to do so.

Judgment for the Court was delivered by **BINNIE J**. The following is a summary of the case and his judgment.

Sylvan's principal was Bell. Sylvan had a right of first refusal to purchase golf club property, and intended ultimately to develop the 18th hole for residential housing. When the opportunity arose to take up the right of first refusal, Bell found that he did not have sufficient funds. O'Connor, the principal of Performance Industries, offered financing, and negotiations for a joint venture ensued. According to their discussions, Bell would have an option to develop two rows of housing on the 18th hole, and this was agreed to verbally between O'Connor and Bell. O'Connor undertook to have his lawyer reduce the verbal terms to writing, and a document was produced. The written terms included Clause 18, that allowed only a single row of housing. Bell did not read the clause or notice the discrepancy between it and what had been agreed to previously. On the basis of their agreement, the parties exercised the right of first refusal.

About four years later, Bell and O'Connor discussed the particulars of Bell's plans to build the housing development. Only then did Bell notice the difference between Clause 18 and what he had negotiated with O'Connor. Clause 18 made the option useless to Bell. Attempts were made to resolve the dispute, but O'Connor insisted that Bell's right to develop was limited under Clause 18 of the written agreement. When Bell refused to relinquish his rights to the property, O'Connor sued for specific performance and won. Later Bell sued O'Connor and Performance Industries in the Alberta Court of Queen's Bench for rectification of the agreement, and for damages for breach of the rectified agreement.

The trial judge held that the written agreement had contained an error that was known to O'Connor who was the "directing mind of Performance Industries." He characterized O'Connor as "fraudulent, dishonest and deceitful" and ordered rectification of the contract. He held O'Connor personally liable jointly and severally with Performance Industries for damages of $1,047,810 including a $200,000 award of punitive damages.

O'Connor appealed to the Alberta Court of Appeal, which upheld the trial judge's award against both O'Connor and Performance Industries, except for the punitive damages, which the Court of Appeal said should be awarded "only if they achieve some rational purpose". The Court of Appeal considered the compensatory damages as sufficient to satisfy any punishment or deterrence objective, and decided that this was not a case where it was necessary to award punitive damages to ensure the defendant did not profit from his misconduct. Performance Industries and O'Connor appealed to the Supreme Court of Canada on the issue of liability, and Bell cross-appealed on the issue of damages.

The Supreme Court of Canada said that where reasonably sophisticated business people reduce their oral agreements to written form, which are prepared and reviewed by lawyers, and changes made, and documents then executed, there is little scope for rectification. The purpose of rectification is to prevent a written document from being used as an instrument of fraud. Usually rectification was allowed only for mutual mistake, but can be available for unilateral mistake provided:

1. There was a prior oral contract whose terms were certain and the terms were not written down properly.

2. At the time the document was executed it must be shown that the defendant was aware of the error and the plaintiff was not. Rectification is not to be a substitute for due diligence, however if permitting the non-mistaken party to take advantage of the written document would be fraud or its equivalent, rectification should be available.

3. The plaintiff must show the precise form in which the writing can be made to reflect the prior oral agreement.

4. There must be "convincing proof" of the plaintiff's contentions.

The Supreme Court of Canada said that the plaintiff had satisfied these four conditions.

It is not necessary for the plaintiff to show due diligence, in fact, lack of due diligence is present in most cases of unilateral mistake. Carelessness on the part of the plaintiff should not be a defence to fraud on the part of the defendant. Here O'Connor did more than "snap" up a business partner's mistake. He became part of a fraudulent scheme to have the document wrongly state the terms of the agreement, fraudulently misrepresented to Bell that it accurately set forth the terms of the verbal agreement, and allowed Bell to sign it knowing he was mistaken. He delayed bringing it to Bell's attention and Bell discovered it when it was almost too late to have exercised his option.

O'Connor said that Bell's damages should be limited to the difference between the market value of the land and the option price, and not include the profits Bell could have made on a fully built residential development. The Supreme Court of Canada said that the damages were for breach of the contract as rectified, and should therefore include losses from any special circumstances known to the parties at the time they made their contract, including, in this case, lost profits. The Supreme Court of Canada agreed with the Alberta Court of Appeal that punitive damages must have a rational purpose and were not warranted here, as they were not required by way of "retribution, deterrence, or denunciation". Even though O'Connor's fraud was reprehensible, only in exceptional cases does it attract punitive damages. The Court dismissed the appeal and the cross-appeal.

QUESTIONS

1. Do you agree that where reasonably sophisticated business people reduce their oral agreements to writing, there should be little scope for rectification? Explain.

2. Why did the court award rectification of this contract?

3. Why did the Court say that lack of due diligence is almost always present in an action for unilateral mistake?

4. Can you envision any circumstances in which a court might award punitive damages in an action for breach of contract? Explain.

chapter nine

Misrepresentation

Collins v. Dodge City East Ltd.

[1999] N.J. No. 285

Newfoundland Provincial Court - Small Claims Division

September 3, 1999

Remedies are available to victims of misrepresentation that are unavailable to those suffering from mistake. It is necessary to show that the mistake destroyed the very foundation of the contract to escape a contract on the basis of mistake. A person claiming misrepresentation need only show that he or she had been misled about some material or important aspect of a contract to receive a remedy.

1   **HYSLOP PROV. CT. J.**:— The plaintiff is suing the defendant corporation for negligent misrepresentation or breach of a sales agreement (or a fundamental part thereof) with respect to the purchase of a used motor vehicle.

2   The plaintiff is a dental hygienist. She had a sporty motor vehicle and wished to upgrade it for a newer model with more options. According to the evidence, she offered her old vehicle on a trade for the newer model which she purchased from the defendant. The defendant corporation is a reputable dealer experienced in the sale of motor vehicles and was represented with respect to all the preliminary negotiations and representations by one Shawn Ryan.

3   I was impressed with the candour and apparent disarming honesty of the plaintiff. She not only presented credible and convincing testimony, but I was impressed with her single minded determination and the caution which she exercised in making her purchase, a purchase which involved an expenditure of a not insignificant amount of money ($15,900.00 + taxes). Prior to consummating the transaction, the plaintiff performed independent research relating to price on the Internet. She ascertained the identity of the prior owner and had a friend check the vehicle for structural damage. I am satisfied that the defendant afforded her the opportunity to have the vehicle independently assessed or evaluated and that there was no improper or unethical conduct that I can attribute to the defendant.

4   Having said all that, I accept that the defendant knew that the plaintiff was interested in viewing with the intention to purchase, a vehicle which had numerous options. I accept that she was shown a vehicle which did not suit her and that in January of 1998, Mr. Shawn Ryan approached her about the availability for purchase of a 1996 model Mazda MX3 Precedia which was described as "fully loaded." The plaintiff went to the sales lot, and since the vehicle was not yet there, returned the next day with a friend, one Paul Goulart who went on a test drive with the agent of the defendant. The control panel clearly indicated that the vehicle was equipped with air conditioning. The designation "A/C" appears on a button on the control panel and the designation was not obscured by a cap or cover. The plaintiff claims that the salesman, Shawn Ryan manipulated the air-conditioning control and demonstrated its operation. She claims that a green light illuminated and that cold air emanated from the vent. She claims that she asked about the air conditioning since she had never had that option before and that the agent said, as he manipulated the controls, words to the effect of "This is how it works." Similar and corroborative evidence was given by Paul Goulart. Shawn Ryan was unable to recall whether or not the conversation occurred or whether or not he manipulated the controls as described. Given the nature of his work and the volume of customers with whom he deals, this is not altogether surprising.

5   I must apply all the common sense rules in the weighing of evidence that is expected of all triers of fact. I have before me a cautious prudent plaintiff who is faced with a considerable expenditure. One of the witnesses described her as "picky." I have no doubt that she was. I accept her evidence as truthful and accurate. It is in sharp contrast, in terms of its clarity of recall, to that of the defendant. I hasten to add that I do not conclude that Mr. Ryan was anything other than honest and truthful. His level of recollection was understandably, not of the level of the Ms. Collins when one considers the situation as a whole. Where the evidence of the plaintiff is in conflict with the evidence of the defence, I accept the evidence of Ms. Collins.

6   The plaintiff used the Internet as a guideline as well as such other advice as she could get in negotiating a fair price. I appreciate that there are variables at play here including the trade in price offered on her old vehicle, the condition of the vehicle to be purchased, as well as its mileage etc. I accept the defendant's position that no two used cars are identical. Nonetheless I am convinced that the plaintiff did at all times consider that she was buying a vehicle with air conditioning, that she factored this consideration into the price that she was willing to pay, and that the presence of air conditioning was a critical factor in her consideration to purchase. She said that she honestly believed that air conditioning was present in the car. I come to this conclusion for the following reasons:

1. She was told the vehicle was "fully loaded."

2. The Option was clearly indicated on the display panel.

3. The agent of the dealer demonstrated the "option" and it appeared to work.

4. I accept that the response of the agent when apprised of the problem was "I didn't know," or words to that effect.

5. The conduct of the plaintiff when the problem manifested itself.

7   With respect to the first point, some narration is necessary. During the "demonstration" of the air conditioner in January, the light came on and cold air was generated. This should not be surprising in our climate. However about seven months later, in June, the plaintiff was on an outing and actually needed the function. She turned it on and found that it did not work. Her first response was to seek to have it repaired. One can only imagine her shock when she learned that it had never even been installed. She tried to negotiate a settlement and was unsuccessful. The matter was brought before this court for a resolution.

8   The defendant seems to place great emphasis on the fact that the buyer had engaged someone to look at the car on her behalf. This is true, but this examination was for structural purposes only. The plaintiff explained that she was interested in seeing if there had been a prior accident involving the vehicle. No examination was done of the air conditioning in view of the impression that had been left with the plaintiff.

9   In short, I conclude that the agent of the defendant demonstrated the air conditioning to the defendant as she described and in a manner that could only have been interpreted as enhancing the attractiveness of the vehicle. I cannot conclude that the misrepresentation was deliberate. The evidence is equally consistent with it having been an innocent misrepresentation. This is all the more likely when I consider the initial response of Mr. Ryan when he was confronted by the plaintiff in June of 1998, as, "I didn't know." Nonetheless I conclude that a misrepresentation was made with respect to an essential aspect of the manner in which the vehicle was equipped. In all other respects, the vehicle was equipped as represented. I am also satisfied that the plaintiff would not have purchased the vehicle without the air conditioning. It was important to her and the conversation with the plaintiff's representative as well as the demonstration should have made that clear. The misrepresentation made by Shawn Ryan was made within the scope of his ordinary duties as a representative of the defendant corporation. It was made with a view to obtaining a sale in a situation where a duty of care was owed to the plaintiff, and it was, however innocent, a negligent misrepresentation that went to the root of what Ms. Collins thought she was bargaining for.

[Paragraphs 10 to 14 have been omitted]

15   It would appear that the defendant takes the position that the plaintiff was somehow negligent in not discovering the absence of air conditioning on her own part. Lest I am misunderstood on that question, I can only state that I have concluded that she exercised a reasonable amount of caution and prudence. I have noted that the defendant was willing to have the vehicle inspected and that a Mr. Hickey was asked by the plaintiff to examine it for structural defects. On the question of air conditioning, I think that the plaintiff was entitled to rely on the words and actions of Mr. Ryan in all the circumstances. I am unable to conclude that there was negligence on her part.

16   Mr. Wadland, who appeared on behalf of the defendant, argued that if the shoe were on the other foot, to the extent, that had he provided an option and erroneously failed to charge for it, he would not be in a position to recover. While it is dangerous to speculate on hypothetical situations, I think it is fair to say that the law does not like to see someone unjustly enriched or deprived at the hands of another.

17   It is my view that the plaintiff's action should succeed on the basis of what amounted to a negligent misrepresentation on a fundamental element which induced her to enter into a contract. I note that her claim is based on an amount that is actually lower than the actual cost of installing air conditioning. She made this claim based on the best information available to her at the time and, quite fairly and reasonably has not sought to amend her claim to the approximate $1,500.00 necessary to install the option in her vehicle.

18   Judgment is entered for the plaintiff for $1,040.00 plus costs of filing ($20.00), the costs of appearance of two witnesses ($8.00), together with the costs of copying and filing photographs and the various documents submitted at trial in accordance with item (i) in the Schedule to the Small Claims Rules ($10.00) for a total judgment of $1,078.00.

Judgment accordingly.

QUESTIONS

1. What is the distinction between an innocent and negligent misrepresentation and why is the distinction important? What remedy was sought in this case?
2. What elements are necessary for the plaintiff to prove in order to establish a claim for negligent misrepresentation?
3. What happens when a misrepresentation becomes a term of the contract?
4. What can a seller do, in circumstances like this case, to protect him/herself from liability for either innocent or negligent misrepresentations?

Crozman v. Ruesch

[1993] B.C.J. No. 2345, [1993] 4 WWR 116, 35 BCAC 236, 87 BCLR (2d) 223
British Columbia Court of Appeal
October 21, 1993

A buyer of real estate under a standard-form real estate contract will likely have difficulty relying on misrepresentation to obtain a remedy, even where the buyer can show that misleading statements were made by the seller. One difficulty is that in a contract for purchase and sale of land, rescission is not usually available after the title has transferred. The other difficulty comes from the fact that the standard exclusion clause in the contract prevents the buyer relying on pre-contractual statements.

1   **TAYLOR J.A.** (for the Court, orally, dismissing the appeal):— This is an appeal from the dismissal by Mr. Justice Arkell of an action for damages for fraud or negligence on the part of vendors in the sale of a house.

2   The appellants, Richard Crozman and his wife Debbie, bought their home in downtown Vernon for $53,000 in May, 1989, from the respondents, Adolph Ruesch and his wife, who had been living there for some three years. Mr. and Mrs. Crozman were advised and assisted in entering into the transaction by Mrs. Crozman's father, Bill Shaw, himself a former real estate salesman who was then in the automobile business.

3   The circumstances leading to the execution of the agreement of purchase and sale, which was recorded on a printed standard-form document produced and completed by Mr. Shaw, are described by the trial judge as follows:

> The Plaintiffs observed a for sale sign on the Defendants' house on May 27th, 1989 and the two Plaintiffs, Mr. and Mrs. Crozman, viewed the house initially and they then accompanied Mrs. Crozman's parents, Mr. and Mrs. Bill Shaw, to further inspect the house. After their inspection and examination of the house Mr. Shaw, on behalf of the Plaintiffs, negotiated the purchase price of $53,000.00 with the Defendant, Adolf Ruesch. Mr. Shaw then drafted an interim agreement that was signed by both of the Plaintiffs and Defendants. The entire transaction, including the inspection of the property and preparation of the interim agreement, took approximately two hours. They arrived at approximately 6:30 p.m. and left somewhere between 8:00 and 8:30 p.m.
>
> During the second examination of the house on May 27th, 1989, by the Crozmans and Mr. and Mrs. Shaw, Mr. Shaw had noticed a crack in the main entrance or foyer and he asked Mr. Ruesch about this crack and Mr. Ruesch said

that it was a minor settling problem and it was common for that area. In the lower rumpus room during this inspection they again asked about the floor sagging and Mr. Ruesch stated that there was a false floor put in and it was carpeted and the boards may be loose. On the upper level in the hallway Mr. Shaw noticed the floor was not level. Mr. Shaw also noticed that the rear screen door was not level. The screen had been ripped and Mr. Shaw asked about the door and Mr. Ruesch replied that with a dog you have got to expect that.

So the Crozmans and their experienced adviser knew from the beginning of their inspection that there had been settlement and that it had caused cracking in the house, which Mr. Ruesch described as "minor" and common to the area. The judge continues:

Before concluding the interim agreement and signing it, Mr. Shaw asked again about the crack in the foyer entrance and Mr. Ruesch again stated it was a settlement problem and, "don't worry, it's been there since we moved in." When Mr. Shaw and Mr. Ruesch were negotiating the price Mr. Ruesch indicated that he was going to list the house for sale with an agent. Mr. Shaw indicated that this statement prompted him to increase his offer from $50,000 to $53,000 to avoid paying the agent commission of approximately $3,500.

Thus, by the time the agreement was signed, the existence of a settlement problem had been mentioned a second time, with the assurance that it had not been getting any worse.

4   The document Mr. Shaw then prepared was an offer, unconditional as to the state of the premises, by his daughter and son-in-law to purchase the property for $53,000. It contains, in capital letters, in its printed portion the following clause:

I/WE HAVE READ AND CLEARLY UNDERSTAND THE ABOVE OFFER TO PURCHASE ACKNOWLEDGE THAT IT ACCURATELY SETS OUT ALL THE TERMS OF MY/OUR OFFER THAT I/WE WAS/WERE NOT INDUCED TO MAKE IT BY ANY REPRESENTATIONS, WARRANTIES, GUARAN-TEES OR PROMISES EXPRESSED OR IMPLIED NOT CONTAINED HEREIN, AND ACKNOWLEDGE HAVING RECEIVED A COPY OF THE SAID OFFER.

Mr. and Mrs. Crozman signed the offer, as completed for them by Mr. Shaw, and Mr. and Mrs. Ruesch then signed a portion below which evidences the vendors' accept-ance of the offer.

5   The judge notes that on leaving Mr. Shaw made a parting remark to Mr. and Mrs. Ruesch to the effect that if there was anything wrong with the home they would hear from his lawyer.

6   When the Crozmans moved in, about five weeks later, they made a number of discoveries, which are described by the trial judge in the following passage:

In addition to the crack in the entrance foyer that had been observed by Mr. Shaw, they found numerous cracks in the walls that were covered by way of wallpaper, wood panelling and drapes or furniture. They also found several cracks in the concrete floor in the basement that was covered by carpets or by the sub-floor. The concrete in the carport was cracked and dropped towards the house. At the time of the inspection on May 27th there were boxes, dressers, and a trailer with a boat located in the carport. The door into the carport from the basement could not be opened due to sagging. On May 27th there was a deep freeze in front of the door so it wasn't opened on that day. On July 1st the Crozmans also noted water seepage in the front foyer. They also noted that the home was not level and some doors and lower front windows were not level, were sagging and binding. The cost of raising one end of the house and repairing the settlement damage was said to have exceeded $12,000, and it was to recover this cost that the Crozmans brought their action.

7 In discussing with the law the trial judge concluded that the rule "caveat emptor" would apply in the circumstances unless there was proof of fraud. While counsel for the appellant seemed to question that conclusion on appeal, I heard nothing in his argument which suggested that it was wrong.

8 There can be no suggestion that the Crozmans suffered from any inequality of bargaining power; quite the contrary. Nor can it be said that the words of the offer would not bind them, having in mind that they were acting under the advice of a person experienced in the real estate business and that it was he who prepared the offer for them. Obviously, Mr. Shaw could have inserted clauses making the purchase conditional on inspection and approval of the premises by someone with appropriate expertise. But, then, the price may have seemed an attractive one to Mr. Shaw and the Crozmans, and good deals can easily be lost by dickering and delay. In any event, the purchase was made by the Crozmans on what is sometimes known as an "as is" basis, and this was done in reliance of Mr. Shaw's expertise.

9 Was there proof, then, of fraud on the part of Mr. and Mrs. Ruesch? In this regard the trial judge said:

> Mr. and Mrs. Ruesch both testified that the house they sold was in the same condition as the house they purchased in 1986. The only changes that they made were to remove the carpet in the kitchen and replace it with lino. Mrs. Ruesch also put some new wallpaper in the two smaller bedrooms and Mr. Ruesch built a fence over the period of some two years while they were living there. Mr. Ruesch also put locks on the lower bedroom window and other windows for security reasons and the windows, according to both the Rueschs, were in the same condition as when the Plaintiffs bought the house in 1989. Mr. and Mrs. Ruesch also testified there were no water problems whatsoever in the house during the period of time they were living there and to their knowledge there were no serious settling problems. Mr. Ruesch indicated that they could open the exterior door to the carport when they moved into the house in 1986 but even at that time it was stiff and binding. They indicated they placed the deep freeze in front of the door because it was a convenient place and they left the deep freeze there until they moved in 1989. When they moved they discovered they could not open the door.
>
> It was also Mr. Ruesch's testimony that the cracks in the carport, cracks in the entry foyer walls and cracks in the livingroom and in the bedrooms and kitchen were all visible to them when they purchased it in 1986 to 1989. The panelling and wallpaper that went on the walls and sub-floor in the basement were all in place when the Rueschs purchased the house in 1986.

The judge rejected the allegations of fraud, observing:

> I may say that after hearing their evidence in the witness stand, that I accept the evidence of Mr. and Mrs. Ruesch. There was no false or fraudulent action by them either knowingly or otherwise. A careful and proper inspection of the house

by the Shaws and Crozmans would have disclosed the same patent defects as were observed by the Rueschs when they bought the house in 1986. When Mr. Shaw asked about the crack in the foyer Mr. Ruesch said it was minor settlement and I am satisfied it was to Mr. Ruesch's knowledge at that time an honest statement. Any other statements made by Mr. Ruesch to Mr. Shaw on May 27th, 1989, as to the sub-floor being spongy and as to the back door damages were also a true statement to the best of Mr. Ruesch's knowledge and belief upon the three years he lived in the house.

The claims of the Plaintiffs as to fraudulent misrepresentation and deceit are not supported by the not concealment of latent defects by the Rueschs and certainly no evidence of fraud. Those are findings made on the basis of the judge's assessment of the credibility of Mr. and Mrs. Ruesch, after hearing and observing them in the witness box, and counsel for the appellant conceded before us that he faced a difficult task in seeking to have this Court overturn such findings.

10   The fact that the judge did not refer to all the evidence of defects discovered is not a ground for disturbing his conclusion as to the motivation and good faith of the respondents. Nor can it be said that the judge ought to have found 'fraud by half truth', as described in *C.R.F. Holdings Ltd. et al v. Fundy Chemical International Ltd. et al* (1980) 21 B.C.L.L. 345. The judge found that the respondents acted with honest intent, and this necessarily negatives, in the present circumstances, fraud by half truth as well as fraud by untruth and fraud by concealment.

11   With respect to the assertion by counsel for the appellants that the respondents must, when they moved out their belongings, have discovered evidence which would have destroyed their former belief that the settling problem was a minor one, and that they then had a duty to disclose this to the purchasers, no authority was referred to us which supports this contention in the context of an executed contract of purchase and sale, nor in a situation where the statement originally made was a statement of opinion. Even if it is true that documents of title had not yet been registered at the time when the respondents moved out — a point not established in evidence we are told — their failure to tell the Crozmans of whatever they then discovered cannot, on the basis of any authority referred to us, constitute fraud.

12   I would dismiss the appeal.

QUESTIONS

1. What did the sellers say that qualified as misrepresentation?

2. Why could the buyers not rely on misrepresentation to get rescission of the contract?

3. What difference would it have made to the outcome of this case if the buyers had proved fraud on the part of the sellers?

4. What should buyers do to protect themselves against unexpected defects in real estate they buy?

Buckwold Western Ltd. v. Sager

[1997] B.C.J. No. 1121

British Columbia Supreme Court

May 13, 1997

When a person is forced or pressured to enter into a contract against his or her will by threats of violence or imprisonment, the contract may be voidable for duress. The type of pressure that some contracting parties are subject to is often more subtle than duress. Undue influence results from a special relationship between parties creating domination of one party over the mind and will of another to such a degree that the weaker party is deprived of the will to make an independent decision. A contract formed as a result of undue influence is also voidable by the weaker party.

1   **SAUNDERS J.**:— On June 27, 1991 the defendant Collyne Sager signed a document guaranteeing payment of monies owing from time to time by London Carpets Ltd. to the predecessor company of the plaintiff. The defendant Laurence Sager had signed a similar guarantee in May of 1991. The plaintiff now claims $77,415.16 against Ms Sager, the sum owing by London Carpets Ltd. Ms Sager admits signing the guarantee but denies awareness of its possible consequences.

2   The issue is the enforceability of the guarantee.

3   London Carpets Ltd. was a business owned by the defendants. Mr. Sager was the principal of the company. Ms Sager received income from the company and helped in the business from time to time. Although she was not aware of her share ownership until after the guarantee was signed, she was at all times an equal owner of the company with her husband. The company provided the family income.

4   Prior to 1991 London Carpets Ltd. purchased carpet from a predecessor company of the plaintiff, Buckwold Western Ltd., to a credit limit of $5,000. In 1991 Mr. Sager wished to increase the credit limit. He was advised by the supplier that credit would only be extended beyond $5,000 if he and Ms Sager signed a personal guarantee of the company debts. Mr. Sager signed such a guarantee in May 1991. When he presented it to the supplier Mr. Sager was advised again that the guarantee of Ms Sager was also required before further credit would be granted.

5   Mr. Sager presented a form of guarantee to Ms Sager and asked her to sign it. Ms Sager was reluctant to do so as she did not want her name on legal documents. She understood that without her signature, the company could not do the volume of business with this supplier that her husband thought was necessary. Without the

advice of a lawyer and after a few hours, she signed the guarantee. Ms Sager did not meet any person from the supplier company in whose favour the guarantee was given.

6   Ms Sager testified that she did not understand what the document represented and that had she understood, she would not have signed it. She agreed that she knew there was a risk that she may have to pay some money as a result of the guarantee.

7   In April 1995 London Carpets Ltd. was assigned into bankruptcy. At that time it owed $77,415.16 to the plaintiff's predecessor company. There have been no payments on that debt.

8   Ms Sager seeks relief from the guarantee on the basis that she did not understand all the consequences of signing the guarantee and signed it only at her husband's insistence that her guarantee was required for the company to do business with this supplier.

9   There are few defences to an action on a guarantee. In this case, Ms Sager's evidence raises the possible defences of duress or undue hardship.

10   The defence of duress is available to excuse a guarantor from payment on the guarantee where improper pressure has been placed on the guarantor. The issue here is foremost a question of the guarantor's free will and the soundness of her consent: *Byle v. Byle* (1990), 65 D.L.R. (4th) 641 (B.C.C.A.).

11   In this case no improper pressure was brought to bear upon Ms Sager. In the circumstances, the pressure imposed on Ms Sager by Mr. Sager was nothing more than standard commercial pressure. The linkage described by Mr. Sager between the guarantee and supply of product was simply an expression of the gist of the commercial arrangements between London Carpets Ltd. and the supplier. The supplier would not extend greater credit unless it had some assurance beyond the company's commitment that the bills would be paid, and unless it had greater capacity to collect amounts that may become owing.

12   I find that the pressure placed on Ms Sager did not have the effect of preventing her from freely exercising her own will in giving her consent. In my view she elected to do what was commercially required to obtain the desired supply of carpet for the business that supported the family.

13   The defence of undue influence is available to a guarantor where the guarantee was entered into under the influence of another person to the extent that the guarantor could not exercise his or her independent will (K.P. McGuinness, The Law of Guarantee: A Treatise on Guarantee, Indemnity and the Standby Letter of Credit, (Toronto: Carswell, 1986) at 67) and where this influence was known or ought to have been known by the creditor (*First Independent Bank v. Proby* (1966), 57 W.W.R. 360 (B.C.S.C.)).

14   In this case Ms Sager did not act under undue influence. She had the document for some time before she signed it, knew correctly that her signature was required for the family company to transact business with the creditor, and chose to take the risk that was represented by signing the documents.

15   In this case, the creditor, who supplied the goods in reliance on the guarantee, is entitled to enforce the guarantee.

16   The plaintiff shall have judgment for $77,415.16 plus pre-judgment interest pursuant to the Court Order Interest Act, R.S.B.C. 1996, c.79 and costs.

QUESTIONS

1. Do you think it is common for a supplier, before extending credit, to require some assurance that the bill will be paid? Would this constitute duress? Would it constitute undue influence?

2. What factors did the court consider important in the case in determining that there was no duress? What factors were important in determining that there was no undue influence?

3. What would you suggest that contracting parties who are concerned about undue influence do before entering into an agreement?

4. Is it likely that courts will enforce an agreement where it can be demonstrated that the weaker party to the contract followed independent legal advice? Would your answer be the same if the agreement was unreasonable or conveyed some great advantage to the stronger party? Explain.

5. Are there circumstances where the burden of proof in claims based on undue influence shifts to the party who is alleged to have exerted such influence? Explain.

chapter ten

Writing

Smith v. Hasegawa

[2000] A.J. No. 1420, 278 AR 335
Alberta Provincial Court
November 29, 2000

The legal requirement as to which contracts require writing varies from jurisdiction to jurisdiction. For example, the scope of the writing requirement is much broader in Ontario than it is in British Columbia. Most jurisdictions require that agreements to do with land be evidenced in writing. This case considers how much evidence is necessary in order to meet the requirement.

LeGRANDEUR PROV. CT. J.:—

Nature of the Proceedings

1   The Plaintiff claims from the Defendant the sum of $500.00 being the sum of money paid to the Defendant by the Plaintiff on or about April 31st, 1993 with respect to a certain lot of land owned by the Defendant and which payment was receipted by the Defendant in writing. (See Exhibit #1)

Issues

2   The issues arising in this matter may be stated as follows:

a.   What is the nature of the agreement, if any, between the Plaintiff and the Defendant with respect to those lands described in Exhibit #1?

b.   Has the Defendant performed the obligations imposed upon him pursuant to the agreement reached between the parties?

c.   Do the provisions of the Statute of Frauds apply to the agreement between the parties, and if so, does the agreement between the parties satisfy the requirements of the Statute of Frauds?

d.   Is the Plaintiff's claim against the Defendant barred by the provisions of the Statute of Limitations?

Facts

3   In April of 1993 the Defendant then owned certain lands which he had subdivided into lots. The Plaintiff expressed an interest in one of these lots and as a result of discussions between the parties, the Defendant paid to the Plaintiff the sum of $500.00. In return he received from the Defendant a written receipt, Exhibit #1, which states as follows:

> April 31/93
>
> Received from Wayne Smith $500.00 deposit on the 1.26 acre lot to the west of our existing house 3905 - 100W.
>
> George M. Hasegawa

4   There is no real dispute as to the circumstances and background that led to the payment of the money by the Plaintiff and the issuance of the receipt by the Defendant. The Plaintiff was not able to afford the purchase of the subject lot, yet expected that in the future he would have the ability to complete such a transaction. He wanted, and I am satisfied Mr. Hasegawa understood his desire, to be able to purchase the lot in the future and it was understood that Mr. Hasegawa would give him the opportunity to purchase it before he sold it to any other party. Mr. Smith testified that the purchase price of the lot in the future was not specifically agreed upon, although Mr. Hasegawa testified that all the lots were valued at $12,500.00.

5   It is clear to me that the true intent of the parties in entering the agreement they did in April of 1993 was to give to Mr. Smith the right to purchase the property should Mr. Hasegawa have a buyer for the same at some time in the future. Mr. Smith was quite content to sit and wait; over and above his initial lack of funds, he didn't want to be the first person to locate in the subdivision, he wanted to see how things went over time, in that regard.

6   He now says Mr. Hasegawa never gave him the chance to purchase the lot before he sold it to a third party.

7   Mr. Hasegawa testified that the Plaintiff phoned him in 1997 about a rumour that the lot had been sold. He told him the lot was still there for him to buy. Six or seven months later, Mr. Hasegawa received another phone call wherein the Plaintiff said he wanted his money back because Mr. Hasegawa had sold the lot. Mr. Hasegawa testified that he told the Plaintiff that he was negotiating with Mr. Tollestrup for the sale of the lot. Mr. Smith did not offer to purchase the lot upon receipt of that information. Mr. Hasegawa told him he would not give him his money back.

8   Thereafter, in 1998, Mr. Hasegawa agreed to sell and did sell the subject lot and others to Mr. Tollestrup. The subject lot was sold for $12,500.00.

9   It is clear that Mr. Hasegawa did not, once he received an offer from Mr. Tollestrup with respect to the subject lot that he was prepared to accept, offer to the Plaintiff the lot for the price he was going to sell it to Mr. Tollestrup. He simply proceeded on the basis that as Mr. Smith did not indicate that he wanted to purchase the property when he was told he was negotiating with Mr. Tollestrup, he therefore did not have any further interest in the same.

Nature of Agreement Between the Plaintiff and Defendant

10   The agreement reached between the parties in April of 1993 is evidenced by the receipt issued by the Defendant and by the oral testimony of the parties. The receipt itself does not purport to be the agreement, but only evidence thereof, and it does not on its own identify its nature.

11   I am satisfied, that the parties intended to enter into a contractual relationship and that which they contemplated, as evidenced by the receipt issued by the Defendant and the testimony of the circumstances and background leading up to the issuance of the receipt, was a contract in the nature of a right of first refusal; such that the Plaintiff would have the right to purchase the subject lot in the future should the Defendant receive an offer for the lot which he would be prepared to accept. It was clear on the evidence of both parties that at that point in time the Defendant would be required to go to the Plaintiff and see if he wished to purchase the subject lot. The receipt itself, Exhibit #1, uses the word "Deposit", however when the receipt is considered in the context of the history of the transaction, it is clear that the aim and purpose of the parties was not to achieve a purchase agreement, but rather a right of first refusal. The fact that the receipt makes no mention of price is supportive of that position as well given that the price in a right of first refusal is fixed by the future act of an offer from a third party.

Defendant's Performance of Agreement

12   Upon the Defendant receiving an offer from Mr. Tollestrup that he was prepared to accept, with respect to this particular lot, he was contractually bound to
advise the Plaintiff of the same, so as to give the Plaintiff the opportunity to purchase
the subject lands at the same price. In this case, the Defendant did not do so. At the
time he advised the Plaintiff that he was negotiating with a third party, he had either
not received an offer from the third party, or at least not received an offer her was prepared to accept. Accordingly, the right of the Plaintiff did not come into play and the
fact that he did not indicate a desire to purchase the property is irrelevant to that right.
The fact that the Plaintiff apparently demanded his money back has no relevance
either as the Defendant at that time had no obligation to return the money to the
Plaintiff as the right of first refusal was not brought into play at that time. It was the
Defendant's choice as to whether he wanted to return the $500.00, which was the con-
sideration for the granting of the right of first refusal agreed upon between the parties
orally and evidenced by Exhibit #1.

13   When the Defendant received an offer from Tollestrup that he was prepared
to accept, he did not notify the Plaintiff and give him a chance to meet it. By not so
doing, he breached his contractual obligations with the Plaintiff as described aforesaid.

Statute of Frauds

14   The Defendant pleads the Statute of Frauds, 1667 (U.K.), 29 Car. 2, C.3; in
defence of the Plaintiff's claim alleging that the agreement was an agreement that is
required to be in writing and as it was not in this instance, the agreement is unenforceable and therefore cannot support the Plaintiff's claim for return of the $500.00.

15   Section 4 of the Statute of Frauds reads:

> *...no action shall be brought whereby to charge any Executor or Administrator
> upon any special promise to answer damages out of his own estate or whereby to
> charge the Defendant upon any special promise to answer for the debt, default or
> miscarriages of another person or to charge any person upon any agreement
> made upon consideration of marriage or upon any contract of sale of lands, ten-
> ements or hereditaments or any interest in or concerning them or upon any
> agreement that is not to be performed within the space of one year from the mak-
> ing thereof unless the agreement upon which such action shall be brought or
> some memorandum or note thereof shall be in writing and signed by the party to
> be charged therewith or some other person thereunto by him lawfully authorized.*

16   By virtue of s. 59.1(1)(a) of the Law of Property Act, RSA 1980, c.L-8 as
amended, a right of first refusal is an equitable interest in land and therefore is an agreement relating to an interest in lands and must therefore comply with the Statute of Frauds.

17   The contract between the parties in this instance is an oral agreement which
is evidenced in writing by the receipt given by the Defendant to the Plaintiff. It is
important to note that the memorandum in the form of the receipt is not the contract,
but only evidence of that contract. (*Walker v. Cusack*, (1982) 16 Man. R. (2d) 114)

18   For a memorandum to satisfy the requirements of s. 4 of the Statute of Frauds as it relates to an interest in land, it must ordinarily at least identify three specific items; the parties to the agreement, the land which is the subject of the agreement and the price, that is the specific amount agreed by the parties or some method or formula of ascertaining the price. (*MacKenzie v. Walsh*, (1921) 1 W.W.R. 1017, S.CC)

19   A receipt is capable of satisfying the requirements of the Statute of Frauds as described aforesaid. (See: *Standard Realty Co. v. Nicholson*, (1911) 24 OLR 46) In this case the memorandum (receipt Exhibit #1) makes no reference to the price of the lot referred to in the memorandum receipt. It is my view however, that the only price the memorandum need evidence is the price being paid for the right of first refusal, not the price to be paid if the right is acted upon in the future. Clearly, the price paid for the right of first refusal, is evidenced in the receipt being Exhibit #1.

20   The price that the holder of an interest in the nature of a right of first refusal will have to pay should that right of first refusal be exercised in the future is not an essential term of the right of first refusal itself. The obligation of the Defendant under the contract was one whereby the Defendant was obliged to offer the land to the Plaintiff at the price at which the Defendant was willing to sell to a third party who had offered to purchase the property. That price is not essential to the contractual obligation of a right of first refusal. In law, the right of first refusal contemplates that the price, should the holder of the right of first refusal exercise that right in the future is determined in the future by the offer of a third party. (See *Smith v. Morgan*, (1971) 2 All ER 1500)

21   Accordingly, given that the memorandum otherwise identifies the parties and the subject lands with sufficient particularity, I am satisfied that the requirements of s. 4 of the Statute of Frauds are satisfied by the memorandum (Exhibit #1) and accordingly the agreement between the parties is an agreement that is enforceable at law. The Statute of Frauds is not an answer to the Plaintiff's claim in this instance.

22   In the event that the requirements of the Statute of Frauds were not met in this instance, it would be my view that the Plaintiff would be entitled to return of the $500.00 paid for the contractual right of first refusal. The Defendant has never denied the oral agreement between the parties, but seeks to set up as a defence to recovery of the money paid for the right, the Statute of Frauds, arguing that there is no enforceable agreement upon which to base any such claim. The deposit paid by the Plaintiff was never put to the use intended, that is, to secure the right of first refusal and the Defendant having so failed to apply the deposit in that regard, ought now to be required to return the $500.00. (See: *Gosbell v. Archer*, 111 ER 193)

[Portions of the judgment dealing with the Statute of Limitations and the applicable limitation period in this case have been omitted.]

QUESTIONS

1. How does the writing requirement affect contracts?
2. Did the right of first refusal for the purchase of land need to be in writing? Explain.
3. What elements generally need to be in writing in order to comply with the Statute of Frauds? In this case, what elements did the court consider important?
4. Why do you think that some people have suggested that the Statute of Frauds has led to more frauds than it has prevented?

chapter eleven

Interpretation

Black Swan Gold Mines Ltd. v. Goldbelt Resources Ltd.

[1996] B.C.J. No. 1458, [1997] 1 WWR 605, 78 BCAC 193, 25 BCLR (3d) 285
British Columbia Court of Appeal
May 29, 1995

The large majority of contractual disputes are not regarding the formation of contracts but are about the meaning, or interpretation, of contracts. Whenever there is a dispute involving the meaning of a specific term or terms, the courts have a choice of applying the literal meaning of the term or adopting a more liberal approach that tries to determine the parties' intent. Even determining the literal meaning of the terms of a contract is not as simple as it might first appear.

1   **DONALD J.A.:**— This case poses a problem in contract interpretation: to what extent should the contextual facts influence the meaning of the text?

2   The appellant, Goldbelt Resources Ltd. ("Goldbelt"), alleges that the learned trial judge improperly ignored crucial features of the factual matrix in which the contract was formed and interpreted the contract in a vacuum. This is the main attack on the judgment below.

3   In that judgment, dated 29 May 1995, the learned trial judge held that Goldbelt was obliged by contract to protect the shareholding of the respondent, Black Swan Gold Mines Ltd. ("Black Swan"), in Goldbelt from dilution and as a result he ordered Goldbelt to issue 3,170,592 of its shares to Black Swan. That figure is derived from the formula set out in an agreement dated 14 January 1992 which settled a dispute between Goldbelt and Black Swan over the taking of a mineral development opportunity in the former Soviet Union.

4   The learned trial judge described the background in this way:

EVENTS LEADING TO THE SETTLEMENT AGREEMENT

2   Black Swan is a public company, trading on the Toronto and Vancouver Stock Exchanges. On October 30, 1991, Black Swan signed an option agreement with a Luxembourg company, Comptoir International du Commerce S.A.R.L. ("Comptoir"), whereby Black Swan acquired 99.5% of Comptoir's issued capital. By this arrangement Black Swan obtained interests which Comptoir had acquired in a copper-silver deposit in Russia (the "Udokan" project), and a gold tailings project in Kazakhstan (the "Leninogorsk" project).

3   Under the terms of its agreement with Comptoir, Black Swan paid an option price of $100,000 (U.S.), and was required to "use its best endeavours" to raise $5,000,000 (U.S.) by January 31, 1992. The funds were to be used to complete feasibility studies and advance the two projects towards production. Comptoir's shareholders were to receive 45.4% of the "fully diluted issued capital" of Black Swan if the $5,000,000 was raised on time.

4   Goldbelt, also a public company trading on the Vancouver Stock Exchange, became interested in the projects and offered to assist Black Swan in financing the feasibility studies. Their negotiations led to the signing of two confidentiality agreements, pursuant to which Black Swan agreed to furnish geological and other project data to Goldbelt.

5   In the confidentiality agreements, which were signed on November 15, 1991, Goldbelt undertook to utilize the information supplied by Black Swan "only for internal evaluation and for the determination of the extent of its interest in acquiring an interest in the Properties." Goldbelt also agreed that it would not, for five years, acquire any property interest in the project areas unless through an agreement with Black Swan, or after obtaining Black Swan's written consent to any such acquisition.

6   However, on December 5, 1991, Goldbelt publicly announced that, independently of Black Swan, it had completed an agreement to fund the feasibility studies and to participate in development of the Udokan and Leninogorsk projects. Goldbelt's announcement included a statement that it had agreed to acquire "the private European company that has negotiated agreements with the U.S.S.R. officials in Moscow." The "private European company" referred to in the announcement was, of course, Comptoir.

7   Goldbelt's ostensible justification for dealing directly with Comptoir was Black Swan's inability to raise the required financing. However, that issue need not be discussed in these reasons since Black Swan's lawsuit is based solely on its claim that Goldbelt breached the terms of a settlement agreement which the two companies entered into on January 14, 1992, in an attempt to resolve their differences over the mining interests.

THE SETTLEMENT AGREEMENT

8   The settlement agreement required Black Swan to assign its interest in Comptoir to Goldbelt. Black Swan also consented to Goldbelt acquiring Comptoir. In return, Goldbelt paid $308,000 (Cdn) to Black Swan and, upon the receipt of Vancouver Stock Exchange approval, issued 1,200,000 Goldbelt shares to Black Swan. The agreement also provided for Black Swan's entitlement to the following percentage interest in Goldbelt:

> 6.   Within the 10 days following the final issue of:
>
> (a)   shares of Goldbelt under its agreement with and in respect of Comptoir (which may be 31.6% of the then fully diluted shares or more); and
>
> (b)   shares of Goldbelt sold from time to time hereafter to raise $5,500,000;
>
> Goldbelt shall (subject to having received the aforesaid approvals to the issue of such shares) issue to Black Swan that number of shares of Goldbelt by which 5% of the number of shares of Goldbelt then outstanding, (calculated on a fully diluted basis as if any warrants, options or other rights to purchase shares of Goldbelt then outstanding had been exercised) exceeds 1,219,500 shares, it being the intention of parties that the share portion of the consideration to Black Swan hereunder shall comprise not less than that number of Goldbelt shares which is 19,500 shares less than 5% of the fully diluted capital of Goldbelt at that time.

9   It is the parties' divergent interpretations of the above provision in the settlement agreement which gives rise to this action.

EVENTS FOLLOWING THE SETTLEMENT AGREEMENT

10   What appears to have been a Russian political decision scuttled Goldbelt's ability to pursue Comptoir's plans for both projects. The Russian government called for tenders on development of the Udokan copper-silver deposit, and development rights were awarded to a third party. Accordingly, since Goldbelt was not called upon to fund the Udokan feasibility study, on June 30, 1993, Goldbelt's agreement with Comptoir was amended to delete the requirement for Goldbelt to advance financing of $3,000,000 (U.S.).

11   Left with only the Leninogorsk project to develop, on March 23, 1994 Goldbelt entered into a loan agreement with Pegasus Gold Inc. ("Pegasus") wherein Pegasus agreed to provide a loan to Goldbelt "to finance a portion of the development costs of such project." The loan agreement called for advances of $3,000,000 and $15,000,000, payable upon satisfaction of conditions precedent which contemplated two distinct phases. Those phases required, among other things, completion of documentation, obtaining of government approvals, satisfaction of regulatory body conditions, and finding a third party lender prepared to commit itself to financing "the entire portion of the capital cost of the construction of the Project."

5   The Pegasus agreement also provided that in certain circumstances Pegasus might convert its loans into Goldbelt shares. The existence of this right was considered by the trial judge in his calculation of the number of outstanding Goldbelt shares for purposes of the top-up formula.

6   The first point to consider in this appeal is whether the learned trial judge ought to have admitted and given effect to evidence presented by Goldbelt and objected to by Black Swan. The reasons do not contain a ruling on admissibility but I think it is clear that if the learned trial judge did admit the evidence, he gave it no weight.

7   Three pieces of evidence are in question. The first is a letter written by Black Swan's solicitor to Goldbelt's solicitor proposing terms for settlement of the dispute over Goldbelt's dealing with Comptoir. Goldbelt tendered this evidence as proof of the commercial objective of the settlement agreement. Pursuant to Goldbelt's agreement with Comptoir, Comptoir's shareholding in Goldbelt would be topped up if additional shares were issued in the course of raising the $5.5 million in the feasibility phase of the projects. Goldbelt says that the Black Swan settlement agreement was intended to provide a top-up formula for protection against the dilution of Black Swan's shares if such an increase in Comptoir's shareholding occurred. The letter in question reads as follows:

December 6, 1991

VIA FAX
WITHOUT PREJUDICE

DuMoulin Black
Barristers & Solicitors
10th Floor, 595 Howe Street
Vancouver, British Columbia
V6C 2T5

Attention: Mr. Brian Irwin

Dear Sirs: RE: Black Swan Gold Mines Ltd.

Enclosed is our client's news release dated Monday, December 9, 1991. Our client has no choice but to assert its legal position. If its claims are not resolved it cannot be equivocal or lax.

We are prepared to meet on Monday as scheduled, or earlier if you wish. You should know that what our client wants is reimbursement of all of its expenses of approximately $300,000 to date plus 1,400,000 shares of Goldbelt (adjusted if the number of shares proposed to be issued to the shareholders of Comptoir International du Commerce S.A.R.L. ("Comptoir") pursuant to Goldbelt's December 3, 1991 agreement changes).

As we discussed with you, we expect you can devise some creative way to accomplish this. As well, a full and final release from Goldbelt and from Comptoir and its principals is a necessity for any settlement.

We look forward to hearing from you.

Yours truly,
SMITH, LYONS, TORRANCE, STEVENSON & MAYER per:

Jonathan A. Rubenstein

[Emphasis added.]

8   The second piece of evidence in dispute is an Information Circular dated 5 February 1992 presented by Goldbelt to its shareholders prior to an extraordinary general meeting called to approve the agreements with Comptoir and Black Swan. It explains the top-up provision in the Black Swan agreement in a way that links it to the operation of Comptoir's top-up clause. The relevant part is as follows:

> 3.   Following acceptance of the Black Swan Agreement by the Vancouver Stock Exchange and approval by the shareholders of Goldbelt, Goldbelt will issue 1,200,000 common shares to Black Swan. On Settlement, as defined in the Comptoir Agreement, Goldbelt will allot and issue to Black Swan that number of additional common shares, if any, which when added to those previously issued to Black Swan will constitute 5% of the then issued shares of Goldbelt computed on a fully diluted basis and after giving effect to the issue of the Goldbelt Shares to the Shareholders of Comptoir in accordance with the Comptoir Agreement, but excluding for purposes of this calculation the additional 385,000 shares to be issued under the Comptoir Agreement.

9   Black Swan's principals would have seen this Information Circular. Black Swan voiced no objection to Goldbelt's description of its top-up right. This, according to Goldbelt, amounts to tacit confirmation of the interpretation put forward by Goldbelt.

10   The third piece of evidence is found in paragraphs 7 and 8 of the affidavit of Goldbelt's solicitor, Brian Irwin, sworn 3 February 1995, in these proceedings:

> 7.   I became directly involved in attempting to resolve the differences between Black Swan and Goldbelt. Mr. Rubenstein acted on behalf of Black Swan. The Goldbelt/ Comptoir Agreement provided for certain top-up rights to allow Comptoir to maintain a 31.6% interest of the then outstanding shares of Goldbelt on a fully diluted basis. This was done for a specific reason. Comptoir required that its shareholdings not be diluted as a result of any shares issued by Goldbelt in order to raise the $5,000,000 (U.S.) under the Goldbelt/Comptoir Agreement. Black Swan was provided with a copy of the Goldbelt/Comptoir Agreement and Mr. Rubenstein insisted that Black Swan also be provided with top-up rights to maintain its percentage of Goldbelt relative to Comptoir's 31.6%. My negotiations with Mr. Rubenstein resulted in a written agreement (the "Goldbelt/Black Swan Agreement") (Exhibit "F" to Mr. Fisher's Affidavit, filed on November 18, 1994).

> 8.   The $5.5 million (Can.) in clause 6(b) of the Goldbelt/Black Swan Agreement is the approximation of the balance of $4.5 million (U.S.) under the Goldbelt/ Comptoir Agreement converted to Canadian dollars at the exchange rates prevailing at that time.

11   Goldbelt emphasizes the importance of paragraph 8 as showing that the top-up formula was related only to the funding target for the feasibility phase of the project. This is advanced in support of the argument that the formula had no relation to the raising of money for production, which is what the Pegasus agreement was concerned with.

12   The admission of the disputed evidence depends on whether it can be said to form part of the factual matrix as that phrase was used by Lord Wilberforce in *Prenn v. Simmonds*, [1971] 3 All E.R. 237 at 240-41.

13   Goldbelt alleges that the learned trial judge erred by construing the contract without regard to the matrix. It argues that, in the context of the surrounding facts, the application of the top-up formula must be confined to the issuance of shares to raise the $5.5 million as set out in the clause, and also that the formula can only be triggered if Comptoir is entitled to a top-up.

14   In my opinion, the learned trial judge was right in disregarding the evidence. All three of the items in contention exceed the bounds of admissibility for contextual facts.

15   The solicitor's letter was simply the opening position in negotiations and there is no way of telling whether the objectives set out in that letter continued to motivate Black Swan when it finally concluded the bargain. The following statement by Wilberforce L.J. in *Prenn v. Simmonds*, supra, at 241 is apposite here: Far more, and indeed totally, dangerous is it to admit evidence of one party's objective even if this is known to the other party. However strongly pursued this may be, the other party may only be willing to give it partial recognition, and in a world of give and take, men often have to be satisfied with less than they want. So, again, it would be a matter of speculation how far the common intention was that the particular objective should be realised.

16   The Information Circular was published after the bargain was struck and so it cannot form part of the matrix in which the deal was made. Also, one party cannot foist an interpretation on another by the expedient of expressing its view of the contract and later arguing that the other party accepted that view by silence.

17   Paragraph 7 of Mr. Irwin's affidavit represents his impression of the course of negotiations from his perspective as Goldbelt's solicitor. Once again, *Prenn v. Simmonds* provides no comfort to Goldbelt: There were prolonged negotiations between solicitors, with exchanges of draft clauses, ultimately emerging in cl. 2 of the agreement. The reason for not admitting evidence of these exchanges is not a technical one or even mainly one of convenience (although the attempt to admit it did greatly prolong the case and add to its expense). It is simply that such evidence is unhelpful. By the nature of things, where negotiations are difficult, the parties' positions, with each passing letter, are changing and until the final agreement, although converging, still divergent. It is only the final document which records a consensus. If the previous documents use different expressions, how does construction of those expressions, itself a doubtful process, help on the construction of the contractual words? If the same expressions are used, nothing is gained by looking back; indeed, something may be lost since the relevant surrounding circumstances may be different. And at this stage there is no consensus of the parties to appeal to. It may be said that previous documents may be looked at to explain the aims of the parties. In a limited sense this is true; the commercial, or business object, of the transaction, objectively ascertained, may be a surrounding fact. Cardozo J. thought so in the *Utica Bank* case [(1918), 118 NE 607]. And if it can be shown that one interpretation completely frustrates that object, to the extent of rendering the contract futile, that may be a strong argument for an alternative interpretation, if that can reasonably be found. But beyond that it may be difficult to go; it may be a matter of degree, or of judgment, how far one interpretation, or another, gives effect to a common intention; the parties, indeed, may be pursuing that intention with differing emphasis, and hoping to achieve it to an extent which may differ, and in different ways. The words used may, and often do, represent a formula which means different things to each side, yet may be accepted because that is the only way to get 'agreement' and in the hope that disputes will not arise. The only course then can be to try to ascertain the 'natural' meaning.

18   If paragraph 8 of Mr. Irwin's affidavit were offered as nothing more than a currency conversion, then it would present no difficulty. However, Goldbelt wants to use it as an evidentiary link between the Black Swan and Comptoir top-up formulae, and it cannot be received for that purpose. If it is taken that way, paragraph 8 is a negotiator's opinion as to why something was included in the contract. That is not context; it is a veiled form of argument or wishful thinking.

19   I am unable to give effect to Goldbelt's contention that the learned trial judge failed to take the relevant surrounding circumstances into account when interpreting this contract. In my respectful opinion, he properly kept the contextual facts in the background and the text of the agreement in the foreground as he examined the picture. The words of the contract must not be overwhelmed by a contextual analysis, otherwise there is little point in writing things down. No certainty could be achieved in choosing words to express a bargain. Contract disputes would have to be resolved by lengthy inquiries into what was fair in light of what happened before, during and after the making of a contract.

20   Extrinsic evidence may be needed to resolve an ambiguity but neither party says there is any ambiguity here.

21   I think that the learned trial judge recited the pertinent facts comprising the factual matrix. He appreciated that the agreement settled a dispute and that the clause in question addressed itself to dilution of the shareholding given Black Swan by the agreement. The kind of detail which Goldbelt seeks to import by way of a contextual reading should have been written into the instrument if Goldbelt wanted it there.

22   Goldbelt submits that the judgment below produces a commercial absurdity: Black Swan's shareholding has been topped up to an extent well beyond any reasonable expectation. Goldbelt argues, firstly, that the result distorts the ratio of shareholding as between Black Swan and Comptoir in Black Swan's favour; secondly, that the Pegasus loan agreement through which monies for the project were raised related not to the feasibility phase of the project but to the development phase; and, thirdly, that the right of Pegasus to acquire shares was subject to so many conditions that it could not be said to be a "right to purchase" within the meaning of the settlement agreement.

23   In *Canadian Delhi Oil Ltd. v. Alminex Limited et al* (1967), 62 W.W.R. 513, the Alberta Court of Appeal considered an agreement between holders of oil and gas leases who joined in a common development scheme. The agreement provided for a formula dividing the production among the leaseholders. A dispute arose concerning the formula and it was contended by some of the leaseholders that the interpretation advanced by their opponents would lead to a commercial absurdity given the surrounding facts. In my opinion, the decision by Smith C.J.A. (whose reasons were endorsed by the Supreme Court of Canada in dismissing an appeal from the judgment: [1968] S.C.R. 775 per Martland J.) accurately states the law regarding the relationship between text and context in the interpretation of commercial contracts. He referred to principles expressed in the authorities as cited in the following quotation from his judgment, at 519: The actual words used by Duff, J. (later C.J.) in *Reddy v. Strople*, supra, at p. 257 are:

> "There is a further rule which must be applied in this case, and that is, (I state it in the words of Coleridge, J., in *Shore v. Wilson* (1842) 9 Cl & Fin 355, at 525, 8 ER 450), that where the language used in the deed in its primary meaning is unambiguous, and that meaning is not excluded by the context, and is sensible with reference to the extrinsic circumstances, then such primary meaning must be taken conclusively as that in which the words are used."

The statement of Coleridge, J. in *Shore v. Wilson*, supra, at 517-8 (ER), was as follows:

> "It is unquestionable that the object of all exposition of written instruments must be to ascertain the expressed meaning or intention of the writer, the expressed meaning being equivalent to the intention; and I believe the authorities to be numerous and clear (too numerous and clear to make it convenient or necessary to cite them), that where language is used in a deed which in its primary meaning is unambiguous, and in which that meaning is not excluded by the context, and is sensible with reference to the extrinsic circumstances in which the writer was placed at the time of writing, such primary meaning must be taken, conclusively, to be that in which the writer used it; such meaning, in that case, conclusively states the writer's intention, and no evidence is receivable to show that in fact the writer used it in any other sense, or had any other intention. This rule, as I state it, requires perhaps two explanatory observations: the first, that if the language be technical or scientific, and it is used in a matter relating to the art or science to which it belongs, its technical or scientific must be considered its primary meaning; the second, that by 'sensible with reference to the extrinsic circumstances' is not meant that the extrinsic circumstances make it more or less reasonable or probable is [sic] what the writer should have intended; it is enough if those circumstances do not exclude it, that is, deprive the words of all reasonable application according to such primary meaning." [Emphasis added.]

24   Having in mind these principles, Smith C.J.A. examined the agreement and concluded, at 520: In my view that language is in no way "ambiguous in its primary meaning and that meaning is not controlled by the context and is sensible with reference to the extrinsic circumstances." There is, therefore, no room for the application for the rule stated by Rigby, L.J. in *Diederichsen v. Farquharson Bros.* [[1898] 1 QB 150, 67 LJQB 103]. and at 521:

> Coleridge J., in the passage in *Shore v. Wilson* already quoted in reference to the phrase "sensible with reference to the extrinsic circumstances," said that this did not mean "that the extrinsic circumstances make it more or less reasonable or probable … what the writer should have intended." In the case at bar these circumstances certainly do not exclude the primary meaning of the words in the clauses under consideration or in the language of Coleridge, J. "deprive the words of all reasonable application according to such primary meaning."

25   For ease of reference, I set out again the clause in question:

6.   Within the 10 days following the final issue of:

(a)   shares of Goldbelt under its agreement with and in respect of Comptoir (which may be 31.6% of the then fully diluted shares or more); and

(b)   shares of Goldbelt sold from time to time hereafter to raise $5,500,000;

Goldbelt shall (subject to having received the aforesaid approvals to the issue of such shares) issue to Black Swan that number of shares of Goldbelt by which 5% of the number of shares of Goldbelt then outstanding, (calculated on a fully diluted basis as if any warrants, options or other rights to purchase shares of

Goldbelt then outstanding had been exercised) exceeds 1,219,500 shares, it being the intention of parties that the share portion of the consideration to Black Swan hereunder shall comprise not less than that number of Goldbelt shares which is 19,500 shares less than 5% of the fully diluted capital of Goldbelt at that time.

26   These words, standing alone, are capable of carrying a meaning and their sense does not depend on the surrounding circumstances. When the admissible evidence as to the circumstances is considered, as it was quite properly by the learned trial judge, it will be seen that the ordinary meaning of the words comfortably fits in the matrix. The context does not contradict the text.

27   The first part of the clause deals with timing: when the top-up formula will be triggered. Goldbelt attempts to read into that part words of limitation as to the scope of the dilution protection, but that is not the plain meaning of the words. Both events described in the first part occurred. Unfortunately for Goldbelt, they occurred at a time when the Pegasus agreement was still alive and, since Pegasus had a right to purchase shares if certain things happened, the right to purchase had to be factored into the computation could have arranged its affairs to avoid this result.

28   Goldbelt's contention that the Pegasus agreement does not grant a right to purchase does not agree with the words of the clause. The extent of dilution was to be determined "... as if any warrants, options or other rights to purchase shares of Goldbelt then outstanding had been exercised". While it is true, as Goldbelt says, that Pegasus's right to purchase shares was subject to many contingencies, nevertheless, on the trigger date, it could not be said that Pegasus would never acquire the shares pursuant to the agreement. I can find no basis in the contract for distinguishing between rights to purchase that are likely to be exercised and those that are not. The trial judge was therefore correct in including Pegasus' right to purchase in his calculation of the number of outstanding Goldbelt shares.

29   There remains the alternative submission by Goldbelt that the learned trial judge erred in failing to imply a term into the settlement agreement to the effect that Black Swan's top-up right would arise only if Comptoir's top-up right arose.

30   Counsel for Goldbelt cites the following passages from Treitel, The Law of Contract, 8th ed. (1991), at 185-6: The principle upon which a court acts in implying terms in fact has been stated by MacKinnon L.J. as follows:

"Prima facie that which in any contract is left to be implied and need not be expressed is something so obvious that it goes without saying; so that, if while the parties were making their bargain, an officious bystander were to suggest some express provision for it in the agreement, they would testily suppress him with a common 'Oh, of course!'"

Shirlaw v. Southern Foundries (1926) Ltd. [1939] 2 K.B. 206, 227 (affirmed [1940] A.C. 701). and at 186:

But if it can be established, as a matter of fact, that both parties regarded the term as obvious and would have accepted it, had it been put to them at the time of contracting, that should suffice to support the implication of the term in fact; for the purpose of such an implication is simply 'to give effect to the intention of the parties'. Luxor (Eastbourne) Ltd. v. Cooper [1941] A.C. 108, 137

31   Goldbelt's argument on this point is summarized at paragraph 94 of its factum:94. The only purpose of either top-up right was to preserve the respective positions of Comptoir and Black Swan in Goldbelt in the event that Goldbelt needed to issue share capital to raise the (U.S.) $5,000,000 to complete the feasibility studies. This assertion depends on the body of evidence which I would exclude as inadmissible. The implication contended cannot be sustained on the language of the clause properly viewed in context.

32   For these reasons, I would dismiss the appeal.

MACFARLANE J.A.:— I agree.

ROWLES J.A.:— I agree.

QUESTIONS

1. How do courts interpret "express terms" in a contract?

2. When is it appropriate for a court to interpret words in a contract in light of the aim of the transaction as well as the factual matrix in which it was formed?

3. When is it that the literal meaning of terms in a contract should not be used? Why do you think the court in this case chose to give the words in issue their literal meaning?

4. In what circumstances may a court imply a term in the contract? Can this be done even if the contract is in writing? Why was a term not implied in this case?

5. What is the primary goal of a court in interpreting a contract? What bias will the court display in choosing between two equally reasonable interpretations of vague wording in a contract?

General Tire Canada, Inc. v. Aylwards Ltd.

[1993] N.J. No. 356 , 1993 St. J. No. 1219

Newfoundland Supreme Court - Trial Division

December 6, 1993

The parol evidence rule states that when the written terms of the contract are clear and unambiguous, the parties will not be permitted to introduce outside evidence to contradict or add to the clear meaning of the contract. The rule prevents a party from relying on a term previously agreed upon but not included in the final written contract. It does not exclude evidence about the formation of the contract, such as legality, capacity of the parties, mistake duress, undue influence, fraud, or misrepresentation.

1   **NOEL J.**:— The plaintiff applied for summary judgment in its claim for money payable under a guarantee. The defendant objected on the ground that it has a good defence.

2   The defendant admits the debt owing by the principal debtor (the debtor) and its guarantee, but, in defence, says that it is not liable because it gave its guarantee:

> "...based on representations made to the defendant by the plaintiff at or about the time the defendant entered into the guarantee, that the plaintiff would extend to the company credit terms no more favourable than those available in the industry generally, and that the plaintiff would use normal diligent credit practices to ensure collection of accounts from time to time owed to the plaintiff by the company." The company referred to is the debtor.

3   In support of that submission the defendant cited the dicta of McIntyre J. in *Bauer v. Bank of Montreal* (1980), 110 D.L.R. (3d) 424 at p. 430:

> "...Various authorities were cited for the proposition that a contract induced by misrepresentation or by an oral representation, inconsistent with the form of the written contract, would not stand and could not bind the party to whom the representation had been made..... No quarrel can be made with the general proposition advanced on this point by the appellant. To succeed, however, this argument must rest upon a finding of some misrepresentation by the bank, innocent or not, or on some oral representation inconsistent with the written document which caused a misimpression in the guarantor's mind, or upon some omission on the part of the bank manager to explain the contents of the document which induced the guarantor to enter into the guarantee upon a misunderstanding as to its nature."

His Lordship went on to say:

> For reasons which will appear later ..., I am of the view that there is no evidence which would support any such finding against the bank. The cases referred to above support the general proposition advanced but rest upon a factual basis providing support for the argument. In each case there is a clear finding of a specific misrepresentation which led to the formation of the contract in question, a circumstance not to be found here."

4   The defendant and the debtor were represented in the credit negotiations with the plaintiff by the defendant's president who was also president of the debtor and the majority shareholder of both. The result was an agreement that the plaintiff would supply goods on credit to the debtor and the defendant's unconditional guarantee to the plaintiff of payment of the debtor's account.

5   The argument that the defendant was induced to give the guarantee by the alleged representations of the plaintiff is not supportable. The guarantee was negotiated by experienced businessmen. The alleged representations are vague, non-specific and incompatible with the guarantee. There were no representations of the kind referred to by McIntyre J. in *Bauer*.

6   The allegation in the defence, that the defendant gave its guarantee because of a representation that the plaintiff would conduct its future affairs with the debtor in the manner alleged, does not permit the defendant to shelter under the general proposition stated. Although worded to take advantage of that general proposition, stated differently, the allegation is that there is an oral collateral contract under which the defendant gave its guarantee in consideration of an alleged undertaking of the plaintiff which was not fulfilled.

7   It is not unusual for the parties to an agreement, after an event, to hold different opinions as to its terms. It is for that reason that experienced businessmen will terminate their negotiations with a formal, written agreement, as was done in this case. It must be presumed that they understand the meaning of their agreements and that they are binding upon them.

8   There are cases in which mistake or representations will affect a formal written agreement, but this is not such a case. The defence is, in essence, that there was a collateral agreement which limited the guarantee. In that regard, the principle of law has been frequently stated:

> If there be a contract which has been reduced into writing, verbal evidence is not allowed to be given of what passed between the parties, either before the written agreement was made, or during the time that it was in a state of preparation, so as to add to or subtract from, or in any manner to vary or qualify the written contract.

9   In *Hawrish v. Bank of Montreal* (1969), 2. D.L.R. (3d) 600 at 605, Judson J., for the court, said:

> "...My opinion is that the appellant's argument fails on the ground that the collateral agreement allowing for the discharge of the appellant cannot stand as it clearly contradicts the terms of the guarantee bond which state that it is a continuing guarantee."

10   The plaintiff shall have judgment in accordance with its statement of claim, with the cost of this application and costs to be taxed.

QUESTIONS

1. What are the risks that may arise when parties have reached an agreement orally about a contract and subsequently record it in writing? How can the parol evidence rule affect the rights of the parties?

2. When business people conclude their negotiations with a formal written agreement, why do courts presume that they understand the meaning of the agreement? What should a party do where terms are unclear?

3. How can mistake or misrepresentation affect a formal written agreement? Explain.

4. What was the effect of applying the parol evidence rule in this case?

chapter twelve

Privity and Assignment

Peacock v. Esquimalt & Nanaimo Railway Co.

[1992] B.C.J. No. 527
British Columbia Supreme Court
March 12, 1992

Contracting parties create a private agreement and outsiders to it can neither enforce it nor be bound to perform its terms. Thus, to succeed in an action in contract law, the plaintiff must prove that he or she has privity of contract with the defendant; that they are both parties to the same contract. The application of the privity rule can have harsh consequences when it prevents an outsider from enforcing a contract that is beneficial to him or her.

MACDONELL J.:— This action came on for trial on the above two dates and did not finish within the time allotted for it. Counsel offered to file written argument and the last argument arrived on March 3rd, 1992.

The plaintiff's claim against the defendants is for the return of the balance of the deposit put up by the plaintiff with respect to the purchase from the defendants of lands and premises at Langford, near Victoria, B.C.

Briefly, the plaintiff's position is that he was a contracting party for the purchase of lands under a contract which was frustrated by an intervening fire before closing, thus entitling him to the return of his deposit under the agreement.

The defendants, on the other hand, argue that there was no privity of contract between the plaintiff and the defendants and that the agreement to purchase the lands was between Wessex Management Ltd. ("Wessex"), West Steel Corp. ("West"), Darrell Brown and Alan Parkin as purchasers and the defendants and that the plaintiff was not a party to any agreement to purchase the land. When the sale was frustrated by the fire, the defendants applied part of the deposit to the cost of the clean-up of the premises, which was a condition of the lease between the defendants and three of the four purchasers, West, Brown and Parkin. By the terms of the offer to purchase the lands, the lease was to be overheld right through to closing. The defendants therefore take the position that as the deposit was put up by the purchasers, it is allocable to the cost of clean-up provided in Clause 7 of the lease.

The plaintiff counters that none of the terms of the lease are applicable to him and that he made an oral agreement with the defendants to purchase the property, albeit that he was planning to take a shareholding in Wessex to the extent of fifty per cent but was not interested in becoming a director or officer as he had been involved in the Northland bank problems as a director.

The case can be summed up by reference to the various documents that were filed as exhibits which, in my view, speak for the transaction. The first agreement of consequence is the lease agreement dated January 7th, 1987 between the defendants and West, Darrell Brown and Alan Parkin. The lease provides in paragraph 7 that:

> (a) If the Premises are not sold by the Lessor during the term of the lease, the Lessee shall ensure that prior to the termination of the lease, the Lessee shall remove at its own expense any buildings, including foundations which are one (1) foot or more above grade level and shall leave the Premises neat, clean, level, free and clear of all waste material, debris and rubbish, and shall ensure that the Premises are left in a safe condition, with such determination to be made by the Lessor.

The next agreement is the offer to purchase dated 23rd February, 1987, made by Wessex, West, Brown and Parkin to the defendants to purchase the property in question for the sum of $850,000.00 with a deposit of $85,000.00 to be held pending acceptance of the offer by the defendants. The offer to purchase provided in paragraph 18 as follows:

> 18. It is understood and agreed that West Steel Corp. is currently leasing a portion of the property until March 31, 1987 and that the Purchaser will overhold its tenancy on the same terms and conditions as the current lease with West Steel Corp. until the Closing Date contemplated by this Offer. If this Agreement does not complete, then the Purchaser will overhold the current lease for a two month period in order that they can complete their obligations under clause 7 of the lease.

When it came time to put up the deposit, Brown and Parkin had persuaded Mr. Peacock to invest in the enterprise. The plan was that Mr. Peacock was to put up the deposit for the purchasers and, in turn, would get a fifty per cent interest in Wessex. Prior to the May 20th acceptance day, the defendants, acting through Marathon Realty, extended the acceptance date to July 15th, 1987; all other terms remained the same. On May 28th, 1987, Mr. Avis, a representative of the defendants, sent along for execution copies of the documents and requested that they be returned with a cheque for $85,000.00 payable to Canadian Pacific. The appropriate parties signed the agreement and the plaintiff gave a cheque for $85,000.00 to Mr. Brown, who took it with the agreement to Vancouver and tendered it to Marathon on behalf of the defendants on May 29th, 1987 (which was the date of Mr. Peacock's cheque). The company, Wessex Management Ltd., was incorporated on the 29th May, 1987. The offer to purchase was accepted on August 31st, 1987; the closing to be the end of September. Following acceptance and before closing, the land and premises were destroyed by fire, thus frustrating the contract. The defendants under the terms of the lease took the position that the clean-up of debris brought onto the site by the purchasers had to be removed under clause 7 of the lease, which was incorporated into and part of the purchase agreement. Accordingly, they requested that it be cleaned up but as this was not done they took steps to do the clean-up and refunded the difference between the $85,000.00 and the amount needed to clean up, which was $28,977.50. The plaintiff claims that money is his and that it is not subject to any set-off by the defendants under a lease to which he was not a party.

For the plaintiff to succeed, he has to satisfy the Court on a balance of probabilities that he was a contracting party with the defendants for the purchase of the property. The plaintiff is faced with a number of obstacles, in my view, not the least of which is that but for the purchase agreement and its various covenants he may not have a right to the refund of the deposit as the agreement calls for the property to be at the risk of the vendor, but if the contract for purchase and sale was verbal, other considerations may apply. Although the plaintiff takes the position that he personally was contracting, nevertheless the evidence he led and part of his testimony concede that he was investing in a company that was acquiring the property, and only when the sale fell through did the matter of the return of the deposit come up. Although the purchasers assigned the $85,000.00 deposit to him, there is no significance to this because, in my view, they had to account to him for the deposit that he put up for them. I do not accept the plaintiff's evidence that he had any oral agreement with Mr. Avis of the defendant companies to purchase the property. Not only is that unlikely, but I accept Mr. Avis's evidence that he had no authority to enter into an oral agreement, nor was it the policy of the defendant companies, nor did it make sense in the circumstances. Accordingly, I accept Mr. Avis's evidence where it conflicts with that of Mr. Peacock.

On the whole of the case, I can come to no other conclusion than that the plaintiff was not a contracting party with the defendants for the purchase of the property and accordingly there was no privity of contract between him and the defendants. This being the case, the plaintiff's action fails against the defendants. There may be an accounting required of the purchasers to the plaintiff but this does not concern the defendants. With respect to the clean-up, it is my view that the lease and purchase agreement are clearly applicable in the circumstances and that the defendants are entitled at law to extract from the purchasers the clean-up cost, which they did from the deposit put up on their behalf by the plaintiff. Therefore, even if the purchasers had brought action, it is my view that they are also caught by paragraph 7 of the agreement and lease and would be required to clean up. The only question then remaining in such a law suit is whether the amount of the cost of clean-up is supportable and in my view the evidence makes it abundantly clear that the costs are justified.

The action is accordingly dismissed with costs.

QUESTIONS

1. What is meant by privity of contract?

2. Why, in this case, did the plaintiff believe he was a party to the contract with the defendant for the purchase of land? Why did the court rule that he was not a party? What effect did this ruling have on the plaintiff's claim?

3. What if a person signs as a party to the contract but has not provided any consideration? Can this person sue to enforce the contract?

4. What could the plaintiff, in this case, have done in order to be able to sue to enforce this contract?

Fraser River Pile & Dredge Ltd. v. Can-Dive Services Ltd.

[1999] 3 SCR 108, [1999] SCJ No. 48, 176 DLR (4th) 257, 245 NR 88, [1999] 9 WWR 380, 127 BCAC 287, 67 BCLR (3d) 213, 50 BLR (2d) 169, 11 CCLI (3d) 1, 47 CCLT (2d) 1, [1999] ILR 1-3717.

September 10, 1999

Supreme Court of Canada on appeal from the Court of Appeal for British Columbia

Present: Gonthier, Cory, McLachlin, Iacobucci, Major, Bastarache and Binnie JJ.

There are cases in which people who are not party to a contract can enforce protection afforded under the contract. This case is an illustration.

The judgment of the Court was delivered by **IACOBUCCI J.** The following is a summary of his judgement.

Fraser River Pile and Dredge Ltd. (Fraser River) carried on the business of providing dredging, pile-driving and related services. It also chartered vessels to others. Can-Dive Services Ltd. (Can-Dive) contracted to charter a barge from Fraser River for use in its work in installing a natural gas pipeline from mainland British Columbia to Vancouver Island. The barge sank while Can-Dive was using it and the trial judge found negligence on the part of Can-Dive. Can-Dive was held liable at trial for damages in the amount of $949,503. Can-Dive did not appeal the finding of negligence, but claimed that Fraser River had been compensated by its insurer, and that according to the terms of its insurance policy with its Underwriters, Fraser River could not bring a claim against Can-Dive for the loss.

The relevant clauses of Fraser River's insurance policy stated as follows:

"1. Additional Insureds Clause

It is agreed that this policy also covers the Insured, associated and affiliated companies of the insured, be they owners, subsidiaries or interrelated companies and as bareboat charterers and/or charterers and/or sub-charterers and/or operators and/or in whatever capacity and shall so continue to cover notwithstanding any provisions of the Policy with respect to change of ownership or management. Provided, however, that in the event of any claim being made by associated, affiliated, subsidiary or interrelated companies under this clause, it shall not be entitled to recover in respect of any liability to which it would be subject if it were the owner, nor to a greater extent than an owner would be entitled in such event to recover.

Notwithstanding anything contained in the Additional Insureds Clause above, it is hereby understood and agreed that permission is hereby granted for these vessels to be chartered and the charterer to be considered an Additional Insured hereunder.

Trustee Clause
It is understood that the named Insured who obtained this Policy did so on his own behalf and as agent for the others insured hereby including those referred to by general description.

17. Subrogation and Waiver of Subrogation clause

In the event of any payment under this Policy, the Insureds shall be subrogated to all the Insured's rights of recovery therefor, and the Insured shall execute the papers required and shall so everything that may be necessary to secure such rights, but it is agreed that the Insurers waive any right of subrogation against:

b)   any charterer(s) and/or operator(s) and/or lessee(s) and/or mortgagee(s)…"

The trial judge held that there was insufficient evidence that Fraser River agreed to extend its own insurance to cover any risk of loss by Can-Dive during the charter period. He also rejected Can-Dive's claim that the insurers were prevented from bringing a subrogated action against Can-Dive arising out of the fact that Can-Dive, as charterer, came within the definition of "Additional Insureds" in the insurance policy. The trial judge said that because Can-Dive was not a party to the contract of insurance, it could not enforce the terms of the insurance policy. He rejected both trust and agency principles as justification for relaxing privity of contract principles in this case.

The British Columbia Court of Appeal reversed the decision of the trial judge and held that the insurer was unable to bring a subrogated claim against Can-Dive. It held that "waiver of subrogation" clauses in contracts of insurance were an exception to the privity of contract rule in a case where the third-party beneficiary is not a party to the policy but comes under the policy's definition of those to whom coverage is extended. An example cited was the *Commonwealth Construction Co. v. Imperial Oil Ltd.* case [1978] 1 SCR 317, in which subrogation was held not to be available against a subcontractor who was not a party to a builder's risk policy, but who met the definition of "Contractor" for the purpose of coverage under the insurance policy. The Court also held that Can-Dive could succeed on the basis of the agency exception. Fraser River appealed the decision.

The Supreme Court of Canada said that it had made an exception to the privity of contract rule in *London Drugs Ltd. v. Kuehne & Nagel International Ltd.* [1992] 3 SCR 299 because it considered the intention of the contracting parties a key factor in whether privity of contract should apply. The questions to ask, the Court said, were:

1. Did the parties to the contract intend to extend the benefit to the third party seeking to rely on the clause?

2. Are the activities performed by the third party seeking to rely on the contractual provision the very activities contemplated as coming within the scope of the contract?

This insurance policy, the court pointed out, specifically mentioned "charterer(s) in its waiver of subrogation clause, so clearly the benefit was intended to be extended to charterers. A concern that the Court had was that, as parties to the contract, the insurer and the Fraser River should be able to modify the provisions of the insurance contract including the waiver of subrogation clause. The Court held, however, that once the insurer and Fraser River contracted in favour of Can-Dive as within the class of potential third-party beneficiaries, the insurer and the Fraser River could not unilaterally revoke Can-Dive's rights. Can-Dive became, for the purpose of relying on the waiver of subrogation clause, a party to the initial contract. Any modification to this provision could be made only with the agreement of Can-Dive.

The court held that the third party was engaged in "contemplated activities", in that the activities were in the context of the relationship of Can-Dive to Fraser River as charterer, the very activity contemplated in the waiver of subrogation clause. The Court added that there were sound policy reasons to relax the privity of contract rule in these circumstances because what the Court was essentially doing was enforcing a commercial bargain entered into freely by the contracting parties.

The appeal was dismissed.

QUESTIONS

1. What are the possible ways in which a party in the position of Can-Dive can protect itself from being financially ruined by a claim arising out of negligence in circumstances such as those in this case? What would you advise Can-Dive to do to protect itself in these circumstances?

2. Explain why the Court expressed a concern that relaxing the rule of privity of contract in the circumstances of this case could impair freedom of contract. Do you think this concern is justified?

3. The Court refers to a principle that the courts must "not abdicate their judicial duty to decide on incremental changes to the common law necessary to address emerging needs and values in society." Is there any other way in which the common law could be changed to create an exception to the rule of privity of contract?

chapter thirteen

Discharge

Poole v. Shanks

[1992] O.J. No. 288, 39 C.C.E.L. 316
Ontario Court of Justice - General Division
February 14, 1992

The doctrine of frustration provides that when, after the creation of the contract, some unforeseen out-side event interferes with the performance of the contract, making the basic object of the agreement unobtainable, the contract is said to be discharged by frustration. A party to a contract cannot willfully disable itself from performing and then claim successfully that the contract has been frustrated. Such a "self-induced" frustration is treated as a breach of contract.

GROUND J.:— This is an action for damages for breach of contract or wrongful dismissal arising out of the termination of an employment contract.

Facts

The plaintiff was employed by the defendant, an orthodontist in sole practice in Toronto as a receptionist/dental assistant pursuant to an oral employment agreement. The plaintiff commenced employment with the defendant in May of 1964 and continued in such employment until February of 1989 at which time her employment was terminated. The reason provided for the termination of her employment was the closure of the defendant's practice due to ill health. The plaintiff was notified by the defendant in mid-February 1989 that her employment would be terminated at the end of February and, by letter dated February 27, 1989 from the defendant's solicitors, a cheque was forwarded to the plaintiff for eight weeks' salary "in lieu of notice" plus an amount of vacation pay equal to 4% of the plaintiff's salary from the date of her last vacation until the end of February 1989.

I find the following additional facts established by the evidence. First, the plaintiff was a loyal and devoted employee who performed her duties in a competent and diligent manner and there were no grounds for termination of the employment contract for cause. The plaintiff made a concerted effort for several months following the termination of her employment with the defendant to find other employment but, due to her age and her lack of any specific educational qualifications as a dental nurse or hygienist, was unable to obtain other employment. There were on at least one occasion discussions between the plaintiff and the defendant regarding her retirement and some vague assurances from the defendant that they would discuss the matter further and some arrangements would be made. As a result of an illness which became critical in December 1988, and surgery in January of 1989, the defendant decided that he was no longer physically able to practice and made arrangements throughout January and February of 1989 to turn his practice over to other orthodontists.

Issues

Three issues arise in this action. First, did the defendant breach a term of the employment contract with the plaintiff by virtue of his failure to make provisions for her retirement? Second, was the defendant's obligation to provide the plaintiff with reasonable notice of termination or a payment in lieu of notice ended as a result of the frustration of the employment contract by virtue of the defendant's illness and inability to continue in practice? Third, if the employment contract was not frustrated, did the plaintiff receive reasonable notice or payment in lieu of notice?

The Law

On the question of breach of the employment contract by the defendant by reason of the failure to provide some sort of retirement benefit for the plaintiff, there does not appear to have been any meeting of minds between the parties as to the nature, extent or amount of such benefit. The discussion between the parties on this subject would appear to be an understanding that the matter would have to be looked into or, at most, an agreement to agree. The courts will not without more specific evidence imply a term of an oral contract. Accordingly, I do not find the defendant was in breach of contract for failure to provide a retirement benefit for the plaintiff.

On the question of the frustration of the employment contract by virtue of the defendant's illness and inability to continue in practice, it appears to be settled law that the doctrine of frustration may apply to an employment contract (Chitty on Contracts, 26th ed., Vol. 2, London: Sweet & Maxwell, 1989 at para. 3964; *The Dartmouth Ferry Commission v. Marks* (1904), 34 S.C.R. 366 (S.(.C.); *Smith v. Tamblyn (Alberta) Ltd. et al.* (1979), 9 Alta. L.R. (2d) 274 (Alta. S.C.).

The issue of whether incapacity of the employer frustrates an employment contract has been addressed by M.R. Freedland in The Contract of Employment, Oxford: Clarendon Press, 1976 at pp. 314-315:

> The question whether it is appropriate for the contract of employment to be treated as frustrated by the death or incapacity of the employer has to be answered in terms of the purpose of the doctrine of frustration in general. If that purpose is seen as being the discharging of liabilities on the ground of the absence of fault on the part of the person prevented from contractual performance by supervening events, then it will appear appropriate to apply the doctrine of frustration to this type of case. . . If, on the other hand, the doctrine of frustration is seen as a method of allocating risk of loss, then it may seem that it should not apply where it is appropriate to treat the employer, or his estate, as an insurer against such events, at least to the extent of being obliged to compensate the employee for loss of employment for the period of due notice.

It is the allocation of risk of loss approach to the doctrine of frustration that has been applied by the courts. The incapacitated employer would therefore be obliged to compensate the employee for the loss suffered due to termination. It was noted in *St. John v. TNT Canada Inc.*, [1991] B.C.J. No. 3217 (B.C.S.C.) that "(t)he authorities indicate that the courts have approached the doctrine of frustration of contract in terms of allocation of risk." It was held in that case that a strike is a foreseeable event and therefore does not constitute frustration of an employment contract such that the employer escapes its liability to provide reasonable notice and severance pay.

Although counsel for the defendant relied on the decision in *O'Connell v. Harkema Express Lines Ltd. et al.* (1982), 141 D.L.R. (3d) 291 (Ont. Co. Ct.) in support of the proposition that an employment contract may be frustrated by an unresolved strike, this case does not reflect the current state of the law. It was not followed in *R. v. Harkema Express Lines Ltd.* (1988), 65 O.R. (2d) 444 (Ont. C.A.) (application for leave to appeal from this decision to the Supreme Court of Canada was dismissed on February 23, 1989). R. v. Harkema, supra, involved the same defendant as O'Connell, supra, and was based on similar facts. The Court of Appeal in *R. v. Harkema* restored the conviction of the employer for failing to give the employee proper notice and failing to pay severance pay. It was held that the doctrine of frustration of contract had no application to this case. The reasons for the doctrine not applying were stated by Zuber J.A. at p. 447 as follows:

> First, it is not every frustrating event which will excuse the parties to a contract from liability. The frustrating event must be one which is outside the contemplation of the parties. I cannot accept the proposition that a strike in the trucking industry can be so described.

Similarly, in the present case, the eventual retirement of the defendant must have been an event which was foreseen and contemplated by the parties to the employment contract.

R. v. Harkema, supra, was followed by the Supreme Court of British Columbia in *St. John v. TNT Canada Inc.*, supra. TNT, the employer, relied on the decision in O'Connell, supra, but such decision was rejected by the court and held to be "an exception to the trend in general in Canadian and British courts."

The Supreme Court of Canada in *Atlantic Paper Stock Ltd. v. St. Anne-Nackawic Pulp & Paper Co.* (1975), 56 D.L.R. (3d) 409 considered the issue of foreseeability of the event alleged to frustrate the contract. It was held at p. 411 that in order for an event to be so radical as to strike at the root of the contract it had to be "unexpected, something beyond reasonable human foresight and skill."

The eventual retirement of the defendant from practice whether by reason of ill health, advancing age or other reason, cannot be an event which was "outside the contemplation of the parties" (*R. v. Harkema*, supra) or "unexpected, something beyond reasonable human foresight and skill" (*Atlantic Paper Stock Ltd. v. St. Anne-Nackawic Pulp & Paper Co.*, supra). Accordingly, I find that the employment contract between the plaintiff and the defendant was not frustrated by the defendant's illness and the closure of his practice and that the defendant was obligated to provide the plaintiff with reasonable notice of termination or payment in lieu of notice.

On the question of the reasonableness of the notice given to the plaintiff, the plaintiff received approximately 2 weeks notice of termination and received 8 weeks salary in lieu of notice for a total of 10 weeks. Taking into account the nature of the plaintiff's position and responsibility, the length of service with the defendant, the age of the plaintiff and the experience and qualifications of the plaintiff, I find that somewhere between 6 months and 9 months would be reasonable notice. Taking the midpoint of 7 1/2 months and deducting the 10 weeks notice and payment received by the plaintiff, I find that the plaintiff is entitled to another 5 months or 22 weeks salary by way of payment in lieu of notice. The plaintiff was paid on a weekly basis at the rate of $582 per week and accordingly the plaintiff is entitled to judgment for $12,804.00 together with pre-judgment interest in accordance with the Courts of Justice Act.

Counsel may speak to me as to the issue of costs.

QUESTIONS

1. Can the doctrine of frustration apply to an employment contract?
2. Under what circumstances does the incapacity of an employer frustrate an employment contract?
3. In a contract of employment, should the doctrine of frustration be seen as a method of allocating risk of loss? If so, which party, the employer or employee, should the risk of loss be allocated to?
4. What is the significance of a court's determination that a contract was frustrated through the fault of one of the parties? Explain.
5. Is substantial hardship in performing a contractual obligation sufficient to excuse a promisor from performing? Explain.

Naylor Group v. Ellis-Don Construction

[2001] SCC 58, [2001] SCJ No. 56, [2001] No. 56, 204 DLR (4th) 513, 10 CLR
(3d) 1, 277 NR 1, 17 BLR (3d) 161, 153 OAC 31.

Supreme Court of Canada on appeal from the Court of Appeal for Ontario

September 27, 2001

Present: McLachlin C.J., Iacobucci, Major, Bastarache, Binnie, Arbour and
LeBel JJ.

Decisions made by third parties that prevent a contract from being performed can sometimes qualify as
frustrating events. In this case, however, the decision of the Ontario Labour Relations Board was held not
to discharge the contract.

The judgment of the Court was delivered by **BINNIE J.** The following is a summary of the
case and his judgment.

In 1991, the Oakville-Trafalgar Memorial Hospital (OTMH) called for tenders for the construction and renovation of an addition to its hospital. It did so through the Toronto Bid
Depository System. The bid depository was a structured bidding process. The owner calling for tenders on a project would notify staff at the Bid Depository, and project documentation was provided. A deadline was set by which pre-qualified subcontractors could
submit tenders on standard form documents containing a breakdown of prices. After the
deadline expired, the subtrade bid documents were made available to interested prime contractors intending to submit a bid on the project.

　　The prime contractors' bids were open for the owner's acceptance for a fixed period of
time, and the subcontractors' bids were open for acceptance by the prime contractor for a fixed
period of time after the award of the prime contract. The process was considered to promote
fairness because all parties were bidding on identical information, and bids were disclosed to
all relevant parties at the same time. This prevented "bid-shopping", the practice of disclosing
one subtrade's bid to other interested parties in the hope of levering their bids downwards.

　　Ellis-Don Construction, one of the largest construction firms in Ontario, intended to bid
on the hospital project. It approached Naylor Group to encourage it to bid on the electrical
subcontract. Naylor informed Ellis-Don that its workers were not affiliated with the
International Brotherhood of Electrical Workers (IBEW); instead Naylor had its own "in-
house" union - The Employees Association of Naylor Group Incorporated. Ellis-Don's representative told Naylor that Ellis-Don was not bound to work with subcontractors affiliated
with the IBEW and could work with anyone. In reality, Ellis-Don had had, over the preced-

ing 30 years, a continuing argument with the IBEW over bargaining rights, and the dispute had gone before the Ontario Labour relations Board (OLRB) in 1990. At the time Ellis-Don was communicating with Naylor over the hospital bid, the OLRB ruling was under reserve.

Naylor put in about six weeks of work and 118 pages of calculations preparing its bid. It tendered a price of $5,539,000. The next lowest bid on the electrical work was submitted by Comstock, whose bid was $411,000 higher than Naylor's. Comstock's workers were members of IBEW.

Ellis-Don incorporated Naylor's bid into its own tender on the prime contract. Ellis-Don was the lowest bidder on the project. When this information became known, Naylor started work on planning the project, even though it had not yet received formal communication from Ellis-Don that its bid had been successful. Awarding of the prime contract had been slower than expected because of a delay in obtaining commitment of government funds for the project. On February 28, 1992, the OLRB released its decision that Ellis-Don was bound to use only electrical subcontractors whose employees had IBEW affiliation.

On March 17, 1992, Ellis-Don submitted a revised bid, incorporating a revised quote that it had requested that Naylor provide. Naylor then found that Ellis-Don was seeking bids from competing electrical subcontractors. Naylor concluded that Ellis-Don was "shopping its bid" to rival firms, and complained to Ellis-Don. On May 5, 1992, Ellis-Don offered to award the electrical subcontract to Naylor, but only if it would affiliate itself with the IBEW. Naylor had its own union and declined to do so.

On May 6, 1992, OTMH awarded the hospital project to Ellis-Don under its revised bid. The prime contract contained Article 10.2 which stated: "The Contractor agrees to employ those Subcontractors proposed by him in writing and accepted by the Owner at the signing of the Contract." On May 13, 1992, Ellis-Don wrote to Naylor saying that because of the OLRB decision, it could not award the electrical subcontract to Naylor. In July of 1992, Ellis-Don awarded the electrical subcontract to Guild Electric, an IBEW subcontractor), at a price of $5,671,192, precisely the amount of Naylor's revised bid. Guild had decided not to submit a bid on the OTMH project and therefore was an ineligible subcontractor under the rules of the Bid Depository.

Naylor sued Ellis-Don and its claim for breach of contract was dismissed at trial because the trial judge said that acceptance was a necessary element to form a contract, and Naylor never communicated acceptance to Ellis-Don, and even if there had been a contract, it would have been frustrated by the OLRB decision dated February 28, 1992. The trial judge said that had Naylor's claim been successful, he would have awarded as damages its lost profits on the project, which he calculated to be $730,286, relying on Naylor's historical profit margins. Naylor appealed.

The Court of Appeal for Ontario held that when Naylor submitted its bid under the bid depository system, it agreed not to revoke its bid during the tendering process, and Ellis-Don agreed to award the subcontract to the subcontractor designated in its bid on the prime contract unless it had some reasonable objection. The Court said that Ellis-Don had not demonstrated that its objection to Naylor was reasonable, and therefore breached its contract with Naylor. The Court reduced damages to $182,500 because it said that the trial judge had not taken into account job site contingencies, and the contingency that the OLRB might not have allowed the subcontract to be awarded to Naylor.

Ellis-Don appealed to the Supreme Court of Canada on the issue of liability for breach of contract, and Naylor cross-appealed that the damages awarded by the Ontario Court of

Appeal were too low. Mr. Justice Binning, for the Supreme Court of Canada, said that indeed Ellis-Don had entered into a contract with Naylor. The rules of the Bid Depository created a bar to "bid-shopping", and in effect required the prime contractor to subcontract to the firm it had designated in its bid on the prime contract.

Ellis-Don said that if there was a contract with Naylor, Ellis-Don had not breached it, because the OLRB decision dated February 28, 1992 requiring Ellis-Don to use IBEW electricians on its projects was a supervening event that frustrated the contract. To succeed, according to the Court, the supervening event would have had to alter the nature of Ellis-Don's obligation to contract with Naylor to such an extent that to compel performance despite the new and changed circumstances, would be to order Ellis-Don to do something radically different from what the parties agreed to under the bid contract.

The Court held that there was no supervening event and therefore no frustration. The OLRB decision of February 28, 1992 recognized an existing obligation that Ellis-Don had to the IBEW. It did not create the obligation; the obligation existed before the bidding process began. This obligation was disclosed to Naylor too late, and Ellis-Don had even given Naylor assurances that there would be no problem. While Ellis-Don was entitled to reasonably object to awarding the subcontract to Naylor, Ellis-Don had known everything relevant about Naylor's qualifications at the time it incorporated Naylor's bid into its bid on the prime contract, so its objection was not reasonable.

On the matter of damages, the Supreme Court of Canada allowed the cross-appeal in part. It agreed with the Ontario Court of Appeal that the trial judge should have taken onto account difficulties encountered in this particular job and not just relied on Naylor's historical profit margins. Ellis-Don had not suggested that labour problems would have awaited Naylor on the job site, and so the Ontario Court of Appeal should not have reduced damages to take account of the contingency that the OLRB might not have allowed the subcontract to be awarded to Naylor. The damage award was set at $365,143.

QUESTIONS

1. What were the obligations under the contract between Ellis-Don and Naylor? When did the contract take effect?
2. Did Clause 10.2 in the prime contract create an obligation that Naylor could enforce against Ellis-Don?
3. Explain why the decision of the OLRB was not considered a frustrating event.
4. Explain what Ellis-Don should have done differently in order to avoid liability to Naylor for breach of contract.
5. Assume that after submitting its bid on the prime contract, Ellis-Don had found that Naylor had lost key personnel, or had become financially insolvent. If either of these events occurred, would Ellis-Don have been justified in refusing to award the subcontract to Naylor? Under what circumstances, if any, might each of these events be considered frustrating events?

chapter fourteen

Effect of Breach

Kinalea Development Corp. v. Ottawa West Developments Ltd.

[1993] O.J. No. 1122.
Ontario Court of Justice - General Division
June 30, 1993

Not every breach of contract justifies termination of the contract. Whether a party is entitled to terminate for breach can be a difficult decision for a party to make. The breach must be of an essential term of the contract. Breach of a minor term may entitle the non-breaching party to damages. If the breach is of an essential term, the party committing the breach is still bound, but the injured party may then elect to terminate the contract.

1   **CHADWICK J.**:— This is an application for summary judgment by the Ottawa West Developments Ltd. a plaintiff by counterclaim as against Kinalea Development Corporation, the defendants by counterclaim.

2   Ottawa West Developments Ltd. (Ottawa West) and Kinalea Development Corporation (Kinalea) entered into an agreement for the purchase and sale of land on the 16th day of November, 1989.

3   Pursuant to the terms of the agreement, Ottawa West agreed to sell 83 building lots in a proposed subdivision located in the Township of Goulbourn to Kinalea. In addition, Ottawa West also granted to Kinalea an option to purchase a further 83 lots in the same subdivision.

4   The purchase price for the lots was $65,000.00 per lot. A portion of the purchase price was secured by a vendor take back mortgage in the amount of $3,798,976.00. As at the filing of the statement of defence and counterclaim in September, 1991 there was $134,064.47 due for interest in addition to the principal.

5   Kinalea did not exercise the option with reference to the balance of the 83 lots and as such paid to Ottawa West a penalty in the sum of $80,000.00, in accordance with the terms of the agreement.

6   Ottawa West has taken a number of actions against Kinalea for payment under the various security documents.

7   On June 12th, 1990 Kinalea commenced this action against Ottawa West for rescission of the November 16th, 1989 agreement along with other relief.

8   The basis for the claim of rescission relates to the failure of Ottawa West to pre-grade and blast the lots in accordance with paragraphs 7.4 and 7.3 of the agreement. In their statement of claim, Kinalea allege the lots are not graded within 12 inches of final grade. In most cases, are 4 to 5 feet of final grade. They also allege that Ottawa West's blasting contractor overblasted the majority of the foundations by approximately 4 or 5 feet.

9   In support of their claim, Ottawa West retained the services of Fairhill, Moffatt and Woodland Limited, Ontario Land Surveyors who have prepared two reports. In addition, they have the engineering opinions of Oliver, Mangione, McCalla & Associates.

10   In response to the motion for summary judgment, Kenneth Baggott the vice-president of Kinalea filed an affidavit on May 3rd, 1993 outlining the substance of their defence and their position relating to the recision of the contract. The affidavit is directed primarily to the grading and overblasting of the building lots. At paragraph 38 of his affidavit he states as follows:

> I estimate the cost to Kinalea prospectively over the entire 83 lots to be in the range of $400,000. More significant than that amount, is the impact of the Ottawa West failure on the ability of Kinalea to continue to build and effectively market homes.

11   Mr. Houston, counsel for Ottawa West acknowledges that there is a triable issue relating to grading and overblasting. There are expert reports prepared for each of the parties which will have to be considered and determined by a trial judge. Mr. Houston's position is, however, that this issue does not justify the rescinding of the con-

tract and as such Ottawa West should be entitled to summary judgment for the amount of principal and interest owing on the agreement and secured by way of mortgage.

12   The issue is one of whether grading and overblasting is a fundamental breach of the contract and would justify rescission of the contract. The British Columbia Court of Appeal in *Standard Precast Limited v. Dywidag Fab Con Products Ltd. et al.* 33 C.L.R. 137 considered the application of a fundamental breach to a commercial contract and whether the breach was such that it would destroy or frustrate the commercial purpose of the contract. In that case, Dywidag sub-contracted the construction and erection of precast concrete panels to Standard Precast. Before Standard had an opportunity of completing the construction of the panels, the general contractor found that the product from Standard's plant to be unacceptable. Also the general contractor had no confidence in the quality of the work or that Standard would meet the delivery schedule. As a result, Dywidag terminated Standard's contract. The trial judge found the termination of the sub-contract was justified since Standard had demonstrated it was incapable of meeting its contractual obligation and dismissed Standard's claim for damages and allowed Dywidag's counterclaim. On appeal, Wallace J. on behalf of the court considers the distinction between breaches of contract for which appropriate remedy is damages and breaches amounting to a total repudiation of one's obligation, thereby entitling the innocent party to terminate the contract. In considering this issue, Wallace J. reviews the decision in *Mersey Steel and Iron Company v. Naylor, Benzon & Co. and Bettini v. Gye* (1876), 1 Q.B.D. 183 at 188. In addition, he also adopts the words of Upjohn L.J. in *Hong Kong Fir Shipping Company v. Kawasaki Kisen Kaisha Ltd* [1962] 2 Q.B. 26 at 64, [1962] 1 All E.R. 474 (C.A.) as follows:

> ". . . the question to be answered is, does the breach of the stipulation go so much to the root of the contract that it makes further commercial performance of the contract impossible, or in other words is the whole contract frustrated? If yea, the innocent party may treat the contract as at an end. If nay, his claim sounds in damages only."

13   The court concluded that evidence did not indicate that Standard's conduct reflected a lack of capability to perform the contract which was to a degree or extent that would destroy or frustrate the commercial purposes of the contract, as such they allowed the appeal. The question of repudiation was also considered by the Supreme Court of Canada in *Townsend v. Moon Motors Co.* [1924] 1 D.L.R. 511.

14   In applying these principles of law to the issues in this case, I am not satisfied that the grading and overblasting destroy or frustrate the commercial purposes of the contract between Kinalea and Ottawa West. As stated by Kenneth Baggott, in his affidavit material, it will cost approximately $400,000.00 to correct the deficiencies if Kinalea's position is correct. This is only a small portion of a major contract and would not frustrate the balance of the contract. It obviously will make the contract more difficult to complete, however, if Kinalea are correct, they can be compensated in damages.

[Paragraphs 15 through 24 of the judgment have been omitted]

QUESTIONS

1. Why does breach of an essential term not always automatically terminate a contract?

2. Is it true that even in the case of a very serious breach, the non-breaching party may be unable to insist that he or she is discharged from his or her obligations? Explain.

3. What needs to be proved by the non-breaching party in order for the court to terminate a contract for breach? Why did the court not terminate the contract in this case?

4. If the breach is not so serious as to terminate the contract, is there any remedy available to the non-breaching party? Explain.

5. What might the parties have done to ensure that their rights and remedies were clearer?

Chrysler Credit Canada Ltd. v. Shipperbottom

[1993] O.J. No. 1707
Ontario Court of Justice - General Division
July 15, 1993

Fundamental breach means that some types of failure to perform are so basic to the contract that they destroy any semblance of performance of the contract, leaving the non-breaching party with no benefit at all from the contract. In the face of such a breach, an exemption or exclusion clause in a contract will, in most cases, not protect the party in breach from liability for damages.

1   **LEACH J.:**— This is a third party claim by Mr. Shipperbottom against Chrysler Canada Ltd. (Chrysler) and Checkpoint Chrysler Ltd. (Checkpoint).

2   This action was commenced by Chrysler Credit Ltd. against Shipperbottom as defendant who issued the third party claim. The plaintiff and the defendant resolved their dispute leaving the third party claim to be determined by the Court.

3   Shipperbottom claims damages from Chrysler and Checkpoint for his losses in leasing from Checkpoint a 1985 Chrysler LeBaron, which was manufactured by Chrysler.

4   Shipperbottom is a chartered accountant residing in the City of Niagara Falls, Ontario.

5   Chrysler is a car manufacturer having its head office in the City of Mississauga, Ontario.

6   Checkpoint is a limited company carrying on business in new and used cars and leasing of the same in the City of St. Catharines, Ontario. It is an authorized dealer for Chrysler.

Facts

7   On the 22nd of July, 1985 Shipperbottom leased from Checkpoint a 1985 Chrysler LeBaron.

8   He tried the car out and found it satisfactory. It was his intention to use it to drive to work and for recreation. The car was equipped with power steering and power brakes and air conditioning. This was important to him as the previous year he had undergone a triple heart by-pass operation. These power features would reduce the manual pressure on him.

9   The parties entered into a lease agreement (Exhibit 1, Tab 7) for 48 months, with monthly payments of $335.50. As is usual in these cases, Shipperbottom did not examine the lease thoroughly. It was his understanding that he was obliged to pay the monthly rental and normal maintenance charges. He made the required monthly payments to Chrysler Credit Canada Ltd., who took an assignment of the lease from Checkpoint. On July 20th, 1988 he returned the car to Checkpoint with a letter (Exhibit 1, Tab 9). The opening paragraph of his letter states:

> "Over the past two and a half years the above automobile has been a great harassment to myself, my family, and probably Checkpoint Services. The car is more than a harassment. It is also a hazard because of the 'power loss problem' and the 'stalling problem'."

The letter further states:

> "The 'power loss' problem has been occurring since March 27, 1986 when it was first reported. The last 'power loss' was April 4, 1988. The 'stalling' problem which is part of the power loss, started June 5, 1988 and as of July 19, 1988 it was still 'stalling'. This car stalls and goes into power loss without warning. It is very dangerous."

10   This letter, in a summary fashion, states the actual problems Shipperbottom experienced with the car. He made no further rental payments after returning the car. Shipperbottom files as Exhibit 1, (Tab 10) a log setting out the dates from March 27, 1986 to July 19, 1988 when he took the car to Checkpoint to have the power problem corrected, without success. The log also indicates the number of hours the vehicle was left with Checkpoint. I find the log accurately indicates the dates, times, and problems when the vehicle was taken to Checkpoint. Hereunder are the relevant entries from the log:

		Time Loss
March 27, 1986	Power loss reported Not corrected	3 hrs.
Sept. 19, 1986	Power loss reported Not corrected	3 hrs.
Sept. 29, 1986	Power loss reported Not corrected	3 hrs.
Feb. 27, 1987	Power loss reported Not corrected	7 hrs.
May 27, 1987	Power loss Air conditioning not working	7 hrs.
May 28, 1987	Power loss Speedometer incorrect	3 hrs.
July 2, 1987	Power loss (sensor)	3 hrs.
Sept. 1, 1987	No heat	5 hrs.
Nov. 1, 1987	No air conditioning in Florida	3 hrs.
Jan. 11, 1988	Power loss-dash not working Call Chrysler Canada Car in garage	72 hrs.
Mar. 8, 1988	Power loss Car in garage Advised trouble water pump	7 hrs.
April 4, 1988	Power loss Battery not charging Speedometer reading when stopped	8 hrs.
May 31, 1988	Air conditioning not working Parts ordered	72 hrs.
June 5, 1988	Son took mother to Toronto Car stopped 4 times on Q.E.W.	8 hrs.
June 6, 1988	Reported above to Checkpoint "Nothing can be done"	4 hrs.
July 6, 1988	Car stalled on 406 and towed to Checkpoint. Left Checkpoint and made it to off-ramp, Car stalled.	3 hrs.
July 8, 1988	Checkpoint installs "pick-up plate" This is problem.	4 hrs
July 19, 1988	Car driven from N.F. office to N.F. N.Y. Car stalled in intersection for four hours.	4 hrs.

11   Shipperbottom testified there were other times the car stalled and it was not taken to Checkpoint. When the vehicle stalled, steering and braking was difficult and "frightening".

12   Shipperbottom's son Alan, testified that on June 5, 1988 he drove the car to Toronto on the Q.E.W. His grandmother was a passenger. The car stalled in heavy traffic. He had to pull into the lane nearest the median. The car lost its power steering and brakes. He described it as "scary". On the return trip, it stalled in Burlington and Port Dalhousie. After waiting 15-20 minutes, the car would start again.

13   Shipperbottom's wife testified about two occasions when she was a passenger and the car stalled. One of the occasions was in Pennsylvannia and the other in Niagara Falls, New York. They were in heavy traffic. After a short time, 15-20 minutes, the car would start up again. She testified "I was too scared to drive the car".

14   Ronald MacDonald testified on behalf of Chrysler. He testified that there is no record of Shipperbottom contacting his firm, and if he did, he would have referred the problem to their dealer Checkpoint. On cross-examination, he stated, " I am not saying Mr. Shipperbottom didn't call." I was not impressed by his evidence as he was evasive and defensive. He stressed Chrysler was a separate legal entity from its dealer, Checkpoint.

15   I am satisfied on the evidence that Shipperbottom contacted Chrysler and that it conferred with Checkpoint to correct the problem. The car was in the Checkpoint garage on January 11, 1988 for three days in a joint attempt to correct the problem. Chrysler did not follow up with Checkpoint or Shipperbottom to see if the problem had been corrected. It was not.

16   Mr. Kent Smith testified on behalf of Checkpoint, where he was service manager for 11 years. I found him to be a credible witness but he could not recall meeting with Shipperbottom. He testified there was no limit on his authority or his actions to satisfy a customer. He explained that there must have been a lack of communication between his mechanics and himself. Significantly, he testified to the effect that he doesn't doubt the accuracy of Mr. Shipperbottom's complaints.

Submission of Chrysler

17   Counsel for Chrysler submitted that Shipperbottom's claim is based in contract and not negligence. The words negligence or fault or manufacturing defect do not appear in the third party claim against his client. He adds that Chrysler and Checkpoint are separate legal entities and there is no privity of contract between Shipperbottom and his client. This is admitted by counsel for the claimant. I reluctantly agree with this submission and therefore dismiss the claim against Chrysler. However, I am satisfied it was aware of the problems with the car.

Submission of Shipperbottom

18   Counsel for Shipperbottom submits that under section 15 of the Sale of Goods Act, Chap 5.1, there is an implied condition in a sale of the car that it will be reasonably fit for the purpose it is to be used.

19   I am unable to accept this argument as the transaction was a leasing of the car and not a sale. S. 18 of the lease provided in part:

"18. Lease only. This agreement is one of leasing only and the lessee has not acquired any right, title or interest to the vehicle..." In the alternative, counsel for the claimant submits there was a fundamental breach of contract.

Submission for Checkpoint

20 Counsel for Checkpoint refers to the warranty provision in the contract.

"S. 17 There is no implied warranty of merchantability of fitness for any particular purpose, or which extends beyond the description of the vehicle as shown on this lease, and there are no conditions, warranties, or representations expressed or implied, statutory or otherwise, with respect to the vehicle, it's quality or this lease unless endorsed thereon." In the alternative, he submits there is no fundamental breach as the claimant drove the vehicle 100,000 kilometres for three years less two days.

Conclusion

21 As previously indicated, I accept the evidence of the claimant as to the troubles he had with the leased car. I do not feel he exaggerated his claim. This view is fortified by the fact he paid all the repair bills for power loss problems, even though Checkpoint did not correct them. One has to admire his patience in putting up with his many visits to the garage without having the problem corrected.

22 In my view, Checkpoint is guilty of a fundamental breach of the contract. Checkpoint leased to the claimant a new car for 48 months. It was the claimant's responsibility to pay maintenance charges, which he did. The claimant leased the car on July 22, 1985, and reported the power loss problem seven months later. From then, as itemized above, he took the car to the garage approximately 14 times complaining of power loss. The car was in the garage for approximately 135 hours in the period March, 1986 to July, 1988.

23 Despite the exclusionary clause, Checkpoint did not provide a rental car that would operate without breakdown and with safety. In my view, when they were unable to correct the power loss problem, they should have provided the claimant with another car.

24 In the case of *Cain, et al vs. Bird Chevrolet - Oldsmobile Ltd. et al* (1976), 12 O.R. (2d) 532 affirmed at 20 O.R. (2d) 569, the plaintiff purchased a truck which he was told was a new truck and sought to use it in connection with a construction project. The truck was found to be wholly unsatisfactory and the trial judge, Weatherston, J. found that there had been a fundamental breach of contract, and the plaintiff was entitled to terminate the contract and recover damages for all loss resulting from the breach of the defendant's obligation to deliver a workable truck, notwithstanding the fact that the contract contained an exclusionary clause.

25 In the present case, we have the claimant leasing a vehicle not purchasing one, but in my view there was a fundamental obligation on Checkpoint to rent a reliable and safe vehicles to the claimant, for the term of his lease. In our society today many persons rent vehicle instead of purchasing them. It is fundamental that they should be trustworthy and safe.

26 The defects in this car could have resulted in a serious accident endangering the passengers and other motor vehicles.

Damages

27   The claimant is asking for $10,000 for general damages for the loss of enjoyment, physical inconvenience and vexation as the result of leasing a defective vehicle from Checkpoint.

28   The vehicle was in the Checkpoint garage for approximately 133.5 hours for repairs to the power problem. This involved 15 trips by the claimant from his residence or office and return. This resulted in a substantial loss of working time. As an accountant, the evidence indicates he earned $85.00 to $92.50 an hour. For 133.5 hours, this would result in a claim of $12,348.75. This amount of loss does not consider the claimant's loss of enjoyment, physical inconvenience and vexation. The latter group of damages is difficult to compute.

29   In his pleadings, the claimant asked for $10,000 and in my view, this is a reasonable figure.

30   The claimant will also have judgment for $4000.00 representing the amount paid to Chrysler Credit Canada Ltd in settlement of the balance owing on the lease after he turned in the car.

31   The claimant will also have judgment for the sum of $849.55 he paid to Checkpoint for repairing the power problem. These repairs did not correct the power problem.

Judgment

32   Mr. Shipperbottom will have judgment against Checkpoint for $14,849.50 plus pre-judgment interest under the Courts of Justice Act from January 9, 1990, the date of issuance of the third party claim. In addition, he will be entitled to post judgment interest under the said Act. He will also have his costs of this claim on a party and party basis. The claim against Chrysler is dismissed. I am not allowing Chrysler costs. I am satisfied it was aware of the claimant's problems but did very little to ensure the vehicle was safe to drive. It was a danger on the highway to the driving public and had an accident occurred, they may have faced a serious claim.

QUESTIONS

1. What is a fundamental breach? Why, in this case, did the court say that there was a fundamental breach?

2. What is the effect of a fundamental breach on an exclusion clause in most cases?

3. The defendant had two defences available in this case. What were they?

4. Why, in this case, did the Sale of Goods Act not apply?

5. Why, in this case, did the court dismiss the plaintiff's claim against Chrysler?

6. Is it feasible to draft an exemption clause that excludes liability for fundamental breach? What should it say?

chapter fifteen

Remedies

Westcoast Transmission Co. v. Cullen Detroit Diesel Allison Ltd.

[1990] B.C.J. No. 942 , 70 DLR (4th) 505
British Columbia Court of Appeal
April 24, 1990

Although damages are designed to compensate the injured party for losses suffered, not all injuries suffered are recoverable. Remoteness and mitigation are two limitations on the recoverability of damages. A breaching party is responsible only for those damages that, at the time the contract was entered into, seem a likely outcome if the contract were breached. A breaching party would also be responsible for any unusual damages for special circumstances when communicated to him or her at the time the contract is entered into. Finally, victims of breach have an obligation to keep the losses as low as is reasonably possible.

TAYLOR J.A.:— This appeal is concerned with the extent to which a supplier of a defective component is required to indemnify the manufacturer to whom it was supplied for compensation paid by the manufacturer to a purchaser of industrial equipment into which the component was incorporated.

The action results from the failure of two generators supplied by the third party Kato Engineering International, Inc., to the defendant Cullen Detroit Diesel Allison Ltd. for incorporation with motors provided by the third party Cooper Energy Services Ltd. into natural-gas driven power units (called 'gensets') for use as an electrical power source for a natural gas processing plant being built by the plaintiff, Westcoast Transmission Company Limited, near Chetwynd, B.C.

On the eve of trial the defendant Cullen settled the claim brought against it by Westcoast, and the action proceeded as a third party claim by Cullen against its suppliers.

The trial judge found that the units failed as a result of faulty manufacture by the third party Kato which resulted in breaches of the warranties of reasonable fitness for the purpose and of merchantable quality implied by Section 18(a) and (b) of the Sale of Goods Act. The judge awarded as damages costs incurred in repairing the machines but did not allow a claim by Cullen for reimbursement of costs incurred by Westcoast in renting portable power units to provide electricity for operation of the plant during the two-month period for which the 'gensets' were under repair. Cullen now appeals the dismissal of that claim.

The claim is for some $120,000 in rental costs incurred by Westcoast because it had no existing alternative source of power to keep its plant in operation.

The trial judge disallowed the claim on two grounds. He held that these rental costs, originally incurred not by the purchaser of the component but by Westcoast as subsequent purchaser of the completed unit, could not be said to have been foreseeable as arising naturally from the breach of the contract between Kato and Cullen, nor could they reasonably be supposed to have been in contemplation by Kato at the time that contract was made as a probable result of such a breach, and therefore fell outside both of the rules in *Hadley v. Baxendale* (1854), 9 Ex. 341, 156 E.R. 145, as elaborated in *Victoria Laundry v. Newman*, [1949] 1 All E.R. 997 (C.A.). The trial judge also held that liability for such 'consequential' damages was excluded by a term of Kato's printed contract of sale, even though that term does not specifically refer to damages for breach of warranties implied by the statute.

In dealing with the claim under the rules in *Hadley v. Baxendale* the trial judge set out the relevant facts as follows (Reasons for Judgment pages 25-27):

1. Kato did not have in its possession a copy of the Westcoast invitation to bid. However, it knew the generators were to provide electricity for the Westcoast Pine River gas plant at Chetwynd which was to process sour gas. It was given certain climatic information, and knew it was to be driven by an engine, unspecified as far as Kato was concerned. It knew that Pine River was in a remote part of British Columbia.

2. When it supplied the generators it did so under a "guarantee" which purported to exclude consequential damage.

3. The goods were ordered early in 1978 and its delivery was made sometime in the late spring of 1978. Cullen's date of delivery was according to a schedule agreed between itself and Westcoast and apparently for some time in September 1978. Kato's knowledge ceased thereafter. On receipt of the machines Cullen assembled and shipped the gensets to Westcoast at Pine River in the late fall of 1978. If there ever was any immediate urgency in Westcoast's order it obviously subsided as the events of this lawsuit occurred some 12 to 14 months after the delivery date. There is no evidence that Kato was ever told that any of Westcoast's

endeavours or success depended on the time of delivery of the generator or the genset. Kato's customer was Cullen, not Westcoast. Kato had nothing to do with Westcoast's timetable and if there were any postponements or deferments it did not know of them.

4. No evidence was offered as to the knowledge of Kato as to any of the operations of Westcoast or the size, configuration or importance of the electrical supply, whether it was the sole electrical supply or was only additional, whether it was to be used for other uses or even whether the generators were a part of a standby operation or not. Specifically, no evidence was offered which showed that Kato knew the facts put pointedly to Cullen in Westcoast's letter of December 24 quoted previously. [A letter in which Westcoast made it clear that it had no other electrical power supply).

5. Kato was never originally scheduled to go on site during startup or at all.

6. The witness Berkeley, senior technical advisor for planning and development, testified that the engineering design started in 1977 and camp and plant construction started in April of 1978 and continued up to July 1979 when he moved to the site for startup as sections were beginning to be completed, tested and commissioned. The plant was to process natural gas and distribute it. Pine River is 30 miles from Chetwynd and was in a remote location totally self-sufficient for utilities.

The appellant Cullen says that the facts are correctly stated with the exception of those stated in Clause 4, where, it says, the trial judge has fallen into error.

Counsel for the appellant points to statements contained in two of the contract documents indicating that the generators were to be incorporated into power plants designated for "continuous use" and as a "prime power" source. Counsel says the judge was wrong when he said there was no evidence before him "as to the knowledge of Kato as to ... the importance of the electrical supply, whether it was the sole electrical supply or was only additional ... or even whether the generators were part of a standby operation or not".

Kato carries on its business in Mankato, Minnesota, and has no office in British Columbia. Cullen invited it to tender by a letter which contained a number of specifications, including "continuous duty", for both units. Kato's quotation contains, under the heading "description", notations which include:

Insulation	Class F
Temperature Rise	105 degrees C.
Duty Cycle	Continuous
Enclosure	Open Drip-proof

Cullen's resulting purchase order repeats under the same heading some or all of these items, including:

Class F insulation	105 degrees C. temperature rise
continuous duty	(prime power application)

There was evidence at trial that "prime power" is "an industry term meaning that the generator set is intended to run continuously as a primary source of power, as against a stand-by type application where it seldom runs". (Transcript pages 47-48).

Counsel for Kato says the references to "continuous use" and "prime power application" are descriptive of the quality or operational standard which the equipment had to meet, and that the trial judge was right in not considering these notations as notice of the service in which they would be used.

Westcoast's intention in fact was that one of the 'gensets' would provide power for the plant while the other would be held in reserve — or that they be alternated in use — so as to provide both 'prime' power and 'standby' power. If the statements referred to in the contract documents should be read as describing the intended use, they would not convey that message. They would indicate that both units were to provide 'prime power' and be in 'continuous use'. It is not apparent from these words that Westcoast would be without any other source of electrical power on which to call in emergencies or while repairs, or regular maintenance, were being carried out. Having in mind that the equipment was to be driven by internal combustion, no one would I think, believe that "continuous use" in this context implied that the equipment would continue indefinitely in operation without any need for maintenance or repair.

Following the failures Kato prepared a repair order in which there appears the note: "These units are being used as prime power and must be returned A.S.A.P.!" While counsel for the appellant lays emphasis on this statement, I do not understand how it adds anything of substance to his case.

In order to foresee that replacement machines would have to be rented in the event of failure of the 'gensets', Kato would have to know that the units were the sole source of power for the gas processing plant operation, and in particular that it had no connection to the ordinary electrical power system — not, I think a normal situation in which one would expect to find a substantial permanent industrial facility.

We were not referred to any evidence which would suggest that a plant powered by such 'gensets' would normally have no alternative source of supply for 'standby' purposes. Indeed the evidence seems to me to suggest the contrary.

No objection was taken on the appeal to the characterization by the trial judge of the law concerning damages recoverable under the rules in *Hadley v. Baxendale*: (1) such as arise naturally, according to the usual course of things, from the breach of contract itself; and (2) such as may reasonably be supposed to have been in contemplation of both parties at the time they made the contract as a probable result of the breach. The trial judge quoted from the judgment of Asquith L.J., in *Victoria Laundry v. Newman*, [1949] 1 All E.R. 997 (C.A.) (at page 1002) which establishes that only those damages "at the time of the contract reasonably foreseeable as likely to result from the breach" are recoverable. Under the "first rule", foreseeability depends on the knowledge which a reasonable person in the position of the party at fault should be taken to have possessed. Under the "second rule" damages are recoverable also which can be considered foreseeable on the basis of knowledge actually possessed by the party in breach of circumstances outside "the ordinary course of things" which would likely lead to greater loss than that recoverable under the first rule.

It is, no doubt, reasonable in some cases to conclude that the supplier of a finished machine would foresee that the purchaser would have to rent a replacement unit in the event the machine was taken out of service for repair. The claim here is not, however, for rental of replacements for the units supplied by Kato but for rental of replacements for the much larger units of which they were merely components.

I do not think it can readily be assumed that the purchaser of electrical power generating equipment will be without any alternative power source to call on when the equipment has to be taken out of service for any reason. At least, that is not something which a reasonable person in the position of this respondent — as supplier of a component for such equipment — should be presumed to foresee. It does not seem to me to be reasonable to assume that a plant which has a locally-generated "prime" power source would not have any alternative or "standby" power available. I agree with the learned trial judge that so far as the claim by Cullen against Kato is concerned the cost of rental of the replacement 'gensets' does not fall under the "first rule" in Hadley v. Baxendale, that is to say as a foreseeable natural result of the failure of the components supplied by Kato.

What, then, of the "second rule"?

Giving the meaning which is urged on us by the appellant to the references to "continuous use" and "prime power" in the contract documents, all that can be said, in my view, is that the two power units were to be used as principal power supply source. I do not think that a reasonable person in Kato's position would conclude from this that there was no source of 'standby' power on site. "Prime" does not, of course, mean "sole" but rather implies that there will also be a "secondary" source, and equipment of this sort cannot be expected to operate "continuously" in the sense that it will not require maintenance or repair. Nothing has been pointed to in the evidence from which it would be reasonable, in my view, to impute such knowledge to Kato. It follows, therefore, that, so far as Kato is concerned, the claim has not been brought within the "second rule" in *Hadley v. Baxendale*.

But it seems to me that the claim is, in any event, one for "consequential damages" for which liability is excluded by the standard terms under which Kato accepted the order.

I am of the view that the claim for rental of replacement 'gensets' falls within the class of consequential damages referred to in Clause 7 of this document, which says:

> The company assumes no liability for consequential damages in case of failure to meet conditions of any guarantee.

I think the term "any guarantee" should be taken to include warranties implied by the statute as well as express warranties, and that the expression "consequential damages", in the context of this document, refers to damages other than cost of repair.

The document provides by Clause 7 a specific guarantee "limited to the replacement of equipment or apparatus proven defective". It then goes on to say that Kato "assumes no liability for consequential damages" in the event of failure to meet the conditions of any guarantee.

It is, of course, well established that very specific terms must be used in order to exclude conditions and warranties implied by Sale of Goods statutes. This rule has recently been applied by the Supreme Court of Canada in *Hunter Engineering Company Inc. v. Syncrude Canada Ltd.*, [1989] 3 W.W.R. 385. Chief Justice Dickson said in that case (at p. 402) that "clear and direct language" is required for this purpose, and Madam Justice Wilson said (at p. 437) that to have that effect the language must be "clear and unambiguous".

But it does not appear that the same approach prevails in the construction of terms intended to limit the extent of damages recoverable in the event of breach of such warranties. This is made clear by the House of Lords in *Ailsa Craig Fishing Co. Ltd. v. Malvern Fishing Co. Ltd.*, [1983] 1 All E.R. 101 and *Photo Production Ltd. v. Securicor Transport Ltd.*, [1980] 1 All E.R. 556.

In the *Ailsa Craig case*, Lord Wilberforce said (at p. 102):

> "Clauses of limitation are not regarded by the courts with the same hostility as clauses of exclusion" for the reason that limitations of liability "Must be related to other contractual terms, in particular to the risks to which the defending party may be exposed, the remuneration which he receives and possibly also the opportunity of the other party to insure". Lord Fraser said (at p. 105) that terms intended to limit liability must be clearly expressed "but there is no reason why they should be judged by the specially exacting standards which are applied to exclusion and indemnity clauses". Lord Fraser said that there is "no such high degree of improbability that (the purchaser) would agree to a limitation of liability".

The distinction is, in my view, one of particular significance in the present case. Kato does business in the United States. It had no knowledge of the extent to which liability had been accepted by its customer toward the purchasers of the equipment into which its generators were to be incorporated. The generators were sold to Cullen for $50,000 each while the 'gensets' into which they were built were supplied by Cullen to Westcoast for about $1,000,000. The cost of rental "gensets" was $120,000, that is to say 120 per-cent of the total price of the components supplied by Kato to Cullen. It seems to me that an equipment manufacturer might well expect a supplier to be unwilling to accept liability for such damages.

I find that even if the rental of equipment to replace the complete 'gensets' provided by Cullen to Westcoast had fallen within either of the rules in *Hadley v. Baxendale*, a claim for indemnity in respect of that cost would nevertheless constitute a claim for "consequential damages" excluded by Clause 7 of Kato's standard terms, and would not be recoverable.

I would dismiss the appeal.

QUESTIONS

1. What is the purpose of an award of damages?
2. Explain what limitations on the recovery of damages were developed from the case of *Hadley v. Baxendale*. Why was the plaintiff's claim for damages denied in this case?
3. What effect did the clause limiting Kato's liability for "consequential damages" have in this case?
4. What might Cullen have done to prevent liability for rental costs incurred by Westcoast in this case?

Blackcomb Skiing Enterprises Limited Partnership v. Schneider

[2000] B.C.J. No. 902, 2000 BCSC 720.
British Columbia Supreme Court
May 2, 2000

Where a party foresees that breach may cause it to suffer damages, the consequences of breach may be built into the contract. Liquidated damage clauses are common in real estate contracts. To be enforceable in a court, the clause must represent a genuine attempt by parties to estimate the damages that would be suffered if the contract were breached. If the amount attempts to punish or impose a penalty for failure to perform, the clause may be void.

1   **HARVEY J.**:— The plaintiff claims for summary judgment under Rule 18A to obtain a declaration that it is entitled to a deposit and accrued interest, pursuant to the default of the defendant under a contract of purchase and sale for property.

2   The defendant submits the deposit clause in the contract is in reality a penalty clause and, in the circumstances here, it would be unconscionable for the plaintiff to retain the deposit.

3   The defendant says further, in the alternative, at the time of closing, there were charges on the title of the property which the plaintiff had not undertaken to discharge and the plaintiff was, therefore, in default under the contract.

4   The parties agree this is an appropriate case for determination under Rule 18A.

5   The facts are set out in the written submissions of counsel as follows:

THE CONTRACT

1. On December 31, 1998, the Defendant Darwin Schneider signed a Contract of Purchase and Sale to purchase Strata Lot 1 of the Pinnacle Heights development being constructed by the Plaintiff Blackcomb Skiing Enterprises Limited Partnership ("Blackcomb") on the Blackcomb Benchlands at Whistler, B.C. (the "Contract"). Pinnacle Heights is a nine unit ultra-luxury detached townhouse project. The Contract was accepted by Blackcomb on January 2, 1999 and provided for a purchase price of CDN $2,290,000 with a deposit of US $150,000 due within 24 hours after Blackcomb's acceptance.

2. Intrawest Resort Corporation ("Intrawest") is the general partner of Blackcomb and signed the Contract in that capacity. A limited partnership cannot hold title to property in its own name and Intrawest as Blackcomb's general partner held title to the subject property in its capacity as the nominee, agent and bare trustee of Blackcomb, which was explained and disclosed in the Disclosure Statement that accompanied the Contract.

3. The Contract provided as follows:

"Purchase Price"	$2,290,000
"Initial Deposit"	$ not applicable (to form part of "First Report" upon subject removal)
"First Deposit"	$150,000 US Funds (this amount and Initial Deposit to equal 10% of Purchase Price)
"Second Deposit"	$ not applicable (to be an additional 10% of Purchase Price)

    THE PURCHASER HEREBY OFFERS to purchase the Property for the Purchase Price on the terms and conditions contained in this Contract, including the terms and conditions set out in Schedule A, which form part of this Contract and are hereby incorporated into this Contract.

    1. Deposits. The Purchaser will pay the First Deposit to the Vendor's solicitors, McCarthy Tetrault, in trust, within 24 hours of the Vendor's acceptance of the Purchaser's offer herein ...

Interest earned on the First and Second Deposits will be for the benefit of the Purchaser unless the Purchaser defaults in any of the Purchaser's obligations hereunder, in which case the Vendor may, at its election, retain the First Deposit and Second Deposit and interest thereon as liquidated damages, the parties hereby agreeing that such amount constitutes a genuine pre-estimate of damages.

4. At all material times, McCarthy Tetrault were Blackcomb's solicitors.

5. The Defendant provided two deposit cheques payable to "McCarthy Tetrault in trust" dated December 31, 1999 totalling US $150,000 drawn on SouthTrust Bank, Georgia, along with the executed Contract. Both cheques were returned to McCarthy Tetrault by its bank marked "NSF". The Defendant provided two replacement cheques dated January 11, 1999 totalling US $150,000 drawn on the Regions Bank, Georgia. These cheques cleared, but by reason of the changes in exchange rate the deposit was $2,246.78 less in Canadian funds.

6. On February 11, 1999, Blackcomb's solicitor, Mr. Benson gave notice to the Defendant pursuant to section 2 of the Contract that the Completion date for the transaction would be March 1, 1999. The notice was faxed to the Defendant at the fax number shown on the Contract, with a copy to his [local] lawyer, Ian Davis of Race & Co. Although the Contract required that a minimum of 10 days' prior notice be given, 17 days' notice was provided.

7. The Defendant's lawyer Mr. Davis requested an extension of the Completion Date to March 10, 1999. This extension was agreed to by letter agreement between Mr. Davis and Mr. Benson dated February 17, 1999.

8. On February 22, 1999, Mr. Benson's office forwarded a draft information sheet containing conveyancing information to Mr. Davis.

9. On March 9, 1999, Mr. Davis requested a further extension of the Completion Date to March 19, 1999. Another letter agreement between Mr. Davis and Mr. Benson reflected the agreed extension.

10. On March 22, 1999, Mr. Davis wrote to Mr. Benson requesting a more lengthy extension to April 30, 1999 (or sooner), with interest at the Royal Bank of Canada prime rate plus 2% from March 19, 1999 to the Completion Date. On behalf of Blackcomb, Mr. Benson's office counter-offered by requesting the deposit be increased by an additional $100,000. A copy of Mr. Davis' March 22, 1999 letter was amended by Mr. Benson's office to reflect this condition. This counter-offer was never accepted by the Defendant, but the Defendant did not close on March 19, 1999.

BANK OF NOVA SCOTIA MORTGAGE

11. Construction financing for the Plaintiff's Pinnacle Heights development was provided by the Bank of Nova Scotia ("BNS"). Its Mortgage BM266394 and Assignment of Rents BM266395 were registered against title to the parent parcel for the project and, on the deposit of the strata plan, was reflected on title to each strata lot, including the subject property Strata Lot 1.

12. McCarthy Tetrault also represented Blackcomb with respect to another town home development on the Blackcomb Benchlands known as "Forest Creek". The construction lender for Forest Creek was Hongkong Bank of Canada ("HBC"). By coincidence, the sale of Strata Lot 1 of the Forest Creek development completed on March 18, 1999.

13. In preparing the partial discharge of the HBC mortgage for Strata Lot 1 of Forest Creek, Mr. Benson's office inadvertently used the partial discharge precedent for Pinnacle Heights. Consequently, the document reflected a partial discharge of BNS's mortgage and assignment of rents from Strata Lot 1 of Pinnacle Heights, rather than the HBC mortgage from Strata Lot 1 of Forest Creek. The partial discharge, reflecting BNS as the lender, was forwarded to HBC. HBC's signing officers inadvertently executed the partial discharge on behalf of BNS and returned it to Mr. Benson's office whereupon it was filed for registration in the Land Title Office on April 6, 1999. Mr. Benson himself did not see the partial discharge at any time before it was filed. The partial discharge was in due course fully registered, thereby partially discharging the BNS's construction mortgage from title to Strata Lot 1 of Pinnacle Heights, the subject property.

CLOSING DATE

14. By letter dated April 23, 1999 and received by Mr. Benson on April 26, 1999, Mr. Davis sent closing documents, ostensibly in preparation for an April 30, 1999 closing.

15. On April 27, 1999, Mr. Benson's office forwarded a revised Vendor's Statement of Adjustments to Mr. Davis, reflecting a slightly different property tax adjustment.

16. On April 29, 1999, Mr. Davis advised Mr. Benson that the Defendant would not be able to close on April 30. On behalf of Blackcomb, Mr. Benson offered to extend the Completion Date to May 14, 1999 on the condition that the Defendant would pay interest at prime rate plus 4% per annum from April 30, 1999 to the Completion Date. This was reflected in his letter to Mr. Davis of May 3, 1999.

17. The Defendant did not complete the purchase on May 14, 1999. Despite discussions between Mr. Benson and Mr. Davis prior to, on and after that date about the Defendant's inability to close, no further formal extension was agreed to.

18. On May 18, 1999, Mr. Davis advised Mr. Benson that the Defendant was involved in a new business venture and was having "money problems". He indicated that the Defendant was unable to raise the required down payment (over and above the amount he was able to finance) of approximately US $600,000 required for the purchase. Mr. Davis made an informal request for Blackcomb to consider financing the difference, or some alternative.

19. Around this time, the Bank of Nova Scotia contacted Mr. Benson's office to enquire when the Defendant's sale would close, as BNS was expecting to receive the net sale proceeds. When Mr. Benson's office checked title to the remaining strata lots in Pinnacle Heights, it was determined that Strata Lot 1 was no longer encumbered by BNS's construction mortgage. It was only then that it was discovered that BNS's mortgage and assignment of rents had been inadvertently discharged from Strata Lot 1. Mr. Benson's office promptly prepared an extension agreement, extending BNS's mortgage and assignment of rents (then still registered against title to three other strata lots in Pinnacle Heights) over Strata Lot 1. The extension agreement was filed for registration on June 2, 1999 under numbers BN141690 and BN141691.

20. On May 28, 1999, Mr. Benson wrote to Mr. Davis re-establishing time of the essence and setting the Completion Date as June 4, 1999. In the letter, Mr. Benson stated the following:

Originally, the Completion Date for the purchase and sale of the Strata Lot was established as March 1, 1999. Subsequently, the Completion Date was extended by agreement to March 10, 1999 and March 19, 1999. A subsequent extension to April 30, 1999 is reflected in your letter of March 22, 1999; however, the Purchaser did not increase the deposit by an additional $100,000 which was a condition of that extension agreement. Notwithstanding the Purchaser's failure to pay the additional deposit, the Vendor subsequently offered to extend the Completion date to May 14, 1999, with additional interest payable from April 30, 1999 to the actual closing date at the prime rate plus 4% per annum. The Purchaser never agreed to the terms of that extension and no subsequent extension agreements have been entered into.

The Vendor has, at all times, been ready, willing and able to complete the transaction. The Purchaser, on the other hand, has not.

In order to clearly re-establish time of the essence, the Vendor hereby gives the Purchaser until Friday, June 4, 1999 to complete the transaction in accordance with the Contract of Purchase and Sale (with interest payable as previously agreed). If the Purchaser fails to complete the transaction, the Vendor will treat the Purchaser as being in default. Such default would give the Vendor the right to exercise any and all of its legal and equitable rights and remedies which could include accepting such default as repudiation of the Contract in which case the Contract would be terminated and the deposit paid, in the amount of $221,367.02, and all accrued interest thereon, would be forfeited to the Vendor as liquidated damages in accordance with section 1 of Schedule A of the Contract.

Please advise us, as soon as possible, as to the Purchaser's specific intentions with respect to completing the purchase and sale of the Strata Lot.

21. The Contract provides as follows:

The Purchaser acknowledges and agrees that the transfer of title may be subject to the Vendor's financing for the Development provided that the Vendor's solicitors undertake to clear title to the Property of encumbrances relating to such financing within a reasonable time after receiving the balance of the adjusted Purchase Price payable to the Vendor on closing.

22. On June 3, 1999, Mr. Benson faxed Mr. Davis a letter indicating that McCarthy Tetrault would be tendering the original Transfer at the New Westminster/Vancouver Land Title Office on June 4, 1999, and attaching copies of all the other closing documentation. In the letter Mr. Benson stated the following:

We advise that the Vendor's representative, Geoffrey Loomer, will be in attendance at the New Westminster/Vancouver land title office near the cashier's wicket between the hours of 2:00 p.m. and 3:00 p.m. on June 4, 1999. We are prepared to provide the Purchaser with the executed Transfer and originals of the other documents referred to above in exchange for cash, a lawyer's or notary's trust cheque, a certified cheque or a bank draft payable to McCarthy Tetrault, "in trust", for the amount of $1,879,869.56, being the net sale proceeds payable by the Purchaser as indicated on the approved Vendor's Statement of Adjustments.

We confirm that we will receive the funds on our undertakings as follows:

(b)   cause registration of a partial discharge of Mortgage BM266394, Assignment of Rents BM266395 and PPSA Notice BM266396 all in favour of The Bank of Nova Scotia insofar as such encumbrances charge the Strata Lot, and advise your office of registration particulars of the partial discharge as soon as available;

Time continues to be of the essence of this transaction. Therefore, if we do not receive the adjusted purchase price from the Purchaser on June 4, 1999, the Vendor reserves all of its rights and remedies, including its right to terminate the Contract without further notice in which event the deposit in the amount of $221,367.02, and all accrued interest thereon, would be forfeited to the Vendor as liquidated damages in accordance with section 1 of Schedule A of the Contract, without prejudice to the Vendor's other remedies.

23. The June 3 closing letter was based on the standard undertaking letter used for all strata lots in the Pinnacle Heights development, and so the undertaking to discharge BNS's mortgage and assignment of rents referred to the registration numbers of the original mortgage (BM266394) and assignment of rents (BM266395) rather than the registration numbers of the extension agreement which extended those same charges to the lot and which had just been submitted for registration on June 2, 1999 and was registered that same day.

24. A copy of the title to the Strata Lot shows all the charges which affected the Strata Lot on June 4, 1999.

25. The material charges are the mortgage and assignment of rents; the extension agreement (Exhibit G) simply incorporated by reference the mortgage BM266394 and assignment of rents BM266395 and caused the mortgage and assignment of rents to charge Strata Lot 1. By Mr. Benson's letter, he undertook to discharge the mortgage and assignment of rents as they affect Strata Lot 1. Pursuant to his letter, upon receipt of the purchase funds he would have caused the BNS mortgage BM266394, assignment of rents BM266395 and the PPSA Notice to be discharged from the Strata Lot, making the title free and clear of all financial encumbrances. The method by which Mr. Benson would effect the discharge of mortgage BM266394 and assignment of rents BM266395 insofar as they affected the Strata Lot would be to effect the discharge of Extension Agreement BN141690 as it extended mortgage BM266394 to the Strata Lot and Extension Agreement BN141691 as it extended assignment of rents BM266395 to the Strata Lot.

26. On June 4, 1999, one of McCarthy Tetrault's articling students attended at the land title office at the appointed time. The Defendant did not attend. Mr. Benson advised Mr. Davis of this by fax on June 7, 1999.

27. On June 16, 1999, Mr. Benson wrote to Mr. Davis advising him that Blackcomb elected to terminate the Contract and claim the deposit and all accrued interest thereon as liquidated damages in accordance with the Contract. Mr. Benson enclosed a form of Direction of Release with respect to

the Deposit and requested that it be signed by the Defendant and returned on or before June 21, 1999. It was not returned.

28. Strata lot one was subsequently sold in August 1999 for the sum of $2,450,000 with title transferred to its owner on August 31, 1999.

Issues

6   The issues are described by counsel for the plaintiff as being:

(1)   did the plaintiff's solicitor's undertaking require him to clear title to the property of encumbrances relating to the plaintiff's financing?;

(2)   was the 10% deposit under the contract a deposit or a penalty?

DID THE PLAINTIFF'S SOLICITOR'S UNDERTAKING REQUIRE HIM TO CLEAR TITLE TO THE PROPERTY OF ENCUMBRANCES RELATING TO THE PLAINTIFF'S FINANCING?

7   As I have stated, supra, the defendant's submission here is that at the time of closing, there were charges on the title of the property which the plaintiff had not undertaken to discharge and the plaintiff was therefore in default under the contract. Counsel for the defendant, with admirable candour, conceded this was the weaker of the defendant's positions in defence of this action.

8   In my view, for the reasons stated in the submission of counsel for the plaintiff, I agree this position is without merit.

9   In this regard, the plaintiff was ready, willing and able to close under the contract on the closing date of June 4, 1999, with a representative in attendance at the Land Title Office for that purpose provided purchase monies were then made available.

10   I am satisfied that the solicitor's undertaking provided here was sufficient such as to have caused title to the property to be cleared of the said financial encumbrances registered against the title on June 4, 1999, the closing date. I place reliance upon the opinion of Mr. McIntyre and agree it is not without significance that no objection to the terms of the undertaking were ever raised by the then solicitor for the defendant at any time.

WAS THE 10% DEPOSIT UNDER THE CONTRACT A DEPOSIT OR A PENALTY?

11   Counsel for the plaintiff submits this is a deposit case.

12   Counsel for the defendant submits this is a penalty case.

13   Upon consideration of the facts and circumstances here, the submissions of counsel and the authority to which I was referred to support their submissions, I find the 10% deposited pursuant to the terms of the contract, was a deposit, not a penalty.

14   It is common ground that the relevant time for consideration as to whether a stipulated sum is a penalty or liquidated damages is at the time of the making of the contract.

15   As the Court of Appeal of this province has stated:

The question whether a sum stipulated is a penalty or liquidated damages is a question of construction to be decided upon the terms and inherent circumstances of each particular contract, judged of as at the time of the making of the contract, not as at the time of the breach. ...

[*See Hughes v. Lukuvka* (1970), 75 W.W.R. 464 at 468, citing Lord Dunedin in *Dunlop Pneumatic Tyre Co. v. New Garage & Motor Co.*, [1915] A.C. 79 at 86, 83 L.J.K.B. 1574].

16   Counsel for the defendant submits in the circumstances here, in what she describes as a rapidly rising market at the relevant times, that the requirement of 10% of the purchase price as a deposit was not a "genuine pre-estimate of damages" and therefore cannot stand as properly a deposit. Apart from the effect of such a submission, making in such circumstances the amount of the deposit or a deposit in itself meaningless, in my view, the submission in itself and its effect, are not supportable in law.

17   The factors and inherent circumstances of this particular contract and the applicable law, I have considered in reaching a conclusion that the 10% deposit is a deposit, include:

(a)   in this case, the contract does not just refer to liquidated damages, but expressly says that the parties hereby agree that the deposit constitutes a genuine pre-estimate of damages;

(b)   the parties were not unsophisticated in the sale and purchase of property in the new construction luxury condominium market. At the material times the defendant was represented by one of the leading realtors in such a market. No objection to the amount of the deposit or any deposit being required in a rising market was taken at that time;

(c)   in relation to (a) and (b), supra, I refer to the dictum of Lord Parmoor in *Dunlop Pneumatic Tyre Co. v. New Garage and Motor Co.*, supra, at p. 101 where he stated:

No abstract can be laid down without reference to the special facts of the particular case, but when competent parties by free contract are purporting to agree a sum as liquidated damages, there is no reason for refusing a wide limit of discretion. To justify interference, there must an extravagant disproportion between the agreed sum and the amount of any damage capable of pre-estimate;

This dictum was cited with approval by Macfarlane J.A. in *Hughes v. Lukuvka*, and thereafter by Gow J. in *Lee v. Skalbania* (1988), 47 R.P.R. 162 at 172;

(d)   the fact that the plaintiff suffered no damages or made a "profit" as a result of the failure of the defendant to complete is irrelevant if the other requirements of a deposit are met.

[*Williamson Pacific Developments Inc. v. Johns, Southward, Glazier, Walton and Margetts* (1997), 11 R.P.R. (3d) at 315; *Lee v. Skalbania*, supra; and DiCastri, Canadian Law of Vendor and Purchaser (3d ed.) which, at paragraph 829, says this:

Whether or not a purchaser is entitled to the return of a deposit depends upon the terms of the contract, the general rule being that, in the absence of an agreement to the contrary, if the contract goes off by the default of the purchaser, the deposit, being a guarantee of performance, becomes the property of the vendor, even if he resells the land at an increased price;]

(e)   here, apart from the parties characterizing the 10% as a deposit, the 10% was half the usual deposit required in the new construction luxury condominium market;

(f)   in *Hughes v. Lukuvka*, supra, Ruttan J. had this to say:

But the courts will not grant relief to a party who has no intention of completing and sues only to recover his deposit. Were it otherwise, a purchaser who repented of his bargain might, by repudiating his contract, bring about a state of affairs which would entitle him to the return of monies paid under the contract; it is not the policy of the law to encourage people to repudiate contracts nor to take advantage of their own wrongs.

18   The plaintiff is entitled to a declaration that it is entitled to the deposit with interest thereon to date. The plaintiff is entitled to its costs related to this application on scale 3.

QUESTIONS

1.   What will a court consider relevant in determining whether a deposit was a genuine pre-estimate of damages?

2.   In what circumstances will a court find that a deposit becomes an "unconscionable penalty"? What is the effect of such a determination?

3.   Is a deal a deal? Explain.

4.   If the requirements of a deposit are met, is the fact that the plaintiff suffered no damages at all or made a profit as a result of the defendant's failure to complete relevant? Explain.

part four

Special Types
of Contract

chapter sixteen

Sale of Goods

Case 29

Borek v. Hooper

[1994] O.J. No. 916, 18 OR (3d) 470, 114 DLR (4th) 570, 71 OAC 312
Ontario Court (General Division), Divisional Court,
May 4, 1994

The Sale of Goods Act provides protection to buyers of goods. A seller of goods will be responsible for fulfilling implied terms, even if the seller was not responsible for the defects or even aware the defects existed. Before the standards in the legislation will apply, though, it must be established that there was a sale of goods.

SOUTHEY J.: — This is an appeal from a judgment of His Honour Judge Lamb, pronounced in Small Claims Court on June 21, 1993, in which he awarded the plaintiff damages of $2,000, plus court costs and added disbursements of $976.93, for breach of an implied condition of merchantable quality under s. 15, para. 2 of the Sale of Goods Act, R.S.O. 1990, c. S.1, in respect of a painting commissioned by the plaintiff from the defendant, a professional artist.

The case is one of first impression. Although counsel referred to several decided cases involving the contractual rights and obligations of artists, none dealt with problems of defective work or materials. The learned trial judge gave careful written reasons for his decision, and it is with regret that I find myself unable to agree with him. He was at a considerable disadvantage, because neither party was represented by counsel before him. I, on the other hand, had the benefit of able submissions from counsel on both sides.

The painting is large. Its dimensions are five feet by eight feet, with the horizontal being the longer edge. It was created expressly to fit a specific space in the plaintiff's home, and to fulfil her wish for a predominantly white painting to hang on a white wall. The painting is abstract. Its composition might be described, albeit crudely, as a relatively narrow, irregular shaped slash or splash of colour across a broad white background.

The artist created the painting in about three weeks. When he delivered it to the plaintiff and hung it, she was thrilled with it and paid him $4,000, which was the price that had previously been agreed upon. About three years later, in 1987, she noticed that the white areas in the painting were yellowing. In addition, by 1991, when the action was commenced, the surface of the painting had cracked and some flaking had occurred in the lower right portion. The plaintiff took the position that the painting she was left with was not the painting she had contracted for.

The learned trial judge found that the painting was of merchantable quality when delivered, but that it maintained its original characteristics for barely five years instead of an expected 10-year economic life, which he found would not have been unreasonable. This was the basis of his judgment for the plaintiff for 50 per cent of the purchase price.

It was held by the Court of Appeal in England in *Robinson v. Graves*, [1935] 1 K.B. 579, [1935] All E.R. Rep. 935, that the oral commissioning of the plaintiff, an artist, to paint a portrait was not a contract for the sale of goods, but was a contract for work and labour. The defendant customer in that case repudiated the contract after the plaintiff had commenced to paint the portrait. The portrait was never completed, but the plaintiff was found to be entitled to recover damages for breach of contract, despite the absence of any memorandum in writing of the contract, as would have been required under the Sale of Goods Act. Greer L.J. said at p. 584:

> I can imagine that nothing would be more surprising to a client going to a portrait painter to have his portrait painted and to the artist who was accepting the commission than to be told that they were making a bargain about the sale of goods. It is, of course, possible that a picture may be ordered in such circumstances as will make it an order for goods to be supplied in the future, but it does not follow that that is the inference to be drawn in every case as between the client and the artist. Looking at the propositions involved from the point of view of interpreting the words in the English language it seems to me that the painting of a portrait in these circumstances would not, in the ordinary use of the English language, be deemed to be the purchase and sale of that which is produced by the artist. It would, on the contrary, be held to be an undertaking by the artist to exercise such skill as he was possessed of in order to produce for reward a thing which

would ultimately have to be accepted by the client. If that is so, the contract in this case was not a contract for the sale of goods within the meaning of s. 4 of the Sale of Goods Act, 1893.

At p. 585, he quoted with approval from the decision of Pollock C.B. in *Clay v. Yates* (1856), 1 H. & N. 73 at p. 78, 25 L.J. Ex. 237: "My impression is, that in the case of a work of art, whether in gold, silver, marble or plaster, where the application of skill and labour is of the highest description, and the material is of no importance as compared with the labour, the price may be recovered as work, labour and materials."

Greer L.J. continued at pp. 587-88:

> But if the substance of the contract, on the other hand, is that skill and labour have to be exercised for the production of the article and that it is only ancillary to that that there will pass from the artist to his client or customer some materials in addition to the skill involved in the production of the portrait, that does not make any difference to the result, because the substance of the contract is the skill and experience of the artist in producing the picture.
>
> For these reasons I am of opinion that in this case the substance of the matter was an agreement for the exercise of skill and it was only incidental that some materials would have to pass from the artist to the gentleman who commissioned the portrait. For these reasons I think that this was not a contract for the sale of goods within the meaning of s. 4 of the Sale of Goods Act, 1893, but it was a contract for work and labour and materials.

Slesser L.J. and Roche L.J. gave reasons to the same effect. During the course of his reasons, Roche L.J. said, at p. 593:

> . . . I have no doubt that the proper conclusion to be drawn is that this was a contract not for the sale of goods but for the employment of an artist to do work which the defendant desired that he should do.
>
> I am satisfied for the reasons given in *Robinson v. Graves* that the contract in the case at bar was not a contract to which the Sale of Goods Act applied, but was a contract for work and labour and materials.

The distinction between the two types of contract may be of no significance in the case at bar, because "a person contracting to do work and supply materials warrants that the materials which he uses will be of good quality and reasonably fit for the purpose for which he is using them, unless the circumstances of the contract are such as to exclude any such warranty" (per du Parcq J. in *G.H. Myers & Co. v. Brent Cross Service Co.*, [1934] 1 K.B. 46, applied in the House of Lords in *Young & Marten Ltd. v. McManus Childs Ltd.*, [1969] 1 A.C. 454 at pp. 468 and 471, [1968] 2 All E.R. 1169).

There was ample evidence to support the finding of a breach of the implied condition of merchantability, if the *Sale of Goods Act* had been applicable. That same evidence would support a finding of a breach of the warranty I have found to have existed that the materials used by the defendant would be of good quality and reasonably fit for a purpose for which he used them. The uncontradicted evidence of the plaintiff was that the defendant, when he saw the yellowing after three years, acknowledged its existence and told the plaintiff that the painting should not do that. The evidence of expert witnesses called by the plaintiff was that the yellowing resulted from the defendant's choice of materials and that the cracks were caused by the materials and techniques of the artist.

In my opinion, the learned trial judge was right in holding the defendant liable to the plaintiff for damages, but I find for the reasons given above that the contractual provision breached was different from the one found by the learned trial judge.

More importantly, I am unable to accept the assessment of damages by the learned trial judge. The reasons for the method of assessment used by him are given in the following passage from his reasons:

> There was really no evidence that the painting in this case had any market apart from the price which the plaintiff was willing to pay initially to have a custom painting of such magnitude. Its very size would undoubtedly be a large factor in resaleability. This of course touches on the question of procuring an acceptable substitute for the particular purpose.
>
> This was considered in the case of Sealand of the *Pacific v. Robert C. McHaffie Ltd.* (1974), 51 D.L.R. (3d) 702 (B.C.C.A.), again referred to by Waddams at p. 265.
>
> There can be no consideration in this instance to the measure of damages by reference to a resale value since the painting is still hanging in the plaintiff's home and had not been even appraised by the date of the trial.
>
> There was no suggestion that the plaintiff would not be content to have the painting continue to occupy its place of prominence in the plaintiff's home were it in a suitable condition. Since I have already concluded from the evidence, that suitable restoration, even if effected, could not be relied on to remedy the problem for any reasonable length of time, resale would only give rise to the problem again in the hands of any new owner.
>
> I have decided however that an expected ten-year economic life of the painting would not be unreasonable, whereas in fact the painting maintained its original characteristic for barely five.
>
> There will be judgment for the plaintiff for 50% of the purchase price, namely $2,000 plus court costs, plus added disbursements of $976.83.

His reference to "Waddams" was to S.M. Waddams, The Law of Damages (1983).

As to the cracking and lifting of the paint, Mr. Poulin, one of the experts, gave the opinion in his report that the paint cracking and lifting could be corrected as defects arose. The cost of such repairs would be a valid head of damages, but there must be evidence as to the amount of those costs. The burden of proving damages is, of course, on the plaintiff.

As to the diminished value of the painting, there was no evidence to support the decision by the learned trial judge that the painting should be taken as having an expected "economic life" of 10 years, or the conclusion, implicit in his assessment, that the painting had lost all its value. He pointed out that the painting was still hanging in the plaintiff's home and that it had not been appraised. The plaintiff cannot have her cake and eat it too.

The plaintiff is not the only person with a wall space large enough to accommodate the painting. As for its colour, there may be prospective purchasers for whom the yellowing is quite acceptable, or who might consider that it enhances the beauty of the painting. In my judgment, the plaintiff cannot recover damages under the heading of diminution in value, unless she offers the painting for sale in whatever is the appropriate manner for paintings of that type, and the response reflects a reduction in value.

For the foregoing reasons the appeal is allowed. The judgment below is set aside, and the action is referred back to the Small Claims Court for a new trial limited to the assessment of damages in accordance with these reasons.

Success on the appeal has been divided, but the plaintiff has successfully defended the finding of liability in her favour. The plaintiff will have one-half of her costs of the appeal, to be paid within 15 days. I fix the amount of that half at $300.

QUESTIONS

1. What standard would the seller have had to meet if this had been found to be a sale of goods?

2. Why did the court find that this was not a sale of goods?

3. The Small Claims judge awarded the plaintiff 50% of the purchase price of the painting as damages. How did the small claims judge justify that award?

4. The court disagreed with the Small Claims court judge's calculation of damages. How should damages be calculated?

Porelle v. Eddie's Auto Sales Ltd.

[1996] P.E.I.J. No. 9, 138 Nfld & PEIR 66

Prince Edward Island Supreme Court - Trial Division

Judgment: January 12, 1996.

Implied terms in the Sale of Goods Act protect purchasers of new and used goods. Those implied terms can be altered or negated by the contract of purchase and sale, though in many jurisdictions, there is consumer protection legislation that can give individual purchasers of new goods protection regardless of what the contract says. In the following case, the plaintiff is an individual purchaser of used goods.

1   **DesROCHES J.**:— The plaintiff, who resides in Cap Pelé, New Brunswick, purchased a used automobile from the defendant company, which is in the business of used automobile sales. The plaintiff testified he was attracted by an entry in Volume 94 Issue 31 of the Auto Trader wherein the defendant advertised for sale a 1988 Oldsmobile Delta 88 Royale. The advertisement includes the words "... just inspected, exc. cond. throughout ...." The advertised vehicle was said to have "127,000 hwy. kms", and the asking price was $4,995.

2   According to the plaintiff, when he spoke by telephone to Eddie Shea, the proprietor of the defendant company, he was informed the Auto Trader had mistakenly listed the vehicle as a 1988 whereas in fact it was a 1987. Eddie Shea's evidence, on the other hand, was that he told the plaintiff the advertised vehicle had been sold but he had in stock a 1987 Oldsmobile Delta 88 for which he was asking $1,000 less than the price of the 1988 model.

3   In any event, on August 6, 1994, the plaintiff, accompanied by his friend, Marie Landry, attended at the defendant's premises where, after taking the vehicle for a test drive, he purchased a 1987 Oldsmobile Delta 88 for a base price of $3,700. The price supports the testimony of Eddie Shea as to the identity of the vehicle purchased by the plaintiff, and had this conflict in the evidence become critical, I would have accepted the testimony of Shea over that of the plaintiff on this point. As will become clear, this case will be decided on a much more narrow basis.

4   The plaintiff also purchased a 12 month Lubrico power train warranty, but that as well does not impact on the determination of the issue between the plaintiff and the defendant.

5   During the test drive the plaintiff noted the engine stalled a few times. He mentioned this to Shea who replied it probably needed a tune-up. The plaintiff paid a total of $4,364.53 for the vehicle, including tax and the warranty, and drove the vehicle to his residence in New Brunswick. He began experiencing difficulties with the vehicle very soon after the sale, to the extent he ultimately on September 3 had to replace the engine at a cost of $2,141.42. He is also claiming for the cost of replacing the radiator and the rack and pinion.

6   In support of his claim the plaintiff relies on the *Sale of Goods Act R.S.P.E.I.* 1988, Cap. S-1 arguing there has been a breach of an implied warranty of fitness. The plaintiff has also argued the defendant engaged in an unfair practice as that phrase is defined in the Business Practices Act, R.S.P.E.I. 1988, Cap. B-7, and relies on ss. 2, 3 and 4 of that Act. In the circumstances of, and based on the evidence presented in, this case, I find the Business Practices Act does not advance the plaintiff's claim.

7   Section 16(a) of the *Sale of Goods Act* reads as follows:

16. *Subject to this Act and any statute in that behalf, there is no implied warranty or condition as to the quality or fitness for any particular purpose of goods supplied under a contract of sale, except as follows:*

   (a) *where a buyer, expressly or by implication, makes known to the seller the particular purpose for which the goods are required, so as to show that the buyer relies on the seller's skill or judgment, and the goods are of a description which it is in the course of the seller's business to supply, whether he is the manufacturer or not, there is an implied condition that the goods are reasonably fit for that purpose; but in the case of a contract for the sale of a specified article under its patent or other trade name, there is no implied condition as to its fitness for any particular purpose;*

8   The *Act* goes on at s. 16(d) as follows:

(d) an express warranty or condition does not negative a warranty or condition implied by this Act unless inconsistent therewith.

9   In this case there certainly are express conditions in the sales contract signed by the plaintiff which are inconsistent with the warranty or condition implied by the Act. In particular, on the front of the contract there is a highlighted portion which contains the following exclusionary clause:

You have purchased a used vehicle. We the dealer are not responsible for any repairs after date of purchase unless stated on contact in writing.

10   There is nothing stated on the contract which would render the defendant responsible for any repairs.

11   In addition to the exclusionary clause quoted above, the back of the sales contract contains the "Conditions of Sale" including:

> It is expressly agreed that there are no Conditions, no Warranties (either legal or conventional or contractual, including the legal Warranty for latent defects, the Warranty printed on the back hereof being hereby expressly accepted in lieu of all other Warranties) or Representations, express or implied, statutory or otherwise, made by the Dealer or the Manufacturer, its Officers or Agents, on the Motor Vehicle, Chassis or Part furnished hereunder, nor shall any Agreement collateral hereto be binding upon the Dealer unless endorsed hereon in writing.

12   The plaintiff testified specifically that he read and understood the exclusionary clause on the front of the contract. Furthermore, immediately above his signature there appears the following wording:

> I HAVE READ THE MATTER on the back hereof and agree to it as part of this Order the same as if it were printed above my signature.

> THE FRONT AND BACK of this order comprise the entire agreement effecting this purchase and no other agreement or understanding of any nature concerning the same has been made.

> THIS ORDER IS NOT BINDING and does not constitute an Agreement on the part of the Dealer until it is Accepted in Writing. I accept delivery of this vehicle with full knowledge of the terms and conditions of sale.

13   The facts in this case are almost identical to those in *Gafco Enterprises Ltd. v. Schofield*, [1983] 4 W.W.R. 135 (Alta. C.A.) in which the purchase agreement for the sale of a used vehicle, a two page document, had on the face of the document in large, clear print the words: "The purchaser understands and agrees that one of the following applies", followed by the applicable alternative clause "no warranty of any kind". Further, on the back of the document were a number of paragraphs setting out the terms of the agreement, including a paragraph similar to that contained on the reverse of the sales contract in the instant case. At the bottom of the front page of the agreement in *Gafco*, just above the purchaser's signature, were the words:

> 1.   I/We have read and understand the terms of the back hereof and agree to them as part of this Agreement as if they were printed above my/our signature.

> The front and back of this order comprise the entire agreement effecting this purchase and no other agreement or understanding of any nature concerning the same has been made.

14   Delivering the judgment of the court, Harradence J.A. applied the decision of Chief Justice Hughes of New Brunswick in *Peters v. Parkway Mercury Sales Ltd.* (1975), 58 D.L.R. (3d) 128 and concluded that, in the circumstances, the defects in the vehicle did not amount to a breach going to the root of the contract. In reaching his conclusion, Harradence J.A. says this at p. 142:

> ... it is now clear that there is no substantive rule of law that nullifies an exclusionary clause where there has been a fundamental breach. The question of whether there has been a fundamental breach or whether an exclusionary clause is applicable to such a breach is to be determined according to a true construction of the entire contract, including any exclusionary or exemption clauses contained

therein. Within the limits that exemption clauses should not be construed so as to deprive one party's stipulations of all contractual force, they must be given effect where their meaning is plain.

15   The learned justice found that the agreement was clearly and unambiguously worded to waive, in that case, the protection of the *Sale of Goods Act*, R.S.A. 1970, c. 327. He concluded that the terms of the agreement when taken together with the words "no warranty of any kind" made it clear the parties contemplated that the risk of defects in the vehicle was to be borne by the buyer.

16   A similar situation arose in *Feucht v. Paccar of Canada Ltd.* (1985), 61 A.R. 328 (Alta. Q.B.) in which Prowse J. applied the decision of the Alberta Court of Appeal in *Gafco*, and the decision of Hughes, C.J.N.B. in *Peters* (supra), and concluded that, although he had some sympathy for the plaintiff, there was no doubt in his mind the plaintiff acknowledged in his evidence he understood the meaning of purchasing a vehicle on an "as is" basis and realized he was waiving in the agreement any claim he might have in the event the vehicle (in that case a used dump truck) was defective.

17   In the case at bar, the exclusionary clause on the face of the contract, the additional clauses on the reverse of the document, and the plaintiff's knowledge of those clauses when he signed the contract, lead me to conclude, reluctantly, that the plaintiff's claim must be dismissed. The often quoted words of Lord Denning, M.R. in *Bartlett v. Sydney Marcus, Ltd.*, [1965] 2 All E.R. 753 are applicable here. At p. 755 the learned Master of the Rolls says:

> A buyer should realize that, when he buys a secondhand car, defects may appear sooner or later; and, in the absence of an express warranty, he has no redress.

18   Were it not for the specific exclusionary clauses of the contract, the plaintiff in the instant case could have relied on the implied warranty contained in the *Sale of Goods Act*. Unfortunately he cannot do so.

19   I do not know if any offers to settle were made. In the absence of such offers affecting the issue of costs, I would exercise my discretion on the matter of costs and, given the plaintiff had to expend some $3,300 to ensure the vehicle he purchased from the defendant continued to function, I would order the parties to bear their own costs.

QUESTIONS

1. The court refers to a statement of Lord Denning in the *Bartlett v. Sydney Marcus Ltd.* case in which he says that generally when a buyer buys a used car, in the absence of an express warranty, the buyer has no redress when defects appear. Explain why this is true.

2. When a buyer can show that there has been a fundamental breach of contract, an exemption clause may not protect the seller. What is a fundamental breach of contract?

3. In *Gafco Enterprises Ltd. v. Schofield*, Harradence J.A. suggested that it may be possible to draft a contract so that liability for fundamental breach is excluded. How might such an exclusion be worded to protect the seller?

4. Would the result of the *Porelle* case have been different had the seller known at the time of sale that the car required substantial engine repairs?

Kovacs v. Holtom

[1997] A.J. No. 775

Alberta Provincial Court

The *Sale of Goods Act* includes rules that apply to determine when property (title) passes from seller to buyer, unless the parties show an intention that differs from those rules. One reason that it is important to determine when property passes, is that generally the party holding title will also bear the risk in the event of loss of or damage to the goods.

LeGRANDEUR PROV. CT. J.:—

Nature of Proceedings

1   In this case the Plaintiff claims from the Defendant the return of the purchase price of a certain motor vehicle she contracted to purchase from the Defendant, or alternatively the value of the vehicle which she contracted to purchase and which was destroyed in a fire while in the possession of the Defendant.

Facts

2   The facts of this case are as follows. In 1992 the Plaintiff attended the home of the Defendant with the view to purchasing a motor vehicle. She had come to know of the Defendant through a friend of his, one Don Pike. When the Plaintiff met with the Defendant he showed her pictures of the work he had done in restoring automobiles and after viewing the photographs and discussing the matter with the Defendant, the Plaintiff agreed to purchase from the Defendant a 1963 Falcon Futura convertible for the sum of $2,500.00. At the root of this transaction was the fact that the Defendant was to retain the vehicle for purposes of restoring it. The Plaintiff was in fact purchasing a restored 1963 vehicle for $2,500.00. The Defendant was to do the restoration and the vehicle remained with him. The Plaintiff paid the $2,500.00 up front.

3   On May 20th, 1995, the vehicle was, for all intents and purposes, destroyed by a fire that occurred in the garage owned by the Defendant and in which the automobile being restored was located. At the time of the fire the Defendant had undertaken considerable work on the vehicle as is shown by the Summary of Material and Labour (Exhibit #1) which reflects the restorative work done. The Plaintiff took no issue with the substance of that exhibit.

4   At the time the fire occurred, the restorative process was not complete, nor had the Defendant notified the Plaintiff that the restoration had been completed. The vehicle was still in the possession of the Defendant for purposes of completing the restoration. The fire destroyed the subject vehicle along with three other vehicles owned by the Defendant located in the garage. The Plaintiff admitted that the presumed cause of the fire was arson by a person or persons unknown.

Issues Before the Court

5   The issue that is presented by the pleadings and the facts as found aforesaid is whether the Defendant is liable to the Plaintiff for the loss of the car and if so, what remedy does the Plaintiff have against the Defendant.

Analysis

6   The Dispute Note filed on behalf of the Defendant denied liability alleging that the Plaintiff had assumed the risk relative to the loss of the motor vehicle. In argument, Defence counsel also argued that at worst, this was a bailment situation and that the Defendant had discharged the onus upon him of demonstrating that he exercised due and reasonable care for the safety of the Plaintiff's motor vehicle in his custody.

7   At the conclusion of the case, I raised with the parties the issue of whether property in the motor vehicle had passed from the Defendant to the Plaintiff at the time of the fire. It is this issue that I intend to address first.

Transfer of Property

8   Whether the property in a specific good has passed or not is dependant upon what the parties intended. Section 20(1) of the *Sale of Goods Act*, R.S.A. 1980. Chap. S-2, as amended provides:

> *"When there is a contract for the sale of specific or ascertained goods, the property in them is transferred to the buyer at the time that the parties to the contract intend it to be transferred."*

9   Lord Watson in the case of *McEntire v. Crossley Brothers Ltd.*, [1985] A.C. 457 stated the principal thus:

> "It does not in the least follow that, because there is an agreement of sale and purchase, the property in the thing which is the subject matter of the contract has passed to the purchaser. That is a question which entirely depends upon the intention of the parties. The law permits them to settle the point for themselves by an expression of their intention upon the point."

10   Section 20(2) of the *Sale of Goods Act*, supra provides:

> *"For the purpose of ascertaining the intention of the parties, regard shall be had to the terms of the contract, the conduct of the parties and the circumstances of the case."*

11   Section 21(1) of the *Sale of Goods Act*, supra provides:

"Unless a different intention appears the rules set out in this section are the rules for ascertaining the intention of the parties as to the time at which the property in the goods is to pass to the buyer."

12   And further Section 21(3) of the said *Act* states:

"When there is a contract for the sale of specific goods and the seller is bound to do something to the goods for the purpose of putting them into a deliverable state, the property does not pass until the thing is done and the buyer has notice thereof."

13   The question thus becomes, whether the terms of the contract, the conduct of the parties and/or the circumstance of the case demonstrate an intention different from that expressed in s. 21(3) of the *Sales of Goods Act*. It is clear on the evidence that if the section applies, property in the subject motor vehicle had not passed to the Plaintiff at the time of the fire. The car purchased by the Plaintiff had been retained by the Defendant for the purpose of putting it into a deliverable state within the context of the agreement between the parties. The thing to be done, that is the restoration of the vehicle had not been completed as at the time of the fire and the item was therefore not in a deliverable state. Section 2(3) of the *Sale of Goods Act*, supra states:

"Goods are in a 'deliverable state' within the meaning of this act when they are in such a state that the buyer would under the contract be bound to take delivery of them."

14   It was fundamental to the agreement that the Falcon motor vehicle be restored. Clearly that restoration had not been completed.

15   The fact that the Plaintiff paid the purchase price to the Defendant prior to restoration does not in my view indicate a mutual intention that property pass. In this regard, I adopt the reasoning of Dennistown, J.A. of the Saskatchewan Court of Appeal in the case of *McDill v. Hillson*, [1920] 2 W.W.R. 877 at pp. 880-81 where he states:

"Payment of the purchase price was not a waiver of the condition which the defendant failed to perform. The Act is silent on this point unless the Court can infer that when the money was paid over it was the intention of the parties, evidenced thereby, that the title should pass. I am unable to draw that inference from the evidence. The plaintiff and his wife were unwilling to buy the furniture in the condition in which they saw it. The defendant agreed to renovate it by an expert at some expense and to deliver it at the plaintiffs address. The plaintiff relying on the defendant's undertaking to have the work done, paid over his money; but the contract remained executory on the defendant's part and on his breach of the stipulated condition was subject to cancellation. Performance having become impossible by reason of the destruction of the specific articles sold, the plaintiff was justified in declaring it at an end and in demanding his money back."

16   Given the contract as a whole and having regard to the circumstance of the case, I can find no evidence that satisfies me that the parties ever put their minds to the issue of when the property would pass. Given the lack of such a clear or identifiable intention otherwise, in the contract itself, or the conduct of the parties, or otherwise, s. 21(3) of the *Sale of Goods Act*, supra, must apply (see *Royal Bank v. Saskatchewan et al.*, [1985] 5 W.W.R. 333) and accordingly title and ownership of the motor vehicle had not passed to the Plaintiff at the time the fire destroyed the subject motor vehicle.

Plaintiff's Remedy

17   Given the finding that the property in the 1963 Falcon Futura had not passed at the time of the destruction of the subject matter of the contract and since the Defendant is not in a position to perform the original agreement within a reasonable time, the Plaintiff is entitled to declare the agreement at an end and receive the return of her money.

18   The Plaintiff will accordingly have a judgment against the Defendant for the sum of $2,500.00.

Judgment Interest

19   The Plaintiff did not claim for interest in her pleadings and the Court accordingly awards no interest.

Costs

20   The Plaintiff shall have the following costs which shall be added to and become part of the judgment:

1. Cost of issuing claim		$25.00
2. Costs of Service		$ 5.00
3. Costs associated with attending Court in Lethbridge		$50.00
	TOTAL:	$80.00

Final Judgment

21   The Plaintiff shall have judgment against the Defendant, inclusive of costs, in the total sum of $2,580.00.

QUESTIONS

1. Why does the court say that this was a sale of specific goods, rather than a sale of unascertained goods?
2. What does the *Sale of Goods Act* say about when property in goods passes to the buyer in this situation?
3. What actions would have had to take place for the court to find that the goods belonged to the buyer?
4. Assume that the facts were as set out in this case, but that the seller had become insolvent as a result of the fire. What position would the buyer have been in regarding recovery of the $2500 she had paid to the seller?

chapter seventeen

Bailment

Lakeside Commission Agency Ltd. v. Saskatchewan Wheat Pool

[1990] S.J. No. 350
Saskatchewan Court of Queen's Bench
July 10, 1990

Bailment is a situation in which someone is in possession of goods belonging to another party. An important issue relating to bailment is what standard of care pertains while the bailee has possession of the goods. The standard of care will vary according to the nature of the bailment.

MacLEAN J.:— This is an appeal by the Saskatchewan Wheat Pool (the Pool) from a judgment of Andrychuk, P.C.J. in which he awarded Lakeside Commission Agency Ltd. (Lakeside) the sum of $931.14.

The trial judge found that on February 17, 1988, Lakeside purchased nine head of cattle from the Pool at an auction sale held at the Pool's stockyard facility at Yorkton, Sask. He found also that Lakeside received only eight of the animals it purchased; one animal having mysteriously disappeared. The issue for determination is which party must bear the loss.

Briefly, the facts are as follows. The Pool conducts regular sales at which large numbers of cattle are sold by auction. John Debalinhard, President of Lakeside, has for many years purchased cattle at these sales. Lakeside is hired by local farmers to purchase cattle on their behalf. On the day in question, Lakeside purchased the nine animals on behalf of a Yorkton area farmer.

Lakeside arranged for Tom Rowley to transport the animals to the customer. Late in the afternoon on the day of sale, Mr. Rowley arrived to take delivery of the cattle. He obtained a "Pass Out" (a document allowing him to obtain possession of the animals) from a Pool employee. Another Pool employee brought all nine head from a holding pen to the loading area. Mr. Rowley has a small stock trailer and was unable to take all nine animals in one load. Five animals were loaded. The four remaining animals were taken by the Pool's employee back to the holding pen to await Rowley's return. An hour or two later when he returned, only three of the animals could be found. Despite an extensive search of its yard and its records, the Pool could find no trace of the missing animal.

The learned trial judge ruled that in the circumstances, title to the animals did not pass to Lakeside when the hammer fell at the auction sale, but rather when they were delivered to Mr. Rowley. Since one animal was not delivered, he ruled the sale as far as this animal was concerned was not complete and hence the price of this animal he ordered refunded. In my respectful opinion, he erred in concluding that title to the animals passed only on delivery.

Section 57(2) of *The Sale of Goods Act* S.S. c. S-1 reads as follows:

> *57. In the case of a sale of auction:*
>
> *2. A sale by auction is complete when the auctioneer announces its completion by the fall of the hammer or in other customary manner. Until such announcement is made a bidder may retract his bid.*

In my view, s.57(2) of *The Sale of Goods Act* applies to all auction sales absent special rules which may be announced by the auctioneer. There is no suggestion in the evidence that the sale in this case was conducted according to any special rules or conditions. In my opinion, this was an ordinary auction sale where the sale was completed and the property passed to Lakeside upon the fall of the auctioneer's hammer.

This, however, does not end the matter. Mr. Grubb submitted, and I agree, the Pool became a bailee of the purchaser pending delivery of the animals. In my opinion, in the circumstances of this case, the Pool was a bailee for value. The standard of care required of such bailee has been outlined in a multitude of cases including several in this court. Among these is *Duncan v. Allen and Gold Dust Manufacturing Jewellers Ltd. et al.* (1984) 28 Sask. R. 177, a decision of my brother Grotsky, who at p. 180 said:

> Where goods are delivered to a bailee to be taken care of by him in return for remuneration to be paid by the bailor, the contract is one of custody for reward. The bailee must take reasonable care of the chattels, according to the circumstances of the particular case.

At p. 181 of the same judgment, Mr. Justice Grotsky adopted the following excerpt from 2 Hals. (3rd Ed.), para. 225, pp. 114-5:

> Care and diligence. A custodian for reward is bound to use due care and diligence in keeping and preserving the article entrusted to him on behalf of the bailor. The standard of care and diligence imposed on him is higher than that required of a gratuitous depositary, and must be that care and diligence which a careful and vigilant man would exercise in the custody of his own chattels of a similar description and character in similar circumstances.

In *Houghland v. R.R. Low (Luxury Coaches Ltd.)*, [1962] 1 Q.B. 694, Ormerod L.J. put the matter thus:

> "... it appears to me that the standard of care required in a case of bailment, or any other type of case, is the standard demanded by the circumstances of the particular case".

A few lines further down he said:

> The question that we have to consider in a case of this kind, if it is necessary to consider negligence, is whether in the circumstances of this particular case a sufficient standard of care has been observed by the defendants or their servants.

The question in this case is can the Pool avoid responsibility for the loss by saying as it does; "we have checked all our records and our stockyard and the animal cannot be found". In my opinion, the Pool cannot absolve itself by establishing that the animal mysteriously disappeared. The Pool failed on a preponderance of the evidence to prove that it cared for Lakeside's animals in a careful and diligent manner. I, therefore, dismiss the appeal with costs.

QUESTIONS

1. Explain why the buyer was the owner of the animals at the time the loss occurred.
2. Was this a contractual or a gratuitous bailment?
3. What standard of care did the court apply?
4. On which party did the court place the burden of proof?
5. Why is it sometimes advantageous to sue under the law of bailment rather than under the law of negligence?

chapter eighteen

Insurance

**Rider v. North Waterloo
Farmers Mutual Insurance Co.**

[1991] O.J. No. 283, 2 C.C.L.I. (2d) 273
Ontario Court of Justice - General Division
January 22, 1991.

A key principle that applies to insurance law is that the insured must have an insurable interest in the thing that is being insured. If there is no insurable interest, the insurer can deny coverage when a loss has been suffered, even though the insured has paid premiums for coverage. In this case, the court considered what constitutes an insurable interest.

COSTELLO J.:— This was a motion for judgment upon an agreed upon Statement of Facts.

The action concerns a claim under a fire insurance policy. The amount of the loss was $27,000.00 and it was caused by a fire of accidental origin. The plaintiff, the registered owner of the property, on which the burned building was situated, and the named insured on the fire insurance policy, made a claim on the policy.

The defense originally consisted of an allegation that there had been a material change in the risk of which the defendant had not been informed. After discoveries the defendant applied for and was granted leave to amend to allege that the named insured was not the owner and therefore had no insurable interest.

Paragraphs 17 to 18.1 of the agreed-upon Statement of Facts deal with the items of defense contained in the amended Statement of Defense. They read as follows

> "17. At the time of the loss, and beforehand, the beneficial owner of the Rider lands was Joe Rider. He looked after payment of insurance proceeds, mortgage payments, taxes, and received the rentals from the property.

> 18. The Plaintiff never received a copy of the policy from the North Waterloo nor did she have any dealings with the agent who issued it. She was not concerned with particulars of the insurance coverage on the property because Joe Rider took responsibility for it.

> 18.1 The property had been transferred to the Plaintiff because her brother Joe Rider could not hold it in his own name for personal reasons. At the time of the fire Joe Rider had the right to direct the Plaintiff to transfer the property as well. The Plaintiff personally did not pay any money for the transfer of the Rider lands to her."

Dealing with the defense raised in the amended Statement of Defense I have read and reread the case law submitted on the motion and with some regret find that that defense must prevail.

The courts have gone a long way to find insurable interests to exist in persons, including corporate persons, who have paid the premium over the years only to be faced with technical objections after a loss. The courts in recent years have pierced the corporate veil to award a sole shareholder an insurable interest although the damaged property was the property of his corporation; going contrary to a line of cases which for a century had rejected claims by insured stockholders who did not themselves own the property they had insured in their own names.

I tried to find in the judgment of Madam Justice Wilson in *Constitution Insurance Co. of Canada v. Kosmopoulos*, [1987] I.L.R. 8297 some justification for not following *Marks v. Commonwealth Insurance Co.* (1974), 2 O.R. (2d) 237 but I could not. All the cases in which an insured had been held to have an insurable interest are cases where, as in the *Kosmopoulos* case, the sole shareholder had in fact an interest and had in fact suffered a loss. There were cases where the lien holder or a lessee was held to have an insurable interest or a corporation in its corporate subsidiary see *Kosmopoulos* at page 8299. Even a lawyer who lost a vault full of clients' wills was held to have an insurable interest and collected for the time and material spent drafting and having the wills re-executed. (*Dudelzak & Landry v. Madill* 13 C.C.L.I. 94.) Always the theme throughout is that the claimant had a financial interest in the thing insured and suffered a financial loss in the thing's destruction.

Marks v. Commonwealth Insurance Co. (1974), 2 O.R. (2d) 37 is binding on me as an Ontario Court of Appeal judgment unless it has been overruled, which it has not been, or can be distinguished on its facts which I am unable to do.

In that case the named insured and registered owner of the burned building was held not to be the beneficial owner of the property. She had not paid for the property. She received no income from the rental property. Her husband, who was held to be the beneficial owner, entered into an agreement to sell the property with a third party.

In the case at bar, Mrs. Agnes Rider took paper title to the property because her brother, Joseph Rider could not hold it in his own name "for personal reasons." Agnes Rider did not pay anything for the property. Joseph Rider looked after insurance payments, mortgage payments, taxes and he received the rentals from the property. She said as well that Joseph Rider had the right to tell her how to dispose of the property.

In Insurance Law in Canada by Craig Brown and Julio Maneses, (1982, Carswell Co. Ltd.) at item 4:3:4 headed "Bare Legal Title" I quote,

> "4:3:4. Bare Legal Title. Notwithstanding that a whole range of interests, such as trustees, etc., with no beneficial claim, have been held to be sufficient as insurable interests, the question has been raised whether bare legal title with no pecuniary interest can support an insurance policy. There is no perceptible basis for this concern. To find against such policies directly on the basis of lack of insurable interest is in fact to argue that legal title is not an interest recognized by the common law, an apparent absurdity. The insured, with no more than legal title to the property may, however, be denied recovery under the policy on the grounds of misrepresentation. Also the principal of indemnity would be violated if the insured were to recover more than he lost. The basis of that defence is not that the legal title is inadequate to support a valid policy, but that the policy only insured the interest of the named insured and since the loss to that insured is nil, that is the extent of the recovery.

The plaintiff Mildred Agnes Rider has not demonstrated an insurable interest and has not shown that she suffers any loss as a result of the fire. As a result she cannot recover and her case is dismissed with costs if asked.

The case proceeded on an agreed-upon Statement of Facts so it is not necessary for me to make any findings of fact or credibility for the benefit of an appellate court.

It is not necessary or desirable for me to make any findings on the other matters raised in the pleadings or the Statement of Fact by either party.

QUESTIONS

1. What would the plaintiff have to demonstrate to show that she had an insurable interest in the property? Why was the plaintiff found not to have had an insurable interest in the property in this case?

2. Does one need to be the owner of property in order to have an insurable interest in it? Explain.

3. Give examples of situations in which non-owners might be found to have insurable interests in the property they insured.

4. Can you think of a reason why the beneficial owner of the property might

   a) not have taken title to the property in his own name?

   b) not have applied for insurance coverage in his own name?

chapter nineteen

Agency and Franchising

Douglas, Symes & Brissenden v. C.M. Oliver & Co.

[1997] B.C.J. No. 1626
British Columbia Supreme Court
Judgment: filed July 7, 1997.

A principal will be liable for contracts made on its behalf by its representative if it gave the representative authority to contract on its behalf, or if it put the representative in a position where the representative appeared to have that authority. A person who puts another party in a position that appears to carry authority must take particular care if there is an intention to avoid responsibility for what the other party does.

1   **DISTRICT REGISTRAR WELLBURN**:— This is a review of a solicitor's bill totaling $3,683.19. There is no dispute as to the amount of the bill or the value of the services. The only issue is whether C.M. Oliver & Company Ltd. ("C.M. Oliver") retained the solicitors.

2   On May 2, 1996, the solicitor, Mr. DeFilippi, met with an existing client, Richard Bullock, who introduced him to Nolan Moss, who was an account broker with C.M. Oliver and Craig Robson, who was introduced as the compliance officer at C.M. Oliver.

3   Mr. Moss described a scheme whereby a Mr. Rodney and some associates and companies within their control opened accounts with a number of brokerage houses including five accounts at C.M. Oliver, where Mr. Moss acted as the broker. The scheme involved a reverse takeover of a company listed on the Alberta Stock Exchange, Ultra Pure, by a company incorporated in the Turks and Caicos Islands. The stock price was inflated by trading between the accounts until the Alberta Stock Exchange ceased trading of Ultra Pure stock. The result was a $2.3 million debt owing to the brokerage houses, including some $800,000 owing to C.M. Oliver.

4   Mr. Moss asked Mr. DeFilippi for his advice as to whether C.M. Oliver had a claim against any of the individuals or companies involved, including Mr. Rodney; what remedies were available; and whether a claim was worth pursuing. Mr. DeFilippi stated that Mr. Moss would be "the point man" with whom he would communicate. Mr. Robson said very little and his presence at the meeting was not explained.

5   Mr. Robson attended the meeting on May 2nd at the invitation of Mr. Moss. Mr. Robson is the compliance officer and the senior vice president in charge of risk management with C.M. Oliver. C.M. Oliver holds its brokers responsible for any losses in their accounts and was pursuing Mr. Moss for the losses arising from the trading activities of Mr. Rodney and his associates. C.M. Oliver withheld Mr. Moss' earnings to recover a portion of the losses.

6   Mr. Robson had suggested to Mr. Moss that he might want to retain a lawyer to try to recover some of the money relating to the transactions. Mr. Robson had advised Mr. Moss that C.M. Oliver had no interest in pursuing the litigation because in Mr. Robson's view pursuing such a claim would be fruitless.

7   The agreement between C.M. Oliver and its brokers that the brokers repay any losses on their accounts is based on industry practice and internal policies of C.M. Oliver which were not communicated to Mr. DeFilippi.

8   After the meeting, Mr. Moss discussed the matter further with Mr. DeFilippi and sent him the account agreements, account statements, trading records and the original C.M. Oliver files, which Mr. DeFilippi arranged to have photocopied and returned to Mr. Moss at C.M. Oliver. There was no retainer agreement concerning the services of the solicitors.

9   Mr. DeFilippi carried out his investigations and learned that Mr. Rodney was a well known scoundrel in the Turks and Caicos Islands, that it was unlikely that any money would be recovered from him, and that there were no assets available for execution in British Columbia or in the state of Washington. He recommended that C.M. Oliver take no action with respect to the matter.

10   Mr. DeFilippi's correspondence indicates that he understood C.M. Oliver to be his client. He did not discuss the necessity of Mr. Moss obtaining an assignment of the debt to C.M. Oliver which would have been necessary for Mr. Moss to pursue the action on his own behalf.

11   On August 23, 1996, Mr. DeFilippi sent his bill to C.M. Oliver to the attention of Mr. Moss. He sent a number of follow-up letters to which he received no response. Mr. DeFilippi telephoned Mr. Robson on March 4, 1997 and was advised that there was an issue as to whether C.M. Oliver ought to pay the account.

12   Counsel for C.M. Oliver argues that Mr. Moss had no authority to retain Mr. DeFilippi, and Mr. Robson, who did have authority, did not have the intention to retain Mr. DeFilippi. Her submission is that Mr. Robson's silence at the initial meeting cannot support a finding that Mr. Moss had authority to enter into a retainer agreement on behalf of C.M. Oliver.

13   The solicitors submit that Mr. Moss had the apparent or ostensible authority to retain them to perform the services rendered and that C.M. Oliver is therefore estopped from denying liability for payment for those services. In my view, these principles govern the situation so it is not necessary for me to deal with the other legal arguments made.

14   The relevant legal concepts are described by Lord Diplock in *Freeman v. Buckhurst Park Properties et al* [1964] 1 All E.R. 630 (at 644):

> The representation which creates "apparent" authority may take a variety of forms of which the commonest is representation by conduct, i.e. by permitting the agent to act in some way in the conduct of the principal's business with other persons. By so doing, the principal represent to anyone who becomes aware that the agent is so acting that the agent has authority to enter on behalf of the principal into contracts with other persons of the kind which an agent so acting in the conduct of his principal's business has normally "actual" authority to enter into.

15   Lord Diplock went on to describe four conditions which must be met to entitle a contractor to enforce a contract against a company entered into on behalf of the company by an agent who had no actual authority to do so (at page 646):

It must be shown:

(a) that a representation that the agent had authority to enter on behalf of the company into a contract of the kind sought to be enforced was made to the contractor;

(b) that such representation was made by a person or persons who had "actual" authority to manage the business of the company, either generally or in respect of those matters to which the contract relates;

(c) that he (the contractor) was induced by such representation to enter into the contract, i.e. that he had in fact relied on it; and

(d) that under its memorandum or articles of association the company was not deprived of the capacity either to enter into a contract of the kind sought to be enforced or to delegate authority to enter into a contract of that kind to the agent.

16   Both Mr. Moss and Mr. Robson attended the meeting of May 2nd when Mr. Moss outlined the nature of the problem and sought advice from Mr. DeFilippi with respect to the debt owed to C.M. Oliver. I find that these facts support a finding that Mr. Robson's attendance at the meeting was a representation to Mr. DeFilippi that Mr. Moss could retain the solicitors to act for C.M. Oliver with respect to the matter.

17   Mr. Robson, senior vice president and compliance officer, had the authority to bind C.M. Oliver to a contractual arrangement. Mr. DeFilippi was induced by the representation to perform legal services for the benefit of C.M. Oliver. There was no evidence that the company, C.M. Oliver, did not have the capacity to enter into an agreement to retain the solicitors. These facts fulfil the remaining three conditions.

18   I find that C.M. Oliver retained the solicitors and is liable for payment of the account. I will sign a certificate in the amount of $3,683.19 plus court order interest.

19   Although the solicitors have been successful, I note that the only issue was that of the retainer. The hearing would not have been necessary if the solicitors had drafted a written retainer agreement or attempted to confirm their retainer in writing. I find that these are special circumstances as provided in s. 78(11) of the Legal Profession Act and award no costs with respect to this matter.

QUESTIONS

1. What circumstances must exist for a principal to be bound by apparent authority?
2. What created the appearance of authority in this case?
3. What should the defendant have done to avoid being responsible for the legal bill?

City Press Inc. v. Green (c.o.b. B & G Print & Litho)

[1996] O.J. No. 1823, 6 OTC 311
Ontario Court of Justice (General Division)
Judgment: May 13, 1996.

When one is representing a principal, it is important to make one's representative capacity clear in all dealings. The following case illustrates the danger that exists if one fails to do so.

1   **LOFCHIK J**.:— The issue in this case is whether the defendant, Edward Green is personally liable to the plaintiff for the cost of goods sold and delivered by the plaintiff to "B & G Litho". The evidence is that the plaintiff company did some printing and provided some material ordered from it by Edward Green to be included in a book being published by "B & G Print and Litho". The plaintiff issued an invoice to "B & G Print and Litho" which remains unpaid.

2   The evidence was that the plaintiff company had had prior dealings with B & G Print and Litho in November of 1974 although the representative of B & G Print and Litho at that time may have been an individual other than the defendant Edward Green, namely Ian Barnes. On the prior occasion invoices were issued by the plaintiff to B & G Print and Litho (Exhibits 4 and 5 dated November 17, 1994) which were subsequently paid by cheques forming part of Exhibit 6 drawn on the Avestel Credit Union Limited, which cheques have the account name at the top as "B & G Printing" and above the signing line have the words "B & G Printing Account 0849285" and were signed by Edward Green.

3   It was the evidence of James Schofield, the President of the plaintiff company that the plaintiff took a Credit Application from B & G when they first commenced their dealing and there was marked as Exhibit 8 in this action a Credit Application in which the company name of the customer is "B & G Print & Litho".

4   There is a line on the application headed "Name of Principals" under which is printed the name Edward Green and his title being indicated as President. The application is dated April 2, 1994 and signed by Edward Green with the title President beside his name at the bottom of the application.

5   It should be noted that there is also a blank space on the Credit Application entitled "Parent Company" which was not filled in on the Credit Application. It was the evidence of Mr. Green that the Credit Application was filled in in all probability by Ian Barnes and signed by himself although he may have signed it before the application itself was completed.

6   There was filed as Exhibit 7 in the action, a Ministry of Consumer and Commercial Relations Registration Form under the Business Names Act indicating that "B & G Printing" was a business carried on by 983074 Ontario Inc. at 31 Bigwin Road, Unit #6, Hamilton, Ontario, the same address as appears on B & G Printing cheques and the same address as to which the plaintiff's invoices in their dealings with B & G were sent.

7   The invoice which is the subject matter of this action is dated December 31, 1994 and marked as Exhibit 1 in this action. It is addressed to "B & G Print and Litho, 31 Bigwin Road, Hamilton, Ontario L8W 3R3" and it is in the amount of $19,912.70.

8   It is the position of the plaintiff that it at all times was contracting with Edward Green, a principal of B & G Print and Litho and was at no time contracting with a limited company. The position of the defendant is that B & G Print and Litho is a business carried on by 983074 Ontario Inc. and that he was contracting on behalf of that entity.

9   By failing to fill in the name of the numbered company on the blank line beside the heading "Parent Company" on the Credit Application provided to the plaintiff company the defendant Green had the opportunity to disclose that he was acting on behalf of a numbered company and failed to do so.

10   The *Business Corporations Act R.S.O.* 1990, c. B.16, s. 10(1) provides as follows:

"10. (1) The word "Limited", "Limitee", "Incorporated", "Incorporee" or "Corporation" or the corresponding abbreviations "Ltd.", "Ltee", "Inc." or "Corp" shall be part, in addition to any use in a figurative or descriptive sense, of the name of every corporation, but a corporation may be legally designated by either the full or the abbreviated form."

11   Section 10.(5) of the same statute provides as follows:

"10.(5) A corporation shall set out its name in legible characters in all contracts, invoices, negotiable instruments and orders for goods or serrvices issued or made by or on behalf of the corporation ... "

12   The *Business Names Act, R.S.O.* 1990, c. B17 as s. 2.(6) provides as follows:

"A Corporation and such other persons as are prescribed carrying on business under a registered name or, in the case of a Corporation, identifying itself to the public under a registered name, shall set out both the registered name and the person's name in all contracts, invoices, negotiable instruments and orders involving goods or services issued or made by the person."

13   Considering all of the foregoing, I find that as no representative of the Plaintiff was advised that B & G Print & Litho was in effect, a registered name of an incorporated company or that the Defendant, Edward Green was acting on behalf of an incorporated company, the representatives of the Plaintiff in dealing with Green and B & G Print and Litho were entitled to assume that B & G Print & Litho or B & G Printing was a proprietorship of which Edward Green was one of the principals.

14   It would appear that one of the purposes of s. 2.(6) of the *Business Names Act* is to protect the public, and as a consequence if someone expects to take advantage of the limited liability available to him through the process of incorporation, he should make the public aware of the existence of such corporation in his dealings with other members of the public. This was one of the factors taken into consideration by the Court in imposing personal liability on the Defendant in *Short's Backhoe and Trucking Ltd. v. Noseworthy* (1992) 101 Nfld. & P.E.I. Reports, p. 277.

15   It was noted in *Excelco Foods Inc. v. Snider* (1991) 95 Sask. R. p. 314 (Sask. Q.B.) p. 316 that if an individual wishes to escape personal liability on a contract, such a person has a duty to make it clear to the person with whom he is contracting that he is negotiating on behalf of his corporation and not in his personal capacity. In that case, the Court imposed personal liability on the Defendant who used the name of his business Candy Connection which was known to the plaintiff but tried to argue that his company Candy Connection Inc. should be liable. It should be noted that in that case, none of the invoices made reference to the Corporation as is the case in the matter before me.

16   Similarly in the case of *Interlake Packers Ltd. v. Vogt and Loewen* (1987) 47 Man. R. (2d) p. 268 (Man. Q.B.) the defendant was held to be personally liable for meat products sold and delivered by the plaintiff instead of his company E.V. Wholesale Meats Limited, because invoices were made out to E & V Meat Whls. and other similar names without the corporate entity being referred to.

17   The same finding was made in the case of *W.R. Benjamin Products Ltd. v. Saulnier* (1982) 40 N.B.R. (2d) 537 (N.B., Q.B.) where the Court indicated at p. 539:

"There is no clear evidence to satisfy me that the Plaintiff was ever made aware of the incorporation of the Defendant's business or that it was doing business with a corporation. And that, in my opinion, is the determining factor."

18   Similar conclusions were arrived at in the Ontario case of *Victor (Can.) Ltd. v. Far Better Addressing and Mailing Ltd. et al* (1978) 3 B.L.R. p. 312 (Ont. H.C.J.) by Morin J. who indicated that the Plaintiff would fully expect that it was dealing with an unincorporated business with "S" as owner and operator and personally liable to the Plaintiff upon the failure of "S" to indicate otherwise and in the British Columbia case of *West Fraser Builder Supplies v. Vanderhorst* [1990] B.C.W.L.D. 436 (B.C.C.A.).

19   Based upon the foregoing, I find the Defendant Edward Green to be liable to the Plaintiff in the amount of $19,912.70. The Plaintiff is entitled to pre-judgment interest on the said amount from August 11th, 1995 to judgment at the rate of 6.6%.

20   The Plaintiff will also be entitled to its cost of the action.

QUESTIONS

1. Why was Green found personally liable in this case?
2. Why would the plaintiff wish to sue Green, instead of his limited company?
3. What should Green have done to avoid incurring personal liability in this case?

Aspiotis v. Coffee Time Donuts Inc.

[1995] O.J. No. 419

Ontario Court of Justice (General Division)

February 21, 1995.

The following case illustrates a typical scenario leading to negotiation of a franchise, and the terms that one would expect to find in a franchise agreement.

1   **GROUND J**.:— In this action, the plaintiff seeks a declaration that an agreement between the plaintiff and the defendant, Coffee Time Donuts Incorporated ("Coffee Time"), dated November 12, 1992 is a binding and enforceable agreement and that the defendants have wilfully breached such agreement. The plaintiff also seeks damages for misrepresentation and breach of contract as well as punitive and exemplary damages.

2   The agreement sought to be enforced (the "November 12 Agreement") is alleged to be the agreement pursuant to which the plaintiff was to purchase a Coffee Time Donuts franchise from the defendant, Coffee Time.

3   I am unable to conclude that the November 12 Agreement is a binding and enforceable contract between the parties. In order to so conclude, I would have to find that the November 12 Agreement contains all of the essential terms of the arrangement between the parties with respect to the acquisition of the franchise. Having considered all of the evidence and the submissions of counsel, it is my view that a number of the essential terms of a franchise acquisition are not contained in the November 12 Agreement and, in fact, that no agreement was ever reached on many of such terms.

4   In particular, I find it very difficult to accept the contention of the plaintiff that the only amount payable for the franchise was to be the $15,000.00 franchise fee referred to in the November 12 Agreement. From the evidence, it would appear that such fee is standard for all Coffee Time franchises and the November 12 Agreement spells out exactly what services are to be provided for such fee. This would mean that in negotiating the sale of franchises, the franchiser does not charge a higher price for a franchise in a very superior location than that charged for a franchise in a rather undesirable location. This does not seem to me to accord with economic reality. In addition, I think it is clear that the plaintiff and his son were both aware that there was a location fee or profit element built into the negotiations for a franchise. They were prepared to pay an additional fee of $25,000.00 to obtain the Dufferin Street franchise which all parties viewed as an excellent location. In addition, they were aware that an associate of theirs had paid fees in the $25,000.00 range for certain franchise locations acquired by him and the various proposals made to the plaintiff by Coffee Time during the course of negotiations all involved the payment of the location fee or "profit". It is clear that it was on this very issue that negotiations broke down between the parties.

5   In addition to failure to agree on price, the question of the exclusive trading area is left open in the November 12 Agreement to be negotiated. The November 12 Agreement does not contain a closing date nor are there are any time periods provided for the performance of obligations or the fulfilment of conditions specified in the document. The November 12 Agreement does not specify whether the store is to be a satellite store or a full producing store which would make a substantial difference with respect to the equipment to be installed. All of these essential terms are not contained in the November 12 Agreement and I find that it is not a binding and enforceable contract for the acquisition of the franchise. The agreement is in my view correctly referred to by certain of the witnesses as a "deposit agreement" reflecting the payment of the deposit by the plaintiff and evidencing the intention of the parties to continue with negotiations for the acquisition of the franchise.

6   Counsel for the plaintiff has urged me to find that the defendant, Coffee Time did not negotiate in good faith and that the contract was not completed due to the wrongful termination of negotiations by Coffee Time. I find no evidence of failure on the part of Coffee Time to negotiate in good faith. The location fee or profit element

was raised at the first instance and meetings and discussions continued from December through to April. The fact that certain of the discussions and meetings may have become rather heated and that the parties were unable to reach an agreement on the question of location fee or profit element does not indicate a failure to negotiate in good faith on the part of either party. To demonstrate a failure to negotiate in good faith, one would have to establish some improper conduct on the part of Coffee Time such as an attempt to mislead the plaintiff or negotiations with third parties at the same time as negotiations with the plaintiff were continuing. There is no such evidence. Failure of parties to agree on an essential term of a contract is not, by itself, evidence of negotiating in bad faith on the part of either party.

7   The action is accordingly dismissed. With respect to the counterclaim, I have some trouble with the declaration sought that the November 12 Agreement is a valid and binding agreement. I have found that the November 12 Agreement was entered into to reflect the payment of the deposit by the plaintiff and to evidence that the parties intended to negotiate the acquisition of a franchise by the plaintiff. With respect to the declaration that Coffee Time is entitled to retain the $5,000.00 deposit, it seems to me that Coffee Time's entitlement to retain the deposit only arises if Coffee Time has approved all matters requiring its approval under the November 12 Agreement and the plaintiff has failed to proceed. The situation in this case is that the parties never got to the stage of approval of the various items referred to in the November 12 Agreement and, accordingly, in my view, the provisions re forfeit of the deposit are not applicable and the deposit should be returned to the plaintiff.

8   The action is therefore dismissed as against Coffee Time Donuts Incorporated and the counterclaim is dismissed.

[*The court considered whether the president and vice-president of Coffee Time Donuts Incorporated should be found personally liable and concluded that there was no basis on which to bring legal action against them either in contract or in tort. That portion of the judge's reasoning has been omitted*].

14   The bringing of this action against Messrs. Michalopoulos and Grammenopoulos personally is in my view symptomatic of a current trend in commercial litigation where individual directors and officers are sued personally for corporate acts whether the actions are framed in contract or in tort. These actions against officers and directors are often, as in this case, totally without foundation and are very often based solely on a pleading that the particular officer or director was "the controlling mind of the corporation." To expose business persons to the considerable inconvenience and expense of being personally involved in litigation, where there is no foundation for an action against them in their personal capacities, is in my view an abuse of the process of the courts. Accordingly, the action against Messrs. Michalopoulos and Grammenopoulos is dismissed with costs payable to Messrs. Michalopoulos and Grammenopoulos on a solicitor and client basis.

15   Although the action has been dismissed as against each of the defendants, I should make some comment on the evidence as to measure of damages. Two conflicting experts' reports were submitted on the quantification of damages. The plaintiff's expert took a valuation of business approach and determined how the proposed franchise business to be acquired would be valued in the open market based on the projected annual earnings of the business. On this basis, he arrived at a measure of damages of somewhere between $145,000 and $174,000. The defendants' expert proceeded on the basis of calculating the anticipated annual profits from the franchise

business and calculated damages based upon the loss of such profits for a reasonable period of time during which the plaintiff might have been expected to pursue an alternative business opportunity. In my view, the latter approach is the correct approach. The claim for damages is based on loss of opportunity and early the plaintiff would have an obligation to mitigate such damages. He is not entitled to claim damages based upon the amount he would have to pay to acquire a business which would earn him annually for the indefinite future the amount of the anticipated profits from the franchise operation. He is clearly obligated to mitigate his losses by pursuing a reasonable alternative business opportunity. In this case, the evidence is clear that there were other business opportunities of a similar nature available and that this particular franchise operation was in no way unique.

16   The action is dismissed. Costs to the defendants Michalopoulos and Grammenopoulos on a solicitor and client basis. Counsel may speak to me or write to me regarding the scale of costs to the defendant Coffee Time and the quantum of costs.

QUESTIONS

1. What are the essential terms of a franchise agreement?

2. The court finds here that there was not a failure to negotiate in good faith. What circumstances could lead a court to find that there was a failure to negotiate in good faith?

3. Under what circumstances would a franchisee's deposit be forfeited? Why was the deposit not forfeited in this case?

chapter twenty

The Contract of Employment

Wynja v. Keir Surgical Ltd.

(1997) BCJ No. 789, 30 CCEI (2d) 85.
British Columbia Supreme Court
Judgment: filed April 3, 1997.

The following case illustrates the very limited circumstances that could justify an employer terminating an employee for cause, and the consequences to an employer of breaching the contract with the employee. It reviews the factors that a court will take into account in assessing damages for wrongful dismissal. It appears that only when exceptional factors are present will damages for mental distress be awarded.

CURTIS J.

Mark Wynja has applied for summary judgment under Rule 18A against Keir Surgical Ltd. for damages for wrongful dismissal including damages for mental distress.

Mr. Wynja was dismissed June 4, 1996 without notice from his position as office supervisor with Keir Surgical Ltd., a company in the business of retail and wholesale supply of hospital and medical supplies. At the time of his dismissal, Mr. Wynja was responsible for the supervision of three office staff and the company's shipper/receiver and for placing orders to suppliers himself. His annual salary was $39,228 in addition to which he had in past years received bonuses of $200 to $400. On June 4, 1996 Mr. Wynja had been in the employ of Keir Surgical Ltd. for 16 years. He was hired in 1980 at 19 years of age as a shipper/receiver. In 1981 he became order desk clerk, in 1986 he went into sales for a year; and in 1988 began working in the position from which he was fired. Following his dismissal, Mr. Wynja suffered a major depression from which he has yet to recover. He has not yet obtained replacement employment.

Keir Surgical Ltd. alleges dismissal for cause, pleading that his behaviour, in particular swearing, slamming down and throwing objects, and criticizing senior management was disruptive, that he had a negative and hostile attitude and failed to perform his function as supervisor.

The first issue is whether or not it is appropriate to decide this matter upon this application. I find that it is. I am satisfied that I can fairly find the facts necessary to decide the issues upon the evidence presented on the application. In doing so, I have considered the guidelines for deciding cases on applications of this nature as set out in the case of *Inspiration Management Ltd. v. McDermid St. Lawrence Ltd.* (1989), 36 B.C.L.R. (2d) 202 (B.C.C.A.).

In order to establish just cause for dismissal without notice an employer must establish conduct by the employee which shows he is repudiating his employment contract or one of its essential conditions. In the case of *John A. Steward v. Director of Employment Standards*, [1995] B.C.J. No. 582, B.C.S.C. March 22, 1995, Vancouver Registry No. A942815, Newbury J., as she then was, stated at p.1:

> At the very least, the conduct must, in the words of the court in *Thompson v. Boise Cascade Canada Ltd.* (1994), 7 C.C.E.L. (2d) 17 (Ont. C.J.) at 34, "be such that by its nature it shows that the employee is repudiating the contract or one of its essential conditions". The Court went on to note:
>
> It is also clear that the employee's conduct, and the character it reveals, must be such as to undermine, or seriously impair, the essential trust and confidence the employer is entitled to place in the employee in the circumstances of their particular relationship. In essence, the conduct must be such as the employer can point to it as a good reason for having lost confidence in the employee's ability faithfully to discharge his/her duties.

In the case of *Carlo Dusconi v. Fujitsu-ICL Canada Inc.* (1996), 22 B.C.L.R. (3d) 62, Spencer J., in deciding a case of alleged dismissal for cause of a 14 year employee held:

In cases such as this, an employee is entitled to have his performance viewed against his previous conduct, good or bad. Where an employee has many years of exemplary service, minor lapses from the employer's requirements, not committed in wilful disregard of its wishes, will not justify dismissal for cause. The employer's contribution to a situation of stress must be considered. The blame must be apportioned by a fair assessment of all the circumstances, as was done in *Roscoe v. McGavin Foods Ltd.* (1983), 2 C.C.E.L. 287.

None of this is to say that the defendant was bound to go on employing the plaintiff if it chose not to. Instead, it is to say that if it chose to dismiss him without sufficient cause it was bound to give him reasonable notice. An employer alleging just cause for dismissal bears the legal onus of proving cause on a preponderance of the evidence.

I find just cause for Mr. Wynja's dismissal has not been proven.

The evidence does establish that by the spring of 1996 Mr. Wynja was becoming frustrated in his work and somewhat depressed which was indeed on occasion evidenced by swearing, slamming down books and a negative attitude. This situation was contributed to by his employer releasing the order desk person, who was not replaced, with the result that Mr. Wynja had to assume a part of that work.

Mr. Keir had a meeting with Mr. Wynja January 10, 1996 which was followed by a letter of January 12, 1996 expressing the concerns of his employer. Thereafter, Mr. Wynja and Mr. Keir met regularly. Mr. Wynja was not advised before his termination that his performance in response to the January meeting and letter was unsatisfactory. Keir Surgical Ltd. takes the position that the reason for that was that Mr. Wynja behaved in one way when his supervisors were present and another when they were absent. I accept that to some extent that was probably the case however, the conduct complained of which resulted in his summary dismissal was not of sufficient gravity to warrant dismissal without further warning to Mr. Wynja. Three of the office staff he was responsible to supervise, happened one day to discuss Mr. Wynja, in particular, his swearing, slamming things on the desk and general bad attitude. One suggested they all report it to Mr. Keir but the other two did not agree. Kate Pugh, the employee who worked most closely with Mr. Wynja, testified on discovery that she got along well with him but in the spring of 1996 he was depressed, unhappy and swearing a lot. She did not expect him to be fired for his conduct and was surprised when he was. Although Mr. Wynja was swearing in frustration and becoming hard to be around, there is no evidence that he swore at customers or staff or that his conduct had got to the point where it harmed his employer's business. In the circumstances of this case where Mr. Wynja had worked from the age of 19 for his employer for 16 years and on the basis of his regular meetings with his supervisor, believed his job performance to be acceptable. It was not fair to terminate that long term employment with no period of notice or pay in lieu of notice on the basis of employee complaints of the gravity the evidence reveals without giving Mr. Wynja specific notification that the conduct complained of if continued would result in his dismissal.

Mr. Wynja's position was not filled after he was fired. He was becoming a difficult employee and rather than attempting to rehabilitate him in the circumstances Keir Surgical Ltd. understandably chose to let him go. The circumstances however did not justify dismissal without notice.

I accept that Mr. Wynja suffered a serious depression after his dismissal. The evidence indicates he was in fact tending toward depression prior to his termination. The manner of dismissal however was not such as to be independently actionable as discussed in the case of *Vorvis v. Insurance Corporation of British Columbia* (1989), 58 D.L.R. (4th) 193, nor was it deceitful as in the case of *Dixon v. British Columbia Transit* (1995), 13 C.C.E.L. (2d) 272, nor done in a manner with the intention of causing mental suffering as in the case of *Campbell v. Willfund Audio-Visual Ltd.* (1995), 14 C.C.E.L. (2d) 240. Keir Surgical Ltd. dismissed Mr. Wynja because he was causing problems and in the circumstances it did not need him as an employee. The cause alleged, although not sufficient to succeed in law, was both understandable and fairly arguable. I find no basis for awarding Mr. Wynja damages for mental distress in addition to his damages for wrongful dismissal.

The matters to be considered in fixing an appropriate period of notice in a case of wrongful dismissal without notice are set out in the case of *Ansari et al v. British Columbia Hydro and Power Authority (1986)*, 2 B.C.L.R. (2d) 33. Mr. Wynja was at a junior management level in a small company when dismissed. He was 36 years old, he had worked 16 years for the company - most of his working life. The opportunities for re-employment in his field are not large - likely he will have to re-train. Considering these factors, I fix 12 months as a reasonable period of notice for Mr. Wynja.

No argument was made on this application that Mr. Wynja failed to mitigate his damages. Mr. Wynja is therefore entitled to damages for wrongful dismissal equal to 12 months pay including the value of holiday pay, benefits and bonuses he would have received during those 12 months. He is also entitled to recover the costs of this action.

QUESTIONS

1. Under what circumstances is an employer entitled to dismiss an employee for cause?

2. Why did the circumstances in this case not justify termination by the employer?

3. What factors does the court take into account in assessing damages for wrongful termination?

4. What would an employee in these circumstances be expected to do to mitigate damages?

5. When might an employee be entitled to damages for mental distress?

chapter twenty-one

Negotiable Instruments

2203850 Nova Scotia Ltd.
(c.o.b. "Money Mart") v. Sarkar

[1995] N.S.J. No. 342, 45 NSR (2d) 101, 23 BLR (2d) 28
Nova Scotia Supreme Court
July 28, 1995.

The law of negotiable instruments was developed to facilitate business transactions. Under certain circumstances it allowed transferees to acquire rights against third parties without having to be concerned about anything surrounding the transaction out of which the rights arose. The law confers on the holder, in due course of a negotiable instrument, greater powers than an assignee of contractual rights. One category of negotiable instrument is a cheque, and this case illustrates that when one writes a cheque, in many cases one is undertaking an obligation that cannot subsequently be revoked.

1   **DAVISON J.**:— This is an appeal from the decision of an adjudicator of the Small Claims Court of Nova Scotia which dismissed the appellant's action against the respondent.

2   The respondent, Dr. Nellie Sarkar hired a Mr. Gardiner to whom she gave a cheque in the amount of $800.00 postdated to September 15, 1994. On September 12, 1994 the respondent placed a stop payment on this cheque with her bank, and on September 13, 1994 Mr. Gardiner negotiated the cheque with the appellant, Money Mart. The appellant was not aware that the respondent had placed a stop payment on the cheque.

3   The appellant commenced an action against the respondent in the Small Claims Court alleging that it was a holder in due course and not susceptible to defences the claimant may have against the payee, Mr. Gardiner.

4   The adjudicator specifically referred to the case of the *Bank of Commerce v. Burman et al.* (1979), 38 N.S.R. (2d) 262, a decision of the County Court for Nova Scotia which held that the plaintiff was not a holder in due course and found that the holder of the cheque was not immune to defences against the payee. Accordingly the adjudicator found in this case that the claimant was not a holder in due course and relying on the Burman case, dismissed the claimant's action.

5   The appellant takes the position and, properly so, that a cheque is a bill of exchange to which the *Bills of Exchange Act* applies. Section 26(d) of the *Act* states that:

> 26.   *A bill is not invalid by reason only that it ...*
>
> > *(d)   is antedated or post-dated, or bears date on a Sunday or other non-judicial day.*

Thus the Bills of Exchange Act permits the postdating of bills of exchange.

6   Crawford and Falconbridge in Banking and Bills of Exchange (8th Ed.) at p. 1741 state:

> A postdated cheque is one that bears, as its only date, a date after the date of its issue. There appears to be no doubt now that such instruments are technically cheques for all purposes of the Act and are fully negotiable by endorsement and/or delivery during the interval between their issue and their ostensible date, and for a reasonable time thereafter.

7   It would appear from the authorities that the practice of postdated cheques is a widespread practice in Canada, although it is discouraged in the United Kingdom.

8   In the *Burman* case the bank took action against the maker and payee of a postdated cheque. The maker stopped payment on the cheque and the bank alleged it was a holder in due course of the cheque and the maker was not entitled to raise the defence against the bank which it had against the payee. Judge Sullivan held the bank was not a holder in due course relying on Falconbridge Banking and Bills of Exchange (7th ed.) at p. 497:

> The fact that a cheque is postdated does not make it irregular within the meaning of s. 56, so as to charge the holder with equities of which he had no notice. ... But a person cashing a post-dated cheque before its ostensible date is not a holder in due course since the drawer can countermand payment under s. 167.

9   The editors of the 8th edition of Crawford and Falconbridge, Banking and Bills of Exchange do not appear to agree with the editors of the 7th edition. That work at 1742 states:

> No doubt such items are a nuisance to banks and could create difficulties for them if processed prematurely by their automated cheque-handling computers, but only in the event of a countermand by the drawer. Presumably such risks are not great and are justified by the economics of automation in any event. Postdated cheques have long been quite commonly used in Canada, and there are some two dozen reported cases concerning them directly. As Brossard J. noted in 1969, more and more, these days, post-dated cheques are being issued and accepted as a method of making instalment or term payments; therefore, except under circumstances...which make them accessory to a fraudulent contract, the fact that they are post-dated cannot affect the rights of a person who is presumed to be a holder in due course.

Where the payee negotiates the postdated item prior to its ostensible date to a person who otherwise qualifies as a holder in due course, the authorities are clear that the mere fact of postdating does not make the instrument less than complete and regular on its face (s. 56) nor ought it to arouse suspicion. Where no value is given, or the transferee acts in bad faith, it is obviously otherwise.

10   A holder in due course is defined by s. 55 of the *Bills of Exchange Act* as follows:

> *(1)   A holder in due course is a holder who has taken a bill, complete and regular on the face of it, under the following conditions, namely:*
>
> > *(a)   that he became the holder of it before it was overdue and without notice that it had been previously dishonoured, if such was the fact; and*
>
> > *(b)   that he took the bill in good faith and for value, and that at the time the bill was negotiated to him he had no notice of any defect in the title of the person who negotiated it.*
>
> *(2)   In particular, the title of a person who negotiates a bill is defective within the meaning of this Act when he obtained the bill, or the acceptance thereof, by fraud, duress or force and fear, or other unlawful means, or for any illegal consideration, or when he negotiates it in breach of faith, or under such circumstances as amount to a fraud.*

11   In this case the cheque was complete and regular on its face. It was not overdue and there was no evidence of it having been dishonoured. I refer again the quote from Crawford and Falconbridge (8th ed.) at p. 1742 which states "postdating does not make the instrument less then complete and regular on its face".

12   There was no evidence Gardiner obtained the cheque by fraud, duress or other unlawful means. The appellant took the cheque in good faith for valuable consideration without notice of a dispute between the respondent and Mr. Gardiner. I find the appellant was a holder in due course.

13   At this point it is of use to refer to the reasoning of the Supreme Court in *Keyes v. Royal Bank of Canada*, [1947] 3 D.L.R. 161. Keyes drew a postdated cheque payable to a Mrs. Mundy on Keyes' account with the Royal Bank of Canada. Keyes

endorsed the cheque and presented it to the credit of Mrs. Mundy's account with the Bank of Commerce. The Commerce had the cheque certified by the Royal with the employees overlooking the cheque was postdated and the monies were credited to Mrs. Mundy's account and Keyes' account with the Royal was debited. Mrs. Mundy withdrew the money on a date preceding the cheque date on which latter date Keyes countermanded payment.

14   In the preceding before me Dr. Sarkar has a role similar to Keyes, and Money Mart's role is similar to the Bank of Commerce. Estey, J., in his reasoning dealing with the issue of estoppel refers to the normal relationship of the Bank and the customer as a creditor and debtor relationship, but in the drawing and payment of cheques the relationship is principal and agent. The relationship between Keyes and the Royal Bank of Canada was debtor and creditor as is the relationship between Dr. Sarkar and her bank. However the Bank of Commerce in receiving the post-dated cheque derives its rights through the negotiation of the cheque and, like Money Mart, was a holder in due course.

15   The rights of a holder in due course are set out in s. 73 of the *Act*:

The rights and powers of the holder of a bill are as follows:

(a)   *he may sue on the bill in his own name;*

(b)   *where he is a holder in due course, he holds the bill free from any defect of title of prior parties, as well as from mere personal defences available to prior parties among themselves, and may enforce payment against all parties liable on the bill;*

(c)   *where his title is defective, if he negotiates the bill to holder in due course, that holder obtains a good and complete title to the bill; and*

(d)   *where his title is defective, if he obtains payment of the bill, the person who pays him in due course gets a valid discharge for the bill.*

16   In my respectful view the adjudicator was wrong in finding the appellant was not a holder in due course. It would also appear she believed that because the holder could countermand payment and that rendered the appellant not a holder in due course. However a postdated cheque is a bill of exchange and a countermand is not effective against a holder in due course.

17   In the Burman case the judge relied on the Ontario County Court decision of *Bk. N.S. v. Kelly Motors Danforth Ltd.*, [1961] O.W.N. 34 which held the postdated cheque which is honoured before its date raises the risk of it being countermanded. I agree with the remarks of Crawford and Falconbridge supra at 1743:

The statutory power of countermand (para. 167(a)) extends to postdated cheques subject, as with ordinary cheques, to the rights of any holder in due course. The decision of the Ontario County Court in Bank of Nova Scotia v. Kelly Motors Danforth Ltd., is (with respect) simply wrong in holding that "anyone honouring a cheque before its ostensible date does so at the risk of countermand of payment".

18   I have also been referred to the decision of Hunter, J. of the Court of Queen's Bench in Saskatchewan in *Wheatland Investments Ltd., operating under the name and style of Money Mart Regina v. Sask Tel* (1994), Q.B.M. No. 89.

19   Madam Justice Hunter states on page 6 of her judgment:

In the case at bar, the conclusion of the learned trial judge was that "...the cheque was not complete and regular on the face of it. To be regular on the face of it, it would have to be presented on or after the date written on the face of it" is wrong in law. There is no evidence to indicate that Money Mart had any notice that the post-dated cheque was overdue and had no notice that it had been previously dishonoured. The cheque was negotiated on June 15, 1993, prior to the notice to the Bank of Montreal to stop payment and prior to the date it was due. Further, the evidence is that Money Mart took the bill in good faith and for value. Accordingly, all the requirements of s. 55 are met and Money Mart is a holder in due course.

The adjudicator in the *Wheatland* case believed that because the respondent had made a countermand this prevented the appellant from becoming a holder in due course. To this Hunter J. replied at p. 7:

SaskTel argues that the countermand is effective and that the drawee of the cheque is protected provided the countermand is initiated prior to the due date on the cheque. In this respect, s. 167 of the *Act* provides:

167. The duty and authority of a bank to pay a cheque drawn on it by its customer is determined by

(a)   countermand of payment; or

(b)   notice of the customer's death.

However, SaskTel can only succeed on this argument if a post-dated cheque is not a bill of exchange. As previously stated, it is a bill of exchange and the countermand is not effective against a holder in due course.

20   In conclusion I allow the appeal. The respondent is liable to the appellant for payment of the amount of the cheque. The respondent shall have its costs as provided in the regulations in the *Small Claims Court Act*.

QUESTIONS

1. What is a bill of exchange? What criteria does an instrument have to satisfy to qualify as a bill of exchange?
2. Why is a postdated cheque considered a bill of exchange?
3. What special rights does a holder in due course have against the drawer of a cheque?
4. If the drawer places a stop payment on a cheque, does the drawer cease to have responsibility under the cheque? Explain.
5. Why might you advise someone not to issue a series of postdated cheques to satisfy future obligations under a contract? Explain.

Bank of Nova Scotia v. Rock Corp. of Canada Inc.

[1992] O.J. No. 2023
Ontario Court of Justice - General Division
Judgment: September 28, 1992

The rights of a holder in due course of a negotiable instrument are superior to those of a regular assignee of contractual rights. In this case, the bank that cashed a cheque for its customer was held not to be a holder in due course, and therefore could not take advantage of the special rights that it might otherwise have had.

HAWKINS J.:— The defendant The Rock Corporation of Canada Inc. drew a cheque on The Royal Bank of Canada for $5,800.00 payable to the order of Bruno Tessoni. Tessoni took the cheque to his bank (the plaintiff Bank of Nova Scotia) and cashed it without endorsing it in any way. By the time the cheque made its way to the drawee bank, payment had been stopped by the drawer as the cheque was dishonoured.

The plaintiff claims to be a holder in due course of the cheque pursuant to the provisions of s. 165(3) of the *Bills of Exchange Act* R.S.C. B-4 which provides as follows:

> "*S. 165(3) Where a cheque is delivered to a bank for deposit to the credit of a person and the bank credits him with the amount of the cheque, the bank acquires all the rights and powers of a holder in due course of the cheque*".

As anyone who has ever had a bank account knows, the cashing (as opposed the depositing) of a cheque by the payee results in absolutely no entry whatever to the payee's account. If the cheque is honoured by the drawee bank the payee's bank account is untouched by the transaction. If the cheque is dishonoured the payee's account will be debited with the amount of the cheque and only then will the payee's account bear any trace of the transaction.

Since the cheque in question was not endorsed by the payee, the plaintiff, having given value for the cheque by cashing it, acquired such title as the payee had in the cheque. See s. 60(1) of the Act which provides as follows:

> "*S. 60(1) Where the holder of a bill payable to his order transfers it for value without endorsing it, the transfer gives the transferee such title as the transferor had in the bill, and the transferee in addition acquires the right to have the endorsement of the transferor*".

Such title is, of course, subject to the equities between the drawer and the payee.

In order to escape the equities between the drawer and the payee, the plaintiff bank must establish itself as a holder in due course which it can do only if it can fit itself within the provisions of s. 165(3).

On the undisputed facts of this case, the transactions between the payee and his bank have absolutely no resemblance whatever to the requirements of s. 165(3). Tessoni did not deliver the cheque to his bank for deposit to the credit of himself or any person. He delivered it to be cashed. The bank did not credit him with the amount of the cheque. It paid him in cash.

The purpose of s. 165(3) is discussed in *Bank of Nova Scotia v. Archo Industries Ltd.* (1970) 11 D.L.R. (3d) 593 at 594 (Sask.Q.B.) in which the following passage from Falconbridge on Banking and Bills of Exchange 7th ed (1969) p. 860 is quoted:

> "Section 165(3), enacted in 1966, makes it clear that a bank becomes a holder in due course of a cheque received for deposit to a customer's credit and so credited. This subsection was added after an Alberta decision that a cheque endorsed "deposit only to the account of A" and signed "A" was a restrictive endorsement and that the bank in which it was deposited was not a holder in due course, *Imperial Bank of Canada v. Hayes and Earl Ltd.* (1962) 35 D.L.R. (2d) 136, 38 W.W.R. 169 (Alta. S.C.). See also 73 Candn. Banker II 34 (1966)".

I have absolutely no idea why the protection afforded by in s, 165(3) was not extended to the case (as here) of a bank cashing a cheque. Presumably Tessoni could have first deposited the cheque to the credit of his account and then withdrawn the whole sum without the bank losing the protection of s. 165(3), but that is not what happened.

Among the ten cases dealing with s. 165(3) referred to me by Counsel, only one deals with the cashing of a cheque as opposed to its deposit. That one case (*CIBC v. Carousel Canada* Ont. Court (P.D.) Bromstein J. released 22 March 1990 unreported) is undistinguishable on its facts but of no assistance because the parties agreed that the cashing bank was a holder in due course.

Counsel advised me that the sole issue is whether or not the plaintiff is a holder in due course and that the answer to that question will be determinative of the party's rights. I find that the plaintiff is not a holder in due course. The plaintiff's motion for judgment is dismissed. The defendant's motion for dismissal is granted. The action is dismissed with costs including the costs of these motions.

QUESTIONS

1. Why did the court hold that the Bank of Nova Scotia was not a holder in due course?

2. What special rights does a holder in due course have?

3. How might the position of the Bank of Nova Scotia have been improved if it had been a holder in due course?

4. What should the bank have done to ensure that it was a holder in due course? Do you agree with the judge's suggestion that the bank would not have been a holder in due course unless the amount of the cheque had been deposited to the customer's account?

5. Under what circumstances would the Bank of Nova Scotia have rights against Rock Corp. of Canada Inc.?

part five

Property

chapter twenty-two

Intellectual Property

Seaward Kayaks Ltd. v. Ree

[2000] B.C.J. No. 2677, 2000 BCSC 1742
British Columbia Supreme Court
December 15, 2000.

A plaintiff's legal action to enforce intellectual property rights usually begins, as this one did, with an attempt to obtain an interim injunction (also called an interlocutory injunction), to halt the defendant's activities pending trial of the action. The courts have established that certain tests have to be met to obtain an interim injunction, and those are set out in this case. This case also illustrates a variety of different ways in which the law can protect intellectual property rights.

1   **SHABBITS J.**:— The plaintiff designs, develops, manufactures and markets kayaks and their accessories. Its president and principal shareholder is Steven Ree. Mr. Ree began the business in 1988, registered the name "Seaward Kayak" in 1990, and incorporated in 1996. It has prospered. Its gross sales for the first ten months of the current fiscal year approximated $2,000,000, and its gross profit for that time period approximated $360,000.

2   The plaintiff claims that it has a unique rudder, which it markets under the trademark "SmartRudder." It claims that its current rudder design was formalized in 1996 in copyright protected schematics. The plaintiff alleges that it has sole proprietary interests in its "SmartRudder" system, and its component parts. The plaintiff's sales in its rudder manufacturing division for the first ten months of the current fiscal year approximated $500,000, and its profit approximated $100,000.

3   The defendant Klaas Ree, is Steven Ree's father. In December of 1998, the defendant had retired from employment with Telus. Mr. Steven Ree alleges that at about Christmas of 1998, the defendant approached him seeking employment to supplement his pension.

4   Mr. Steven Ree hired his father to work for the plaintiff and he was employed from January 27, 1999 until June 22, 1999. During that period of time, the defendant was responsible for managing the plaintiff's machine shop in Summerland, British Columbia. When the plaintiff moved its manufacturing operations from the Okanagan, where the Defendant lived, to Ladysmith on Vancouver Island, the defendant's employment ended.

5   Earlier this year, the defendant established his own business manufacturing kayak rudders that directly competed with the plaintiff. The plaintiff alleges that the defendant began manufacturing kayak rudders and kayak rudder assemblies that are identical to the "SmartRudder" that the plaintiff manufactures. The plaintiff also alleges that the defendant has solicited its customers.

6   Ms. Sheila Gras, Steven Ree's sister and the defendant's daughter, swore an affidavit filed October 20, 2000, that her father showed her his kayak rudder manufacturing operation, and that he told her that they were the same rudders the plaintiff developed. She also says that the defendant told her that he was approaching the plaintiff's customers for business.

7   The plaintiff seeks an injunction restraining the defendant from using its business and trade secrets, and from manufacturing or marketing the "SmartRudder". The plaintiff also seeks an order requiring the defendant to return its property, including design schematics, customer lists, price lists and related documentation.

8   The defendant denies that the plaintiff's method of manufacturing kayak rudders is a trade secret. He says that the plaintiff's method is available to any of the plaintiff's competitors. The defendant denies that the rudder and rudder components he produces are identical to those the plaintiff produces. He also denies that his position as the plaintiff's employee made him a fiduciary with the power and ability to direct and guide the plaintiff's affairs. He alleges that he is entitled to compete with the plaintiff in the business of rudder manufacturing. The defendant submits that since the plaintiff has produced more than 50 rudders, it is not an infringement of The Copyright Act for him to reproduce the design of the plaintiff's rudder. The defendant denies having any documentation belonging to the plaintiff.

9   In *Canadian Broadcasting Corp (CBC) v. CKPG Television Ltd.* (1992), 64 B.C.L.R. (2d) 96 (B.C.C.A.), Lambert J.A. said this for the court at 101:

> The long-standing test for the granting of an interim injunction in British Columbia is a two-pronged test. The test has never been altered and its force has never been affected by a decision of the Supreme Court of Canada. The two-pronged test is this: "First, the applicant must satisfy the court that there is a fair question to be tried as to the existence of the right which he alleges and a breach thereof, actual or reasonably apprehended. Second, he must establish that the balance of convenience favours the granting of an injunction."

10   The applicant submits that there are these triable issues:

(a)   that the defendant breached his duty of confidentiality that arose out of his employment and was an implicit part thereof by appropriating and using the plaintiff's intellectual property and trade secrets, by taking the plaintiffs designs and customer or trade information;

(b)   that the defendant breached his trust and fiduciary duty to the plaintiff that arose out of the terms of his employment by converting and using trade secrets acquired solely by virtue of his employment to compete with the Plaintiff in the manufacture and sale of rudders for the plaintiff's rudder system;

(c)   that the defendant infringed the plaintiff's copyrights by the unauthorized appropriation and use of the plaintiff's copyright protected rudder design, and by the manufacture and sale of rudders.

11   In an affidavit sworn September 21, 2000, Steven Ree says this in paragraphs 21 to 32:

21.   The Defendant had access to Seaward Kayaks Ltd.'s trade secrets, including books, manuals, building schedules, schematics, drawings, specifications, client lists, costings, client profiles, purchasing requirements and other trade secrets of Seaward Kayaks Ltd.

22.   The Defendant's access to the above trade secrets was solely by virtue of his employment by the Plaintiff.

23.   The Defendant was aware of the confidentiality clause of his employment contract, but as he is my father, the Defendant was not requested to sign a standard Confidentiality Agreement.

24.   The Defendant's management duties included supervising employees. In that capacity, he was required to have new employees sign the Confidentiality Agreement.

25.   Exhibit "B" to this my Affidavit, is a true reproduction of the standard Confidentiality Agreement.

26.   The Defendant had no authority to use any trade secrets obtained by virtue of his employment for his own benefit.

27.   The Defendant had no authority to keep or use any trade secrets obtained by virtue of his employment once his employment had ceased.

28.   The defendant was entrusted with communicating with clients and suppliers and representing the interests of the Plaintiff as his employer.

     29.   The Defendant was authorised to bind the Plaintiff in contract.

     30.   The Defendant was given, by virtue of his employment, access to the Plaintiff's confidential client pricing information.

     31.   This information constitutes a major asset of the company and is essential to the competitive viability of the company.

     32.   The Defendant has no authorization to use this information for any purpose.

12   Mr. Steven Ree alleges that the defendant obtained information about the design of kayak rudders from the plaintiff in circumstances where confidentiality was expected. He also alleges that it was and is tortious for the defendant to use the confidential information he gained as a result of his employment with the plaintiff for his own benefit after his employment ended.

13   Steven Ree alleges that the only reason he did not have the defendant sign the standard confidentiality agreement that all other employees had to sign was because the defendant is his father.

14   In *R.J.R. Macdonald Inc. v. Canada* (Attorney General) (1994), 111 D.L.R. (4th) 385 (S.C.C.) Sopinka and Cory J.J. in delivering the judgment of the Court, said this at pages 402 and 403:

> What then are the indicators of "a serious question to be tried"? There are no specific requirements which must be met in order to satisfy this test. The threshold is a low one. The judge on the application must make a preliminary assessment of the merits of the case. Once satisfied that the application is neither vexatious nor frivolous, the motions judge should proceed to consider the second and third tests, even if of the opinion that the plaintiff is unlikely to succeed at trial. A prolonged examination of the merits is generally neither necessary nor desirable.

15   In *Danik Industries Ltd. v. Just Right Bumpers and Accessories Ltd.* (1993), 48 C.P.R. (3d) 20 (B.C.S.C.), affirmed (1993) 81 B.C.L.R. (2d) 91 (B.C.C.A.), Madam Justice Saunders granted an interlocutory injunction restraining the defendant company from manufacturing and selling bicycle racks using the same design as those marketed by the plaintiff.

16   At page 25, she noted that the main issue at trial was the right of the defendants to use the plaintiff's ideas for bicycle racks.

17   At page 26, she said this:

> These cases establish there is a fair issue to be tried. The plaintiff brought to Canada the idea of manufacturing and distributing the bicycle racks and started into that enterprise before the defendants became involved. Through Mr. Morris' imagination, there is a new design for bicycle racks in North America; he developed the marketing plan for this niche product. The draft contract presented by Mr. Morris to Mr. Justesen before Mr. Justesen had spent any significant amount of time making these products referred to confidentiality, yet Mr. Justesen did not tell him a term on confidentiality was out of the question. Mr. Justesen was not in the business of manufacturing bicycle racks or any sporting goods when he started to make the racks for Mr. Morris. Funds from sale were collected by Danik; this was not a license arrangement by which royalties were paid by a manufacturer to the plaintiff. Nor was this a situation in which the defendants made substantial fixed cost investments before starting to manufacture the product.

18   Prior to his employment with his son's company, the defendant was neither an industrial designer, nor a manufacturer, nor a marketer. The plaintiff alleges that the defendant's position as its production facility manager provided him with the intellectual property he needed to begin a business that directly competed with the plaintiff. Kayak rudders are a niche product. It is not a coincidence that the defendant began to produce and market the same niche product developed by the plaintiff.

19   I am of the opinion that the question of whether the defendant obtained information in a way that makes it tortious for him to use that information for his own gain after his employment with the plaintiff ended, is a serious and fair question to be tried.

20   In the *CKPG Television Ltd.* decision, when referring to the second prong of the test, Mr. Justice Lambert said this at 102:

> I would also adopt and follow the approach of Madam Justice McLachlin to the second prong of the test, namely, the assessment of balance of convenience. I would summarize that approach in this way: in assessing the balance of convenience, a judge should consider these points: the adequacy of damages as a remedy for the applicant if the injunction is not granted, and for the respondent if an injunction is granted; the likelihood that if damages are finally awarded they will be paid; the preservation of contested property; other factors affecting whether harm from the granting or refusal of the injunction would be irreparable; which of the parties has acted to alter the balance of their relationship and so affect the status quo; the strength of the applicant's case, any factors affecting the public interest; and any other factors affecting the balance of justice and convenience.

21   The question of whether or not irreparable harm will ensue if the injunction is not granted depends, in part, on whether or not damages would be an adequate remedy if the plaintiff succeeds at trial. In the *R.J.R. Macdonald Inc.* decision, Sopinka and Cory J.J. wrote this at page 405:

> At this stage the only issue to be decided is whether a refusal to grant relief could so adversely affect the applicants' own interests that the harm could not be remedied if the eventual decision on the merits does not accord with the result of the interlocutory application. "Irreparable" refers to the nature of the harm suffered rather than its magnitude. It is harm which either cannot be quantified in monetary terms or which cannot be cured, usually because one party cannot collect damages from the other. Examples of the former include instances where one party will be put out of business by the court's decision (*R.L.Crain Inc. v. Hendry* (1988), 48 D.L.R. (4th) 228, 67 Sask.R. 123, 8 A.C.W.S. (3d) 380 (Q.B.)); where one party will suffer permanent market loss or irrevocable damage to its business reputation (*American Cyanamid*, [1975] A.C. 396); or where a permanent loss of natural resources will be the result when a challenged activity is not enjoined (*MacMillan Bloedel Ltd. v. Mullin*, [1985] 3 W.W.R. 577, 61 B.C.L.R.145 (C.A.)).

22   I am of the view that the plaintiff's potential losses if the injunction is not granted do amount to irreparable harm. The plaintiff's kayak and kayak rudder business are closely interrelated. The plaintiff's business is highly profitable. The defendant has solicited the largest of the plaintiff's customers, representing a substantial portion of its rudder sales. The plaintiff company is concerned that competition by this defendant would cause disruption and confusion among its customers. If an injunction is not granted, and the plaintiff then succeeds at trial, it may not be able to reestablish its market presence.

23   The plaintiff has undertaken to compensate the defendant in damages for loss he sustains because of the interlocutory injunction, if the defendant succeeds at trial. In the event that the defendant succeeds at trial, he will be able to recommence his manufacturing business, starting from virtually the same market presence that he now has. His business is but several months old.

24   Finally, I am of the opinion that the overwhelming balance of convenience favours the plaintiff.

25   It is the plaintiff's business to design, manufacture and market kayaks and kayak rudders. In contrast, the defendant was formerly employed by a telephone company.

26   I have considered the relative strengths of the case as the matter appears from the affidavits. The defendant's argument that the plaintiff may no longer claim copyright protection, having failed to obtain protection under the Industrial Design Act, may prevail at trial. However, the plaintiff's allegation that the defendant wrongfully used the plaintiff's confidential information, and that he breached the confidentiality required by the terms of his employment, cannot be lightly cast aside.

27   I am of the opinion that the interlocutory injunction sought by the plaintiff ought to issue.

28   Until trial or until further order of this court, the defendant shall be restrained from manufacturing, assembling, or marketing kayak rudders, or kayak rudder components, or from directly or indirectly making use of any information imparted to him directly or indirectly by the plaintiff.

29   The defendant was not entitled to remove the plaintiff's customer lists or other confidential material from the plaintiff's facility. The plaintiff seeks a mandatory injunction requiring that all such material be returned to it. Sheila Gras, the defendant's daughter, deposes that she saw that the defendant had a binder containing design schematics and specifications for rudder production bearing the name of the plaintiff with the titles of the plaintiff's various rudder designs including the plaintiff's newest design, the "viscaya."

30   In his affidavit filed November 3, 2000, the defendant flatly denies this allegation. This issue cannot be resolved from conflicting affidavits.

31   In my opinion, an order for a mandatory injunction ought not to be made on the basis that no harm can flow from it, if the defendant does not have any material ordered to be returned. Such an order could be incapable of compliance. If a mandatory injunction is made, it ought to specify what materials are to be returned. Based on the evidence before me, I cannot make a finding that the defendant has possession of any of the plaintiff's materials; therefore, I decline to make an order for the "return" of documentation.

32   The costs of this application shall be costs in the cause.

QUESTIONS

1. What does copyright protect? Which of the plaintiff's intellectual property rights is he seeking to protect by copyright?

2. What is the basis for the defendant's assertion that since the plaintiff produced more than 50 rudders, there is no infringement of copyright?

3. What test does the plaintiff have to meet to be entitled to an interim injunction?

4. What facts did the court rely on in granting the interim injunction?

5. Would it have been necessary or desirable for the plaintiff to have had the defendant sign a confidentiality agreement? Why?

6. Could the plaintiff have obtained protection through patent? Discuss.

Essentially Yours Industries Corp.
v. Infinitec Marketing Group Inc.

[1999] M.J. No. 479, 41 CPC (4th) 342, [2000]5 WWR 283

Confirmed in Manitoba Court of Appeal (2000) MJ No. 212, MBCA 25, [2000] 7 WWR 297

Manitoba Court of Queen's Bench

November 10, 1999.

The advent of the Internet has made accessible much information which would previously have been difficult or impossible to obtain, though often through tedious and time-consuming searching. In our "information age", what is considered confidential? The scope of information considered confidential is the issue that the court had to grapple with in the following case.

1   **KENNEDY J.**:— The plaintiff, Essentially Yours Industries Corp. (EYI), seeks an injunction against the defendants prohibiting them from selling or distributing a list of names they acquired while under contract with the plaintiff.

2   The plaintiff is in the business of selling wellness and weight loss products accessible through the Internet. The plaintiff directly sells the product through a distribution network of Independent Business Associates (IBA's). EYI claims to have in the vicinity of some 350,000 IBA's enlisted for this purpose, of which only about

65,000 are active. For the purposes of this application, the plaintiff's concern is with respect to a list of approximately 7,000 IBA's which is in the hands of the defendant, Infinitec Marketing Group Inc. (Infinitec), and its principal officer, Alan Rosenberg.

3   The sale of the plaintiff's product is carried out through the network of IBA's and their downline IBA's, recruited by them in a multi-level distribution system which operates similar to a pyramid, with IBA's selling product and recruiting downline IBA's. The downline IBA's also sell the product with each level deriving a commission on the sale of the product ultimately purchased from the plaintiff.

4   The distribution begins with the plaintiff's web site which offers the product, but also enlists IBA's to sell the product. The plaintiff's business derives its revenue through the sales made by the IBA's, who in turn purchase the product from the plaintiff.

5   In recruiting IBA's, EYI retains a closely held list of its membership and the computerized ability to contact them. Various safeguards are put in place allowing only certain persons access, with the permission of the plaintiff, to the full list of IBA's.

6   The plaintiff regards the list of IBA's as the lifeline to its business and it keeps the names a closely guarded secret. The plaintiff refers to its list as its database since its marketing distribution system relies totally upon the IBA's and their down-lines. The list of IBA's may not technically be a database, but its recruitment of and reliance on the IBA's is the ultimate source for generating income. In my opinion, the list is a valuable asset of the plaintiff's business.

7   The defendant, Infinitec, signed a web site development agreement with EYI, the main feature of which was to engage Infinitec to prepare individual web sites for the IBA's and their downlines, in order to complete the multi-level distribution system through the use of Infinitec's expertise in reaching the plaintiff's market.

8   The IBA's are recruited from all over the world on the World Wide Web, and the web sites developed by the defendants through their "Virtual Web Site" program purports to allow purchasers and IBA's superior access to the distribution and purchase of the plaintiff's products.

9   The web site allows the IBA's to order product through a confidential number provided to each IBA when signed up under a standard agreement with the plaintiff. The agreement also governs the sale of the plaintiff's product to the individual IBA's, and provides for the recruitment of other IBA's and the revenue for doing so.

10   To provide the service of constructing individual web sites for the IBA's, Infinitec was necessarily given access to the plaintiff's downline tracking system of all online distributors who have signed up for the Infinitec "Virtual Web Site".

11   The Infinitec Virtual Web Site is the primary service provided by the defendants to the plaintiff as it affords the IBA access to the plaintiff's services, including its accessibility to customers and EYI's product.

12   The development of the web site for the individual IBA is done at a cost to the IBA.

13   The agreement between the plaintiff and the defendants contains provisions regarding the confidentiality and protection of EYI's distribution list and these provisions were clearly known to the defendants.

14   Under the agreement with Infinitec, one of the objectives articulated was as follows: "to ensure a high level of security to protect EYI's distribution list from unau-

thorized use". (See Agreement Exhibit A to the Affidavit of Brian Lavorato sworn July 20, 1999). One need not speculate that an unauthorized use was to provide the names to a competitor of the plaintiff.

15   Under the contract with EYI, Infinitec generated a list of approximately 7,000 names for whom it did work in establishing a web site with new IBA's and its downline members. Infinitec and EYI terminated their agreement, and Infinitec now seeks to sell the list of approximately 7,000 names or parts thereof to the plaintiff's competitors.

16   It is respecting the sale of these names that the plaintiff seeks to enjoin the defendants from so doing.

17   The parties have examined the various headings governing when an interim injunction ought to be allowed and argued the following factors:

   (a)   On a cursory review of the merits of the case, is there a serious question to be tried?

   (b)   Would the party seeking the injunction suffer irreparable harm?

   (c)   Which of the two parties will suffer the greater harm from refusing or granting the interlocutor injunction pending determination on the merits?

18   While this case involves the burgeoning litigation that is likely to arise out of e-commerce, it is clear that in developing the list of 7,000 IBA's, the list has considerable value. It represents numerous entrepreneurs who are disposed to selling a product through the Internet, and were the list to be sold to the plaintiff's competitors who may sell similar products, it leaves the plaintiff vulnerable in that a competitor might easily solicit the individual IBA and use his/her customer list to sell a competitor product at a lesser or more competitive price than the plaintiff. The list in its present form is also valuable to the defendants.

19   Inasmuch as the defendants obtained the list while under contract with the plaintiff, the list would not have come to them in the form that it is were it not for being engaged by the plaintiff to prepare web sites for the IBA's who have contracted with the plaintiff.

20   The defendants make the obvious argument that once the web site is prepared, the individual IBA is accessible to any member of the public by searching the Internet for persons selling the plaintiff's product. Those searches would reveal many of the names or the companies which have signed an agreement as IBA with the plaintiff. The defendants argue in that respect that the identity of the individual IBA's is within the public domain, and, therefore, the lists could hardly be referred to as confidential.

21   Accessibility, however, to this list involves a considerable degree of searching, though not providing all of the information available on the list which the defendants possess as a result of developing the individual web sites. The plaintiff argues that the discrete list of 7,000 persons, representing approximately 10% of the plaintiff's overall IBA list, is in a form and contains information which would take any other individual a considerable length of time to amass, even though the possibility of being able to do so is real.

22   The availability of the names in the public domain by culling them from a huge list involving considerable difficulty speaks to the issue of confidentiality. The effort needed to search for the list on an individual basis would, to say the least, be tedious, as each individual web site must be accessed through individual computer search and, therefore, would involve a considerable degree of time and energy.

23   The defendants, on the other hand, have a ready-made discrete list of all of the information without the need to tediously obtain it through individual searches on the Internet.

24   The process of sophisticated searching on the Internet might simplify the process although, if easily carried out, it was not made known to the court. I am left with the belief that, although it is possible to ultimately obtain much of the information contained in the list, the defendants could have avoided this litigation had the names been readily available. In my view, having the names in the organized fashion the defendants have it, renders it confidential information and worthy of protection.

25   In considering the foregoing, I am satisfied that there is a serious question to be tried, having to do with the ownership and control of the plaintiff's list of IBA's. If the defendants are not entitled to that list and it is in fact sold to competitors, which appears to be the intention of the defendants, there would be considerable losses incurred by the plaintiff, which to some extent would be difficult to calculate given the anonymity of the downline IBA's. In considering the harm that might be caused by the distribution of the plaintiff's list to others, it may not be incalculable, but would be based more or less on speculation than on real facts given the nature of the multi-level selling process. Finally, the defendants have never been involved in selling lists of this nature before, and their principal area of business is in the marketing of web sites and their particular ability to create web sites which are more readily accessible than others. It would therefore be the plaintiff's business that would be injured if the interlocutory injunction were not granted as opposed to the defendants, who haven't until this point relied upon the revenue of selling lists.

26   In considering these matters and concluding that the lists appear to be protected by the agreement entered into between the plaintiff and the defendants, and considering the nature of the lists and how they were acquired, I have no difficulty in concluding that the lists are confidential notwithstanding their availability on the Worldwide Web. By virtue of the ongoing nature of the plaintiff's business and the short term profit to be gained from the sale of these lists if it were to take place, the balance of convenience in my view favours the plaintiff.

27   It should be observed that the defendant, Alan Rosenberg, who is a principal of Infinitec Marketing Group, was also an IBA and has access to the lists through the same channel as his company. Hence, in the result, both defendants will be enjoined on an interlocutory basis from disposing and/or selling or releasing the lists.

28   If necessary, the settling of the terms of the injunction beyond the foregoing can be spoken to.

29   Interim injunction allowed.

QUESTIONS

1. In spite of the Internet access that the defendant had to the plaintiff's distribution list, what convinced the court that these lists were the confidential property of the plaintiff?

2. The defendant had entered into an agreement with the plaintiff. What provision was included in the agreement that related to the accessing of distribution lists? Could the provision have been improved?

3. What factors did the court rely on to grant the interim injunction?

Tele-Direct (Publications) Inc. v. Canadian Business Online Inc.

[1997] F.C.J. No. 1387, 138 FTR 245, 77 CPR (3d) 23
Federal Court of Canada - Trial Division
Judgment: September 17, 1997

Business names should be protected by trademark but registration of a trademark does not necessarily guarantee the right to use a business name. In this case, the defendant challenges the right of the plaintiff to police use of its trademark, and illustrates how carefully a plaintiff should guard this intellectual property right.

1   **JOYAL J**. (Order and Reasons for Order):— The Plaintiff applies to the Court for an interlocutory injunction pursuant to Rule 469 of the Federal Court Rules. This motion arises out of a trade-mark infringement action. The motion was very ably and professionally argued by counsel for the parties, who submitted to the Court a mass of affidavits, exhibits and supporting argument. For purposes of the case, however, I will not respond specifically to anything which was said or noted in the course of the two-day hearing.

1.   Facts

2   The Plaintiff company produces and distributes business and telephone directories in Canada. It also provides access to business listings on the Internet. It is the owner of the "Yellow Pages", "Pages Jaunes" and "Walking Fingers" (word and design) trade-marks in Canada. In its advertising, the Plaintiff has used the expression "Yellow Pages" since 1948 and the "Walking Fingers" logo since 1975.

3   The corporate Defendant, Canadian Business Online Inc., operates an internet site in association with electronic business directory services. On its internet site, the Defendant uses the expression "Canadian Yellow Pages on the Internet" alongside a representation of the "Walking Fingers" logo. The individual Defendant, Sheldon Klimchuk, is the sole director of Canadian Business Online, and according to the Plaintiff, its directing mind.

4   On June 20, 1997, the Plaintiff filed a statement of claim wherein it alleged that the Defendants had infringed the Plaintiff's proprietary rights in its trade-marks by using them without proper authorization. In particular, the Plaintiff claims that:

    (a)   the Defendants have made false and misleading statements tending to discredit the Plaintiff's business, contrary to s. 7(a) of the *Trade-marks Act, R.S.C.* 1985, c. T-13 (hereinafter "the Act");

    (b)   the Respondent has created confusion in Canada between the Plaintiff's and the Defendants' wares, services and businesses, contrary to s.7(b) of the *Act*;

    (c)   the Defendants have passed off their wares and services as those of the Plaintiff, contrary to s. 7(c) of the *Act*.

5   As a result, the Plaintiff maintains that it has suffered irreparable harm in that the distinctive character of the trade-marks has diminished and the value of the goodwill attaching the trade-marks has diminished. Thus, the Plaintiff states that it is entitled to remedies provided for under s. 53.2 of the *Act*. It is also seeking the award of punitive and exemplary damages for the willful infringement of its proprietary rights and for the Defendants' unwillingness to resolve the matter.

6   The Plaintiff applied for an interlocutory injunction pursuant to Rule 469 on June 20, 1997. A series of temporary injunctions were granted until the application came on for hearing on the merits, starting in Montreal on August 12, 1997, and continuing and concluding in Ottawa on September 8, 1997.

2.   Interlocutory Injunction

7   The test for granting an interlocutory injunction is the same three-part test outlined in *American Cyanamid Co. v. Ethicon Ltd.*, [1975] A.C. 396 (H.L.), as revised from time to time by the Supreme Court of Canada:

    (a)   the Plaintiff must demonstrate a serious question to be tried;

    (b)   the Plaintiff must convince the Court that it will suffer irreparable harm if the relief is not granted;

    (c)   the Court must consider whether the balance of convenience lies in favour of the granting or the refusing of the interlocutory injunction.

3.   The Case for the Plaintiff

8   In support of its motion, the Plaintiff has filed the affidavits of Patrick F. Crawford dated June 20 and August 5, 1997.

9   In these affidavits, lengthy evidence is presented on the history of the Plaintiff's trade-marks and their wide use throughout Canada. "Yellow Pages" and "Walking Fingers" are well-known in both official languages. The exposure to these marks is such that the public is compulsively identifying them with telephone business directories.

10   The affidavit material goes on to explore the many intrusions by some people into the exclusive field of use of the marks enjoyed by the Plaintiff. This requires vigilance and, at times, cases of infringement on the Internet cannot be immediately discovered. Generally speaking, however, the Plaintiff has jealously guarded its property in this field and has been reasonably successful in putting a stop to unlawful use, thereby maintaining the pristine legitimacy and integrity of the marks.

11   I might add here that for reasons which are not particularly well-known, the marks "Yellow Pages" or "Walking Fingers" and Design are not registered trade-marks in the United States. Recognizing the constant spillover of paper or electronic print into Canada, the Plaintiff is required to increase surveillance and wariness in order to keep its field of protection lean and clean.

12   Further allegations in the Plaintiff's evidence deal with the doctrine or criteria of irreparable harm. In particular, loss of distinctiveness is not easily quantifiable and cannot be adequately compensated.

13   Furthermore, the marks involved are licensed to a number of local, regional or provincial concerns. The Defendants' activities have seriously jeopardized the commercial value of such licensable property as well as the commercial relationship between the Plaintiff and its licensees and down the chain to the advertisers. In fact, by reason of medium of use, the conduct of the Defendants is an open invitation to others to encroach upon the Plaintiff's territory with seeming impunity.

14   Finally, the Plaintiff stresses the fact that it has been in the business of telephone directories for many years. The conduct of the Defendants constitutes a blatant appropriation of someone else's property, with no resources available to satisfy any claim for damages.

4.   The Case for the Defendants

15   The strongest case for the Defendants is that the trade-marks at issue are not trade-marks. Counsel argues that through a proliferation of the use of the trade-marks by the Plaintiff and its licensees, the words "Yellow Pages" and "Walking Fingers" and Design have become merely descriptive of business directories generally, In support, Defendants' counsel has filed over 700 pages of affidavits and exhibits showing the frequent uses of "Yellow Pages" for advertising solicitation in telephone directories.

16   Furthermore, the Defendants argue that the impugned marks are being widely used in a "descriptive" context by themselves. Added to this are examples of "Yellow Pages" being used with no indication of its trade-mark character.

17   As a result, conclude the Defendants, the Plaintiff has no assertible trade-mark rights against the Defendants because the trade-marks are not distinctive of the Plaintiff in Canada or elsewhere.

18   Examples galore are set out in the exhibits of electronic origin, respecting the so-called "generic" use of the trade-marks. Many of these examples are from use by licensees of the Plaintiff, of which there are in excess of 15 throughout Canada and who are directly or indirectly involved in the providing of yellow pages telephone directory services to their clientele. Other examples are provided, again of electronic origin, but the very characteristics of the Internet make their origin, source, purpose and finally use in Canada and in the neighbouring U.S. somewhat ambiguous or unclear.

5.   Findings

19   In my respectful view, the case has been made by the Plaintiff of the unlawful use in Canada by the Defendants of its trade-marks "Yellow Pages" and "Walking Fingers" and Design. This use is well established by the exhibits attached to the Plaintiff's affidavits. Furthermore, this Court can rely on admissions of use of the

marks by the Defendants themselves, their real defence being the non-existence of the marks as "trade-marks" on grounds of descriptiveness and generic meaning.

20   The Defendants obviously place a great reliance on the volume of yellow pages and walking fingers references found in the exhibits of electronic origin. Looking at this phenomenon in isolation, it would be easy to conclude that the marks have lost their distinctiveness in Canada and are no longer enjoying trade-mark status.

21   With respect, I do not believe that such a conclusion may be made. Messages on the Internet are not the only mode of communication. Apart from trade-marks, words and phrases can be found in the whole field of electronic commerce, with attendant problems relating to certainty, predictability and permanency. Certain statutes now carry specific provisions reelating to electronic transfer and records [See Note 2 below]. In "Leading Issues in Electronic Commerce" [See Note 3 below], Michael Erdle of Toronto sets out a series of these new dimensions requiring judicial and judicious attention.

Note 2: See the *Proceeds of Crime (Money Laundering) Act, R.S.C.* 1991, c. 26; and the *Bank Act*, R.S.C. 1991, c. 46, ss. 440 et seq.

Note 3: 12 C.I.P.R. p. 252.

22   In that same issue, at p. 245, Robert M. Frank speaks at length of the travails of the International Trade-Marks Association, whose views on the open range of the Internet and intellectual property rights are set out as follows:

> My views on the current Internet domain name crisis were sought. I replied that sooner or later, a case will go to trial over domain names conflicting with trade-marks. I anticipated that it will be decided that domain names are trade-marks. Once that case is closed, trade-mark owners will have to monitor domain names as they now monitor trade-marks and prosecute those who violate their trade-mark rights.

23   It may perhaps be said that the case before me is already one in which, notwithstanding the peregrinations of the Internet in terms of its seamless borders and its obtrusive presence across whole continents, the basic principles of property ownership require continuing protection. In so doing, the current historical doctrines surrounding the concepts of use, of making known, of distinguishing, of acquiring or losing proprietary interests in trade-marks, may require jurisprudential and statutory revision. In the meantime, however, this Court should eschew making a Frigidaire case out of the one before me or making a finding of multiple third party use of the impugned marks when such use is in the United States. In that respect, I do not believe that this Court should rely on the case law [See Note 4 below] submitted by the Defendants, where the context or the surrounding circumstances were radically different from the ones before me.

Note 4: See *N.W.L. Ltd. v. Woods*, [1979] W.L.R. 1294 (H.L.); *Caterpillar Inc. et al v. Chaussures Mario Moda Ltd.*, (1995) 62 C.P.R. (3d) 338; and *Centre Ice Ltd. v. National Hockey League*, (1994) 53 C.P.R. (3d) 34.

24   Much was said, in argument by counsel for the Defendants, of the affidavit of Sheldon Klimchuk as well as the affidavits of staff of counsel for the Defendants which in volume, are meant to create a cumulative effect that the trade-marks involved have lost their distinctiveness. I am not satisfied, however, that the exhibits cited are evidence of third party use of the marks in Canada. They are mostly, in my respectful view, spillover from usage in the U.S., where the marks are not protected. That use of Canadian trade-marks abroad might have some evidentiary weight in some cases is

not disputed. I should doubt, however, that it is very cogent when dealing with the alleged disappearing distinctiveness of a well-known trade-mark.

25   With respect to the affidavit of Sheldon Klimchuk and the transcript of his cross-examination thereon, I regret not being able to draw many inferences in his favour. His answers on cross-examination are often at considerable variance with facts alleged in his affidavit. The company he formed a few months ago appears to be a paper company and its owner, as sole director, has provided no evidence of any activity under corporate status. Nor has he provided any tangible evidence by way of supporting documents, minutes, contracts, lists, bank accounts and the like which would reflect to any extent the financial stability and viability of his operation, or his ability to satisfy Court costs in the successful after trial. Admittedly, the inordinately stretched nature of his evidence might have little to do with the validity of the trade-marks before me, but it does suggest that there is an element of charade somewhere in his scenario.

6.   Conclusions

26   It is my view that the case for the Plaintiff is strong. The evidence of unauthorized use knowingly made by the Defendants is pretty conclusive. Both sides of the issue were thoroughly canvassed by very able and persuasive counsel for the parties, and for that, I am duly thankful. Nevertheless, I am unable to endorse the Defendants' substantive strategy and the case for interlocutory relief for the Plaintiff becomes more convincing.

27   In this respect, I should adopt the comments of my colleague Dubé J. in *Tele-Direct (Publications) Inc. v. American Business Information Inc.* [See Note 5 below], where the allegations of infringement of the Plaintiff's trade-marks were substantially the same. Interlocutory relief was granted in that case and I see no reason why it should be refused in the case before me.

Note 5: 58 C.P.R. (3d) p. 10.

Order

28   Unless sooner varied, amended or terminated on consent of the parties or otherwise, the interim injunction dated September 8, 1997, is hereby made interlocutory and is to remain in force until final disposition of the action.

29   Costs in the cause.

QUESTIONS

1. What defence to trademark infringement does the defendant offer?
2. What should the holder of a trademark do to protect ownership of the trademark?
3. The plaintiff said that infringement of its trademark by the defendant could devalue the plaintiff's business. In what ways could the plaintiff's business be devalued?
4. The judge in this case seemed to question the true purpose of the president of the defendant when he says that "there is an element of charade in his scenario." What do you suppose the judge meant by this?

chapter twenty-three

Interests in Land

Lockmac Holdings Ltd. v. Earle

[1997] N.B.J. No. 35, 185 NBR (2d) 360, 12 RPR (3d) 142
New Brunswick Court of Queen's Bench
Judgment: January 17, 1997.

Common Law has established certain tests that agreements must meet in order to qualify as interests in land. If the agreement meets the tests, it will be enforceable against successors in title to the property to which it pertains, provided that it meets statutory requirements such as registration. Those requirements may vary from jurisdiction to jurisdiction.

1   **McLELLAN J.**:— The applicant Lockmac Holdings Limited owns land on Lancaster Avenue, Saint John. In 1937 when that land was deeded to a former owner, the deed was subject to restrictions. Those restrictions included that "any buildings . . . shall be single or semi-detached houses only". That sort of wording in a deed is a restrictive covenant.

2   The 1937 deed with the restrictive covenant was from the late William E. Earle, Jr. and his parents to the Ford Motor Company of Canada, Limited. It was registered in the Saint John County Registry office as Number 122942 in Book 225 at Page 229. The applicant is a successor in title to Ford. Thus the applicant knew about the restrictive covenant when the applicant acquired the land in 1994.

3   Now the applicant asks the court to order that the restrictive covenant:

> . . . does not run with the land and is therefore invalid against the applicant, a successor in title to Ford . . . .

4   When the Earles signed the 1937 deed to Ford, they also owned the adjacent property. The respondent Margaret M. Earle, the widow of William E. Earle, Jr., now owns that adjacent property. The other respondents own other property near the applicant's land.

5   The respondents Mrs. Earle and Mrs. May oppose this application. As they see it, the restrictive covenant means what it says, remains in full force and effect and may be enforced by them. They fear that the values of their homes will suffer if the Court rules that the restrictive covenant is invalid.

Wording of 1937 Deed

6   The 1937 deed is worded as follows:

THIS INDENTURE made this fifth day of February, A.D. 1937;- BETWEEN WILLIAM E. EARLE SR. of the Parish of Lancaster in the County of the City and County of Saint John and Province of New Brunswick, Retired, ANNIE E. EARLE, of the same place, wife of the said William E. Earle and WILLIAM E. EARLE, Jr., of the same place, Barrister (hereinafter called the Grantors) of the first part, and FORD MOTOR COMPANY OF CANADA, LIMITED, a Company duly incorporated under the laws of the Dominion of Canada, having its head office at the City of Windsor in the Province of Ontario, (hereinafter called the Grantee), of the second part.

WITNESSETH that the said Grantors for and in consideration of the sum of ONE DOLLAR of lawful money of Canada to them in hand well and truly paid, at or before the ensealing and delivery of these presents, by the said Grantee, the receipt whereof is hereby acknowledged, HAVE granted, bargained, sold, aliened, released, conveyed and confirmed and by these presents DO grant, bargain, sell, alien, release, convey and confirm unto the said Grantee, its successors and assigns -

"ALL that certain lot, piece and parcel of land situate, lying and being in the Parish of Lancaster, in the County of the City and County of Saint John and Province of New Brunswick lying to the southwest of Lancaster Avenue, bounded and described as follows, viz:- Beginning at the southerly corner of a lot of land deeded by Sterling Realty Limited to Norman J. Cabeldu and wife and running thence northwesterly along the rear line of said Cabeldu lot 81.2 feet or until it meets the southeasterly side line of a lot of land owned by Emma E. Duffy, thence southwesterly along said side of said Duffy lot until it meets the north-easterly side line of lot number 15 on a plan of land owned by the Estate of the late James S. Gregory, thence southeasterly along said side line of said lot Number 15 to the southeasterly corner thereof, thence in a straight line in a north-easterly direction to the place of beginning."

Subject, however, to the following restrictions: If any buildings are erected on the said lot of land, the said buildings shall be single or semi-detached houses only, and no house to cost less than Twenty-five Hundred Dollars ($2500.00); no fences to be erected around said property more than two feet in height, nor no erections shall be placed thereon or anything done thereon which might be deemed a nuisance. Subject also the [sic] right of the Vendors to remove any and all buildings on the said above described lot of land at any time within one month after the transfer of said property.

TOGETHER WITH all profits, privileges and appurtenances to the same belonging or in any manner appertaining, and the reversion and reversions, remainder and remainders, rents, issues and profits thereof and also all the estate, right, title, right and title, homestead, interest, use, possession, property, claim and demand either at law or in equity of them the said Grantors of, in, to or out of the same and every part and parcel thereof with the appurtenances.

TO HAVE AND TO HOLD the said lot, piece or parcel of land and premises hereby granted, bargained and sold or meant, mentioned or intended so to be and every part and parcel thereof with the appurtenances unto and to the use of the said Grantee, its successors and assigns, subject to the restrictions hereinbefore set forth, forever.

IN WITNESS WHEREOF the said Grantors have hereunto set their respective hands and seals the day and year first above written.

7   The restrictive covenant in that deed is not expressly stated to run for the benefit of described lands owned by the Earles or "covenantees". There is no indication in that deed that the Earles owned any other land, although in fact they owned adjacent land. Nor is there anything in the deed to suggest that the parcel conveyed was part of a common building scheme or subdivision.

Restrictive Covenants

8   The applicable rules distinguish between "personal covenants" and "covenants that run with the lands". Personal covenants are enforceable only by or against the original parties to the deed. Covenants that run with the lands can be enforced by or against subsequent owners of specific lands.

9   The New Brunswick Court of Appeal said in *Woolworth (F.W.) Co. v. Hudson's Bay Co. et al* (1985), 61 N.B.R.(2d) 403, at pp. 426-427:

> As Dickson, J., pointed out in *Friesen v. Valleyview Estates Ltd.* (1977), 18 N.B.R. (2d) 1; 26 A.P.R. 1, a restrictive covenant will run with the land in two circumstances. He said at page 5:
>
>> "I take it to be well settled in law that a restrictive covenant can be deemed to run with the land only in two circumstances, viz., (a) where the covenant, whether or not expressly made binding upon the successors and assigns of the grantee to whom it is initially conveyed, is expressly stated to run for the benefit of described lands of the covenantee; or, even if failing that, (b) the land against which the covenant is to run and the land for the benefit of

which the covenant is to run are both part of a common building scheme, all parts of which are subject to - if not totally then at least substantially - to the same restrictions."

As Article 31 of the Woolworth lease does not meet the first requirement, can the Woolco and Hudson's Bay stores be considered part of a common building scheme?

Before a restrictive covenant in a building scheme can be upheld, four requirements must be met: (1) there must have been a common vendor under whom the various owners derive title; (2) before the lands were sold there was a scheme relating to a defined area for sale in lots containing restrictions which were to be imposed on all the lots and which, though varying in details as to particular lots, were consistent only with some general development; (3) the restrictions were intended by the vendor to be and were for the benefit of all the lots, whether or not they were also intended to be and were for the benefit of other land retained by the vendor; and (4) that the original purchasers bought on the understanding that the restrictions were to enure for the benefit of the other lots included in the general scheme. See 14 Halsbury (4th Ed.) at p. 912 ff.; *Elliston v. Reacher*, [1908] 2 Ch. 374, at p. 384; *Scharf v. Mac's Milk Ltd.*, [1965] 2 O.R. 640, at p. 645.

10   Mr. Justice P.S. Creaghan elaborated on the rules as follows in *Arthur v. Nelson* (1988), 88 N.B.R. (2d) 217 at pp.221-222:

> The principal question here is whether the land for which the benefit is reserved is clearly defined. In order that the parties have intended that the restrictions be covenants that run with the land, the land retained by the covenantee and which is to be benefited by the restrictions, must be clearly defined.
>
> In this case there is no reference to the land to be benefited in the conveyance from Steeves to Probert which sets out the restrictions. DiCastri, the Law of Vendor and Purchaser (2d Ed. 1976), states at page 331.
>
> ". . . the mere fact that at the date of the agreement the vendor owns other land capable of being regarded as a 'dominant tenement' but not expressly referred to in the agreement, is not a sufficient compliance with the rule that at the date of the agreement there must be a coexistence of the dominant and servient tenements . . . the land to be benefited must be referred to or described in the deed itself."

In the case before us this criterion has not been met. The doubt, therefore, arises as to whether the restrictions were intended to benefit remaining lands of the covenantee or simply were covenants designed to personally benefit him. In such a case the question should be resolved in favour of the free use of the property and against the restriction with respect to whether they should bind subsequent assignees of the covenantor.

11   The Supreme Court of Canada in an Ontario case has also recognized that a deed with restrictive covenants must describe the land to be benefited. That court said:

> There is nothing in the conveyance from the Club to Mrs. Firth which attempts to annex the benefit of the covenant to any land retained by the Club. Further, there is no evidence anywhere in the record to indicate whether the Club had any such land capable of being benefited. The grantee simply covenants for herself, her heirs, executors, administrators and assigns, with the grantor, its ssuccessors and assigns, to the intent that the burden of the covenants should run with the lands during the corporate existence of the Club but nothing is said about any other lands. This fails to meet what I think must be regarded as the minimum requirements that the deed itself must so define the land to be benefited as to make it easily ascertainable. *Galbraith v. Madawaska Club Ltd.*, [1961] S.C.R. 639, at p. 653.

Derogation from Grant

12 As well, a classic New Brunswick case adopts the traditional rule of interpretation of deeds expressed by Chief Justice Robinson of Upper Canada in 1852 that:

> ... deeds shall be construed most strongly against the grantor, and therefore that he shall not be allowed to contradict or retract, by any subsequent part of the deed, the gift made in the premises. And it is in many books given as the common illustration of this rule, that if land were given in the premises to A. and his heirs, habendum to A. for life, the habendum is void, because it is utterly repugnant to and irreconcilable with the premises. *Ahearn v. Ahearn* (1894), 1 N.B. Eq. 53, at pp. 55-56, quoting *Meyers v. Marsh* (1852), 9 U.C.Q.B.242 at p. 245.

Precedents

13 Those previous decisions are called precedents. By following precedents and other legal authorities, courts decide similar cases the same. In that way the law remains equal, predictable and common.

Opinion

14 In this case the 1937 deed itself did not "define the land to be benefited as to make it easily ascertainable", contrary to the "minimum requirement" in *Galbraith v. Madawaska Club* and *Arthur v. Nelson*. Nor was the restrictive covenant made in the context of a building scheme within the requirements of cases such as *Elliston v. Reacher* and *Woolworth v. Hudson's Bay*.

15 For these reasons in my opinion the restrictive covenant in the 1937 deed was a personal covenant between Ford and the Earles who signed that deed. It does not run with the land because the deed itself did not define the land to be benefited, nor was it part of a building scheme. Thus the restrictive covenant is invalid against the applicant and cannot be enforced by the respondents.

16 The restrictive covenant also purports to take away or derogate from the grant made in the previous paragraphs of the deed, contrary to the rule in *Meyers v. Marsh* and *Ahearn v. Ahearn*.

Conclusion

17 For these reasons I allow the application. The restrictive covenant in the 1937 deed is now invalid. That covenant does not affect the applicant's title to the property.

QUESTIONS

1. Why did the court hold that the restrictive covenant in the 1937 deed was not a restrictive covenant? Does this mean that the restriction was unenforceable? Explain.

2. How should the restriction have been worded to qualify as a restrictive covenant?

3. Why did the restriction not qualify as a building scheme?

chapter twenty-four

Landlord and Tenant

Mac Investments and Consultants Ltd. v. Gittens/Casey Management Co.

[1993] N.J. No. 263, 110 Nfld & PEIR 350
Newfoundland Supreme Court - Trial Division
Judgment: filed August 12, 1993.

When faced with a situation where a tenant may be in the process of abandoning premises, a landlord must proceed carefully in order to preserve a right to be compensated for losses incurred. This case is an illustration of what the result may be if a landlord does not consider its position carefully enough before the landlord takes action.

1   **MERCER J.**:— The Plaintiff (Lessor) seeks judgment against the Third Defendant (Casey), as guarantor of a lease. The claim covers (a) rent for the final five months of the lease and (b) compensation for the removal of fixtures and resultant damage.

Issues

2   The chief issues are:

1. (a) Was the Lease terminated when the Lessor changed the lock to the exterior access door?

   (b) Is the Lessor entitled to compensation for rent for the period following termination?

2.   The extent of liability arising from the removal of certain items from the leased premises.

Findings

1. (a) The Lessor terminated the Lease by changing the lock to the exterior access door.

   (b) The Lessor cannot claim compensation for rent due after the date of termination.

2.   The Lessor is entitled to compensation for the removal of fixtures other than trade fixtures, and for damages caused by the removal of fixtures and chattels.

Summary of Facts

3   In early 1992 a law firm, Gittens/Casey, carried on its practice from leased premises at the former Evening Telegram Building 271 - 275 Duckworth Street, St. John's (the Building). The First Defendant (Lessee), the firm's management company, had taken a five year lease (Lease) expiring April 30, 1993. The Lease was guaranteed by the firm's parties, the Second Defendant and Casey. A Guaranteed Investment Certificate (GIC) for $4500.00 was deposited as security.

4   The Lease expressly provided for rent to be paid on the first day of each month. The Lessee in practice paid on or after the fifteenth of the month. The evidence did not establish an agreement, express or implied, to amend the due date for rent.

5   The Lessor bought the Building on June 12, 1993 and received an assignment of the Lease. The law firm had vacated the leased premises prior to the purchase. At that time Casey provided written assurance that the Lease would be honoured for the balance of its term.

6   In the following months the monthly rent payments (agreed to be $5333.33 plus GST) were continually in arrears. The last rent payment, made on December 2nd, was for November 1992. The Lessor did not seek to terminate the Lease or accelerate the rent prior to January 1993.

7   In late October or early November Casey directed a contractor to remove four bookcases from the leased premises. The bookcases were part of a set which were not built-in or attached to the premises. The Lessor learned of their removal and objected. Casey had left the key to the premises with his contractor and had authorized him to take the remaining cabinets, if he wished. The contractor returned in late December or early January and removed (a) free-standing bookcases, (b) several office cabinets, some of which were screwed to the wall, and (c) kitchen cabinets and a sink. The walls of the leased premises were damaged by the removal of these items.

8   In early January the Lessor learned of the contractor's action. He assumed it had been done by Casey or the Second Defendant. At that time the Lessor also received a statutory notice advising that Gittens/Casey and the First Defendant were insolvent and a receiver had been appointed to realize upon an assignment of book debts and a debenture. The Lessor was then due rent for December 1992 and January 1993.

9   The Lessor consulted its lawyer on its remedies and on January 6, 1993, against the advice of its lawyer the Lessor changed the lock to the exterior door of the Building. The lock of the interior door to the leased premises was not changed and the leased premises were therefore accessible during normal business hours. The Lessor was not subsequently contacted by any of the Defendants seeking admission to the leased premises.

10   The Lessor's president stated that the exterior lock was changed to protect its property and to ensure nothing further was taken from the leased premises. He testified that the Lessor did not intend to exclude the Defendants and that the Lessor did not therefore retake possession. However a different position was stated in his affidavit filed in support of an application for summary judgment which stated:

> "The Plaintiff had no reason to believe that the Defendants would not continue to remove fixtures from the Premises and in an effort to protect the Premises and preserve its assets and because the Plaintiff considered the removal of assets from the Premises a default under the Lease, the Plaintiff repossessed the Premises pursuant to clause 10 of the Lease by changing the locks on the Premises on or about January 8, 1993." (Cl.9; Affidavit of May 7/93).

11   On January 15, 1993 the Lessor's lawyer wrote Casey as guarantor of the lease. Pursuant to the guarantee and the acceleration clause of the Lease the letter demanded payment of $28,466.66 (including $5000 for removal of fixtures and resultant damage) by January 29, failing which "we will assume you have repudiated the lease". No reply was received and on February 1st the Lessor advised it had terminated the Lease claiming damages for losing the benefit of the Lease over its unexpired term.

12   Casey admits his guarantee and states it is limited to monies properly due and owing by the Lessee.

Relevant Lease Provisions (Summarized)

Access

Cl.1.   "Normal Business Hours" are defined and followed by an explicit acknowledgement by the Lessor that the Lessee intended to make use of the premises outside Normal Business Hours.

Cl.7(d)   The Lessor agreed the Lessee was to have use during Normal Business Hours of the entrances, stairways and halls leading to the premises.

Rent - Due Date

Cl.4 Rent was to be paid on the first day of each month.

Removal of Fixtures and Chattels

Cl.5(c)(11). Trade fixtures and chattels belong to the Lessee, and may be removed if rent is current. Leasehold improvements are the Lessor's property and are not to be removed.

Liability of Lessee for third parties

Cl.5(b). Damage or loss to the premises deliberately or negligently caused by the Lessee or a third party is the responsibility of the Lessee if it permitted the third party to be on the premises.

Acceleration/Default

Cl.10. Upon the occurrence of numerous specified events (including non-payment of rent, vacating the premises, appointment of a receiver of the lessee, breach of any covenant) the current month's rent and the next six months rent are stated to be due and payable. The Lessor may claim the rent immediately. Further, at the Lessor's option, the terms shall immediately be determined and the Lessor may, without notice, re-enter and take possession.

Non-Waiver

Cl. 11. A waiver of a default or breach of any covenant or condition shall not operate as a waiver of the Lessor's rights respecting any continuing or subsequent default or breach.

Application of Law to Facts

1.(a) Termination of Lease

13   The Lease expressly addressed use of the leased premises outside normal business hours. It follows that the Lessor's fundamental obligation to provide access was not limited to normal office hours. The changing of the exterior lock restricted the Lessee's access in clear breach of the Lessor's obligation. Objectively viewed it was an act inconsistent with the continuance of the Lessee's term. (*Country Kitchen Limited v. Wabush Enterprises Ltd. et al* (1980) 35 Nfld. & P.E.I.R. 391 (Nfld. C.A.) at pp. 395-396; *Re Cooper & Lybrand Ltd. and Royal Bank of Canada* (1982) 137 D.L.R. (3d) 356).

14   The Lessor therefore had forfeited the term by its action on January 8, 1993. It was entitled to do so under Clauses 10 and 11 of the Lease as the Lessee had defaulted in paying rent.

1.(b) Compensation for Rent

15   The Lessor is entitled to rent for December 1992 and January 1993. January's rent was due prior to the termination of the Lease. Is the Lessor entitled to compensation for the rent due for February, March and April 1993, the balance of the term of the Lease? The claim must be based on either (i) common law or (ii) Clause 10 of the Lease.

(i) Common Law

16   The Lessor would be entitled to damages for losing the benefit of the Lease over its unexpired term if the Lease was properly terminated by the Lessor following repudiation by the Lessee (*Highway Properties Ltd. v. Kelly, Douglas & Co. Ltd.* (1971) 17 D.L.R. (3d) 710 (S.C.C.)).

17   Repudiation occurs where a party clearly indicates that its obligations will not be honoured. Not every lease default, even one in, the payment of rent, constitutes a repudiation. Whether a breach amounts to repudiation is not to be lightly found or inferred and in the words of a leading text: "What has to be established is that the defaulting party has made his intention clear beyond reasonable doubt no longer to perform his side of the bargain". (Cheshire and Fifoot's Law of Contract, 11th ed., M.P. Furmston, Butterworths, 1981, p. 523).

18   In this case (a) rent was overdue on January 8 but rent had previously been overdue and then paid. (eg. November's rent was paid December 2); (b) the premises were vacant for many months during which rent payments were accepted by the Lessor; (c) fixtures had been removed by a contractor. The Lessor assumed (but did not make reasonable inquiries to confirm) that Casey or the Second Defendant had removed the fixtures.

19   In these circumstances I do not consider that the Lessee had repudiated the Lease prior to January 8, 1993. I also note that the Lessor had not indicated its intention to seek damages (for losing the benefits of the unexpired term) prior to or coincident with the termination. The principles outlined in *Highway Properties* therefore do not apply.

  (ii) Clause 10

20   Clause 10 states that where rent is overdue (or other obligations breached) the current month's rent and the ensuing six months' rent immediately become due and payable and the Lessor may immediately claim the same. The Lessor is further provided with the option of forfeiting the term and re-taking possession.

21   Clauses providing that leases are void for breach of conditions are interpreted to mean they are voidable at the option of the Lessor. (See Williams & Rhodes, Canadian Law of Landlord & Tenant, 6th ed., Carswell v. 2, para. 12:8:1). A similar rule of interpretation applies to rent acceleration clauses. The Lessor must clearly claim the benefit of the clause. If this is not done prior to termination of the Lease the Lessor is left with its common law remedies.

22   No claim for accelerated rent was made prior to January 8 when the Lessor changed the lock and thereby forfeited the term.

23   The Lessor is therefore entitled to rent for December 1992 and January 1993 against which must be credited the amount realized by the Lessor on the GIC deposited as security.

2.   Removal of Items from Leased Premises

24   The prohibition against the Lessee removing trade fixtures and chattels provides security for the Lessor's remedy of distraint. Ownership of trade fixtures and chattels is not affected and remains with the Lessee. The Lessor cannot therefore recover for rent and for loss of trade fixtures and chattels.

25   I classify the items removed as follows:

(a)   bookcases. I accept that these were free-standing. These were therefore chattels and not fixtures to which the Lessor had a claim.

(b)   office cabinets and shelves. The evidence establishes that only some of these were attached to the wall by screws. They were therefore easily removable and not sufficiently attached to the premises to alter their fundamental nature. (Williams & Rhodes, Canadian Law of Landlord and Tenant, supra, para. 13:2:4, citing Birch v. Dawson (1834) 6 Cr. & P. 658). Had I concluded that these items were sufficiently affixed to be considered fixtures I would further consider the same to be trade fixtures. (c) kitchen cabinets and sink. Casey has acknowledged that these items were leasehold improvements.

26   At common law and under Clause 5 of the Lease the Lessee was responsible for any damage caused to the leased premises by the removal of chattels or trade fixtures. This includes damages caused by the contractor who was permitted access by Casey.

27   The Lessor is therefore entitled to compensation for (a) the removal of the kitchen cabinets and sink and (b) damages caused to the leased premises by the removal of all items. The quantum of damages were not proven at the hearing and I exercise my discretion under Rule 44 to direct that judgment be entered with damages to be assessed.

Other Defendants

28   The Lessor seeks judgment against Casey alone and not against the Lessee and Second Defendant, neither of which filed a defence. This has been challenged by Casey. The guarantee makes Casey jointly and severally liable with the Lessee and permits the Lessor to proceed against Casey without first exhausting its remedies against the Lessee.

29   The Court will not force a plaintiff to enter judgment against other defendants who are jointly liable with the party against whom judgment is sought. Casey has legal remedies to prevent overpayment of the Plaintiff and to pursue contribution from the Lessee and Second Defendant.

Judgment

30   Judgment shall be entered for the Plaintiff for:

(a)   Rent for December 1992 and January 1993 less the amount realized by the Plaintiff on the GIC security;

(b)   Damages to be assessed for (a) removal of kitchen fixtures and (b) damages to the leased premises as noted;

(c)   Costs to be taxed on a party and party basis.

QUESTIONS

1. When the landlord bought the building from a previous owner, the court said that the tenant "provided written assurance that the lease would be honoured for the balance of its term." Was this assurance necessary? Explain.

2. Why might the tenant have had the contractor remove the bookshelves and cabinets from the premises?

3. What right did the landlord forfeit when it changed the locks? Explain.

4. Why did the court hold that the landlord was not entitled to rely on the acceleration clause in the lease?

5. When the landlord changed the locks on the premises, the tenant was in arrears of rent, and had removed the bookshelves and cabinets. What should the landlord have done instead of changing the locks?

6. What liability would the tenant have incurred if the cabinets and shelves were found to be ordinary fixtures, and not trade fixtures? Explain.

chapter twenty-five

Mortgages

Monarch Trust Co. v. Low

[1993] O.J. No. 499
Ontario Court of Justice - General Division
February 26, 1993

It is fairly common when property is transferred, that purchasers agree to assume the obligations of the vendor under an existing mortgage, rather than negotiating their own financing with another lender. Of concern to a vendor in this situation may be the possible liability that could accrue if the purchaser fails to meet the obligations under the mortgage.

1   **ADAMS J.**: (Orally):— This is an appeal from an order of a Master on an application for summary judgment where the summary judgment was refused. No affidavit was filed by the defendants and accordingly the matter must be examined on the plaintiff's material including the related cross-examination of the affiant for the plaintiff on his affidavit.

2   The action is by Monarch Trust Company on the covenant of a mortgage it took from Stephen and Theresa Low to support the advance of $250,000 on a commercial property. The mortgage was dated March 31, 1989 at 13% per annum. It provided a maturity date of April 1, 1991. There was no restriction in the mortgage preventing its assumption by a transferee of the equity of redemption without the mortgagee's consent. The Lows in fact transferred the property for more than they paid for it to Wing Chan Inc. on or about December 6, 1989. Wing Chan did not enter into any formal assumption agreement with Monarch Trust and Monarch accepted its payments as the mortgage progressed. The Lows as well did not seek a release from their mortgage covenant nor did they choose to pay the mortgage off as they were entitled to on the receipt of the funds from Wing Chan. The Lows heard no more from Monarch until the commencement of this action on August 10, 1992. Monarch accepted a further twelve post-dated cheques from the new owner. There was no formal extension or renewal agreement in writing but Monarch accepts it effectively committed to a further year on the same terms and conditions. In September, 1991 Wing Chan requested from Monarch and received a discharge statement indicating what was required to pay the mortgage off. However, the mortgage was not paid off. On April 1, 1992 Monarch asked for and received twelve more post-dated cheques. Some of these cheques were not honoured but were replaced until the cheque of July, 1992. That cheque was neither honoured nor replaced whereupon Monarch elected to sue the Lows on their covenant and not Wing Chan Inc. A key term of the mortgage is paragraph 17. Known colloquially as a "no prejudice" clause, it provides:

> No extension of time given by the Chargee to the Chargor or anyone claiming under him, or any other dealing by the Chargee with the owner of the land or of any part thereof, shall in any way affect or prejudice the rights of the Chargee against the Chargor or any other person liable for the payment of the money secured by the Charge, and the Charge may be renewed by an agreement in writing at maturity for any term with or without an increased rate of interest notwithstanding that there may be subsequent encumbrances. It shall not be necessary to register any such agreement in order to retain priority for the Charge so altered over any instrument registered subsequent to the Charge. Provided that nothing contained in this paragraph shall confer any right of renewal upon the Chargor. (emphasis added).

3   The plaintiff relies on several cases materially similar to the instant matter in asserting that the transfer of the equity of redemption and subsequent extensions or renewals accorded a new owner do not release the original mortgagors from their covenant. (See *Forster v. Ivey*, (1901), 2 O.L.R. 480 (C.A.); *Malaviya et al. v. Lankin et al.* (1986), 53 O.R. (2d) 1 (Ont. C.A.); and *Financeamerica Realty Ltd. v. Holloway* (1986), 53 O.R. (2d) 3 (Ont. H.C.)). There can, of course, be a release and discharge of the original mortgage covenant directly or by way of novation but the constituent elements of such transactions are crucial. In considering the requirements to support the finding of a novation, Wilson J. in *National Trust Co. v. Mead et al.* (1990), 71 D.L.R. (4th) 488 (S.C.C.) at pp. 500-501 stated:

The common law has long recognized that while one may be free to assign contractual benefits to a third party, the same cannot be said of contractual obligations. This principle results from the fusion of two fundamental principles of contract law: (1) that parties are able to make bargains with the parties of their own choice (freedom of contract); and (2) that parties do not have to discharge contractual obligations that they had no part in creating (privity of contract). Our law does, however, recognize that contractual obligations which a party has freely assumed may be extinguished in certain circumstances and the doctrine of novation provides one way of achieving this.

A novation is a trilateral agreement by which an existing contract is extinguished and a new contract brought into being in its place. Indeed, for an agreement to effect a valid novation the appropriate consideration is the discharge of the original debt in return or a promise to perform some obligation. The assent of the beneficiary (the creditor or mortgagee) of those obligations to the discharge and substitution is crucial. This is because the effect of novation is that the creditor may no longer look to the original party if the obligations under the substituted contract are not subsequently met as promised.

Because assent is the crux of novation it is obvious that novation may not be forced upon an unwilling creditor and, in the absence of express agreement, the court should be loath to find novation unless the circumstances are really compelling. Thus, while the court may look at the surrounding circumstances, including the conduct of the parties, in order to determine whether a novation has occurred, the burden of establishing novation is not easily met. The courts have established a three-part test for determining if novation has occurred. It is set out in *Polson v. Wulffsohn* (1890), 2 B.C.R. 39, as follows:

1. The new debtor must assume the complete liability;

2. The creditor must accept the new debtor as principal debtor and not merely as an agent or guarantor; and

3. The creditor must accept the new contract in full satisfaction and substitution for the old contract.

There has been some disagreement among courts across the country as to the weight to be attributed to these elements and it might be helpful to review some of the authorities. Indeed, such a review makes it clear that these three factors are not the only ones to be considered. The courts are usually confronted with an amalgam from which they must distil their finding of fact as to whether novation has occurred or not.

4   The defendants submit that a novation may have occurred at the time of the two informal extensions or renewals and that a trial is required to explore that issue where representatives of Wing Chan Inc. and a real estate agent retained by that company can be called as witnesses. The defendants also intend to examine the relationship of Monarch and Wing Chan in the context of a falling real estate market in order to argue that Monarch's conduct in suing the original mortgagors is harsh, oppressive and unreasonable and not contemplated by an "implied" term in paragraph 17 of the mortgage to this effect. Finally, the defendants submit paragraph 17 cannot be relied upon by the plaintiff because the extensions were not in writing as required by that clause.

5   The approach on summary judgment is set out by Henry J. in *Pizza Pizza Ltd. v. Gillespie* (1990), 75 O.R. (2d) 225 at pp. 237-238 as follows:

In my opinion, there is a lower threshold that is contemplated by the new Rule 20 and the case law developing. It is that the court, in taking a hard look at the merits, must decide whether the case merits reference to a judge at trial. It will, no doubt, have to go to trial if there are real issues of credibility, the resolution of which is essential to determination of the facts. That aside, however, the rule now contemplates that the motions judge will have before him sworn testimony in the affidavits and other material required by the rule in which the parties put their best foot forward. The motions judge, therefore, is expected to be able to assess the nature and quality of the evidence supporting "a genuine issue for trial"; the test is not whether the plaintiff cannot possibly succeed at trial; the test is whether the court reaches the conclusion that the case is so doubtful that it does not deserve consideration by the trier of fact at a future trial; if so then the parties "should be spared the agony and expense of a long and expensive trial; if so then the parties "should be spared the agony and expense of a long and expensive trial after some indeterminate wait" (per Farley J. in Avery).

In my view, the general thrust of the seminal decisions of the court of Rule 20, where the moving party is the defendant, may be summarized thus for present purposes:

Rule 20 contemplates a radically new attitude to motions for judgment; the objective is to screen out claims that is the opinion of the court, based on evidence furnished as directed by the rule, ought not to proceed to trial because they cannot survive the "good hard look".

It is not sufficient for the responding party to say that more and better evidence will (or may) be available at trial. The occasion is now. The respondent must set out specific facts and coherent evidence organized to show that there is a genuine issue for trial.

Apparent factual conflict in evidence does not end the inquiry. The court may, on a common sense basis, draw inferences from the evidence.

6   In *Financeamerica Realty Ltd. v. Holloway*, supra, the plaintiff was the assignee of a mortgage granted by the defendants. The mortgage provided that no extension of time given by the mortgagee to anyone claiming under the mortgagor should affect the rights of the mortgagee against the mortgagors. The respondents sold to third parties who covenanted to assume the mortgage and to indemnify and save the respondents harmless therefrom. The plaintiff thereafter entered into an extension agreement with the third parties at a substantially higher interest rate. When the third parties defaulted, the plaintiff brought action on the covenant against the defendants and the parties stated a case for the opinion of the court on the defendants' liability. In finding for the plaintiffs, Krever J. stated at p. 8:

It is true that there are distinctions between the facts of *Malaviya et al. v. Lankin et al.* and the facts of this case. The first extract reproduced above makes it clear that, unlike this case, in the Malaviya case, the rate of interest payable under the mortgage was not altered and no agreement extending the term of the mortgage was entered into with the purchaser of the equity of redemption. As I read the reasons of the Court of Appeal, however, these distinctions do not affect the matter. The critical point is that s-s.19(2) [now s-s.20(2)] of the Act does not have the effect of converting the original mortgagors from primary debtors to sureties and the sale by them of the equity of redemption did not affect their liability as mortgagors for payment of the moneys secured by the mortgage. Indeed, in the light of that interpretation of the subsection, it can be said that in this case the plaintiff is in even a stronger position than the appellants were in the Malaviya case. The proviso set out above is an express agreement by the defendants that no extension of time given by the mortgagee and no other dealing between the mortgagee and the owner of the equity of redemption would prejudice the right of the mortgagee to proceed against the defendants for payment of the moneys secured by the mortgage.

7   Against this legal and factual backdrop this appeal must be allowed and summary judgment granted. On these facts, there can be no genuine issue of novation or implied terms. Paragraph 17 is clear and all embracing on these facts. In my view, the plaintiff "extended" the mortgage for Wing Chan or engaged in an "other dealing" with that owner within the meaning of paragraph 17. There is, as well, nothing harsh or oppressive concerning the plaintiff's conduct. Rather, Monarch is exercising a contractual right granted to it by the Lows and for which they derived a commercial benefit. They could have paid the mortgage off when they transferred the property to Wing Chan. Alternatively, they might have sought a release on their personal covenant from Monarch. Further still, they could have required a personal indemnification from the principals of Wing Chan as a condition of the transfer. It is not for a court to step in now and alter the terms of the mortgage contract between Monarch and the Lows. It is also not sufficient for a responding party to say that more and better evidence "may" be available at trial. The respondent must set out specific facts organized to show there is a genuine issue for trial. It has failed to do so.

8   Judgment will go accordingly.

9   The endorsement on the Record reads:

Motion for extending time to appeal granted. Appeal allowed and order granting summary judgment to go for reasons given orally. Costs to the appellant fixed in the amount of $2,500.

QUESTIONS

1. What is a novation?
2. Why did the court hold that there had been no novation in this case?
3. Would it have made a difference if the lender had consented to the purchasers assuming the mortgage? Explain.
4. What would the borrowers have had to do to ensure that they were free of obligations under the mortgage when they sold the property to the purchasers?

part six

Business
Organizations

chapter twenty-six

Sole Proprietorships and Partnerships

Punjab Foods Centre Ltd. v. Bailie

[1999] B.C.J. No. 2331
British Columbia Supreme Court
October 20, 1999

A sole proprietorship is an owner-operated business that is not incorporated. A major disadvantage of this form of business association is that the owner-operator has unlimited personal liability for the debts and obligations of the business. In order to avoid this personal liability, the owner has to form a corporation and ensure that the corporate name is used in connection with all business dealings.

1   **BAUMAN J.**:— This is an appeal under the *Small Claims Act*, R.S.B.C. 1996, c. 430 from the decision of Rae P.C.J. dated 25 June 1999.

2   The learned judge allowed the claimant's claim of $6,023.64 for goods sold and delivered against the personal appellant.

3   The issue before the courts here and below is simply whether the appellant and/or his incorporated company, Tandoori Taj Restaurant Ltd., is legally responsible for the admitted debt.

4   I have concluded that Judge Rae was correct in her disposition of the claim for the reasons given by her.

5   Briefly the facts are these.

6   The claimant is in the business of supplying food to restaurants and temples.

7   For a number of years the claimant supplied Tandoori Taj Restaurant when it was operated through the corporate defendant by Ranjit Walia, a friend of the claimant's principal.

8   Upon sale of the restaurant, Walia advised the claimant's Harinder Toor, that Bill Bailie was taking over the business and that after 14 August 1997 he would be responsible for payment of the bills.

9   Thereafter, the claimant took the usual orders from the restaurant and made deliveries until November 1997.

10   In September 1997, Mr. Toor attended at the restaurant and picked up a cheque from Bill Bailie in payment of the then outstanding account. It was a personal cheque. It was the only payment received on the account.

11   The restaurant ceased operations in February 1998.

12   Mr. Toor maintains that he was never informed that the restaurant was being operated through an incorporated company. The claimant's invoices were addressed to "Bill Tandoori Taj" or "Tandoori Taj".

13   Mr. Bailie had no dealings directly with the claimant or Mr. Toor until after the purchase of the restaurant and these discussions concerned payment of the outstanding account.

14   The trial judge concluded her recital of the evidence and the facts found by her (at 3):

> He [Mr. Bailie] did not discuss with Mr. Toor at that point that the restaurant was being operated by a company. He agrees that he paid one invoice with a personal cheque because there was some difficulty with information printed on the company cheques for a brief period of time. He says that the suppliers were advised by letter subsequent to this of the reason for the use of the personal cheques. There is no copy of that letter in evidence, and Mr. Toor was not asked directly about that letter, although he did say when asked that he had never received any documents from Mr. Bailie. Mr. Bailie maintained that Mr. Walia was well aware that the company would be operating the restaurant and that Mr. Walia had volunteered to pass that information on to the suppliers.

15   That review of the evidence gives sufficient context for these reasons.

16   The trial judge applied the decision in *Con-Force Products Ltd. v. Rosen and Boyle* (1967), 61 W.W.R. 129, 64 D.L.R. (2d) 63 (Sask.Q.B.). Con-Force follows a line of cases which hold that, in determining the terms of a contract, including which parties are liable on that contract, "the question is not what the parties had in their minds, but what reasonable third parties would infer from their words and conduct" (Con-Force at 141, citing Cheshire and Fifoot, Law of Contract, 6th ed., at p. 204).

17   *Con-Force* also stands for the proposition that a person acting in a representative capacity can be found to be personally liable on a contract in certain circumstances (at 141):

> Again, a specific identifiable person may act either for himself or in a representative capacity for another, for example: as an agent, as a partner for the partnership, or as an officer or director for a body corporate. It is sufficient to state at this point that in general a person who renders services to another at the latter's request, without notice that the latter is acting in a representative capacity, may enforce the individual liability of such other, notwithstanding no inquiry was made as to the capacity in which the latter acted: 17A Corpus Juris Secundum, at p.342.

18   The court in *Con-Force* held that the party claiming to act in a representative capacity, Mr. Rosen, was personally liable for the contract in question:

> It is quite clear that Rosen believed that he was acting as the president of and for the company in accepting the plaintiff's offer, and that he had no intention of entering into the contract in his personal capacity. But Rosen in his personal capacity and Rosen in his presidential capacity was still one and the same specific and identifiable person. It was equally clear that at that time the plaintiff had no knowledge of even the existence of the company. There was no duty upon the plaintiff when it made an offer to Rosen to inquire as to whether he was acting for himself or in a representative capacity. It was for Rosen to advise the plaintiff that he was acting in a representative capacity for the company in order to escape from personal liability by accepting an offer made to him. The plaintiff would then have had the opportunity to contract or not with the company as it saw fit, because the company could not accept the offer made to Rose, another person.

19   Similarly, the court in *Selby's Electrical Ltd. v. Bruce* (1984), 3 C.L.R. 314, 46 Nfld. & P.E.I.R. 240 (Nfld.D.C.), at 321, cited Halsbury's Laws of England, 3rd ed. (1 Hals. (3d) 228, para. 516), as authority for the proposition that:

> Where a person makes a contract in his own name without disclosing either the name or the existence of a principal, he is personally liable on the contract to the other contracting party, though he may be in fact acting on the principal's behalf. Nor does he cease to be liable on the discovery of the principal by the other party unless and until there has been an unequivocal election by the other contracting party to look to the principal alone.

20   Other decisions follow similar reasoning: see e.g., *Lohnes v. Corkum* (1981), 121 D.L.R. (3d) 761, 43 N.S.R. (2d) 477 (S.C.A.D.); *McLellan v. Geldert* (1982), 38 N.B.R. (2d) 310 (Q.B.); *Leland Brown Electric Ltd. v. Hansen*, [1988] A.J. No. 529, [1988] A.W.L.D. 1183, (Alta. C.A.); *Lambur Scott Architects Ltd. v. 404577 Alberta Ltd.* (1993), 142 A.R. 241, 9 C.L.R. (2d) 268 (Alta.Q.B.); and *CHED-CKNG FM, a division of Westcom Radio Group Ltd. v. Goose Loonies Inc.* (1995), 172 A.R. 117, 31 Alta.L.R. (3d) 242 (Alta.Q.B.).

21   Although not cited by counsel for the appellant, there is a line of cases that purport to establish a duty on a supplier of goods or services to inquire as to the legal status of the purchaser in certain circumstances: *Provincial Bandag Tire Ltd. v. McCoy* (1990), 109 N.B.R. (2d) 174 (Q.B.T.D.); *Curtis (c.o.b. Solid Gold) v. Dupuis* (1991), 112 N.B.R. (2d) 361, 281 A.P.R. 361 (Q.B.T.D.); and *Hartland Publishers Ltd. v. McCarthy* (1991), 115 N.B.R. (2d) 172 (Q.B.T.D.).

22   In *Provincial Bandag*, Stevenson J. held that the defendant, Mr. McCoy, was not personally responsible for the contract with the plaintiff company, stating (at para. 7):

> It must be recognized in today's business world that most businesses, even small businesses such as that run by Mr. McCoy, are incorporated. While it may be putting it too strongly to say there is an onus on one selling goods or services to inquire as to the exact identity of the purchaser, the fact that employees of the plaintiff had opportunities to see the name of the corporate defendant (or a contraction thereof) on the vehicles and on the cheques it received and negotiated was enough to put the plaintiff on notice that it was dealing with the company rather than Mr. McCoy personally.

23   The decision in Curtis cited Provincial Bandag with approval and held that the plaintiff had a duty to inquire because he was put on notice by a liquor licence which was posted in a conspicuous place and bore a corporate name.

24   Similarly, in *Hartland Publishers* the court held that the plaintiff had a duty to inquire because employees of the plaintiff had opportunities to see a corporate name on business cards and cheques that they received.

25   Finally, in *Wellington Stove Sales Ltd. v. Perry*, [1999] N.B.J. No. 41 (Q.L.) (Q.B.T.D.), the court held that the plaintiff had a duty to inquire, citing factors that should have put the plaintiff on notice, such as orders, warranty claims, business cards and a business sign all bearing a corporate name.

26   It should be noted, however, that this line of cases does not overrule the law as stated in *Con-Force* and impose a duty to inquire on a plaintiff in all circumstances. Indeed, the New Brunswick Court of Appeal, in *Pontbriand v. Taylor*, [1996] N.B.J. No. 462 (Q.L.), N.B.R. (2d) (Supp.) No. 74 (C.A.), stated, at 2, that "although it may be good business practice to do so, neither of these decisions [*Provincial Bandag and Curtis*] should be taken to establish any duty in law on a person selling goods or services to inquire as to the legal status of the purchaser."

27   Instead, these cases indicate that a person selling goods or services will have a duty to inquire into the legal status of the purchaser only where there are factors present which give notice to that person that the purchaser may be acting for an undisclosed principal.

28   In the case at bar, the defendant Bailie made no attempt to bring it home to the claimant that he was contracting in a representative capacity on behalf of the defendant company. Mr. Bailie was apparently content to have Mr. Walia advise the supplier of the new arrangement and Mr. Walia told the claimant that Bill Bailie would be responsible for payment of the account and the claimant's invoices reflect that understanding. In saying this I am not suggesting that Mr. Walia was Mr. Bailie's agent. I am simply saying that in the circumstances Mr. Bailie can hardly complain that the claimant misunderstood his unstated intent to contract through the company.

29   For these reasons and those of the trial judge the appeal is dismissed.

30   I should add that I also agree with the trial judge's disposition of the argument that the claimant did not make an election to pursue the defendant company alone. The claimant sued the personal defendant, Tandoori Taj Restaurant, and the corporate defendant. The claimant obtained default judgment against all of the defendants, but the personal defendant was successful in setting it aside as against himself. That does not amount to an unequivocal election to pursue the defendant company for the debt.

31   The appeal is dismissed with costs on scale 3.

QUESTIONS

1. What risk does a business person face in a sole proprietorship that is avoided in a corporation?

2. What is meant by a corporation being a separate legal entity? What are the implications?

3. In this case, why was it important that Mr. Bailie inform Mr. Toor that the restaurant was being operated through an incorporated company?

4. What is the consequence of a person making a contract in his/her own name without disclosing either the name or the existence of the principal? Explain.

5. Is there an onus on the seller of goods to inquire as to the exact identity of the purchaser? Explain.

Lanz v. Lanz

[1998] S.J. No. 392
Saskatchewan Court of Queen's Bench
May 28, 1998

A partnership is essentially two or more persons acting together for a business purpose with a view of making a profit. What does this mean? The court considers whether there has been a joint contribution of capital, an intention to share expenses, profits or losses, and joint participation in management in deciding whether a partnership existed. Whether two or more persons are partners depends on all the circumstances of the case.

1   **WIMMER J.**:— In the summer of 1975 the plaintiff, Robert Lanz, then 22 years old, became associated with his father, the defendant, in a trucking business which had been operating for many years under the name of F. Lanz Trucking. They worked together until the late fall of 1990 when there was a falling out. The plaintiff claims that the business was a partnership and that he never received all of the monies due to him. He now wants a final settlement of all partnership accounts. The defendant denies there ever was a partnership and says there is no money owing to the plaintiff.

2   The arrangement between the parties was never properly formalized and whether, as a matter of law, it constituted a partnership is unclear. In the course of his testimony, the plaintiff acknowledged that he was merely to share in the profits of the business to the extent of 40 percent. He had no responsibility for debts and there never was any discussion about who owned the assets. It was always the defendant who acquired and disposed of assets and arranged for financing on his own credit. When the business finally wound up and all assets were disposed of, the defendant paid the income tax on recaptured depreciation. It is true that income tax returns prepared for the parties by accountants described them as partners. Also, when asked during his examination for discovery if the plaintiff was a partner in the business for some period of time, the defendant replied, I guess so. However, describing people as partners does not necessarily mean they are, and calling a business a partnership does not, without more, create one.

3   Section 3(1) of *The Partnership Act, R.S.S.* 1978, c. P-3 states that partnership is the relation that subsists between persons carrying on a business in common with a view to profit. Paragraph 3 of s. 4 says that the receipt by a person of a share of the profits of a business is prima facie evidence that he is a partner in the business, but the receipt of such share, or of a payment contingent on or varying with the profits of a business, does not of itself make him a partner in the business. The plaintiff not only

assumed no liability for debts of the business, either as a guarantor of loans or otherwise, he also had no role in its management or operation. He worked as a truck driver in return for 40 percent of the profits. With the defendant attending to everything except driving one truck it is difficult to see that the parties were carrying on the business in common. Even if there was some sort of partnership arrangement, its terms were limited to a sharing of profits. The only question is whether the plaintiff has succeeded in establishing that he did not receive his full share.

4   No adequate accounting records for the business now exist or, for that matter, were ever kept. The plaintiff engaged James Pettigrew, a chartered accountant, to reconstruct the Capital Account Balance of the business as at December 31, 1990, using such records as are available, and calculate the plaintiff's share including his share of profits. Pettigrew assumed that there was a partnership and did his best taking as much information as possible from income tax returns. But he also had to rely upon information given him by the plaintiff—information that he could not verify or investigate. He also did not seek independent evidence to support any of the material provided to him. He acknowledged that the task assigned him could not be completed in a truly accurate way because of the inadequate records and, in the end, his final conclusion was only an estimate grounded upon the assumption that everything he had been told was true.

5   The plaintiff's own testimony was mostly non-specific and not clearly directed at verifying under oath all of those facts relied upon by Pettigrew. In response to questions, he often said he was guessing or that he assumed things. His evidence generally is that he never received all the money disclosed as income in tax returns. But he signed the returns year after year without raising any question with the accountants who prepared them. He says that when the business operated a joint bank account he possibly wrote cheques to himself but he does not know how often or in what amounts. Before there was a joint bank account, according to him, all he got from the business was fifty dollars a week. Registered Retirement Savings Plan and other investments were made by the business in his name but he was unable to answer many questions about these assets. He agrees that he brought nothing into the business. He believes that his earnings were continuously rolled back into the business but he cannot demonstrate it. This is not the evidentiary fibre of successful lawsuits.

6   The onus of proof of a fact is upon the person asserting it. I cannot accept that for almost 15 years the plaintiff got by on $50 a week even though he was living with his grandmother and may have had modest demands upon him. I also cannot accept that he is as naive as he presents himself in respect of his personal affairs. He is simply not credible. The case is not made out. The action is dismissed with costs which, with a view to possible reconciliation, the defendant might consider forgiving.

QUESTIONS

1. What are the basic elements of a partnership relationship? Were they met in this case?
2. What is the difference between sharing profits and sharing gross receipts?
3. If a partnership relationship is deemed to exist by a court, how are profits and losses split?
4. Does describing a person as a partner necessarily make that person a partner? Does calling a business a partnership, without more, create one? Explain.

Foothills Dental Laboratory Ltd. v.
Naik (c.o.b. Apple Dental Group)

[1996] A.J. No. 583, [1996] 8 WWR 448, 40 Alta LR (3d) 434, 29 BLR (2d) 130.

Alberta Provincial Court

June 14, 1996

Because of the liabilities that attach to being a partner in a partnership, people co-operating in a common enterprise may try to prevent a conclusion that they are partners by disclaiming that relationship in an agreement between them. Such an agreement came under consideration from the court in the following case.

1   **McDONALD PROV. CT. J.**:— In this action Foothills Dental Laboratory Ltd. ("plaintiff") claims the sum of $2,535.99 from Dr. Rajiv Naik ("Naik") and Dr. Martin Goldstein ("Goldstein") individually, as well as them jointly carrying on business as Apple Dental Group, being the balance remaining for dental laboratory services provided to the defendants by the plaintiff for the month of April 1994. The plaintiff has demanded payment from the defendants, both individually and jointly and has not been paid.

2   This matter was originally commenced in the Court of Queen's Bench as Action Number 9401-08922 and by Consent Order before Master Alberstat dated March 17, 1995 was transferred to the Provincial Court of Alberta, Civil Division, Calgary, Alberta as action P9590101942.

3   As Goldstein has made a Proposal to Creditors under the provisions of the *Bankruptcy and Insolvency Act R.S.C.* 1985, c. B-3, all actions against Goldstein are stayed. The claim in this Court is proceeding solely against Naik and Naik carrying on business as Apple Dental Group, who collectively I shall refer to as the defendants hereafter.

4   The plaintiff has alleged that the defendants together with Goldstein at all material times were carrying out business as partners or in a partnership under the style or firm name of Apple Dental Group at Calgary, Alberta. The defendant denies that a partnership relationship existed between Goldstein and Naik. They allege that the laboratory services of the plaintiff were performed for Goldstein solely, and that Goldstein alone is responsible for the outstanding debt owing to the plaintiff.

5   Naik and Goldstein commenced association for the practice of dentistry under the firm name of Apple Dental Group on March 1, 1993. An Associateship Agreement ("Agreement") dated March 19, 1993 was executed by Naik and Goldstein

together with each of their professional corporations. They practiced together until the end of April 1994.

6   Pursuant to the Agreement, Goldstein joined Naik as an associate in the practice of dentistry, with Rajiv Naik Professional Corporation providing management services both to Naik and Goldstein on the terms and conditions set out thereunder. The following provision, Clause 2 in the Agreement, expressly negatives a partnership relationship between the two. It provides:

> 2.   It shall be an express term of this agreement that the Association herein provided for shall, under no circumstances, be deemed to create an employer and employee or partnership relationship between Naik and Goldstein respectively.

7   The Agreement set out the working relationship between Goldstein and Naik. In the Agreement, Goldstein sold his dental practice to Naik and all of Goldstein's billings from his dental practice with Apple Dental Group were assigned to Naik. Laboratory costs and other costs were to be deducted from Goldstein's gross billings, and Goldstein's net billings would then be split between Goldstein and Naik based on the formula set out in clause 3(f) of the Agreement, which provides as follows:

> 3(f)(i) To pay to Naik from the actual amount of fees collected by Goldstein personally or by Naik or the Corporation directly attributable to services rendered by Goldstein, or auxiliary staff working on Goldstein's patient's under his direct supervision, in each calendar month
>
> (a) laboratory fees attributable to Goldstein; and
>
> (b) sixty (60%) percent of the actual amount of fees collected by Goldstein after deducting the amounts set out in subclause (a) hereof. The actual amount of fees collected by Goldstein directly attributable to services rendered by Goldstein, or auxiliary staff working on Goldstein's patients under his direct supervision, in each calendar month less the amounts set out in subclause a) hereof is hereinafter referred to as "Goldstein's net billings". . . .
>
> It shall be an express term hereof that any receipts of fees by Goldstein personally (except for fees generated by Goldstein for work done outside of the practice) shall forthwith and immediately be turned over to Naik or to the Corporation's authorized representative, as hereinafter provided.

Further, clause 9(b) of the Agreement provides:

> 9(b)   Goldstein hereby acknowledges and confirms that in consideration of Naik providing to him the association created by the agreement herein and the certain equipment, instruments, supplies, facilities and services hereinbefore described, Goldstein shall pay to Naik the amount or amounts from time to time payable as hereinbefore described in subparagraph 3(f) hereof and shall additionally assign to Naik or as directed by Naik the collection of all fees and receivables payable to Goldstein or collectible by Goldstein in connection with Goldstein's practice of dentistry and dental surgery; provided that Goldstein shall be paid the balance of the gross billings collected by or on behalf of Goldstein after deducting the same amount or amounts payable to Naik.

8   Prior to commencing his association with Naik, Goldstein had an existing laboratory relationship with the plaintiff in his practice of dentistry. Unknown to Naik, Goldstein had an outstanding account with the plaintiff, which Goldstein paid off in monthly instalments to the plaintiff by November 1993.

9   At the commencement of Naik's and Goldstein's association, an Open House was held at the premises of the Apple Dental Group to which John Zakokut, the principal of the plaintiff was invited. Zakokut, Naik and Goldstein had a casual discussion at the Open House. Goldstein indicated that the plaintiff was fortunate that he was now in association with Naik as Naik was fastidious about paying bills on time. Naik specifically said to Zakokut either on that occasion, or on one of Zakokut's periodic visits to the office to pick up Goldstein's prescriptions, that Zakokut, on behalf of the plaintiff, should let him know if Goldstein was not paying the plaintiffs invoices and Naik would ensure that they were paid. Naik commented that he was not in the habit of running his business with outstanding bills to suppliers.

10   The plaintiff initially provided Apple Dental Group with monthly invoices showing a global amount outstanding for services provided in the previous month. The plaintiff explained that this methodology was used as Apple Dental Group would already have been provided with an itemized copy of each invoice when the ordered laboratory item was delivered by the plaintiff. In approximately June or July 1993, Naik called the plaintiff and asked for a full itemization on a monthly basis of the amounts being billed to Apple Dental Group for services provided the preceding month. The plaintiff changed its methodology of billing at Naik's request. Subsequently, the plaintiff listed each separate invoice number together with the cost of that laboratory service on its monthly invoice.

11   The plaintiff produced the invoices for the period of time that Goldstein was associated with Naik in Apple Dental Group to show how the invoices were issued. The monthly invoices had the plaintiff's name printed on top, and were addressed to either Apple Dental Group re: Goldstein or to Dr. Goldstein c/o Apple Dental Group.

12   In addition, the plaintiff presented as evidence the prescriptions issued by Goldstein or the dental assistance staff of Apple Dental Group. Both Goldstein and Naik agreed that Goldstein, with one possible exception, solely made use of the plaintiff's laboratory services. Naik had an existing relationship with another dental lab and the only time that he made use of the plaintiff's services was in respect of one of Goldstein's former clients, Mr. Keenan, whom he agreed to treat midway through a procedure. As remedial work was required on Keenan's bridge which was supplied by the plaintiff, two prescriptions were issued by Naik to the plaintiff. The plaintiff, as acknowledged, performed the remedial work on Keenan's bridge for Naik on a no charge basis. Other than that, Naik did not make use of the laboratory services of the plaintiff.

13   The usual method of payment of the plaintiff's monthly invoices was for Goldstein to authorize payment to the plaintiff on his personal Visa account. He therefore got the benefit of Air Mile points on the amounts charged. Goldstein would then invoice Naik, his professional corporation or Apple Dental Group for the plaintiff's monthly laboratory services, and would be reimbursed monthly.

14   In January 1994, Naik contacted the plaintiff to indicate that from then forward he was going to pay the plaintiff's monthly invoices addressed to Apple Dental Group on either his personal Mastercard or Visa accounts. He was just as interested as

Goldstein in earning Air Mile points. However, the plaintiff was contacted a short time later by Goldstein indicating that with the agreement of Naik, the payment scheme would go on as usual with Goldstein paying the plaintiff's invoices by charging monthly to his Visa account the invoice amount billed to the Apple Dental Group for the previous month's laboratory services. The plaintiff indicated that it really didn't care as to how the individual defendants made arrangements to pay, as long as its invoices were paid monthly.

15   Subsequent to January 1994, Naik and Goldstein mutually agreed that rather than Naik through Apple Dental Group or his professional corporation reimbursing Goldstein for laboratory expenses by way of cheque, Naik would do so by paying on his Mastercard so that Naik could also get the benefit of Air Mile points on the plaintiff's monthly laboratory charges. The new scheme resulted in a loss to Goldstein of approximately one and one half per cent on the amount of the monthly invoices, to which he acquiesced.

16   The relationship between the plaintiff, the defendants and Goldstein continued as previously until April 1994, which was the last month Goldstein was associated with Naik in the Apple Dental Group. The April 1994 monthly invoice was issued by the plaintiff to Apple Dental Group re: Dr. Goldstein in the total amount of $5,035.99. Goldstein retired a $2,500.00 portion of that debt by issuing five monthly post dated cheques of $500.00 each dated November 1994 to March 1995, thus leaving a balance of $2,535.99 owing to the plaintiff, which is the amount claimed in this action.

17   Both Goldstein and Naik confirmed to the Court that the plaintiff's laboratory fees were paid out of Goldstein's gross billings prior to any money being distributed between the parties according to the formula set out in Clause 3(f) of the Agreement, which was set out earlier in this judgment.

18   The defendants argued that the laboratory costs billed by the plaintiff were solely Goldstein's responsibility and that Goldstein was only reimbursed after he provided the defendants with confirmation that he had paid the plaintiff's invoices. The defendants further argued that there had been no formal arrangement with the plaintiff regarding payment. Rather, based on social chatter at the Open House and the odd discussion with John Zakokut when he dropped by the office to pick up Goldstein's prescriptions, a course of dealings had been set up wherein the plaintiff looked solely to Goldstein for payment of the monthly laboratory costs. Naik testified his only responsibility to the plaintiff was that if the plaintiff advised Naik that Goldstein had not paid the monthly laboratory invoices, he undertook to pay them. Accordingly, he instructed the plaintiff to advise him of any non-payment so that he could then ensure that the plaintiff was paid directly rather than him reimbursing Goldstein.

19   In cross-examination, Naik did admit that he, the Apple Dental Group or his professional corporation ultimately took the laboratory fees paid to the plaintiff as a tax deduction in filing Income Tax Statements with Revenue Canada reporting the statement of income and expenses of the Apple Dental Group.

20   The plaintiff argued that it was entitled to rely on its belief that Goldstein and Naik were carrying on business with a view to profit and accordingly they were both individually and jointly liable for the debt owing by Apple Dental Group to the plaintiff. The salient provisions of the *Partnership Act, R.S.A* 1980, Chapter P-2 provide as follows:

> *1   In this Act,*
>
> > *(d) "partnership" means the relationship that subsists between persons carrying on business in common with a view to profit;...*
> >
> > *16(1) Each person who by spoken or written words or by conduct represents himself, or who knowingly permits himself to be represented, as a partner in a particular firm is liable as a partner to any one who has on the faith of that representation given credit to the firm.*
> >
> > *(2) Each person liable as a partner under subsection (1) is so liable whether the representation has or has not been made or communicated to the person so giving credit by or with the knowledge of the apparent partner making the representation or permitting it to be made...*
> >
> > *17 An admission or representation made by a partner concerning the partnership affairs and in the ordinary course of the business of the partnership is evidence against the firm.*

21   The plaintiff argued that notwithstanding the provision contained in Clause 2 of the Agreement between the parties clearly stating that a partnership was not created, nevertheless the plaintiff is entitled to rely on the provisions quoted above from the Partnership Act to infer that a partnership existed.

22   The defendants contended that Naik and Goldstein did not share the profits of Apple Dental Group. Accordingly, they argued that Goldstein was not Naik's partner and that the defendants were therefore not individually or jointly liable to the plaintiff for dental services supplied to Goldstein. They also argued that the failure to share profits should be sufficient to cause the Court to apply the 1958 case of *Big Ben Construction Ltd. v. Donald et al* of Justice Riley of the Supreme Court of Alberta 25 W.W.R. 281, wherein Justice Riley stated at p. 284 as follows:

> The absence of evidence as to profit participation strongly suggests that no partnership exists. Further a partnership is really a relationship produced by a contract, express or implied. In the present case there is not a scintilla of evidence that an express contract existed and if there is no evidence of a contract in writing, the intention of the parties must be looked to. No intention to be become partners existed...

23   S. 4 of the *Partnership Act* sets out various indicia to assist in determining whether a partnership does or does not exist. S. 4(c) provides:

> *4   In determining whether a partnership does or does not exist, regard shall be had to the following rules: ...*
>
> > *(c) the receipt by a person of a share of the profits of a business is prima facie proof that this person is a partner in the business, ...*

24   I conclude that the Agreement does not provide that Naik and Goldstein are to share in the profits of the dental practice carried on by them under the name of Apple Dental Group. Rather, Naik merely shared in a portion of Goldstein's net billings after payment of laboratory fees from Goldstein's gross billings, as provided in clause 3(f)(i) of the Agreement cited earlier. Goldstein did not share in the general profits of Apple Dental Group. Rather, he solely received a portion of his own net billings. However, I find that the sharing of profits is merely one of many indicia set out in s. 4 of the Partnership Act indicating that a partnership exists.

25   The defendant's counsel also discussed the *Hayes v. British Columbia Television Broadcasting System Ltd.* [1993] 2 W.W.R. 749 and quoted from p. 754 as follows:

> The second branch of the analysis requires the Court to inquire into whether the conduct of the parties during the currency of their joint project constituted a partnership relationship notwithstanding their contrary intention and the provisions of their agreement. The evidence in this case does not disclose conduct which would convert the relationship from one of no partnership to one of partnership. . . .
>
> What the evidence demonstrates is that the conduct of the parties conformed to the terms of their agreement.

26   I find that the verbal discussions between the plaintiff and Naik takes the analysis in this case to the second step and converts what between Naik and Goldstein was clearly not intended to be a partnership, to one of partnership as it relates to the third party, the plaintiff in this case. This is evidenced by Naik not refuting Goldstein's statement to Zakokut "that the plaintiff was fortunate that Goldstein was now associated with Apple Dental Group as Naik always paid his bills on time" made in Naik's presence at the Open House, and Naik's further statement to the plaintiff that the plaintiff should let him know if Goldstein did not pay his accounts in a timely fashion. Relying on section 16(1) and section 17 of the *Partnership Act* together with the definition of partnership as set out in section 1(d), I hold that a partnership existed between Naik and Goldstein.

27   In coming to the conclusion that Naik and Goldstein were partners, I am also persuaded by the evidence which indicated that the plaintiff's laboratory expenses were claimed by Naik or his professional corporation in filing annual Income Tax Returns of the Apple Dental Group. The profits of Apple Dental Group eventually flowed solely to Naik. Further, the evidence of Naik asking the plaintiff to change its methodology of monthly billings was persuasive in convincing me that Naik was more than just an innocent bystander in the relationship between the plaintiff and Goldstein. I find that Naik's statement to the plaintiff that the plaintiff was to advise him should Goldstein not pay his bills and Naik would see that the plaintiff was paid, falls squarely within the provisions of s. 17 of the Partnership Act and means that Naik is liable to the plaintiff in respect to the laboratory fees.

28   Accordingly, judgment is hereby granted in favour of the plaintiff against the defendants Naik and Naik carrying on business as Apple Dental Group for $2,535.99 together with interest pursuant to the *Judgment Interest Act* S.A 1984 c. J-0.5 from the 30th of April 1994 to today's date. In addition, the plaintiff is entitled to $25.00 for filing of the Civil Claim, $300.00 Party/Party Costs and other out of pocket disbursements as may be spoken to by counsel of the plaintiff with the Clerk of this Court.

QUESTIONS

1. Describe the liability of partners in a partnership.
2. Can one avoid being a partner by including a clause to that effect in the agreement between the parties? Explain.
3. What danger exists when a third party is led to believe that two people are partners who in fact are not? This situation is an example of what principle?

chapter twenty-seven

Nature of a Corporation and its Formation

Universal Property Management Ltd.
v. Westmount Windows and Doors Ltd.

[1996] N.S.J. No. 570
Nova Scotia Supreme Court
December 10, 1996

A shareholder is generally not liable for the debts and obligations of the corporation. There are exceptions to this immunity. Shareholders of a corporation are occasionally held responsible for debts and liabilities incurred by the corporation. This is known as piercing or lifting the corporate veil. Courts are reluctant to lift the corporate veil except in certain circumstances.

1   **TIDMAN J.** (orally):— The plaintiff seeks reimbursement from the defendant, Patrick Copeland, a corporate officer and shareholder of the defendant, Westmount Windows & Doors Limited, for an alleged debt of that now bankrupt company. Both defendants deny the existence of the debt.

Basic Circumstances

2   The defendant, Copeland, at the times material here, owned 50% of the common shares and was vice-president of the corporate defendant Westmount. Two other persons also owned shares of Westmount. Westmount was in the business of manufacturing, selling, installing and servicing doors and windows for residential and commercial properties. On February 13, 1996, Westmount was petitioned into bankruptcy.

3   Centennial Management Ltd. is a property management company to whom Westmount had provided product and service. Centennial, for some time, had owed a debt to Westmount in the amount of $20,154.46, plus interest. On June 27, 1995, the plaintiff, Universal Property Management Ltd., in error, sent a cheque to Westmount, payable to Westmount in the amount of $30,635.41 which was credited to Centennial's indebtedness to Westmount and deposited to Westmount's general bank account.

4   On July 11, 1995, Menachem Suissa, president of Universal, telephoned Copeland, advised him of the error and demanded repayment. Copeland refused him and on July 27, 1995 this action was commenced for a return of the funds and for exemplary or punitive damages against the defendant Copeland.

Extenuating Circumstances

5   On those basic circumstances, liability for repayment appears obvious. There are, not surprisingly, however, extenuating circumstances which provide argument in defence of the action. There is little factual dispute between the parties even as to the extenuating circumstances.

6   Westmount, for some time, had had difficulty in collecting from Centennial. In an attempt to do so, Copeland attended the offices of Centennial to discuss payment with Centennial's president, Ralph Medjuck. Medjuck assured Copeland he would do what he could to see the debt paid and introduced Copeland to his son-in-law, Suissa, as president of Universal. Universal had taken over several building management contracts formerly held by Centennial. Westmount in the past had provided service or product to the buildings which were managed under those contracts. Universal and Centennial share the same suite of business offices and have a common receptionist. Universal had also taken over from Centennial the computer accounting systems and some furnishings in relation to the management contracts, but did not take over the accounts payable and receivable related to those contracts.

7   On the same day they were introduced by Medjuck, Copeland and Suissa had discussions during which Suissa said he was interested in doing business with Westmount. He offered to pay $12,000.00 in full satisfaction of Centennial's debt to Westmount and stated that he had made arrangements to do business with other companies by paying them up-front amounts, such as $10,000.00, indicating to Copeland that such an arrangement could be made with Westmount. Copeland refused the offer.

8   At the time the Universal cheque was received by Westmount, Universal owed Westmount Draperies Limited, an out of province company unrelated to the defendant company, the sum of $30,635.41. Universal's accounts payable clerk wrote a cheque in that amount and in error made it payable to and forwarded it to the defendant, Westmount Doors and Windows Limited. The cheque was received with surprise by Westmount's accountant, Bruce Whitman, who unknown to Copeland at the time, deposited the cheque to Westmount's general account. All of the key employees of Westmount, including Whitman, believed that a close business relationship existed between Universal and Centennial.

9   Testimony was given by the office secretary of Westmount, who says that in the past she was told not to send out service personnel for either Centennial or Universal because of Centennial's bad payment history.

10   On the day the cheque was received by Whitman, he reported its receipt to Copeland and told him he could not reconcile the amount of the cheque with the amount owed by Centennial. Copeland, based on his discussions with Medjuck and Suissa, believed the account was for credit to Centennial's account and attempted to reconcile the amounts. After adding late payment interest and legal fees paid in attempting to collect the debt, the amount of the cheque approximated the amount owed by Centennial.

11   At the time Suissa demanded repayment and Copeland refused, Copeland was not satisfied that an error had been made by Centennial. Later, after this action was commenced, he says he still was not satisfied that Westmount Draperies' invoices, which added up to the exact amount of the Universal cheque, were bona fide invoices.

12   During that time, Westmount was experiencing its own financial difficulties and Copeland, in order to pay company debts, meet payrolls and continue operations, was periodically injecting amounts of his own personal funds.

Issues

13   There are two issues before the court:
(1)   Is the plaintiff entitled to judgment against Westmount for the amount paid?
(2)   Is the plaintiff entitled to judgment against Copeland personally for the same amount as part of or together with exemplary or punitive damages?

Issue No. 1 - Is the plaintiff entitled to judgment against Westmount for the amount paid?

14   The defendants claim that Westmount is not obliged to repay Universal based on the extenuating circumstances previously set out. In my view, the extenuating circumstances do not alter the basic circumstances, that is, that no debt was owing by Universal to Westmount. I accept the evidence on behalf of Universal that there was no intention on the part of Universal to pay Centennial's debt to Westmount. The cheque went to Westmount as a result of a clerical error by Universal. That conclusion is supported by the fact that the amount of the Universal cheque was not in the exact amount of Centennial's debt to Westmount, even after applying interest and legal fees calculated unilaterally by Westmount and that the cheque was in the exact amount of the debt owed by Universal to Westmount Draperies.

15   The negotiations that took place between Copeland and Suissa with respect to satisfaction of Centennial's debt to Westmount led to no conclusive agreement. I agree with Mr. Stern's submission that the harshness of the old adage once taught in our law schools of "finders keepers loser weepers" no longer applies in our courts.

16   The plaintiff is entitled to judgment against Westmount for the amount of $30,635.41.

Issue No. 2 - Is the plaintiff entitled to judgment against Copeland personally for the same amount as part of or together with exemplary or punitive damages?

17   In relation to the dispute Copeland was acting as a corporate officer of Westmount: In order to find Copeland personally responsible for the return of the funds paid in error, the court must consider whether there are circumstances here sufficient to warrant the piercing of Westmount's corporate veil. The legal principle that corporate bodies are distinct entities separate and apart from their shareholders and officers was established in *Saloman v. Saloman and Co. Ltd.*, [1897] A.C. 22. That general principle remains intact today, but not without exceptions. Courts have pierced the corporate veil and held company officers personally liable where their conduct was fraudulent or improper or where there were other unusual circumstances. (See *J.W. Bird & Co. Ltd. v. Newell Electric Ltd. et al* (1991) 104 N.S.R. (2d) 343 and *Lockharts Ltd. v. Excaliber Holdings Ltd. et al* (1987) 83 N.S.R. (2d) 181.)

18   From a review of the case law, it appears that the terms "improper conduct" and "other unusual circumstances" in all cases involve an element of unconscionability.

19   It is the plaintiff's position that Copeland's conduct in refusing to return the funds after being advised they were paid in error was unconscionable to an extent that justifies a lifting of the corporate veil. In fact, Mr. Stern, on behalf of the plaintiff, submits that Copeland's conduct may be characterized as improper, high-handed, reckless, reprehensible, unethical and morally wrong.

20   At trial, Mr. Stern, relied upon this court's recent decision in *Wolfson v. Corkum* [1996] N.S.J. No. 391, S.H. #121503. Mr. Stern submits that the case provides authority for piercing the corporate veil solely on the grounds of mistake and unjust enrichment. He argues that the circumstances in Wolfson are similar to those in the case at bar.

21   In the Wolfson case, a limited company borrowed money by way of a mortgage loan. The solicitor for the mortgagee lender erroneously advanced excess funds to the sole shareholder of the company. The funds were used by the shareholder for his own personal benefit and not for the purposes of the borrowing company. The company subsequently went bankrupt. The mortgage was foreclosed and sold at a foreclosure sale. Funds from the sale were insufficient to satisfy the mortgage and the solicitor, because of his error in advancing excess funds, reimbursed the mortgage company for its loss. The solicitor, Wolfson, then sued the shareholder Corkum personally for return of the funds. The court, in considering the element of fraud, strongly suspected that the shareholder Corkum at the time of or soon after the disbursement of the mortgage funds, knew that the solicitor had erroneously advanced excess funds. The court, however, made no finding of fraud based on the fact that Corkum's evidence that he had no such knowledge could have been true. The court, however, still found in favour of the plaintiff and ordered reimbursement.

22   I cannot agree that the case stands as authority for the proposition that the court will pierce the corporate veil based solely on mistake and unjust enrichment.

The case simply illustrates that the court will take into consideration all of the circumstances when deciding whether the corporate veil should be pierced. After doing so, in this case, I cannot find circumstances which justify holding the defendant, Copeland, personally liable.

23   The circumstances in Wolfson, however, are useful for comparative purposes. In Wolfson, the court strongly suspected, if not actually believed, that the defendant knew of the solicitor's error at the time the funds were disbursed. Also, the funds were not used for the company's purposes, but for the shareholder personally and the shareholder had personally guaranteed repayment of the mortgage loan. In contrast here, Copeland did not receive the funds, nor did he do or omit to do anything to cause the plaintiff to make the erroneous payment. The funds were received by another company employee who deposited the funds to the company's own corporate account. That employee knew at the time of payment that there was a close association between Universal and Centennial. The funds were used for company purposes not for Copeland's personal benefit. Mr. Stern argues that Copeland did, in fact, receive a personal benefit. He submits that the company with Copeland still on the payroll, survived longer as a result of the Universal payment, and the funds were used to pay company debt thus reducing Copeland's liability on personal guarantees held by the company's banker. Those submissions may in fact be correct, but while the company may have survived longer by reason of the Universal payment, I accept Copeland's evidence that during the latter period of the company's life he was injecting his own money into the company in attempting to meet payroll and other company financial obligations. It is noted also that Copeland was not the only guarantor of the company's debt nor was he the sole shareholder of the company. Therefore, I would hold that Copeland was not unjustly enriched.

24   Copeland was aware of the close relationship between Universal and Centennial and was a party to negotiations whereby Universal would undertake to satisfy the Centennial account with Westmount. These were circumstances upon which Copeland could reasonably hold the belief that the cheque was intended for the Centennial account. When Suissa telephoned Copeland to tell him of the error, the funds had already been used for company purposes and Westmount was struggling financially to continue operations and pay its debts. Under all of the circumstances there was, in my view, some justification for Copeland not immediately acceding to Suissa's demand.

25   Although, as I have already decided, Westmount had no basis in law to retain the funds, the conduct of Copeland in refusing to cause an immediate return of the funds was not fraudulent and does not, in my view, amount to unconscionable conduct warranting a piercing of Westmount's corporate veil.

26   Thus, I would dismiss the action against the defendant Copeland. Copeland is entitled to costs of the action under the mid-scale of Tariff "A" based on the amount of the claim.

QUESTIONS

1. What is meant by "limited liability"? Whose liability is limited?
2. What is meant by the phrase "lifting the corporate veil"? What is the consequence of lifting the veil?
3. In what circumstances will the court lift the corporate veil?
4. Will a court pierce the corporate veil based solely on mistake or unjust enrichment or must the court take into consideration the circumstances of the case? Explain.

chapter twenty-eight

Internal Affairs
of a Corporation

Malcolm v. Transtec Holdings Ltd.

[2001] B.C.J. No. 413, 2001 BCCA 161, 150 BCAC 20, 86 BCLR (3d) 344, 12
BLR (3d) 66.

British Columbia Court of Appeal

March 7, 2001

Under Common Law, a director has always owed a duty to the corporation to be careful. In addition to this duty to be careful, directors also have a duty based on their fiduciary relationship with the corporation. The fiduciary duty of a director is to act in the best interests of the corporation, to be loyal, to avoid conflict and to otherwise act honestly and in good faith towards the corporation. This duty can become particularly difficult to meet when the director is making a decision to distribute a dividend to shareholders.

1   **McEACHERN C.J.B.C.**:— This is an appeal against a decision made by a trial judge, [2000] B.C.J. No. 1233, holding the defendant directors of a company liable for breach of fiduciary duty to a shareholder. At the hearing, we allowed the appeal with reasons to follow. These are the reasons.

2   The circumstances are technical but they may be described quite briefly. Mr. Malcolm, the Plaintiff at trial (hereinafter the "plaintiff"), was one of three senior operating officers of a group of companies (the "Johnston Group") that was in serious financial difficulty. These three each held different amounts of preferred shares in a subsidiary known as Transtec Canada Limited.

3   The personal defendants, who were executive officers and directors of the Johnston Group expressed interest in protecting as best they could the financial position of these three operating officers. In a letter to the plaintiff dated December 6, 1985, the terms of which had already been accepted by his two colleagues, the parent company proposed as "... part of a program of recapitalizing the company and addressing the needs of the senior shareholders, a uniform proposal ... to redeem the shares held by [the plaintiff] and others." It was stated the plan was not yet complete and was being reviewed by solicitors. The letter further suggested that the plan would require these officers to convert their shares in Transtec to a new class of redeemable preference shares in the new company, (Transtec Holdings Ltd.).

4   It was stated first, that the plaintiff's salary would be increased by $6,000 annually, plus automobile and other benefits; second, that on retirement, "early or otherwise", he would have a pension equal to 50% of his increased salary, and there would be dividends on his exchanged shares of $15,740 per annum that, with dividend tax credits would be equal to $23,610 for a total income of $56,610; third, after a three year moratorium commencing in 1986, his shares would be redeemed over a seven year period (1989 to 1995) at a price of $32.60 per share; fourth, he would be provided with funds annually to service the debt he owed on his shares; and fifth, the company would maintain life insurance that would fund complete redemption upon his death.

5   The plaintiff accepted this proposal "in principle subject to the completed final program, plan, terms & details being satisfactory to me." I take this to mean he subscribed to the plan, which was very much to his advantage because his shares were otherwise worthless. This becomes important when considering his relationship with the defendants.

6   The actual transaction by which the plaintiff exchanged his shares was carried out by documents dated December 27, 1985, that described the plaintiff's benefits which were substantially but not precisely the same as described in the earlier letter.

7   It was well known by all parties, including the plaintiff, that Transtec was without assets or income and that these programs for the senior officers could only be carried out with funds furnished by the parent company to Transtec. Thus, although the plan contemplated the payments of dividends to retired members, this was obviously a tax saving device because the company would never be in a position to pay dividends.

8   What then happened is that one of the three senior officers retired and then died. His shares were redeemed with insurance monies arranged for that purpose. The other officer retired and his shareholder benefit was paid out to him by way of dividends which, from 1988 to 1992, amounted to $97,280.76. Each year, after the first three years, a number of the plaintiff's shares were redeemed.

9   It appears that the plaintiff received funds through redemption of shares as follows:

a)   December 31, 1988 - $38,598.40

b)   December 31, 1989 - $12,485.80

c)   December 31, 1990 - $12,518.40

d)   December 31, 1991 - $12,518.40

e)   December 31, 1992 - $2,086.40

10   In 1992, Mr. Malcolm was presented with another document headed "Waiver", for his signature. That "waiver", addressed to the directors of Transtec Holdings, recited that the directors proposed to cause dividends to be paid for the years 1988 through 1991 in the amounts and on the dates specified in a resolution of the same date purporting to declare dividends in specific amounts in each of the years, 1988, 1989, 1990, and 1991. After such recitals the waiver document ends with this paragraph:

> THE UNDERSIGNED hereby waives any rights they may have to receive a dividend in respect of Preference Shares held by them in the aggregate amounts described above to the holders of Preference Shares of the Company, and the undersigned hereby consents to the Directors of the Company declaring and causing such dividends to be paid to the holders of the Preference Shares without causing such dividends to be paid to them even though the undersigned are entitled to receive such dividends.

11   The plaintiff refused to sign the waiver. The trial judge held, that the company did actually declare dividends that were paid to the retired officer, but not to the plaintiff whose shares were being redeemed. As already mentioned, the company had no funds and for that reason it could not declare or pay dividends even though it issued T5 slips to the retired officer indicating that he had received dividends.

12   In this way Mr. Malcolm learned that the retired officer had been receiving "dividends".

13   Even though he remained employed, and was receiving salary and redemptions, the plaintiff brought this action against the company (which he knew had no assets) and against the three defendant directors. They were found personally liable in the sum of $64,758.48, being the amount the plaintiff says he should have received in dividends based upon the number of shares he held, and a further $35,895.88 for interest.

14   The trial judge found that the retired member of the group actually received dividends (obviously with funds furnished by the parent company) and that:

> [42] Accordingly, I find that the plaintiff's action must succeed. He has established, on a balance of probabilities, that the defendants, as directors of Transtech, indeed declared dividends payable to the holders of record of preference shares of Transtec on December 31, 1989, and for each of the succeeding years 1990 through 1992. I find that no such dividends were paid to Malcolm and that as a holder of preferred shares he was entitled to such payments. It is a fundamental principle of corporate law that the rights carried by all shares to receive a dividend declared by a company are equal unless otherwise provided in the articles of incorporation. (*McClurg v. Canada* (1990) 76 D.L.R. (4th) 217 (S.C.C.))

[43] I find that by declaring dividends for the years 1988 through 1992 by way of resolution and not making any payments of such dividends to Malcolm, the defendants have discriminated against Malcolm.

[44] Here, given the language of the Articles of Incorporation, the preferred shareholders were particularly vulnerable. They had no right to receive notice of or to attend any meeting of the members of the company or to vote at any such meeting. The directors were empowered to declare and authorize the payment of dividends, as they deemed advisable, without any requirement to give any notice of such declaration to any member. In these circumstances, the defendants held broad powers to unilaterally exercise their discretion or power as they saw fit, with no consideration of Malcolm's interests. (*Dusik v. Newton* (1985) 62 B.C.L.R. 1 (C.A.); *Coleman v. Myers* (1977) 2 N.Z.L.R. 297 (C.A.))

[45] In these circumstances, I am satisfied the plaintiff has established that the defendants, as directors of Transtech, were in a fiduciary relationship with Malcolm and that they owed him a fiduciary duty with respect to the declaration and payment of dividends.

[46] Here Malcolm was not made aware of any of the declarations of any of the dividends until after the fact. He has lost the benefit of the payment of the dividends when they were declared. Further he will never recover the dividends that otherwise would have been paid to him when declared since the corporate defendants have been dissolved.

15   In my judgment the judge's finding that the defendants personally breached a fiduciary duty to the plaintiff cannot stand.

16   Assuming for the purposes of this decision that the defendants as officers of the parent company and as directors of Transtec Holdings were wrong in believing that the plaintiff had subscribed both to the purpose of the plan as set out in the original letter of intent and to the actual agreement to exchange his shares, and also assuming that the directors should have ensured that all surviving shareholders were entitled to the same "dividends", (even though the plaintiff was receiving his increased salary and redemption monies), it does not follow that such error on their part, if any, constituted a breach of fiduciary duty to the plaintiff. The trial judge relied upon the fact that the plaintiff was vulnerable and more or less at the mercy of the defendant directors because of their position with the holding company. That is true in the sense that Transtec could not pay any dividends or redeem any shares except with funds provided by the parent company. Such error on their part, I suppose, might give rise to an empty claim against the company for its failure to pay the plaintiff the dividends it purported to declare.

17   But the law seems clear that, except in exceptional cases, the fiduciary duty of a director is to the company and not to shareholders.

18   In this respect appellants' counsel refers to *McClurg v. Canada*, [1990] 3 S.C.R. 1020 where Dickson C.J., writing for the Court at p. 1040, quoted with approval a passage from a treatise written by Professor Bruce Welling, Corporate Law in Canada - The Governing Principles (Toronto: Butterworths, 1984) at p. 614:

> The directors' general managerial power is a fiduciary one, owed to the corporation. It must always be exercised in what the directors' from time to time think is likely to serve the best interests of the corporation...

19   In *Pelling et al. v. Pelling et al.* (1981), 130 D.L.R. (3d) 761 (B.C.S.C.) Berger J. at p. 762 said this:

> Dealing first with the claim at common law: there is no fiduciary obligation as between shareholders, and no general fiduciary obligation owed by a director to shareholders. A director's duty is to the company; he has no fiduciary obligation to the shareholders. There are some exceptions to this rule (Gower, Principles of Modern Company Law, 4th ed. (1979), p. 573) but the plaintiff has been unable to persuade me that the case at bar falls within any of them. The common law has not thus far provided a remedy in a case such as this.

20   In a more general sense Mr. Holmes referred to *Litwin Const. (1973) Ltd. v. Kiss* (1988), 29 B.C.L.R. (2d) 88 (B.C.C.A.) where the Court said at 105:

> It would surely be an exceptional case where parties who have different commercial interests and who have entered into a contract to bring about diverse results for each of them, ought to be considered, from the circumstances, to have assumed a fiduciary relationship in which one of them owes a duty of loyalty and selflessness to the other. That is not the normal expectation between commercial parties contracting at arm's length.

21   I pause to point out that there is no suggestion the defendant directors profited in any way from these transactions.

22   There are some authorities where directors have been found to have a fiduciary duty towards other shareholders. In this respect see *Dusik v. Newton* (1985), 62 B.C.L.R. 1 (C.A.); *Coleman v. Myers* (1977), 2 N.Z.L.R. 297 (C.A.); *Edelweiss Credit Union et al. v. Cobbett* (1992), 68 B.C.L.R. (2d) 273 (B.C.C.A.) at 280. In all those cases, however, there was either a family relationship or a special relationship of trust and dependency between the plaintiffs and defendants where the latter were seeking to take unfair advantage of the others for personal gain or profit. Those cases have no application to the facts of this case where the defendants, without any prospect of personal gain, were attempting to assist the plaintiff and his fellow officers in circumstances where, without their help, there would be no possibility of recovering anything for their shares.

23   In my judgment, no breach of fiduciary duty against the plaintiff has been made out. As no judgment was ever taken against the defendant Transtec Holdings Ltd., against whom the plaintiffs may have had a doubtful cause of action for non-payment of "dividends", I would allow the appeal, set aside the judgment against the three individual defendants and dismiss the action.

SAUNDERS JA: I agree.

LOW JA: I agree.

QUESTIONS

1. What standard must the directors' duty to the corporation meet?

2. Are there any circumstances where a director might owe a duty to a shareholder? If so, what would the circumstances be? Why was there no breach of fiduciary duty in this case?

3. What duties does a shareholder owe to the corporation? What duties do shareholders owe to each other?

Grizzly Ropes Ltd. v. Hymax Engineering Ltd.

[1992] B.C.J. No. 1406
British Columbia Supreme Court
June 22, 1992

According to traditional principles of corporation law, aggrieved minority shareholders received little or no help from courts of law. Statutory remedies have greatly improved the situation of minority shareholders, who, in non-reporting companies, are often at the mercy of the majority. Today, in many jurisdictions, both shareholders and creditors have the right to go to court and seek and order for relief from oppression or unfairly prejudicial conduct.

CURTIS J.:— Jack Parrish and Frank and Elizabeth Weinzierl were friends when they went into business together. Mr. Parrish's company, Grizzly Ropes Ltd., now seeks relief as a minority shareholder of Hymax Engineering Ltd. under section 224 of the *Company Act*, R.S.B.C. 1979.

The *Company Act* provides:

"*224.(1) A member of a company may apply to the court for an order on the ground*

    (a)   that the affairs of the company are being conducted, or the powers of the directors are being exercised, in a manner oppressive to one or more of the members, including himself; or

    (b)   that some act of the company has been done, . . . that is unfairly prejudicial to one or more of the members, including himself.

  (2) On an application under subsection (1) the court may, with a view to bringing to an end or to remedying the matters complained of, make an interim or final order it considers appropriate, and, without limiting the generality of the foregoing, the court may

    (a)   direct or prohibit any act or cancel or vary any transaction or resolution;

    (b)   regulate the conduct of the company's affairs in future;

    (c)   provide for the purchase of the shares of any member of the company by another member of the company, or by the company;

    (d)   in the case of a purchase by the company, reduce the company's capital or otherwise;

    (e)   appoint a receiver or receiver manager;

    (f)   order that the company be wound up under Part 9;

(g)   *authorize or direct that proceedings be commenced in the name of the company against any party on the terms the court directs;*

(h)   *require the company to produce financial statements;*

(i)   *order the company to compensate an aggrieved person; and*

(j)   *direct rectification of any record of the company."*

In the early 1970's Jack Parrish was a forestry engineer employed in supplying wire rope to logging and other industry. Frank Weinzierl had a small wire rope shop in Nakusp. They worked together on a transmission line project which Mr. Parrish's company Grizzly Ropes had undertaken, following which it was decided to make their business relationship more permanent. Mr. Parrish's company bought shares in Demac Engineering Ltd. (later renamed Hymax) a company in which Mr. Weinzierl had an interest. Demac was in receivership at the time because of problems with a former business associate of Weinzierl's. Grizzly Ropes paid $20,000 for 40 shares; Mr. Weinzierl held 52 and his wife Elizabeth 9. The parties agreed to draw modest salaries, initially $800/month, in order to build up equity in the company which they could realize through sale for their retirement. There was no buy/sell agreement between the shareholders.

Mr. Weinzierl became the president of the company, his wife the secretary and all three were directors. Mr. Weinzierl, being a machinist by trade was in charge of the shop, Mrs. Weinzierl kept the books and Mr. Parrish concentrated on marketing and customer service which involved frequent and extensive travel. The Weinzierls' looked after the day to day management of the company but in the early years business matters were frequently discussed amongst the shareholders although formal company meetings were never held.

The company carried on business out of leased premises in Vancouver where it prospered and grew. The foundation of its work was the manufacture of grouser bars, which are used to rebuild vehicle tracks, and wire rope fittings. The company expanded into the design and installation of cable systems, such as those used for reaction ferries. It also became involved in manufacturing sophisticated track vehicles, and successfully obtained a patent for an undercarriage to convert highway trucks to all terrain vehicles using tracks. One of its vehicles was sold for desert use in Iran, another was being tested by the Canadian army. The company was a small, innovative engineering company which was making significant advances in its field through the personal efforts of its shareholders. By 1975 the company had a gross revenue of $568,000 and retained earnings of $75,000, with the parties receiving management salaries and expense monies as agreed and holding large shareholders loans payable to them by the company for patents they had sold to it.

It was over the sale of patents that the first significant disagreement arose. Mr. Weinzierl held a patent for grouser bars and another for wire rope fittings. In or about 1977, without consulting Mr. Parrish he sold these to the company for $70,000 which he paid himself. Mr. Parrish considered the price too high and was annoyed about not being consulted. He refused to sign financial statements of the company approving of the sale. Because of this refusal the Weinzierls as majority shareholders of the company removed Mr. Parrish as a director. According to the company's books he ceased to be a director May 27, 1978. Mr. Parrish appears to have accepted this situation as he never took any action to regain his position. The result however was a significant change in the manner in which the company was operated. The Weinzierls ceased to consult Mr. Parrish concerning the management of the company and completely shut him out from that function, denying him access to the books and records of the company, and failing to consult him or inform him of important company decisions.

On the 21st of June, 1978 Frank Weinzierl signed an interim agreement to buy 10 acres of industrial land in Surrey for $495,000. The agreement was in the name of "Frank and Marlies Weinzierl and Assigns". Frank Weinzierl signed as "Pres", the position he held with Demac Engineering. Only part of the property was conveyed to Demac however when the transfer was completed. Demac received the 5 acre portion of the property on which there were buildings for $460,000 while a company named W L & S Investments (later Surrey Veneer Ltd.) received the other 5 acres for $35,000. W L & S Investments Ltd. had been incorporated July 20th, 1978, the shares of that company being held as follows: Elizabeth Weinzierl 40%; David Lindley (the Weinzierl's son-in-law and a Demac employee) 20%; Irmtraud Lindley (the Weinzierl's daughter) 20%; Susan Banwell (the Weinzierl's daughter) 20%.

Mr. Parrish knew nothing of any of this until he returned from a holiday in late October, 1978. Mr. Parrish testified "Frank told me we had bought property in Surrey and he took me to see it. He said we'd bought 10 acres at 144th Street in Surrey". Mr. Parrish was pleased. The company had outgrown its leased premises in Vancouver and the back 5 acres, which was very rough looked ideal for testing their track vehicles. Mr. Weinzierl told him "we are going to build a demonstration sawmill on the unused portion" which also pleased Mr. Parrish because the company was planning to manufacture a vertical band saw they would want to demonstrate.

Demac moved its business to the Surrey location in December, 1978. The back portion of the property was, as contemplated, used to test track vehicles. Sometime later, Mr. Parrish noticed a lot of levelling work and filling taking place on the back five acres and asked Frank Weinzierl about it, saying they needed only a small portion for their demonstration mill. Mr. Weinzierl told him David Lindley owned the property (which was not true as it was registered in the name of the family company). This was the first information Mr. Parrish had the company did not own the full 10 acres. Parrish was not pleased, and became suspicious that he, as a minority shareholder was being taken advantage of. However, he was 58 years of age, and having no desire to start over, he took no action.

Frank Weinzierl drew up plans for a sawmill. The engineering company's skid loader was used to excavate the site. Used veneer mill machinery started to arrive and was stored at the Demac premises.

Mr. Weinzierl became completely involved with the sawmill construction. Demac equipment, labour and shop facilities were used to prepare structural members, steel doors, the band saw base and whatever else was needed. Demac's business, particularly its track vehicle business fell into neglect. Mr. Weinzierl told Mr. Parrish not to worry "we'll just give David a hand for two or three months and then we'll get back into production". When Parrish inquired about all the work Demac was doing on the project Frank Weinzierl told him repeatedly it was business just like other customers and the engineering company was being paid for it. Work orders for the project were kept posted by the time clock where work orders usually were and appeared to be being filled in appropriately. However, at trial these work orders were no where in evidence. There was no evidence of any billing to Surrey Veneer Ltd. for the years 1979, 1980 and 1981, or any evidence of payment for such work. On the evidence before me at trial I conclude the engineering company probably did well over $100,000 of work for Surrey Veneer Ltd. for which it was not paid. Frank

Weinzierl lied to Mr. Parrish about this; both as to the ownership of the mill, which he said was David Lindley's when in fact his wife owned 40% of the shares, and as to the engineering company being paid for its work. Mr. Parrish however, was not given an opportunity to see the records, and remained deceived.

On the 8th of March, 1979, Frank Weinzierl as president of Demac signed an agreement granting Surrey Veneer Ltd. an easement over its property for roads, water lines and vehicles. According to the agreement the consideration was $10.00. The Surrey Veneer property had no road access at all and without the easement could not have been developed. Mr. Parrish knew nothing of the granting of the easement, although of course he knew Surrey Veneer used the Demac property for access, until his counsel in this action did a land registry search. Demac Engineering Ltd. changed its name to Hymax Engineering Ltd. June 10th, 1979.

On the 28th of October, 1982, Frank Weinzierl as president of Hymax Engineering Ltd. signed a $461,000 mortgage to the Toronto Dominion Bank in support of loans to Surrey Veneer Ltd. The mortgage was discharged, September 14, 1985, when FBDB financing was arranged, $48,000 of the proceeds of which was advanced as shareholders loans to Frank and Elizabeth Weinzierl and put into Surrey Veneer. A further $126,718.83 was used to pay Hymax tax arrears as the company had allowed it's property to go to tax sale. All of this was unknown to Mr. Parrish when it occurred.

Surrey Veneer's financial statement show that it never made a profit until 1982. In 1980 it lost $12,187; in 1981 $107,640 and in 1982 $232,526. The Hymax guarantee of $461,000 in 1982 was obviously a serious risk for the company. There is no evidence of any payment or consideration to Hymax for taking this risk. It appears that Frank Weinzierl simply risked the business and assets of Hymax to advance the interests of Surrey Veneer.

In the beginning of 1980 the Weinzierls, as directors of the company, stopped paying Mr. Parrish's expense accounts. Because Mr. Parrish had to travel extensively during his work this created a serious problem. Mr. Parrish continued to travel at his own expense and ultimately sued the company for $23,000. Numerous projects came up which Mr. Parrish wanted to, or tried to tender, including cabling for the roof system at B.C. Place Stadium, and a railing contract for the stadium, but Frank Weinzierl would not agree. He told Mr. Parrish that Hymax did not have the resources to do the work, all the while devoting his time and attention to the running of the sawmill, negotiating log purchases, lumber sales and construction of the veneer mill. The Hymax shop continued to be used to support the adjacent sawmill and veneer mill.

In 1982 and subsequent years invoices were sent for Hymax work to Surrey Veneer and payments were made, however this in no way lessened the damage caused to Hymax's business as a result of Mr. Weinzierl, one of its key personnel, turning his time and attention to the other family venture. Rather than continuing to expand, the engineering company's business slipped. It ceased to manufacture tracked vehicles and fell back on making grouser bars and wire rope fittings. At present it has only one employee. A serious loss of $125,000 occurred in 1982, followed by losses in 1984, 1985, 1986 and a loss of $128,239 in 1989. The only significant profit in recent years was $61,405 in 1990, by which time rental income from the property was a significant factor.

Mr. Parrish's employment with the company ceased in 1985. Frank Weinzierl told him there was no money to pay him a management salary and if he wanted a job he would have to work as an hourly employee. Mr. Parrish treated this as a firing, stopped working for the company, and has not been employed since. He is now 72 years of age, his only income being old age security and his Canada pension plan.

Despite the allegations made against them the Weinzierls chose not to testify at the trial. The evidence called by the defence was limited to valuation of the company land and shares, and matters pertaining to the easement. The only challenge to Mr. Parrish's version of the facts was cross examination. This did reveal some contradictions, however it did not cause me to doubt the substance of what Mr. Parrish had to say. Accordingly I have found the facts as I have stated them to be.

The evidence clearly establishes that following Mr. Parrish's removal as a director in 1978 the Weinzierls used the engineering company to serve the interests of Surrey Veneer Ltd. and in doing so repeatedly acted contrary to the engineering company's interests in order to favour those of their family company; to the prejudice of Hymax Engineering Ltd., and its shareholders, and in breach of their fiduciary duties as directors.

The defence has argued strongly that Mr. Parrish's complaints even if true are long barred by the Statute of Limitations, or by laches and acquiescence.

The answer to those arguments is found in the provisions of section 224(1) when considered in light of the facts of this case.

Mr. Parrish joined a small company in which all the shareholders were actively employed in the business. He did so on the basis of his friendship with the Weinzierls and the mutual understanding that they would continue to work together to further the company's interests. Since his departure as a director the Weinzierls have seriously subverted the interests of the company to benefit Surrey Veneer Ltd., both directly by using and pledging its assets, and indirectly by turning their time, attention and energy to promoting the business of Surrey Veneer. They have done so in breach of their fiduciary duties as directors, and in contravention of the original understanding between the members. I have no difficulty in finding "that the affairs of the company are being conducted. . . in a manner oppressive to one of the members. . . " I read the case of *Diligenti v. RWMD. et al* (1976) 1 B.C.L.R. 36 (S.C.) as authority for the proposition that such considerations are appropriate in this case. To leave the company in the control of the Weinzierls would be to continue the oppression that has occurred since 1978. That being the case the limitation arguments are to no effect.

Even if Mr. Parrish "sat on his rights" the facts in this case are such that the equitable defence of acquiescence and laches ought not to be available to the defendants. Furthermore as I find the continued control of the company by the Weinzierls to be oppressive, the remedy is available on the circumstances existing both at the date of issue of the writ and at trial.

There is conflicting evidence concerning the value of the company's real estate, and therefore the value of its shares. The parties agree the company has no good will value as a going concern. According to the Plaintiffs' appraisers the land and buildings are worth $850,000. The Defendants' appraiser places the value at $750,000. Using the $750,000 figure Hymax's accountant estimates the liquidation value of the company after commission and taxes at $577,000, making Grizzly's shares worth $230,800. A higher land value would increase that. There is also a dispute over the value of the inventory. The best method of determining the true value is to sell the assets.

Grizzly, in addition to claiming the value of its shares also seeks compensation for the actions of the Weinzierls in breach of their duties as directors. Although the provisions of section 224 of the *Company Act* appear to allow such a remedy in my opinion these claims are more properly the claims of the company itself.

I conclude the proper remedy in this case is to order that a receiver be appointed and the company wound up, in order that the parties may receive the value of their respective interests. With regard to the claims concerning the Weinzierl's breach of their duties as directors I authorize the company's receiver to take whatever action he deems advisable on behalf of the company against the Weinzierl's or Surrey Veneer Ltd.

I also direct that the easement granted by Demac to Surrey Veneer, negotiated as it was by the Weinzierls who were using the engineering company to serve the interest of Surrey Veneer Ltd, shall be cancelled. The Receiver shall have authority to grant to Surrey Veneer Ltd. whatever easement or right of passage if any he sees fit, for appropriate compensation. Cancellation of the easement in this manner was suggested by the defendants as being preferable to attempting to value it.

Grizzly Ropes Ltd. shall have the costs of its action.

The parties may apply for further directions should that be necessary.

QUESTIONS

1. Section 224 of the *Company Act, R.S.B.C.* 1979 requires that a plaintiff prove either "oppression" or "unfairly prejudicial" conduct in order to obtain a remedy from the court. What conduct was considered "oppressive" in this case and why?

2. What remedies are available to a plaintiff bringing an action for oppression? What remedy was awarded to the plaintiff in this case?

3. Why, in this case, was the equitable defence of acquiescence and laches not available to the defendants?

chapter twenty-nine

External Responsibilities of a Corporation

Forbes v. Wellsley Investments Inc. (c.o.b. Hasty Market)

[1997] B.C.J. No. 175
British Columbia Supreme Court.
January 18, 1997

It is considered trite law to say that a director or officer of a corporation acting within his or her actual or apparent authority binds the corporation to contracts made with third parties. The question that has arisen is whether an innocent third party can rely on the regularity of a corporate act if it is reasonable to do so in the circumstances. The rule that has developed is that a person dealing with a corporation is entitled to assume that its internal procedural rules (found in the corporation's constitutional documents) have been complied with unless it is apparent that such is not the case. This is known as the "indoor management rule."

1   **KIRKPATRICK J.**:— On January 29, 1990, Wellsley Investments Inc. ("Wellsley") executed a distress warrant under the *Rent Distress Act*, R.S.B.C. 1979, c. 362, to recover the balance of rent in the amount of $5,406.64 it claimed was due from Forbes Marketing Ltd. ("Forbes") and Sandy Forbes. The distraint effectively brought an end to a short-lived franchising agreement between Wellsley as franchisor and Forbes as franchisee of a Hasty Market convenience store located at 8900 No. 1 Road, Richmond, B.C.

Background

2   In August 1989, Sandy Forbes saw an advertisement in the Vancouver Sun newspaper for the franchise of a Hasty Market outlet. In September 1989, Mr. Forbes arranged a meeting with Carl McGowen, the president of Wellsley. Mr. Forbes had been employed as a sales representative with a number of food companies prior to 1985, and from 1985 had operated two video stores owned by Forbes Marketing Ltd., a company wholly owned by his wife, Kathy Forbes.

3   Mr. Forbes and Mr. McGowen had several meetings and telephone conversations concerning the franchise and Mr. Forbes' plans for the convenience store. Mr. Forbes hoped to combine his experience in the food and video industries and planned to feature the rental of videos at that Hasty Market location. Mr. Forbes visited six other Hasty Market locations and interviewed the previous franchisee of the 8900 No. 1 Road Hasty Market location.

4   Mr. McGowen was interested in Mr. Forbes' concept of combining the video and convenience store features in one store. Mr. McGowen knew that the 8900 No. 1 Road location was not performing well, as did Mr. Forbes. Mr. McGowen felt that converting one-third of the floor space to video rentals as suggested by Mr. Forbes might improve the commercial viability of the store. Mr. McGowen and Mr. Forbes discussed at some length the reconfiguration of the layout of the store as well as those things which Mr. Forbes would have to instal in order to give effect to the video rental aspect of the operation.

5   On September 1, 1989, shortly after their initial meetings, Mr. Forbes completed a franchise questionnaire for Hasty Market in which he described himself as the operations manager for Forbes Marketing Ltd. which he described as the operator of a video and Nintendo rental business. He also represented that he held the sole interest in the matrimonial home occupied by him and Mrs. Forbes (with a market value of $300,000 and a cost of $140,000) as well as an investment property (with a market value of $150,000 and a cost of $108,000). In addition, Mr. Forbes completed the personal financial statement attached to the franchise questionnaire in which he disclosed that he had "readily marketable investments" valued at $160,000 which, he told Mr. McGowen, were two video stores. Mr. Forbes' net worth was shown to be $488,000, according to the personal financial statement attached to the franchise questionnaire.

6   Mr. Forbes' declarations of his financial worth were clearly false. At most, he held a one-half interest in the real property. He held no interest in the video business.

7   Shortly after completing the franchise questionnaire, Mr. McGowen provided to Mr. Forbes an offer to franchise dated September 4, 1989; a dealer's franchise agreement dated September 11, 1989; a store sublease dated September 11, 1989; and an equipment lease dated September 8, 1989. Mr. Forbes took those documents home

and read them carefully. It is unclear from the evidence as to the precise time at which Mr. Forbes discussed those documents with his wife. However, it is clear from Mrs. Forbes' evidence that she was unwilling to participate in the franchise agreement and did not wish to have her company, Forbes Marketing Ltd., participate in the agreement. Nevertheless, Mr. Forbes signed all of the franchise documents under the name of Forbes Marketing Ltd., although he did not affix the seal of the company to the documents, nor did he have the execution of the documents witnessed.

8   It was evident from the remarks made by Mr. and Mrs. Forbes during the trial that they understood that the absence of witnesses and the fact that the documents were not signed under seal somehow rendered void the agreement between the parties. However, in *Stone Creek Hotel Ltd. v. Symons General Insurance Co. et al.* (1986), 24 C.C.L.I. 131, (B.C.S.C.) the Court held, at p. 135:

> There is no requirement in the Company Act that a company must have a seal for use in the province, let alone use it in the execution of any type of particular document.

Furthermore, under the *Property Law Act*, R.S.B.C. 1979, c. 340, s. 16 provides that:

> *16. (1)   An instrument purporting to transfer, charge or otherwise deal with land or to transfer, release or otherwise deal with a charge need not be executed under seal. Therefore, the execution of the sublease not under seal does not affect its validity. Further still, there is no requirement for the signature of a witness under the Company Act nor under any applicable legislation relating to franchises or leases.*

9   For reasons which were not made clear at trial, Mr. Forbes did not obtain possession of the store until November 17, 1989. However, it is clear that on November 17, 1989, Mr. Forbes paid a franchise fee of $32,500, purchased inventory of $12,683 and was charged with a float of $150, for a total of $45,333. That initial investment was paid from $80,000 in funds borrowed by Mr. Forbes from the Richmond Savings Credit Union. In the days following November 17, 1989, Mr. Forbes, Mr. McGowen, three or four other employees of other Hasty Market locations and employees of Wellsley, as well as casual labour hired by Mr. Forbes, worked to prepare the store for reopening.

10   During the initial period of the franchise, an employee of Wellsley, Elmer Tomniuk, helped to train employees hired by Mr. Forbes. Mr. Tomniuk also visited the store on a weekly basis after the initial take-over. A special feature of Hasty Market at the time was an in-store bakery. Mr. McGowen's wife was responsible for training the staff of new franchisees in the bakery aspect of the business. Mrs. McGowen trained two young female employees hired by Mr. Forbes to work in the Hasty Market. However, both of those employees apparently returned to work shortly thereafter in the video stores owned by Mrs. Forbes.

11   Within a matter of weeks of November 17, 1989, the store seems to have been barely functioning and relations between Wellsley and Mr. Forbes had deteriorated. Mr. Forbes now complains that Wellsley refused to reimburse him for repairs he paid for after taking possession of the store premises. He also complains that Wellsley refused to credit him for unnecessary and infested merchandise. In particular, the Forbes allege that, some time in late December 1989, Wellsley removed a juice cooler from the 8900 No. 1 Road Hasty Market without Mr. Forbes' consent or knowledge and placed it in another Hasty Market location in New Westminster. Mr. Forbes testified that when he became aware of removal of the juice cooler (when visiting the New Westminster Hasty

Market) he immediately placed a stop payment on a $1,649.70 cheque dated December 27, 1989 which represented the monthly payment under the equipment lease.

12   Mr. McGowen was evidently unhappy with the manner in which Mr. Forbes was operating the franchise. Mr. Forbes failed to complete weekly sales sheets from which royalty payments payable under the franchise agreement were to be calculated. After his initial period of involvement in the opening of the store, Mr. McGowen visited the store on three to five occasions in November and December. Contrary to his understanding that video rentals were to form part of at least one-third of the floor area, Mr. McGowen testified that videos were not displayed on shelves. He was concerned that the store did not have sufficient inventory and that the baking aspect of the store was conducted only sporadically. Further, under the terms of the franchise agreement, the store was required to be open 24 hours a day, seven days per week. Mr. Forbes, for reasons he attributed to safety of his employees, unilaterally changed the store hours from 24 hours a day to 6 a.m. to midnight. As to the juice cooler, Mr. McGowen testified that he removed it prior to November 23, 1989. Furthermore, Mr. McGowen testified that the juice cooler never formed part of the equipment leased to Mr. Forbes and is not listed on the schedule attached to the equipment lease. Mr. McGowen testified that Mr. Forbes knew that the cooler was never to form part of the equipment lease as he had discussed with Mr. Forbes the necessity of removing it to make room for the video display aspect of Mr. Forbes' operation.

13   By early January 1990, the business relationship between the parties can at best be described as tenuous. Mr. McGowen called a meeting. Mr. McGowen remembers the meeting as taking place on January 5 at the store. Mr. Forbes remembers the meeting taking place at Mr. McGowen's home on January 10. In any case, it is clear that the grievances held by both sides were discussed at that meeting. Mr. Forbes was accompanied by Keith Lowe, who managed, in Mr. Forbes' words, "the operation of the store." Mr. McGowen was particularly concerned that Mr. Forbes had failed to pay the January 1 rent of $7,200. Mr. McGowen was aware that Mr. Forbes had placed a stop payment on the $1,649 equipment lease payment of December 27, 1989. Further, Mr. Forbes had not paid royalties (except to the extent of $490). Mr. McGowen complained to Mr. Forbes that the store was not really operating. He testified that Mr. Forbes responded to his complaints by saying that he did not have the money to pay and had not been able to "get around" to preparing the revenue statement on which the royalty payments were calculated.

14   Mr. Forbes' recollection of the meeting was that Mr. McGowen offered to accept $5,000 in lieu of the full amount due to Wellsley to January 1, 1990, including rent of $7,203.56, the equipment lease of $1,688.30, and royalty payments. According to Mr. Lowe, Mr. McGowen agreed to accept the $5,000 as "a compromise solution to continue the franchise agreement." Mr. McGowen testified that no such arrangement was made. He said that he left that meeting after advising Mr. Forbes that he wanted the balance of the monies due immediately.

15   No further money was received from Mr. Forbes by Wellsley after that meeting. Furthermore, no sales summaries were delivered to Wellsley upon which royalties could be calculated.

16   On January 29, 1990, Wellsley retained Accurate Bailiff to execute a warrant of distress. On the same day, Wellsley advised Mr. Forbes by letter that Mr. Forbes had committed a "material breach" of the franchise agreement and that Wellsley was terminating the franchise agreement.

17 Mr. Forbes left the store shortly after the bailiff attended on the warrant of distress. Mr. McGowen testified that he attempted to discuss the dispute with Mr. Forbes on January 29 and 30, but was unable to do so to any effect. On January 30, 1990, the then counsel for Mr. Forbes notified Wellsley that Mr. Forbes had elected to treat the contract at an end and claimed return of the franchise fee of $32,500.

Determination

18 By the statement of claim filed November 8, 1990, Mr. Forbes and Forbes Marketing Ltd. claimed rescission of the franchise agreement and repayment of the franchise fee; or in the alternative, claimed against the defendants for damages for breach of contract, loss of investment, loss of income and loss of opportunity as well as damages for fraudulent misrepresentation, deceit, negligent misrepresentation and negligence; or alternatively for an order that the defendants pay damages for wrongfully distraining for rent.

19 At the commencement of the trial, the plaintiffs, who represented themselves, purported to rely on a document entitled "Statement of Claim" which was inserted in what can loosely be described as the trial record in this matter. They also disavowed any claim for negligent or fraudulent misrepresentation, and stated that the focus of their claim was for wrongful distraint. At the conclusion of the plaintiffs' case, counsel for the defendants applied for an order under R.40(10) that the plaintiffs' case be dismissed for insufficient evidence. The application was not granted. Insofar as the application related to the plaintiffs' claims of misrepresentation, the defendants' motion was amply supported. There was no evidence that Wellsley or Mr. McGowen made any fraudulent or negligent misrepresentations to Mr. Forbes. Most significantly, Mr. Forbes testified unequivocally that he relied on his own business judgment in entering into the agreements and did not rely on the statements of anyone else.

20 Notwithstanding the Forbes' assertion that their claim at trial was limited to the wrongful distraint of rent, it is clear from the evidence, particularly that of Mrs. Forbes, that she regarded the action against Forbes Marketing Ltd. as improper. The foundation of Mrs. Forbes' position is that Mr. Forbes entered into the franchise agreement under the name of Forbes Marketing Ltd. without her consent, and Mr. McGowen, on behalf of Wellsley, subsequently refused to alter the franchise documents to properly reflect the real contracting parties.

21 The defendants rely on the old authority of *The Royal British Bank v. Turquand* (1856), 6 E. & B. 327, 119 E.R. 886 (Ex. D.). The rule in Turquand's case, which is also referred to as the "indoor management rule", is helpfully explained in Canadian Business Corporations, (Agincourt: Canada Law Book Ltd., 1977) at p. 104:

> The indoor management and constructive notice doctrines were devised to draw a balance between two conflicting interests. On the one hand, there is the interest of the property owner, in this case a corporation, to protect itself against the dissipation of its property by the unauthorized acts of its agents. On the other hand there is the general interest in promoting and facilitating smooth commercial intercourse. The doctrine of constructive notice is basically designed to further the former policy by placing a duty of enquiry on the outsider. The rule in Turquand's case is designed to further the latter policy as "business could not be carried on if everybody who had dealings with a company had meticulously to examine its internal machinery in order to ensure that the officials with whom he dealt had actual authority".

22   In my view, the rule in Turquand's case prevents the plaintiffs from denying that the contract was with Forbes Marketing Ltd. However, more importantly, it was plain from Mrs. Forbes' evidence that she agreed to have this action commenced under the name of Forbes Marketing Ltd. and, indeed, when Forbes Marketing Ltd. was struck from the Registrar of Companies for failure to make filings, Mrs. Forbes paid $1,600 in order to reinstate the company in order to maintain the action. Accordingly, Forbes Marketing Ltd. adopted the position taken by Mr. Forbes by taking steps to enforce its rights under the contract and through its proximity to the defendants.

23   It was plain from Mrs. Forbes' testimony at trial that she was frustrated and resentful that her company was drawn into the agreement and subsequent litigation without her initial consent. However, her complaint in that regard is more properly directed to her husband than to either Wellsley or Mr. McGowen notwithstanding her belief that an experienced businessman would undertake a more detailed investigation of the party with whom he is contracting.

[*The Court went on to consider whether there was a fraudulent misrepresentation and held that Wellsley did not misrepresent the viability of the store. Furthermore, Forbes did not rely on any representations. The counter-claim was dismissed because Wellsley did not give notice to Forbes of its intention to seek general damages for the unexpired term of the contract on termination of the agreement.*]

QUESTIONS

1. Is a person dealing with a corporation expected to know the contents of the corporation's articles of incorporation or its by-laws?

2. What is the effect of invoking the indoor management rule in this case?

3. Should the failure of the plaintiff in this case to affix the seal of the company to the documents and to have the documents witnessed have put the defendants on notice that the plaintiff had not complied with its internal laws?

4. Would you recommend that a business person dealing with a corporation undertake a detailed investigation of the corporation with whom he or she is contracting? Explain.

part seven

Creditors and Debtors

chapter thirty

Secured Transactions

Bank of Montreal v. Polar Pandas Developments Ltd.

[1992] N.W.T.J. No. 186

Northwest Territories Supreme Court

Judgment: October 30, 1992

Priority amongst secured creditors often arises as an issue when the debtor becomes insolvent. When making a loan, it is important to ensure that you have taken all the necessary steps to entitle you to the priority you expect. This case is an illustration of a contest between competing creditors.

DE WEERDT J.:— This dispute over priority of interest in the proceeds of a court-ordered sheriff's sale of goods seized on behalf of the defendant landlord must be resolved, by and large, in favour of the plaintiff bank, having regard to the provisions of the *Bank Act, R.S.C.* 1985, c. B-1 and the circumstances of the case.

The seizure was made on March 17th 1992 by way of distraint upon goods on premises then under lease by the defendant to Anna Marie's Boutique Limited, a corporation. The goods, which consisted of an inventory of women's clothing belonging to Marie Coe, carrying on business as the proprietor of Anna Marie's Boutique, had been valued by her in May 1992 at $70,000. On sale by the sheriff pursuant to the order of the Chambers Judge made on August 24th 1992, the amount realised on the goods was $17,888. This amount was paid into court in compliance with that order and comprises the proceeds in dispute.

It is not in any real doubt that the plaintiff acquired a security interest in the goods pursuant to section 178 of the *Bank Act* on February 1st 1992, the requirements of registration under that section then having been met. The security is in standard form and purports to have been given by Marie Coe as proprietor of the business carried on in the leased premises. The documentation provided by Ms. Coe to the plaintiff subsequently identified the business as that of Anna Marie's Boutique, a proprietorship dealing in ladies wear and accessories.

The relationship between Ms. Coe and the proprietorship, on the one hand, and the corporation Anna Marie's Boutique Limited, on the other hand, is not stated in the affidavit material. There is nothing in evidence to suggest a sublease by the corporation to the proprietorship or Ms. Coe. Nor is there any mention of a licence to them by the Corporation to use the premises in any way. In the absence of such details, I can only infer that some arrangement existed for that purpose. Whatever the arrangement may have been, it is apparent that the goods belonged to the proprietorship and not to the corporation. On the evidence before me, I find that to be the fact.

Nevertheless, it is equally apparent that there was, in the arrangement between Ms. Coe, her proprietorship and the corporation, a joint venture relationship of some sort. It is quite common for individuals in small businesses to have a corporation created to carry on the operations of the business for tax purposes, and to limit personal liability, but without always taking the steps required to show that the business is being conducted by the corporation rather than by themselves as individuals. Not infrequently this manifests itself in banking documents, such as cheques signed without showing the corporate name (or the corporate capacity of the individual signing for the corporation). In the present case, the banking documents do not display this sort of confusion, however. It is made emphatically clear that they are not documents of the corporation. That being so, I find that the plaintiff bank dealt only with Ms. Coe as the proprietor of the unincorporated business known as Anna Marie's Boutique.

The defendant landlord, for its part, dealt only with the corporation, to whom the lease in question had been assigned by another corporation (the tenant of the premises until January 31st 1992), the assignment taking effect on February 1st 1992. Ms. Coe and another person appear as signatories for "Anna Marie's Boutique Ltd.", under the corporate seal of the corporation, on the lease assignment document.

It is the defendant landlord's position that the assignee corporation was in arrears of rent on February 1st 1992, since rent was payable in advance on that day. There being no specific time during the day by which this rent was to be paid, I can only conclude that the rent was not in arrears, at the earliest, until midnight of that day had passed. In other words, the rent was not in arrears until February 2nd 1992 or some later date.

This alone is enough, in my respectful view, to disentitle the defendant landlord to any claim to priority over the plaintiff bank in respect of the proceeds of sale of the goods seized in distraint for rent. As of February 1st 1992, the defendant, as landlord, could have had no interest in those goods, there being nothing at common law or in the lease (or lease assignment), or any other instrument, conferring any such interest on the defendant. The plaintiff bank's section 178 security under the *Bank Act* took effect on February 1st 1992. And it does not make any difference whether the goods were then being held or used by Ms. Coe, the proprietorship, the corporate assignee of the lease or some venture of any kind at that time.

It was argued on behalf of the defendant that it was entitled to believe that the goods belonged to Anna Marie's Boutique Limited, the assignee of the lease, there being nothing to show otherwise so far as it was concerned. I have considerable sympathy for that view, since it assumes that Ms. Coe and her proprietorship were operating in some regular and open business relationship on behalf of the corporation. The defendant was, in my view, entitled to make that assumption. But, as I believe the foregoing will have shown, the defendant would be no better off even if that assumption was more or less correct. The plaintiff's Bank Act security attached before the defendant could claim any right to distrain upon the goods for non-payment of rent and there was no other right in or over the goods which the defendant can successfully claim in priority to that security. See *Royal Bank of Canada v. Digital Video & Sound Inc.* (1990), 76 Alta. L.R. (2d) 390 (Q.B.) at page 393.

The fact that the plaintiff obtained its security on the same day that the lease assignment took effect is in my view immaterial. The assignment did not, in itself, vest any then existing right to or in respect of the goods in the defendant landlord; nor did the lease do so.

As to the costs of seizure and storage, as well as of sale, of the goods — the considerable delay before the goods could be sold appears to have been due to the inability of the parties to agree on ultimate responsibility for those costs, primary responsibility resting with the defendant who had authorised the seizure. The delay evidently resulted in a considerable loss of value due to the nature of the goods and the passage of time, so that the summer was over before the sale took place, the goods consisting of fashionable summer wear.

Being unable to determine which of the parties brought about the delay, the costs of storage shall be divided equally, each party to bear an equal share of those costs in that reckoning. The costs of the seizure and sale, apart from those storage costs, shall be credited to the defendant in that reckoning.

The plaintiff shall have its costs of the present application in triple column 2 of the tariff.

QUESTIONS

1. How does the collateral held by the debtor qualify for security under s.178 (now s. 427) of the *Bank Act*?

2. At what point was the Bank entitled to priority over the debtor's collateral?

3. When was the landlord entitled to distrain for arrears of rent?

4. Assume that the bank had registered its security interest on February 3rd. What step would the landlord have had to have taken to establish priority over the debtor's goods?

5. Assume that your financial institution plans to loan money to a retail outlet, using the retailer's inventory in stock as collateral for the loan. What searches should be made to ascertain whether your financial institution will be able to assert first priority against the inventory in stock in case the retailer defaults in its obligations under the loan agreement?

Willi v. Don Shearer Ltd.

[1993] B.C.J. No. 2218, 107 DLR (4th) 121, [1994] 2 WWR 312, 35 BCAC 170, 85 BCLR (2d) 393, 5 PPSAC (2d) 179

British Columbia Court of Appeal

September 29, 1993.

The mercantile agency rule is an exception to the rights that a secured creditor obtains by registering a security instrument against collateral. The mercantile agency rule is embodied in personal property security legislation. In the following case, it is section 30(2) of the *B.C. Personal Property Security Act* that is under consideration, but similar provisions exist in the personal property security legislation of other jurisdictions in Canada.

1   **HOLLINRAKE J.A.** (for the Court, dismissing the appeal):— This is an appeal from the order of a judge in chambers made under Rule 18A of the *Rules of Court* in which he held for the plaintiff/respondent in a priority dispute as to property in a motor vehicle. To be more precise the chambers judge held that the respondent purchased a motor vehicle from a third party free and clear of a chattel mortgage registered as a perfected security under the provisions of the *Personal Property Security Act*, R.S.B.C. 1979, c. 321.5 which had been assigned to the defendant/appellant.

2   These are the facts.

3   The appellant carries on the business of leasing motor vehicles.

4   On May 1, 1990 the appellant purchased a 1990 Ford truck for use in its rental fleet. The purchase price was financed 100% by Ford Credit Canada Limited (Ford) and was secured by a chattel mortgage which was duly registered at that time with the Registrar General on May 8, 1990.

5   On December 7, 1990 the appellant sold this vehicle to Connaught Auto Sales Ltd. (Connaught) taking in payment a cheque in the sum of $17,000 post-dated to January 6, 1991. At the time of this transaction Connaught was advised that the vehicle was encumbered by the Ford chattel mortgage. It was understood that on the sale of this truck by Connaught the balance owing on the Ford chattel mortgage would have to be paid to Ford. Whether this meant payment would be from the sale proceeds from the post-dated cheque or from the proceeds of the Connaught sale to a third party is not clear from the record before us.

6   On December 12, 1990 the vehicle was registered in the name of Connaught.

7   On December 21, 1990 the respondent purchased the vehicle from Connaught. Payment by the respondent to Connaught was a trade-in and cash which was paid at the time of the transaction. The respondent had no knowledge of the dealings between Ford and the appellant or those between the appellant and Connaught. The respondent has deposed, and this was accepted, that he believed that having purchased from an automobile dealer his interest was one free and clear of any other interest.

8   Sometime soon after this transaction from Connaught to the respondent Connaught went out of business. When, precisely, is unknown.

9   On January 16, 1991 the Connaught cheque to the appellant was returned "NSF". The appellant made inquiries and satisfied itself that these funds were not collectible which led it to paying to Ford the funds owing on the chattel mortgage. At the same time as paying Ford the appellant took an assignment of the Ford chattel mortgage. The appellant then learned through the Motor Vehicle Branch that the respondent was the registered owner of the vehicle. Payment was sought from the respondent by the appellant, and when this was refused the appellant seized the vehicle priority by reason of the Ford chattel mortgage which had been assigned to it.

10   Before the time the appellant had paid Ford and taken this assignment Ford had registered its security interest under the provisions of the *Personal Property Security Act*.

11   The respondent then sued the appellant claiming delivery up of the truck to him and succeeded before the chambers judge on a Rule 18A summary trial.

12   Before turning to the law there are other facts which should be referred to. These are:

(1)   The Ford chattel mortgage was not before the court and thus it cannot be asserted that there was a clause in it that prevented the appellant from dealing with the vehicle before payment to Ford.

(2)   There are no facts from which it can be inferred there was fraud on the part of Connaught at the time it purchased from the appellant.

(3)   The appellant did not register the purchase and sale document between it and Connaught which transaction the appellant now says was a conditional sale reserving title to it until the cheque from Connaught cleared the banking system which it never did. The lack of registration of this purchase or sale document is inferred from the fact that the appellant asserted the Ford chattel mortgage in seizing the vehicle from the respondent.

(4)   There is no direct evidence that the appellant knew or thought Connaught would sell the truck before January 6, 1991 nor is there any evidence as to what Connaught had in mind at the time of the transaction between itself and the appellant. It is this latter fact that negatives any fraud on the facts before us.

13   The agreement of sale or purchase between the appellant and Connaught contained the following terms:

2.   The right and title to the motor vehicle ordered herein and hereinafter referred to as "the motor vehicle" shall remain in the Vendor until the unpaid cash balance stated on the reverse side hereof and all other sums including interest owing by the Purchaser to the Vendor according to the terms, conditions and warranties herein, are fully paid to the Vendor.

3. The Purchaser agrees that he will not, without first obtaining the Vendor's permission in writing, suffer or permit any charge, lien or encumbrance whether possessory or otherwise, to exist against the motor vehicle until all sums owing by the Purchaser to the Vendor or its assigns according to the terms, conditions and warranties herein or set out in any applicable conditional sales contract or chattel mortgage, are fully paid to the vendor or its assigns.

14   The issue before the Court is whether s.30(2) of the *Personal Property Security Act* insulated the respondent from the property interest asserted by the appellant as the assignee for value of the Ford chattel mortgage.

15   I reproduce here s.30(1) and (2) of the *Personal Property Security Act*.

30.(1) In this section

"buyer of goods" includes a person who obtains vested rights in goods under a contract to which the person is a party as the consequence of the goods becoming a fixture or accession to property in which the person has an interest;

"seller" includes a person who supplies goods that become a fixture or accession under a contract with a buyer of goods or under a contract with a person who is party to a contract with the buyer;

"the ordinary course of business of the seller" includes the supply of goods in the ordinary course of business as part of a contract for services and materials.

(2) A buyer or lessee of goods sold or leased in the ordinary course of business of the seller or lessor takes free of any perfected or unperfected security interest in the goods given by the seller or lessor or arising under section 28 or 29, whether or not the buyer knows of it, unless the buyer or lessee also knows that the sale or lease constitutes a breach of the security agreement under which the security interest was created.

16   Both counsel agree, as is clear, that the contest, in substance, is one between Ford and Connaught. Both counsel agree that the bona fides of the appellant or the respondent are not in issue. Both counsel agree that the transaction is not covered by s.30(2) because the security interest here was not "given by the seller" (Connaught) but rather was given by a third party, in this case the appellant. And so the issue here is whether on the sale from the appellant to Connaught, Connaught was protected by s.30(2) of the *Act* against the Ford chattel mortgage security interest. If Connaught was so protected then the respondent would take from Connaught free of the Ford security interest.

17   The appellant asserts these errors in the judgment of the chambers judge:

(a)   holding that Section 30(2) of the *Personal Property Security Act* operated so as to have extinguished the perfected security interest held by Ford Credit Canada Limited upon the sale of the truck from Don Shearer Ltd. to Connaught Auto Sales Ltd., and finding therefore that Connaught Auto Sales Ltd. purchased the truck free and clear of the chattel mortgage given by Don Shearer Ltd. to Ford Credit Canada Limited;

(b)   holding, in effect, that Connaught Auto Sales Ltd. was a bona fide "buyer of goods", thereby entitled to the protection of Section 30(2) of the *Personal Property Security Act*;

(c)   finding that the sale of the truck from Don Shearer Ltd. to Connaught
Auto Sales Ltd. was made in the ordinary course of the business of
the seller;

18   The case for the appellant is this. Connaught was not a "buyer" within
s.30(2) of the *Act* because the sale from the appellant to it was not a completed one in
that payment had not been concluded because the cheque taken by the appellant from
Connaught was post-dated and title was reserved to the appellant by clauses 2 and 3 in
the agreement of purchase or sale which I have set out above. This argument has as its
foundation the position, as asserted by the appellant, that before one can be a "buyer"
within s.30(2) of the Act the transaction must be a "sale". As there is no definition of
"sale" in the *Personal Property Security Act* one must turn to the *Sale of Goods Act*,
R.S.B.C. 1979, c. 373 to determine whether or not this is a sale. Section 6 of the *Sale
of Goods Act* provides in part:

(4)   *where the transfer of the property and the goods is to take place at a
future time or subject to some condition thereafter to be fulfilled, the
contract is called an agreement to sell.*

(5)   *an agreement to sell becomes a sale when the time elapses or the conditions are fulfilled subject to which the property and the goods is to
be transferred.*

19   The appellant goes on to say that because payment was taken by a post-dated
cheque it follows that this is an agreement to sell (a conditional sale) under s.6(4) of
the *Sale of Goods Act* and this agreement to sell cannot become a sale until the conditions are fulfilled subject to which the property is to be transferred as dictated by
s.6(5) of that Act.

20   Thus, says the appellant, there never was a "sale" concluded and Connaught
never achieved the status of "buyer of goods" within s.30(2) of the *Personal Property
Security Act*.

21   In advancing this submission the appellant relies on what he submits are
principles enunciated by the Saskatchewan Court of Appeal in *Royal Bank of Canada
v. 216200 Alberta Ltd.*, 6 P.P.S.A.C. 277. The respondent says this case does not stand
for the principles asserted by the appellant.

22   The appellant also submits that in any event the transaction between it and
Connaught was not one "in the ordinary course of business" within s.30(2) of the *Act*
and thus that section cannot apply to defeat the security interest of Ford held by the
appellant as assignee.

23   The respondent counters by saying that the appellant seeks to place a narrow
interpretation on the word "buyer" in s.30(2) which cannot be justified on policy
grounds. He says a "buyer" within s.30(2) must be both a buyer and one who agrees to
buy. Otherwise s.30(2) would not protect a person who purchases from a dealer in the
market place from the security interest of the party who provides financing for that
dealer's inventory. That cannot be so, says the respondent, because this would be a
marked step backward in the statutory protection that has been given for years to buyers for value in good faith in the market place.

24   I should say here that I confess to some hesitation in turning to the *Sale of
Goods Act* when interpreting the words "buyer", "sold" and "sale" in the *Personal
Property Security Act*. I say no more about this in view of the conclusion I have

reached in this case. I also note that s.30(8) says a "... sale ... may be ... on credit ...". No submissions were made to us as to what, if any, significance s.30(8) has in interpreting s.30(2) and who is a "buyer". I note this to emphasize that these reasons reflect the arguments made by counsel that I have set out above and should not be taken to go beyond those arguments.

25   Counsel for the appellant conceded that even on his argument if the full consideration for this transaction between the appellant and Connaught was Connaught's cheque, albeit post-dated, then there would be a completed "sale" with s.30(2) and Connaught would be a "buyer" within that section.

26   In my opinion, the facts before us lead to the conclusion that it was the intention of the parties (the appellant and Connaught) that title to this vehicle would pass on the execution of the agreement of sale or purchase on December 7, 1990.

27   I draw this inference in the face of clauses 2 and 3 of the agreement of sale or purchase which I have reproduced above. On the facts before us I think it must be taken that on the cheque being handed to the appellant by Connaught its obligations under the contract were "fully paid".

28   These facts are:

(1)   The cheque given by Connaught to the appellant was a bill of exchange capable of negotiation for value as such. See s.26(d) of the *Bills of Exchange Act*, R.S.C. c. B-4.

(2)   It must be taken the appellant knew Connaught to be a dealer whose business it was to sell vehicles.

(3)   The appellant did not register its agreement of sale or purchase under the appropriate legislation as a security interest.

(4)   The appellant delivered the vehicle to Connaught prior to December 12, 1990 well before the date of the cheque, and executed the forms required to effect registration of the vehicle in Connaught's name on December 12, thereby enabling Connaught to sell the vehicle to an innocent third party for value before the date the cheque was to clear. In the absence of any evidence to the contrary I infer that this transfer was agreed to at the time of the transaction on December 7, 1990.

29   I repeat, I think that the appellant was "fully paid" when it took the cheque from Connaught on December 7, 1990. This being so I conclude there was a completed sale on December 7 and thus, even if the word "buyer" is interpreted narrowly as the appellant would have us do, Connaught was a "buyer" within s.30(2) of the *Personal Property Security Act* and so took from the appellant free and clear of the Ford security interest. Connaught, having taken free and clear of the Ford security interest, the respondent also took clear of that interest when it purchased from Connaught. To put it in the words of the chambers judge:

> Applying the words of section 30(2) Connaught, as buyer of the vehicle, in the ordinary course of business took the vehicle free of any perfected security whether or not Connaught knew of the security interest in it given by Don Shearer Ltd., the seller, unless Connaught knew that the sale constituted a breach of the agreement under which the chattel mortgage was created. There is no evidence that Connaught knew of such a breach. Under the terms of the statute Connaught bought the truck free of the chattel mortgage given by Don Shearer Ltd.

30   I wish to emphasize that it must not be taken that in my opinion the approach of the appellant to the construction of the word "buyer" in s.30(2) of the *Act* is the correct one. My conclusion is that even if the appellant's position is correct, (without deciding), it nevertheless fails on this issue.

31   The last point I must deal with is the appellant's submission that the sale from the appellant to Connaught was not in the ordinary course of the appellant's business.

32   This is what the chambers judge said on this issue. Whether or not the sale from Don Shearer Ltd. to Connaught was in the ordinary course of business is a question of fact. The fact is, as deposed to by Mr. Shearer is his company purchases vehicles and at other times sells vehicles from its rental fleet in order to maintain a proper inventory of vehicles for hire." In other words, it is ordinary and usual for Don Shearer Ltd., carrying on business as Canuck Truck Rental, to sell vehicles such as the one in question. I find nothing in the statute which suggests that interpreting "ordinary course of business" to include transactions which are usual and ordinary for the business in question is not appropriate. The sale of the vehicle by Don Shearer Ltd. to Connaught was in the ordinary course of business.

33   I agree with what the chambers judge said on this issue and his conclusion that this was a transaction in the ordinary course of the business of the appellant.

34   It follows that I would dismiss the appeal.

TOY J.A.:— I agree.

GOLDIE J.A.:— I agree.

QUESTIONS

1. What protection does a buyer get under s. 30(2) of the *B.C. Personal Property Security Act*?

2. Why did the respondent in this case not qualify for protection under s. 30(2) of the *Personal Property Security Act*?

3. Why did the court say that the appellant ie., the party (that had obtained an assignment of the chattel mortgage from Ford Ltd.) was not entitled to seize the vehicle from the respondent?

4. Though the respondent ultimately won this case, undoubtedly much time and money was spent in doing so. How could the respondent have prevented this waste of resources?

5. Could the respondent have sued Connaught Auto Sales Ltd. for damages incurred as a result of the seizure? Explain. Would this have provided the respondent with a practical solution? Why?

chapter thirty-one

Creditors' Rights

Bowering (Re)

[1995] B.C.J. No. 966, 33 CBR (3d) 267
British Columbia Supreme Court (In Bankruptcy)
Judgment: filed May 2, 1995.

Statutory provisions have been designed to nullify transactions that defeat the legitimate claims of creditors. In the following case, the judge refers to the *Bankruptcy and Insolvency Act RSC* 1985 c.B-3 as amended by SC 1992, c.27, that provides for review of payments or transfers to an unrelated person within three months preceding bankruptcy, and to a related person within 12 months preceding bankruptcy. Provincial legislation contains remedies for fraudulent preferences and conveyances, but if the provisions of the provincial legislation conflict with those in the federal *Bankruptcy and Insolvency Act*, the provisions of the federal statute prevail.

1   **MACZKO J.**:— This is an appeal from a Master who made a finding that the payment of funds paid by the bankrupt (the Bowerings) to the Alberta Treasury Branch (ATB) was a fraudulent preference.

2   On March 29, 1993 the Bowerings gave an irrevocable assignment of proceeds of the sale of their home to the ATB. The house was sold and the funds actually passed from the Bowerings' solicitor to the ATB on April 30, 1993. The Bowerings made an assignment in bankruptcy on July 19, 1993.

3   The *Bankruptcy Act*, s. 95, provides that any transfer of property or funds is deemed to be a fraudulent preference if it is made within three months of the bankruptcy.

4   The Master made a finding that on March 29, 1993 when the Bowerings made an irrevocable assignment to the ATB they were insolvent and therefore it brought the assignment within the three month period. He concluded his findings as follows:

> In view of the finding of insolvency on the part on the Bowerings at March 29, 1993, the defence of prior agreement fails. It follows that the presumption stated in s. 95 of the Bankruptcy and Insolvency Act has not been rebutted, and consequently the trustee is entitled to the declaration sought.

The Master set out his findings of fact as follows:

> The bankrupt made an assignment in bankruptcy on July 19, 1993, and E. Sands and Associates Inc. was appointed as their trustee. On April 30, 1993 the sum of $10,360.76 was paid to Alberta Treasury Branch out of the sale proceeds of the Bowering's home in Alberta. The payment was made by the solicitor handling the transfer of the home pursuant to an irrevocable assignment of proceeds executed by the Bowerings on March 29, 1993. The assignment is as follows:

> > In consideration of Alberta Treasury Branches accommodation made available to Bowerings Automotive Services Ltd., loans for which we have personally guaranteed, we, the undersigned, do hereby irrevocably assign net sale proceeds of our home, scheduled to close April 30, 1993, to Alberta Treasury Branches, 217 - 16th Avenue N.W., Calgary, Alberta, for application on outstanding loans to Bowerings Automotive Services Ltd. (approximately $11,000.00).

> > Dated this 29 day of March, 1993.

> > "Kelly Bowering"
> > KELLY BOWERING

> > "Noreen Bowering"
> > NOREEN BOWERING

Prior to that date, the Bowerings had been operating a company in the auto repair business known as Bowerings Automotive Services Ltd. The company had borrowed money from Alberta Treasury Branches for company purposes and the loan was guaranteed by Mr. and Mrs. Bowering personally. The company had got into difficulty with its main customer and the bankrupts had decided in 1992 to liquidate the company's assets in an orderly fashion. As of December 30, 1992 the company's loan with Alberta Treasury Branches was in good standing. Throughout the period from December 30, 1992 to March 29, 1993 the company reduced the amount owing to Alberta Treasury Branches by the sale of equipment and by continuing the monthly payments. By March 29, 1993 the amount owing to Alberta Treasury Branches was approximately $11,000. At that time, Alberta Treasury Branches learned that the Bowering's home had been sold, and in consideration for waiving the requirement for continued monthly payments and the forbearance from seizing further equipment, agreed to accept the irrevocable assignment of proceeds of the sale. Subsequent to the April payment, the balance owing to Alberta Treasury Branches of some $500 was paid by Bowering Automotive Services Ltd. and the remaining security held by Alberta Treasury Branches was released.

It appears that Alberta Treasury Branches had no knowledge of the bankruptcy of the Bowerings until August 1993. It also appears that Alberta Treasury Branches was unaware that the Bowerings were insolvent, either on March 29 or April 30,1993.

5   Counsel for the trustee characterized the case as follows. The actual transfer of funds was made on April 30, 1993 which is within the three month period, and therefore, the presumption of fraudulent preference arises pursuant to s. 95 of the *Bankruptcy Act*. It is now for the ATB to rebut the presumption of fraudulent preference. The trustee argues that the March 29, 1993 assignment is not effective to rebut the presumption because the Bowerings were insolvent at the time of the assignment.

6   Counsel for the ATB argues that the transfer of all property interests in the proceeds of the sale of the house took place when the irrevocable assignment was given on March 29, 1993 which was outside the three month period. The date on which the funds moved is irrelevant because on that date the ATB was already the owner of the funds, and therefore the presumption of fraudulent preference does not arise because no transfer occurred within the three month period.

7   Counsel referred me to a line of cases which found that where there has been a transfer of funds within the three month period, but was made pursuant to a prior agreement, the prior agreement would be a defence only if the bankrupt was solvent at the time the agreement was made.

8   It is my view that the question of prior agreement only arises once there has been a finding that the transfer took place within the three month period.

9   The issue therefore is whether the transfer of property occurred on March 29, 1993 at the time of the irrevocable assignment or whether the transfer of property took place on April 30, 1993 when the monies moved from the Bowerings' solicitor to the ATB.

10   A finding on this issue must be made before a finding on the prior agreement and the state of insolvency of the bankrupt can be made.

11   I find that the transfer of property took place on March 29, 1993 with the irrevocable assignment. The fact that the money did not move until April 30 is in my view irrelevant because on that date the money was already the property of the ATB and not the Bowerings. The Bowerings had no claim on the funds because all property in the money had passed on March 29, 1993. The key to this case is to decide the true nature of the assignment.

12   In *Cowichan Native Heritage Society (Trustee of) v. Toronto Dominion Bank*, [1994] 1 W.W.R. 713 (B.C.C.A.) the bank provided interim financing for its customer prior to bankruptcy secured by an irrevocable authorization from the customer to the government to pay grant installments to the bank. The irrevocable authorization was provided in September, 1990 and the bank's customer went bankrupt in

March, 1991. The court said that the test for whether an assignment is absolute is whether the assignor has unconditionally transferred to the assignee the sole right to the debt in question as against the debtor. Once the irrevocable assignment has been made property transfers to the assignee and the intervention of a trustee cannot affect the validity of the assignment. At p. 716 the court said:

> In my opinion, the appointment of the Trustee did not in itself affect the equitable assignment in favour of the Bank if it was validly created on September 4, 1990. ... Nor can the trustee point to any provision, statutory or otherwise, that supports the bold proposition that an equitable assignment, given for valuable considera-tion as was the case here, is defeated by an assignment in bankruptcy.

13   In *Alberta (Director of Employment Standards) v. Sanche* (1992), 15 C.B.R. (3d) 58 (Alta. Q.B.), the bankrupt gave a creditor a written assignment of up to $40,000 out of monies owing or accruing to him by his employer. The court held that in order for an assignment to be a fraudulent preference under the *Act*, it had to be made within three months of the debtor's bankruptcy. At page 65 the court said:

> The transaction that gives Sanche the "preference" over other creditors is the assignment given to him on June 8, 1990. That is the time when Evans executed and delivered to Sanche the legally enforceable assignment of funds which authorized Terra to pay funds to Sanche. That is the transaction that the trustee is now contesting. The assignment was granted on June 8, 1990, which date pre-cedes the December 30, 1991 date by approximately 18 months, far exceeding the three month limit in the statute. It follows that this assignment is not deemed to be fraudulent and void by operation of s. 95(1), supra.

14   I accept counsel for the ATB's argument that this is not a case where a prior agreement is being put forward to support a transfer of property within three months of bankruptcy. The issue here is whether or not a transfer in fact occurred at all within the three months. In my view the transfer of property took place on March 29 which is outside the three month period. That is the point in time when the ATB was legally entitled to the proceeds of the sale of the Bowering home. Having made this finding it follows that there is no presumption in favour of the trustee.

15   My finding does not preclude the trustee from proceeding under other legis-lation to prove that the assignment was a fraudulent conveyance. The effect of my finding is that the presumption of fraudulent preference does not arise because there was no transfer of property or money within three months of the bankruptcy.

QUESTIONS

1. Why did the court hold that the transfer to the Alberta Treasury Branch was not a fraud-ulent preference, in spite of the fact that the funds were transferred on April 30, 1993?

2. When would the assignment in bankruptcy have had to occur for the transaction to have been considered a fraudulent preference?

3. What would have happened if this transaction had been found to be a fraudulent pref-erence?

Gates (Re) (1998) A.J. No. 374 (Alberta Court of Q.B.)

[1998] A.J. No. 374, ABQB 465, 3 CBR (4th) 263.

Alberta Court of Queen's Bench

Judgment: March 27, 1998. Filed: March 30, 1998.

One purpose of bankruptcy legislation is to allow honest but unfortunate debtors to make a new start. The courts are wary of allowing people to use bankruptcy legislation to escape debts they incur in circumstances when they knew or should have known that the debts could not be repaid. If such circumstances are present, legislation allows the court to refuse to grant a discharge, or to impose conditions that must be fulfilled to obtain a discharge.

1   **REGISTRAR LAYCOCK**:— The bankrupt Gates filed her assignment in bankruptcy April 8, 1997 and on March 17, 1998 applied for her discharge.

2   Ms. Gates was in financial difficulties in 1992 and unable to pay all of her creditors. She entered into an arrangement with her creditors through orderly payment of debts which provided for payment of $500.00 per month which was later reduced to $250.00 in the fall of 1995. In 1995 she was forced to take early retirement after 25 years employment with the Canadian Imperial Bank of Commerce. She received a severance and retirement package of approximately $36,000.00 which was placed into a registered retirement income fund (RRIF).

3   In January 1996 she withdrew $18,000.00 from the RRIF and with her son departed for Australia to visit her daughter Susan and tour the continent for 3 months. From her withdrawal from the RRIF she spent $7,762.00 on the Australia trip. In March 1996 she withdrew a further $7,000.00 from her RRIF obtained a further $2,000.00 for her Australia holiday and paid over to her daughter Christina $3,000.00 for her wedding. In April 1996 she withdrew a further $2,500.00 which was used to cover her expenses after her return from Australia. In August 1996 she withdrew a further $4,200.00 from RRIF and paid out $2,780.00 to her son for tuition, books and clothing and a further $1,000.00 for Christine's wedding expenses and to help pay for her daughter Susan's transportation costs from Australia to attend the wedding. In December 1996 she withdrew a further $3,406.00 to close out the RRIF using $2,400.00 to buy a computer for her son's education and the balance for utility bills and Christmas presents.

4   The bankrupt continued to make payments to her creditors of $250.00 per month to and including December 1996. When she defaulted in making payments there was approximately $6,700.00 still outstanding to her creditors.

5   The bankrupt is now 57 years of age and supports herself on $900.00 pension and employment income of $700.00 to $800.00 per month earned as a part time employee with IGA. The trustee reports an average monthly income during bankruptcy of $1,865.00. Her son Billy is now 21 years of age and attending the S.A.I.T. in civil engineering where he expects to graduate in spring of 1998. He works part time at Radio Shack and uses his income for his personal expenses and pays no room and board to his mother.

6   The trustee's report indicates that in March 1997 the bankrupt realized that with reduced monthly income and tax debt due from the de-registration of her RRIF she could no longer continue the payments to her creditors and decided to make an assignment into bankruptcy.

7   The trustee's report indicates that only 2 of her creditors Revenue Canada for $14,331.49 and Hudsons Bay Company for $1,694.77 have filed a proof of claim in the bankruptcy. Other creditors who are participating in the OPD payments have not filed a proof of claim to date. The trustee recommends that at as a condition of discharge the bankrupt pay into the estate $160.00 per month for 12 months plus any tax refunds that she may be entitled to receive would apply to the condition. None of the creditors have filed an objection to the bankrupt's discharge.

8   Pursuant to the *Bankruptcy Insolvency Act*, section 172(2)(c) the court may require the bankrupt as a condition of discharge to pay monies as the court may direct on proof of any facts mentioned in section 173.

9   The facts that have been proven as enumerated in section 173(1) include:

   (a)   the assets the bankrupt's assets not of a value equal to 50 cents on the dollar, and;

   (e)   the bankrupt has brought on the bankruptcy by unjustifiable extravagance in living.

10   Ms. Gates could have avoided bankruptcy by making proper provision for payment to Revenue Canada for tax incurring from the deregistration of the RRIF and by using those funds to pay off the balance of the amounts payable under the orderly payment of debt's program. She chose instead to use the funds to pay for an extravagant holiday. One of the prime purposes of the Bankruptcy & Insolvency Act is to permit an honest but unfortunate debtor to obtain a discharge from his debts subject to reasonable conditions. Several principles must be kept in mind in dealing with applications for discharge in bankruptcy, some of which are set out by Hallett J. in *Re Crowley* (1984) 54 C.B.R. (N.S.) 303 at pages 306 to 308:

> "First, each case must be decided on its facts.... Second, in considering the application for discharge, the court must have regard to not only the interests of the bankrupt and his creditors but also the interest of the public....Third, if as is usually the case the assets of the bankrupt are not of a value equal to 50 cents in the dollar of the bankrupt's unsecured liabilities, the onus of proving that this fact arose from circumstances for which the bankrupt can not justly be held responsible as on the bankrupt.... Seventh, in considering if an order should be made that involves the payment of money by the bankrupt as a condition of his discharge, the court must bear in mind that he is entitled to have available for the maintenance of himself and his family a reasonable amount out of his after-acquired income."

Hallett, J. further stated at page 309:

> "In recent years there has been a trend by this court to impose conditions of payment on the bankrupt as a price for his discharge. This reflects the feeling of the

public as stated through the decisions of this court that abuses of the bankruptcy process are perceived. While the vast majority of the public are wrestling with their finances to make ends meet, there is a small percentage, albeit a large number of persons, who are availing themselves of the provisions of the Bankruptcy Act and, in particular, the discharge provisions, to walk away from debts which they have accumulated. Imposing a condition that a bankrupt consent to judgment in a reasonable percentage of his unsecured liabilities under certain circumstances is not to frustrate the objects of the *Bankruptcy Act*. In fact, not to do so in many cases may offend the integrity of the discharge procedure. Where a debtor owes a substantial number of creditors, it is reasonable that he be freed from their harassment and get on with earning a living under peaceful conditions but subject to a reasonable judgment in favour of the trustee who, based on his knowledge of the debtor's circumstances, can exercise a sensible discretion in collection procedures; it being understood that under no circumstances should a judgment be entered against a bankrupt which he would be unable to pay over a reasonable period of time."

11   An alternative to requiring the bankrupt to consent to a judgment is to provide as a condition of a bankrupt's discharge that funds be paid into the estate prior to the discharge being granted. The advantage of the judgment entered against a bankrupt with a discharge being granted immediately is that the bankrupt receives a discharge while knowing exactly the debt that must be paid in the future. The disadvantage is that circumstances may change which may make it virtually impossible for the now discharged bankrupt to pay the judgment amount. When a conditional order is made the bankrupt may re-apply to the court on a change of circumstances to vary the amount of the conditional payment. The disadvantage is that the individual remains a bankrupt until a condition has been satisfied. Each case will dictate which approach is to be implemented.

12   What is a reasonable period of time over which the bankrupt should pay money to his estate has been considered in numerous decisions. In *Re: Toal* (1996) 37 Alta. L.R. (3rd) 296 the Alberta Court of Appeal considered a payment period of 4 to 6 years as not being unreasonable. In *Re: Clark* 26 C.B.R. (3rd) 44 British Columbia Registrar Wilson directed the bankrupt to pay for a period of 6 years.

13   Having regard to the bankrupt's financial circumstances the amount recommended by the trustee is appropriate but the time period of 12 months is not reasonable in these circumstances.

14   The bankrupt will be required to pay a further $7,680.00 to her estate as a condition of her discharge with minimum payments of $160.00 per month commencing May 1, 1998, any tax refunds received in the estate may be applied against the payment.

QUESTIONS

1. What conditions did the court impose on the bankrupt for her to obtain a discharge in bankruptcy?

2. Under what circumstances can the court impose requirements before allowing the bankrupt to be discharged in bankruptcy? What circumstances justified the court in imposing requirements here?

3. Instead of imposing conditions that had to be fulfilled before the bankrupt could obtain a discharge, the court could have required the bankrupt to consent to a judgment against her, then granted the discharge. Why did the court not use that approach here?

part eight

Modern Legal
Environment
for Business

chapter thirty-two

Government Regulation of Business

R. v. 279707 Alberta Ltd.

[1991] A.J. No. 364, 35 C.B.R. (3d) 570, 81 Alta. L.R. (2d) 100, 116 AR 13
Alberta Court of Appeal
Judgment: April 25, 1991

When directed to the public at large, an advertisement is not usually considered an offer, so the advertiser is not usually bound in contract to sell the goods at the advertised price. There is, however, legislation at both the federal and provincial level containing sanctions against false advertising. In the following case, the court applies the federal *Competition Act*.

THE COURT:— The criminal charges here consisted of a series of counts. For each of a number of days, the accused was charged with

(a)   misleading advertising under s. 52 of the *Competition Act* and

(b)   not supplying bargain goods advertised under s. 57 of the *Competition Act*.

Competitors and investigators tried repeatedly to buy from the accused a certain model of television set which it repeatedly during the period advertised for sale at a bargain price. Sales people told these would-be buyers that the sets were sold out, had been sold out for some time, and there was not much hope of getting other sets in. The would-be buyers tried in most cases to get rainchecks. In some cases they failed, and in other cases they got rainchecks which the accused, although requested to do so, never honoured.

The Provincial Court convicted the accused on virtually all the counts. The Court of Queen's Bench allowed the appeal and entered acquittals. The Court of Queen's Bench therefore did not have to deal with a sentence appeal which had also been filed.

The Crown now appeals to us. In our view, the appeal should be allowed and the convictions entered in Provincial Court should be restored, except for four counts described below. These are our reasons.

The Crown showed that the wholesaler had on hand at all times a large and ready supply of this model of television set. It could have filled an order by the accused within half a day. An experienced officer of the wholesaler testified that under the conditions then operating, a reasonable supply of that model to keep on hand would have been 100. The President of the accused testified and strongly disputed that estimate, saying that quantity was excessive. Evidence by the accused's President seemed to indicate that during the period in question the accused had on hand a very small number of the right model of television set. Their inventory records indicated that they had five shortly before the period in question, and two fairly late in the period in question. They acquired none during that time.

Though would-be buyers were told that the store had been sold out of that model for some time, the President testified that was not true. He said he really had no idea what made his sales people say that.

The Appellant first suggests that the charge of false advertising must stand or fall on facts existing at the time the advertisement was run, and that later acts or omissions cannot make an advertisement punishable which was not punishable beforehand. The Appellant does concede, however, that events after the advertisement is run can be evidence of what were the facts at the time the advertisement was run.

There is a second reason why the time distinction drawn by the Appellant is not so helpful in this case as it might be. During the time that the various shoppers were attempting to buy such a television set from the accused, the accused repeatedly ran advertisements with identical wording. Therefore, times were really intermingled.

The Crown submitted to the trial judge that the accused never had an honest intent and that the whole thing was a scheme from start to finish. The trial judge agreed without hesitation, saying that he had no doubt at all that was the case. We note the number of experiences which the shoppers had, and the comparative baldness and unconvincing nature of the explanations given in evidence by the President of the company. The trial fact finding is not surprising. In any event, the learned trial judge saw and heard the witnesses, which we and the Court of Queen's Bench have not done. We have no inclination whatever to interfere with that fact finding by the trial judge.

In the second place, whether or not 100 television sets would have been an excessive number to keep on hand was not really the issue. We have no hesitation in saying that two to five sets was far too small a reserve to fulfil these advertisements. The accused appears to have been in a large way of business, and to have had two branches in Calgary alone. The advertisement clearly related to both Calgary stores and was run repeatedly. It expressly stated that the particular model of television set in question was "Priced to Move". Even if it could be argued that the advertisement was not technically false, it was clearly misleading. It was placed in the Calgary Sun which obviously has a large circulation. It would therefore induce thousands of readers to believe that they had the ability to attend at the store and buy that particular model for that particular price. Plainly almost none of them, if any, had that chance. The fact that the distributor had a large untapped supply is not what the advertisement suggested. Nor would it have been, nor was it, of any practical use whatever to the shoppers.

Therefore the convictions for false or misleading advertising sound proper.

Section 57 is obviously directed toward "bait-and-switch" advertising. While the "switch" is not part of the section or the charge, it is interesting to note that the "switch" was very plainly present here. The shoppers were not merely rebuffed in their attempt to buy this particular model of television set; they were also steered toward other more expensive television sets.

The charge is failing to supply the goods advertised in reasonable quantities. In the first place, for the reasons given, we do not regard two to five sets as reasonable quantities. We regard a supply in the hands of the wholesaler which the accused retailer refused or neglected to draw upon, as not being a supply for practical purposes.

In the second place, we do not interpret the section as does the Appellant accused. It submits that the meaning of the verb "supply" in s. 57 is to have on hand or available. We disagree. In our view a retailer who advertises goods would not comply with this section by having a museum with items on hand in glass cases displayed on velvet cushions with spotlights shining upon them. He must sell them on demand. Among the definitions of the word "supply" which are found in the Shorter Oxford Dictionary are the following:

> "2. To furnish with (additional) troops; to reinforce. 5. To fulfil, satisfy (a need or want) by furnishing what is wanted 1567. 6. To furnish, provide, afford (something needed, desired, or used): now usu. with impersonal subj. 1520.7. To furnish (a thing) with what is necessary or desirable; in early use, without const., to make provision for 1529."

If a government or large company calls for tenders for the "supply" of goods or services, a tender would not be responsive if it proposed to leave the goods or the workmen untouched at the "supplier's" place of business.

It cannot possibly be said that there was any "supply" whatever here to these customers. They were repeatedly rebuffed, and none succeeded in getting one of the television sets advertised.

It is true that a defence of due diligence might be open in such a case, and that some elements of it might have been provided by the evidence of the accused's President. However, the circumstances make that defence most improbable, and the learned trial judge who saw and heard the witnesses plainly did not believe any of it. Again we see no reason to interfere with his fact finding. We are not making a finding of automatic vicarious liability. Instead, there is a clear admission that the accused ran the advertisements, and so s. 57 put a duty upon the accused. The trial judge has found that the accused had no intent to carry out that duty. Even on the evidence of its President, the accused took what were obviously completely inadequate steps to carry out that duty.

The accused suggested that the profusion of counts violated the rules against multiplicity. We have no doubt that each new advertisement laid the foundation for, or constituted, another offence. We see no multiplicity in counts.

The Appellant also argued that the *Kianapple* principle should apply. He suggested that virtually all the elements of the charges under s. 52, and those under s. 57, were the same. He therefore suggested that half the convictions were redundant. We do not agree. The essence of the false advertising charge is publishing an advertisement which is then untrue. The essence of the s. 57 charge is failing to sell after the advertisement has come out. It is true that a fully implemented "bait-and -switch" scheme would in many cases entail violation of both sections. But such full implementation might not occur. On the one hand, a retailer who had adequate supplies of the goods and had been selling them and advertising them, might decide to neglect or refuse to sell and instead switch customers to more profitable lines. He would violate s. 57 only. On the other hand, a retailer who had published an advertisement which was then totally false might have a change of heart; he might get supplies from his wholesaler and thereafter live up to the implicit promise in his advertisements. He would violate s. 52 only. Therefore there is no double punishment by allowing the two sets of convictions to stand.

For these reasons the convictions under s. 57 sound proper also. The Crown's factum "concedes that acquittals were proper on Counts 15-18 inclusive". We allow the Crown appeal and restore the convictions made in Provincial Court on Counts 1-14 inclusive and or Counts 19-28 inclusive.

The sentence appeal has never been heard on its merits. It was agreed at the end of argument before us that, should we restore any of the convictions, we would remit the sentence appeals to the Court of Queen's Bench.

Thus the sentence appeals may be dealt with on their merits. We so order.

We were told that an arrangement had been made (hold the fines "in abeyance"). Counsel agreed that we should leave that arrangement in place until the sentence appeals in the Court of Queen's Bench are disposed of. We so order.

LIEBERMAN J.A.

MASON J.

COTE J.A.

QUESTIONS

1. Why was the appellant found to have violated s. 52 of the *Competition Act*?

2. The appellant's president said that he had no knowledge that his salespeople were saying that the store had been sold out of the advertised televisions for some time. Would the president's lack of knowledge have provided a defence to liability under s.52?

3. What was the appellant's defence to the charge under s.57 of the *Competition Act*? Why did the defence fail?

chapter thirty-three

International Business Transactions

Eastern Power Ltd. v.
Azienda Communale Energia and Ambiente

[1999] O.J. No. 3275, 178 DLR (4th) 409, 125 OAC 54, 50 BLR (2d) 33, 39 CPC (4th) 160

Ontario Court of Appeal (Appeal to the Supreme Court of Canada dismissed with costs and without reasons – June 22, 2000.)

Judgment: September 14, 1999.

Two important issues arise when a party transacts business with someone in another jurisdiction - which court can deal with a dispute between them, and which law governs resolution of the dispute. Jurisdiction and choice of law are two different issues. Courts in more than one jurisdiction may have the ability to exercise authority, but the court must decide which law applies to resolve the dispute. Many of the same factors are relevant in determining both issues.

MACPHERSON J.A.:—

Introduction

1   This is an appeal from the judgment of Juriansz J. dated November 26, 1998, [1998] O.J. No. 4908 in which he set aside service in Italy of a statement of claim by an Ontario company and stayed the company's action in Ontario on forum non conveniens grounds. In addition to the standard forum non conveniens factors that need to be addressed, the appeal poses the interesting question of where a contract is formed when the acceptance of an offer is communicated by facsimile transmission. Is the contract formed, in accordance with the general rule of contract law, in the place where the acceptance is received? Or should the postal exception to the general rule, which says that a contract is formed when and where an acceptance is placed in the mail, apply to acceptances communicated by facsimile transmission?

Factual Background

2   The appellant, Eastern Power Limited ("EP"), is a corporation organized under the laws of Ontario with its principal place of business in Toronto. Its business is the generation of power from non-conventional sources of energy such as landfill gas.

3   Azienda Communale Energia and Ambiente ("ACEA") is a corporation under the laws of Italy with its principal place of business in Rome. ACEA provides power to the City of Rome. ACEA generates some of its own power; however, it also purchases power from other sources.

4   In September 1994 representatives of ACEA came to Toronto to learn about EP's operations and to explore the possibility of developing power from non-conventional sources in Rome. In order to facilitate these discussions, a confidentiality agreement was prepared and signed. ACEA agreed to maintain as confidential any information specific to the proposed joint venture or related to proprietary processes and systems developed by EP. ACEA also agreed that it would not utilize such information and proceed independently or apart from EP.

5   In December 1994 EP met with ACEA in Italy. The parties drafted a Co-Operation Agreement. ACEA signed the agreement on December 9 and faxed it to EP in Ontario. EP signed the agreement in Ontario and faxed it to ACEA in Rome on December 21. It was an express term of the agreement that the two companies would co-operate and use their best efforts to enter into a project agreement. This agreement, relating to the implementation of the alternative energy project, would be based on proposals to be developed by EP and submitted to ACEA for approval. The project was described as "an electricity generating plant fuelled by landfill gas, sewage sludge and fossil fuel(s) located near Rome, Italy."

6   On January 29, 1996 ACEA signed a Letter of Intent relating to the project. The Letter of Intent was faxed by ACEA to EP in Ontario. On February 14 EP accepted and signed the Letter of Intent in Ontario and faxed it back to ACEA in Rome. The Letter of Intent indicated that the parties wanted to proceed with the project and set out how EP would structure itself in order to be permitted to carry out its work in Italy. The Letter of Intent contained these two provisions:

The terms of reference between the parties of the new company are governed according to the Joint Venture Agreement which will be later signed by the parties. The intended contents of the present letter are subject to conditions such as:

a) The acquisition of a favourable written opinion from the Ministry of Industry regarding the award of CIP 6 subsidy to the plant to be built, and also in relation to the Italian Law N. 481 dated 14.11.95 and every subsequent change and integrations which could occur in the meanwhile;

7   The parties worked to conclude a Joint Venture Agreement. Many drafts were prepared. However, none was ever signed. During these further negotiations EP was concerned that ACEA was not diligently pursuing the important CIP 6 subsidy. On January 24, 1997 the Ministry of Industry amended the subsidy program in a way that made it inapplicable to the proposed joint venture.

8   On February 14, 1997, ACEA wrote to EP and effectively terminated their relationship. The letter, signed by ACEA's General Manager, Mario Diaco, cited three reasons: an inability to agree on some terms of the Joint Venture Agreement, the apparent inapplicability of the government subsidy to the project, and the legal requirement that ACEA award large contracts, like the proposed Rome generating plant, by way of public tender.

9   On March 19, 1997 EP forwarded an invoice to ACEA for $478,547 for development and legal costs relating to the project. The time frame for this invoice was stated to be October 1994 - March 1997.

10   On September 11, 1997 ACEA filed a summons with the Rome Civil Court. The summons essentially seeks a declaration that ACEA has no liability whatsoever to EP. EP was served with a copy of this claim about a week later. There is nothing in the record to indicate whether the court in Rome has disposed of the matter.

11   On December 4, 1997 EP commenced its action against ACEA in Ontario. EP sought damages of $750,000 for development costs incurred and $160,000,000 for loss of profits as a result of the alleged negligence and breach of contract by ACEA with respect to the Co-operation Agreement.

12   On January 19, 1998 ACEA was served with the statement of claim. ACEA did not serve a statement of defence and on March 25 was noted in default. EP then brought a motion for default judgment. This motion was adjourned to permit ACEA to bring its motion to set aside service of EP's statement of claim and to stay the action.

13   Juriansz J. heard ACEA's motion on October 27, 1998. On November 26, 1998 he released his judgment. He set aside the service in Italy of EP's statement of claim and he stayed EP's action in Ontario on forum non conveniens grounds. By endorsement released on February 9, 1999, he awarded ACEA its costs of the motion fixed at $44,000.

14   EP appeals from both components of Juriansz J.'s order of November 26, 1998 and from his costs award of February 9, 1999.

Issues

15   The issues on this appeal are:

Was the motions judge correct to stay EP's action in Ontario on the basis of forum non conveniens?

Was the motions judge correct to set aside service in Italy of EP's statement of claim?

Was the motions judge correct to award ACEA costs of the motion fixed at $44,000?

16   In the view I take of the appeal, the disposition of the first issue makes it unnecessary to consider the second issue. Accordingly, in these reasons I will address only the forum non conveniens and costs issues.

C.   Analysis

Forum non conveniens

17   On a motion to stay a proceeding on the basis of forum non conveniens, the test is whether there is clearly a more appropriate jurisdiction in which the case should be tried than the domestic forum chosen by the plaintiff: see *Amchem Products Inc. v. British Columbia (Workers' Compensation Board)* [See Note 1 below], [1993] 1 S.C.R. 897 at 921 and 931; *Frymer v. Brettschneider* (1994), 19 O.R. (3d) 60 (C.A.); and *Mutual Life Assurance Co. of Canada v. Peat Marwick*, [1998] O.J. No. 5119 (C.A.).

18   In determining which forum, domestic or foreign, is the more appropriate forum, the courts will look at a wide range of factors. The general approach was enunciated by Arbour J.A. in *Frymer v. Brettschneider*, at p. 79:

The choice of the appropriate forum is designed to ensure that the action is tried in the jurisdiction that has the closest connection with the action and the parties. All factors pertaining to making this determination must be considered.

19   What, then, are the relevant factors? *Amchem* mentions several of them - the connection of the parties to the competing jurisdictions, where the acts that are the foundation of the claim took place, and legitimate juridical advantage in the domestic forum. A useful catalogue of factors which various Ontario courts have considered is contained in *SDI Simulation Group Inc. v. Chameleon Technologies Inc.*, (1994), 34 C.P.C. (3d) 346 (Ont. Gen. Div.), wherein Borins J. stated, at pp. 350-51:

The law with respect to forum non conveniens has been subject to a number of recent cases: *Amchem Products Inc. v. British Columbia (Workers' Compensation Board)*, [1993] 1 S.C.R. 897; *Upper Lakes Shipping Ltd. v. Foster Yeoman Ltd.* (1993), 14 O.R. (3d) 548 (Gen. Div.), leave to appeal refused; *Guarantee Co. of North America v. Gordon Capital Corp.* (1994), 18 O.R. (3d) 9 (Gen. Div.), leave to appeal refused; *Frymer v. Brettschneider* (1994), 19 O.R. (3d) 60 (C.A.). In my view, on the basis of these authorities the test is not one of convenience, but one of "a more appropriate jurisdiction based on the relevant factors in which to litigate the plaintiff's claim". In the *Gordon Capital* case Ground J. identified the following as the factors to be considered in determining the appropriate forum and, in the case of two appropriate forums, which is the more appropriate:

the location where the contract in dispute was signed,

the applicable law of the contract,

the location in which the majority of witnesses reside;

the location of key witnesses,

the location where the bulk of the evidence will come from,

the jurisdiction in which the factual matters arose, and

the residence or place of business of the parties.

20   In his judgment, Juriansz J. focussed on this catalogue of factors from *Gordon Capital and SDI Simulation Group*. He added to this list one other factor, the loss of juridical advantage, because it was identified as an important factor by the Supreme Court of Canada in Amchem. The appellant does not quarrel with the relevance of any of these factors, and indeed has made submissions on all of them. Hence, I will review these factors.

(a)   Location Where the Contract Was Signed

21   The contract which forms the basis of EP's action in contract and tort against ACEA is the Co-operation Agreement: see Statement of Claim, paragraphs 5, 26, 30 and 31. The motions judge found that the Co-operation Agreement was made in Italy because "acceptance was communicated to Italy." Since EP's acceptance was communicated by facsimile transmission, this raises the interesting question of the legal relationship between a faxed acceptance of an offer and the place where a contract is formed.

22   The general rule of contract law is that a contract is made in the location where the offeror receives notification of the offeree's acceptance: see Fridman, The Law of Contract in Canada, 3rd ed., (1994), at p. 65; and *Re Viscount Supply Co.,* [1963] 1 O.R. 640 (S.C.). However, there is an exception to this general rule. It is the postal acceptance rule. As expressed by Ritchie J. in *Imperial Life Assurance Co. of Canada v. Colmenares,* [1967] S.C.R. 443 at 447:

> It has long been recognized that when contracts are to be concluded by post the place of mailing the acceptance is to be treated as the place where the contract was made.

See also: Fridman, The Law of Contract in Canada, supra, at pp 67-68.

23   EP contends that the rule with respect to facsimile transmissions should follow the postal acceptance exception. With respect, I disagree. EP has cited no authority in support of its position. There is, however, case authority for the proposition that acceptance by facsimile transmission should follow the general rule, which would mean that a contract is formed when and where acceptance is received by the offeror.

24   In *Brinkibon Ltd. v. Stahag Stahl G.m.b.H.,* [1983] 2 A.C. 34 (H.L.), a contract was concluded when the buyer in London transmitted its acceptance to the seller in Vienna. The mode of acceptance was a message sent by telex, a form of instantaneous communication like the telephone. The law lords were unanimous in concluding that the contract was formed in Vienna where the acceptance was received by the offeror. Lord Brandon of Oakbrook analyzed the issue in this fashion, at p. 48:

> Mr. Thompson's second and alternative case, that the contract was concluded by the buyers transmitting to the sellers their telex of May 4, 1979, seems to me to

be the correct analysis of the transaction. On this analysis, however, the buyers are up against the difficulty that it was decided by the Court of Appeal in *Entores Ltd. v. Miles Far East Corporation* [1955] 2 Q.B. 327 that, when an offer is accepted by telex, the contract thereby made is to be regarded as having been so made at the place where such telex was received (in this case Vienna) and not in the place from which such telex was sent (in this case London). Mr. Thompson invited your Lordships to hold that the Entores case was wrongly decided and should therefore be overruled. In this connection he said that it was well-established law that, when acceptance of an offer was notified to an offeror by post or telegram, the concluding of the contract took place when and where the letter of acceptance was posted or the telegram of acceptance was dispatched. He then argued that the same rule should apply to cases where the acceptance of an offer was communicated by telex, with the consequence that the contract so made should be regarded as having been made at the place from which the telex was sent and not the place where it was received.

My Lords, I am not persuaded that the *Entores case* [1955] 2 Q.B. 327, was wrongly decided and should therefore be overruled. On the contrary, I think that it was rightly decided and should be approved. The general principle of law applicable to the formation of a contract by offer and acceptance is that the acceptance of the offer by the offeree must be notified to the offeror before a contract can be regarded as concluded, *Carlill v. Carbolic Smoke Ball Co.* [1893] 1 Q.B. 256, 262, per Lindley L.J. The cases on acceptance by letter and telegram constitute an exception to the general principle of the law of contract stated above. The reason for the exception is commercial expediency: see, for example, Imperial Land Co. of Marseilles. In *re (Harris' Case)* (1872) L.R. 7 Ch. App. 587, 692 per Mellish L.J. That reason of commercial expediency applies to cases where there is bound to be a substantial interval between the time when the acceptance is sent and the time when it is received. In such cases the exception to the general rule is more convenient, and makes on the whole for greater fairness, than the general rule itself would do. In my opinion, however, that reason of commercial expediency does not have any application when the means of communication employed between the offeror and the offeree is instantaneous in nature, as is the case when either the telephone or telex is used. In such cases the general principle relating to the formation of contracts remains applicable, with the result that the contract is made where and when the telex of acceptance is received by the offeror.

25   In my view, this analysis is equally applicable to facsimile transmissions, another form of instantaneous communication. Indeed, there is at least one Canadian authority that has reached this conclusion. In *Joan Balcom Sales Inc. v. Poirier* (1991), 49 C.P.C. (2d) 180 (N.S. Co. Ct.), an acceptance of a real estate listing offer was communicated by two vendors in Ottawa to a real estate company in Berwick, Nova Scotia. The mode of communication was a facsimile transmission. The vendors' position was that the contract was formed in Ottawa; they argued that the "mailbox doctrine" should be applied to communication by facsimile transmission.

26   Haliburton Co. Ct. J. did not accept the vendors' argument. He reviewed the English academic writing about the postal acceptance exception to the general rule of contract formation. He then concluded, at p. 187:

The writers then discuss the practical need of special rules to be applied to contracts entered into by post in the age when post was the primary method of commercial communication. The considerations which made it highly practical, if not imperative, in the interests of commerce, for the offeree to have knowledge in a timely fashion that he had a firm contract do not apply to facsimile transmissions. The communication is instantaneous. The offeree could easily have confirmed within minutes that they had a binding contract. I, therefore, find that the contract was executed at Berwick.

27   I agree with this analysis, and with the analysis of the law lords in Brinkibon. I would hold that in contract law an acceptance by facsimile transmission should follow the general rule of contract formation, not the postal acceptance exception.

28   I do not say that this rule should be an absolute one; like Lord Wilberforce in his separate speech in Brinkibon, "I think it a sound rule, but not necessarily a universal rule" (p. 42). Lord Wilberforce discussed some of the factors that might suggest caution about applying the general rule to telex communications in all cases, including the many variants in such communications and whether the message was sent and received by the principals to the contemplated contract. However, he concluded, at p. 42:

> The present case is ... the simple case of instantaneous communication between principals, and, in accordance with the general rule, involves that the contract (if any) was made when and where the acceptance was received.

29   In my view, the present appeal is also "the simple case." The acceptance was faxed by the principals of EP in Ontario to the principals of ACEA in Italy. There is nothing to suggest that the communication between these principals was not instantaneous. Hence, applying the general rule, the contract was formed in Italy.

The Applicable Law of the Contract

30   The Co-operation Agreement contained no provision specifying which system of law, Ontario or Italy, was to govern issues arising under it. In such a situation, a court must infer which jurisdiction should be the proper law of the contract. In reaching a conclusion on the proper law, the court will consider a number of direct and contextual factors. Many of these factors are contained in a passage in Professor Castel's book, Canadian Conflict of Laws, 4th d., (1997), at pp. 596-98:

> If there is no express choice of the proper law, the court will consider whether it can ascertain that there was an implied choice of law by the parties ... [I]f the parties agree that the courts of a particular unit shall have jurisdiction over the contract, there is a strong inference that the law of that legal unit is the proper law. Other factors from which the courts have been prepared to infer the intentions of the parties as to the proper law are the legal terminology in which the contract is drafted, the form of the documents involved in the transaction, the currency in which payment is to be made, the use of a particular language, a connection with a preceding transaction, the nature and location of the subject matter of the contract, the residence (but rarely the nationality) of the parties, the head office of a corporation party to the contract, or the fact that one of the parties is a government.

31   In my view, the motions judge was alive to the full range of factors as he determined the proper law of the Co-operation Agreement between EP and ACEA. He made a full and careful analysis of the factors (Reasons, p. 10):

In my view, the applicable law of the cooperation agreement and letter of intent is Italian. While there is no express choice of governing law, the cooperation agreement provided that the Italian version would "bear witness", only the Italian version of the letter of intent was executed, currency was expressed in lira, the subject matter of the contracts was the building of a power plant near Rome, the project was subject to Italian regulation, the plaintiff was to participate in the project through a company organized under Italian law, and the defendant was associated with the municipal government of Rome. The plaintiff's intent and recognition that Italian law would govern is indicated by the fact it regarded as finalized the draft joint venture agreement which provided that Italian law would govern and the Italian courts would have exclusive jurisdiction.

32   Some of these factors are direct - they involve an interpretation of the Co-operation Agreement. Other factors, including those relating to the Letter of Intent (which the parties signed) and the draft Joint Venture Agreement (which was never signed) are contextual. All, in my view, are relevant. They point overwhelmingly to the conclusion reached by the motions judge: the proper law of the contract was Italian law.

Location Where the Majority of Witnesses Reside

33   The motions judge did not address this factor. There is little in the record on EP's side to indicate how many witnesses it would call. In the affidavit of Gregory Vogt, a director of EP, dated September 2, 1998, there is this brief allusion in paragraph 30: "None of the witnesses who would be called to testify on behalf of EP speak Italian, with the exception of Mr. De Vuono." Unfortunately, all this establishes is the unsurprising fact that EP intends to call more than one witness at the trial.

34   The record on ACEA's side is better. In his supplementary affidavit dated October 21, 1998, Vincenzo Puca, the Head of the Legal Department at ACEA, stated:

[T]he persons that ACEA would call to testify in this proceeding reside in Italy, and the majority of them do not speak English. Besides the undersigned, the following ACEA employees would be probably called to testify as witnesses: none of them speaks English fluently, and the services of an interpreter would become necessary to receive their testimony: Francesco Sperandini, Alfonso Messina, Massimo Cortesi, Biagio Eramo and Maria Gemma Pisano. The testimony of some Italian public officials may also be necessary.

35   Based on the record, it appears that the majority of witnesses reside in Italy. Having said that, in a case involving two large corporations and hundreds of millions of dollars it does not strike me that this factor is a particularly important one.

Location of Key Witnesses

36   Presumably, the key witnesses for EP would be Canadians and the key witnesses for ACEA would be Italian. This factor is neutral.

The Location Where the Bulk of the Evidence Will Come From

37   The motions judge concluded that the location where the bulk of the evidence will come from is Italy. He offered no reasons for this conclusion.

38   In my view, this is a difficult factor to assess on the record before the motions judge. There is no question that EP performed its part of the contract in both Ontario and Italy. ACEA's performance obviously was anchored in Italy; however, its representatives made at least one trip to Ontario. Without knowing the identity of the witnesses and something about the evidence to be tendered, it would be wrong to reach a conclusion on this factor.

The Jurisdiction in Which the Factual Matters Arose

39   The motions judge did not consider this factor. EP argues that it performed some of the development work on the power plant in Toronto. This preliminary work would have been done, likely in Toronto, even if the Joint Venture Agreement had been finalized.

40   However, the design, construction and operation of the plant would have taken place almost entirely in Italy. The Letter of Intent required EP to acquire an Italian construction company to undertake the project. A new Italian company, owned 51 percent by ACEA and 49 percent by EP, was to acquire the construction firm. The final draft of the Joint Venture Agreement proposed that meetings of the board of directors of the new company were to take place in Rome. In addition, throughout the two and a half year relationship between EP and ACEA, almost all of the negotiating sessions for the project took place in Italy; it appears that only one meeting, in October 1994, took place in Ontario.

41   Moreover, a significant part of EP's claim relates to the alleged failure of ACEA to secure a major subsidy for the project from the Italian government. No part of this sequence of events took place in Ontario and none of the persons responsible for the subsidy program or ACEA's attempt to secure a subsidy has any connection with Ontario. EP had nothing to do with that portion of the project.

42   For these reasons, I conclude that this factor tells in favour of Italy as the proper forum for the litigation between the parties.

The Residence or Place of Business of the Parties

43   EP's place of business is Ontario; ACEA's is Italy. This is a neutral factor.

Loss of Juridical Advantage

44   A substantial portion of EP's claim against ACEA is for damages for alleged loss of profits. These damages flow, asserts EP, from ACEA's breach of contract and from its negligence. EP asserts that Italian law does not permit a claim for loss of profits. This is, EP concludes, a huge juridical disadvantage.

45   Accepting, arguendo, the truth of EP's assertion that Italian law does not permit a claim for loss of profits does not, in my view, assist EP. The proper law of the contract between the parties is, as discussed above, Italian law. If the action is heard in a court in Ontario the court will have to apply Italian law, including the Italian law with respect to damages flowing from breach of contract.

46   EP's tort claim suffers the same fate. In *Tolofsen v. Jensen,* [1994] 3 S.C.R. 1022, a case dealing with conflict of laws principles in a tort context, La Forest J. said, at pp. 1049-1050:

From the general principle that a state has exclusive jurisdiction within its own territories and that other states must under principles of comity respect the exercise of its jurisdiction within its own territory, it seems axiomatic to me that, at least as a general rule, the law to be applied in torts is the law of the place where the activity occurred, i.e., the lex loci delicti ... In short, the wrong is governed by that law. It is in that law that we must seek its defining character; it is that law, too, that defines its legal consequences. [Emphasis added]

47   In paragraph 31 of its Statement of Claim, EP sets out the conduct which it alleges constituted negligence on the part of ACEA. All of the impugned conduct relates to ACEA's efforts, or lack thereof, in relation to the Italian government's subsidy program and ACEA's position with respect to the negotiation and finalization of the Joint Venture Agreement. ACEA's activities in both of these domains took place in Italy.

48   EP makes one other argument, a procedural one, on the juridical advantage point. It is that Italian law does not permit a jury trial, whereas a jury trial is possible if this action proceeds in Ontario. I must confess my surprise that EP would advance this argument; it did not file a jury notice when it served its Statement of Claim and it has not done so in the 20 months since then.

49   For these reasons, I would conclude, as did the motions judge, that EP will suffer no juridical loss, in contract law, tort law or procedure, if its dispute with ACEA is resolved by the Italian courts.

Conclusion

50   Of the eight factors I have considered, five tell in favour of ACEA. Four of the five strike me as particularly important factors - the location where the contract was formed, the law of the contract, the jurisdiction in which factual matters arose, and the absence of a loss of juridical advantage for EP. The other three factors are neutral. No factors favour EP's position. Accordingly, the motions judge was correct to stay EP's action in Ontario on forum non conveniens grounds.

51   In light of this conclusion, it is not necessary to consider the motions judge's second basis for staying EP's action in Ontario, namely that EP could not serve its statement of claim on ACEA ex juris in Italy because EP could not bring itself within rule 17.02(h) of the Rules of Civil Procedure which requires that the plaintiff's claim be "in respect of damage sustained in Ontario." If, as I have concluded, EP's action cannot be brought in Ontario, then it is irrelevant how EP effected service of its statement of claim.

Costs

52   In supplementary reasons dated February 9, 1999, the motions judge fixed costs of the motion payable by EP to ACEA at $44,000. EP does not object to the fact that the motions judge fixed costs; it appears that both parties agreed to this format. EP does object to the $44,000 amount of the award, which it characterizes in its factum as "grossly excessive".

53   A trial or motions judge has a large discretion as to costs: see *Murano v. Bank of Montreal* (1998), 41 O.R. (3d) 222 (C.A.). The motions judge in the case under appeal was familiar with the issues and he received extensive submissions on costs. In his supplementary reasons, he described the motion as "a moderately complex matter in an action in which some $163,000,000 was claimed" (p. 2). He also characterized the motion as "a matter of great importance to the parties and counsel for both sides, justifiably, devoted time to it" (p. 2).

54   Both parties submitted bills of cost and supporting affidavits and dockets to the motions judge. ACEA asked for a costs order of $50,014.50 inclusive of disbursements and GST.

55   In my view, there is nothing to indicate that the motions judge did not properly consider the submissions made by the parties or the factors in rule 57.01. Although his costs award was a substantial one, he did not simply rubber stamp ACEA's request. Accordingly, in my view there is no basis on which this court should interfere with the motions judge's discretion in ordering EP to pay costs of $44,000 inclusive of disbursements and costs.

Disposition

56   I would dismiss the appeal with costs.

ABELLA J.A — I agree.

LASKIN J.A. — I agree.

QUESTIONS

1. What is the postal acceptance rule? Does it apply to facsimile transmissions? Explain.

2. Where was this contract made? Explain.

3. What factors did the court consider in determining whether the courts of Ontario should hear this dispute? Explain why the Ontario court decided that Ontario was not an appropriate location for trial of this action.

4. What could the parties have done to make it less likely that they would be involved in a dispute over what court would have jurisdiction in the dispute, and which law to apply to it?

Rudder v. Microsoft Corp.

PROCEEDING UNDER the Class Proceedings Act, 1992

[1999] O.J. No. 3778, 106 OTC 381, 47 CCLT (2d) 168, 40 CPC (4th) 394, 2 CPR (4th) 474

Ontario Superior Court of Justice

Judgment: October 8, 1999.

When a party is transacting business with someone in another jurisdiction, there will often be a clause in the contract whereby the parties agree where any litigation in connection with the contract will take place. The court will usually, but not always, give effect to such a clause. In this case, the plaintiffs argued that there were a number of factors that should influence the court in refusing to enforce the forum selection clause.

1   **WINKLER J.**:— This is a motion by the defendant Microsoft for a permanent stay of this intended class proceeding. The motion is based on two alternative grounds, first that the parties have agreed to the exclusive jurisdiction, and venue, of the courts, in King County in the State of Washington in respect of any litigation between them, and secondly, that in any event, Ontario is not the appropriate forum for the conduct of this proceeding and that the service ex juris of the Statement of Claim ought to be set aside.

2   The Microsoft Network ("MSN"), is an online service, providing, inter alia, information and services including Internet access to its members. The service is provided to members, around the world, from a "gateway" located in the State of Washington through computer connections most often made over standard telephone lines.

3   The proposed representative plaintiffs in this action were subscriber members of MSN. Both are law school graduates, one of whom is admitted to the Bar in Ontario while the other worked as a legal researcher. They were associated with the law firm which originally represented the intended class. The plaintiffs claim under the *Class Proceedings Act,* 1992, S.O., C.6 on behalf of a Canada-wide class defined as:

All persons resident in Canada who subscribed for the provision of Internet access or information or services from or through MSN, The Microsoft Network, since September 1, 1995.

This class is estimated to contain some 89,000 MSN members across Canada.

4   The plaintiffs claim damages for breach of contract, breach of fiduciary duty, misappropriation and punitive damages in the total amount of $75,000,000.00 together with an accounting and injunctive relief. The plaintiffs allege that Microsoft has charged members of MSN and taken payment from their credit cards in breach of contract and that Microsoft has failed to provide reasonable or accurate information concerning accounts. The Statement of Claim was served on Microsoft at its offices in Redmond, Washington on January 5, 1998.

5   The contract which the plaintiffs allege to have been breached is identified by MSN as a "Member Agreement". Potential members of MSN are required to electronically execute this agreement prior to receiving the services provided by the company. Each Member Agreement contains the following provision:

> 15.1   This Agreement is governed by the laws of the State of Washington, U.S.A., and you consent to the exclusive jurisdiction and venue of courts in King County, Washington, in all disputes arising out of or relating to your use of MSN or your MSN membership.

The defendant relies on this clause in support of its assertion that the intended class proceeding should be permanently stayed.

6   Although the plaintiffs rely on the contract as the basis for their causes of action, they submit that the court ought not to give credence to the "forum selection clause" contained within. It is stated in support of this contention that the representative plaintiffs read only portions of the Member Agreement and thus had no notice of the forum selection clause. Alternatively, the plaintiffs contend, in any event, that the Washington courts are not appropriate for the conduct of this lawsuit.

7   I cannot accede to these submissions. In my view, the forum selection clause is dispositive and there is nothing in the factual record which persuades me that I should exercise my discretion so as to permit the plaintiffs to avoid the effect of the contractual provision. Accordingly, an order will go granting the relief sought by the defendant. My reasons follow.

Analysis and Disposition

8   Forum selection clauses are generally treated with a measure of deference by Canadian courts. Madam Justice Huddart, writing for the court in *Sarabia v. "Oceanic Mindoro"* (1996), 4 C.P.C. (4th) 11 (B.C.C.A.), leave to appeal denied [1997] S.C.C.A. No. 69, adopts the view that forum selection clauses should be treated the same as arbitration agreements. She states at 20:

> Since forum selection clauses are fundamentally similar to arbitration agreements, ... there is no reason for forum selection clauses not to be treated in a manner consistent with the deference shown to arbitration agreements. Such deference to forum selection clauses achieves greater international commercial certainty, shows respect for the agreements that the parties have signed, and is consistent with the principle of international comity.

9   Huddart J.A. further states at 21 that "a court is not bound to give effect to an exclusive jurisdiction clause" but that the choice of the parties should be respected unless "there is strong cause to override the agreement." The burden for a showing of a "strong cause" rests with the plaintiff and the threshold to be surpassed is beyond the

mere "balance of convenience". The approach taken by Huddart J.A. is consistent with that adopted by courts in Ontario. (See *Holo-Deck Adventures Ltd. v. Orbotron Inc.* (1996), 8 C.P.C. (4th) 376 (Gen. Div.); *Mithras Management Ltd. v. New Visions Entertainment Corp.* (1992), 90 D.L.R. (4th) 726 (Ont. Gen. Div.)).

10   The plaintiffs contend, first, that regardless of the deference to be shown to forum selection clauses, no effect should be given to the particular clause at issue in this case because it does not represent the true agreement of the parties. It is the plaintiffs submission that the form in which the Member Agreement is provided to potential members of MSN is such that it obscures the forum selection clause. Therefore, the plaintiffs argue, the clause should be treated as if it were the fine print in a contract which must be brought specifically to the attention of the party accepting the terms. Since there was no specific notice given, in the plaintiffs' view, the forum selection clause should be severed from the Agreement which they otherwise seek to enforce.

11   The argument advanced by the plaintiffs relies heavily on the alleged deficiencies in the technological aspects of electronic formats for presenting the terms of agreements. In other words, the plaintiffs contend that because only a portion of the Agreement was presented on the screen at one time, the terms of the Agreement which were not on the screen are essentially "fine print".

12   I disagree. The Member Agreement is provided to potential members of MSN in a computer readable form through either individual computer disks or via the Internet at the MSN website. In this case, the plaintiff Rudder, whose affidavit was filed on the motion, received a computer disk as part of a promotion by MSN. The disk contained the operating software for MSN and included a multi-media sign up procedure for persons who wished to obtain the MSN service. As part of the sign-up routine, potential members of MSN were required to acknowledge their acceptance of the terms of the Member Agreement by clicking on an "I Agree" button presented on the computer screen at the same time as the terms of the Member Agreement were displayed.

13   Rudder admitted in cross-examination on his affidavit that the entire agreement was readily viewable by using the scrolling function on the portion of the computer screen where the Membership Agreement was presented. Moreover, Rudder acknowledged that he "scanned" through part of the Agreement looking for "costs" that would be charged by MSN. He further admitted that once he had found the provisions relating to costs, he did not read the rest of the Agreement. An excerpt from the transcript of Rudder's cross-examination is illustrative:

Q. 314. I will now take you down to another section. I am now looking at heading 15, which is entitled "General", and immediately underneath that is subsection

15.1. Now, do I take it, when you were scanning, you would have actually scanned past this, and you would have at least seen there was a heading that said "General"? Is that fair? Or did you not even scan all the way through?

A.   I did not go all the way down, I can honestly say. Once I found out what it would cost me, that is where I would stop.

Q. 315. So, I take it that you did not read 15.1?

A.   No, I definitely did not read this, no.

Q. 316. I now have 15.4 on the screen, and presumably you did not read that either?

A. No, I did not.

Q. 317. I take it, during the whole signup process that you did, you did the whole thing online on the computer ...

A. Yes.

Q. 318. ... using the disk? And we will come to the connection. You did not have any voice communication with MSN?

A. No.

Q. 319. Or with Microsoft Corporation?

A. No.

Q. 320. You did not have any written correspondence with them at the time of signup?

A. No.

Q. 321. All right. Now, I take it that, after doing the review of this that you did do, you clicked, "I agree"? Is that what you did?

A. After I was satisfied with what it was going to cost me, I agreed.

14   I have viewed the Member Agreement as it was presented to Rudder during the sign up procedure. All of the terms of the Agreement are displayed in the same format. Although, there are certain terms of the Agreement displayed entirely in upper-case letters, there are no physical differences which make a particular term of the agreement more difficult to read than any other term. In other words, there is no fine print as that term would be defined in a written document. The terms are set out in plain language, absent words that are commonly referred to as "legalese". Admittedly, the entire Agreement cannot be displayed at once on the computer screen, but this is not materially different from a multi-page written document which requires a party to turn the pages. Furthermore, the structure of the sign-up procedure is such that the potential member is presented with the terms of membership twice during the process and must signify acceptance each time. Each time the potential member is provided with the option of disagreeing which terminates the process. The second time the terms are displayed occurs during the online portion of the process and at that time, the potential member is advised via a clear notice on the computer screen of the following:

> ... The membership agreement includes terms that govern how information about you and your membership may be used. To become a MSN Premier member, you must select "I Agree" to acknowledge your consent to the terms of the membership agreement. If you click "I Agree" without reading the membership agreement, you are still agreeing to be bound by all of the terms of the membership agreement, without limitation ...."

15   On cross-examination, Rudder admitted to having seen the screen containing the notice. In order to replicate the conditions portions of the cross-examination were conducted while Rudder was being led through an actual sign-up process including the online connection portion. While online, and after having been shown the notice posted above, Rudder responded to questioning as follows:

Q. 372. All right. You see immediately below the printing that we have just read, a rectangular box that says, "MSN Premier Membership Rules"?

A. Yes.

Q. 373. And, below that, a larger white box that says, "Please click MSN Membership Rules and read the membership agreement"?

A. Yes.

Q. 374. Did you read the phrase that I just stated in the big white box?

A. No. What I probably did ... I can't say for sure ... is I probably just went to "I Agree", and then "Next".

Q. 375. Did you understand, when you clicked "I Agree" on this occasion, that you were agreeing to was something that was going to govern your legal relationship surrounding your use of MSN?

A. If you are asking me if I made a mental note, or if I had knowledge of that, no, I did not really pay attention to that. That is a common practice when I sign up on anything. Like I said, my main concern is what the costs are.

16   It is plain and obvious that there is no factual foundation for the plaintiffs' assertion that any term of the Membership Agreement was analogous to "fine print" in a written contract. What is equally clear is that the plaintiffs seek to avoid the consequences of specific terms of their agreement while at the same time seeking to have others enforced. Neither the form of this contract nor its manner of presentation to potential members are so aberrant as to lead to such an anomalous result. To give effect to the plaintiffs' argument would, rather than advancing the goal of "commercial certainty", to adopt the words of Huddart J.A. in *Sarabia,* move this type of electronic transaction into the realm of commercial absurdity. It would lead to chaos in the marketplace, render ineffectual electronic commerce and undermine the integrity of any agreement entered into through this medium.

17   On the present facts, the Membership Agreement must be afforded the sanctity that must be given to any agreement in writing. The position of selectivity advanced by the plaintiffs runs contrary to this stated approach, both in principle and on the evidence, and must be rejected. Moreover, given that both of the representative plaintiffs are graduates of law schools and have a professed familiarity with Internet services, their position is particularly indefensible.

18   Having found that the terms of the Member Agreement, including the forum selection clause, bind the plaintiffs, I turn to a consideration of whether it is appropriate to exercise my discretion to override the forum clause agreed to by the parties. In my view, the submissions made by the defendant are compelling. On the facts of this case, it would not be appropriate for this court to permit the plaintiff to continue this action in Ontario contrary to the forum selection clause.

19   Simply put, I find that the plaintiffs have not met the burden of showing a "strong cause" as to why the forum selection clause should not be determinative. In *Sarabia*, Huddart J.A. referred to the English case, *"Eleftheria" (The) (Cargo Owners) v. "Eleftheria" (The),* [1969] 2 All E.R. 641, as the decision most often followed in Canada in setting out the factors that a court will consider in determining whether it should exercise its discretion and refuse to enforce a forum selection clause in an agreement.

20   The factors to consider may be paraphrased as follows:

(1)   in which jurisdiction is the evidence on issues of fact situated, and the effect of that on the convenience and expense of trial in either jurisdiction;

(2)   whether the law of the foreign country applies and its differences from the domestic law in any respect;

(3)   the strength of the jurisdictional connections of the parties;

(4)   whether the defendants desire to enforce the forum selection clause is genuine or merely an attempt to obtain a procedural advantage;

(5)   whether the plaintiffs will suffer prejudice by bringing their claim in a foreign court because they will be

(a)   deprived of security for the claim; or

(b)   be unable to enforce any judgment obtained; or

(c)   be faced with a time-bar not applicable in the domestic court; or

(d)   unlikely to receive a fair trial.

21   When these factors are applied within the factual matrix of this case, it is apparent that the plaintiffs cannot meet the threshold of a "strong cause". Most of the activities associated with the provision of services pursuant to the Member Agreements that are the subject of the allegations in the Statement of Claim are carried out in King County, Washington. This includes the business management of accounts of MSN members, member authentication, policy-making regarding member accounts, billing and customer service. All of the computers in which MSN content and information are contained are located in King County. The sheer size of the intended class means that there is a potential that voluminous amounts of billing statements and related information, which is most likely to be located in Washington, will be required as evidence. Furthermore, the MSN witnesses are located at the company's center of operations in King County.

22   Since I have found that the forum selection clause applies in this case, by operation of that clause the choice of law agreed to by the parties is the law of the State of Washington. Regardless of whether this action where tried in Ontario or elsewhere, the law to be applied would remain the same.

23   Microsoft has demonstrated substantial connection to the State of Washington, and in particular to King County. The plaintiffs, on the other hand, propose to represent a Canada-wide class whose connections to Ontario are not readily apparent on the evidence before the court. Class proceedings may be conducted under both the federal and state court systems in the State of Washington and while the test for certification may be somewhat more advantageous to the plaintiffs in Ontario, it is not sufficiently so as to permit me to ignore the other factors which clearly favour the defendant in this case. Moreover, in the interests of international comity, and in the absence of any evidence to the contrary, there is nothing to suggest that the plaintiffs would not receive a fair trial in the State of Washington. Indeed, considering that the defendant is resident there, it would be more advantageous to the plaintiffs, in respect of enforcement, if a judgment were obtained from a court in that jurisdiction.

24   I note in passing that this forum selection clause has been upheld on appeal in an intended class proceeding in the State of New Jersey. (*Caspi v. The Microsoft Network*, L.L.C., 732 A.2d 528 (N.J. App. 1999).

25   In view of my disposition on the first point, it is unnecessary to deal with the forum non conveniens and service ex juris arguments.

26   The defendant shall have the relief requested. The action brought by the plaintiffs in Ontario is permanently stayed. The defendant shall have its costs of this motion, which, by agreement of the parties will be fixed by the court and payable forthwith. Counsel may make brief written submissions with respect to costs within two weeks of the date of release of these reasons.

QUESTIONS

1. The plaintiffs thought that the clause in the contract with Microsoft that determined jurisdiction should not bind them. What were their arguments? Did the court agree? Explain.

2. Even if they were bound by the jurisdiction clause, the plaintiffs said that it would be inappropriate for the court to give effect to it. What were their arguments in this regard? Did the court agree? Explain.

3. Why did the court say that "regardless of whether the action was tried in Ontario or elsewhere, the law to be applied would remain the same"?

4. Why did the court say that "it would be more advantageous to the plaintiffs, in respect of enforcement, if a judgment were obtained from a court in that jurisdiction [i.e. Washington state]"?

Rozsa v. Barclays Bank, Darier Hentsch

[2000] O.J. No. 4158

Application for leave to appeal dismissed May 2, 2001 in the Ontario Superior Court of Justice.

Ontario Superior Court of Justice

October 17, 2000.

Even though there was a choice of forum clause in this case, the court decided not to give effect to it.

1   **COO J**. (endorsement):— This is a motion by the moving Darier Hentsch defendants, Swiss bankers, for an order staying the action against them and also staying the crossclaim against them by the Barclays defendants.

2   The action against the rest of the defendants is for fraudulent misconduct on their part in connection with how approximately $1.5 million US disappeared from the plaintiff's grasp and control. There is a claim that the Barclays defendants were involved in a conspiracy with these defendants that led to the plaintiff's loss of funds.

3   The money was borrowed by the plaintiff from Darier Hentsch, ultimately placed in an account in a Bahamas branch of the defendant Barclays, and came to be withdrawn in circumstance giving rise to the claims of fraud. There are claims against the moving defendants and the Barclays defendants founded on negligent money transfer or transfers in clear violation of instructions as to how the money was to flow electronically from Darier Hentsch to its destination.

4   The defendants alleged to have been directly involved in the fraudulent conduct have been served, have not defended and have been noted in default.

5   The Barclays defendants were served outside Ontario without leave, in reliance on rule 17.02(o), as necessary or proper parties to a proceeding properly brought against another person served in Ontario. The defendant, United Investment Funds Inc., is an Ontario company that was served in this province and is alleged to have been a participant in the fraud upon the plaintiff that produced his loss. The Barclays defendants attorned to the jurisdiction of this Court, delivered a statement of defence and have crossclaimed against the moving party defendants for indemnity for any sum they might be found liable to pay the plaintiff. They deny participating, through their Nassau manager of the time, the co-defendant Wallace, in the conspiracy alleged. Wallace is one of the Barclays defendants, represented by the same law firm. There is no crossclaim brought against him by Barclays themselves.

6   The moving party defendants have brought this motion and have not yet delivered a statement of defence to the claim or crossclaim. They assert that they and the plaintiff agreed in writing that any legal dispute between them of the sort reflected in these proceedings would be governed by Swiss law and that the courts in Geneva would have exclusive jurisdiction to deal with such litigation. They also take the position that, any proper law or jurisdiction agreement aside, Ontario is not a proper forum for the claim and crossclaim against them, and Switzerland is.

7   I have concluded that there was the agreement alleged between the plaintiff and the Swiss bankers and that it applied to the transaction that is the subject matter of the plaintiff's claim against them. The language applicable and circumstances in which it came to be accepted and made part of the banking arrangements between the parties will support no other interpretation. There is no need for the moving parties to rely on general conditions to which there is repeated reference in the banking documents. The original and follow-up account material will support no other conclusion. I cannot accept that there is any possibility that the parties, or either of them, were under a misunderstanding about the applicability of the proper law and forum terms to the issues raised in the main action.

8   It is conceded that does not end the matter. There is authority in the Court to override such forum provisions to avoid chaos in the litigious process and to accomplish the interests of justice, recognizing that such terms are entitled to great respect, their reliability being of major importance in the electronic world of finance in which transactions such as the present ones play out, with perhaps little or no regard to geography.

9   The moving parties make a second point equally relied on, that wherever the proper forum may be for this case, it is not Ontario. All counsel agree that there is no obvious right place for this trial. Much of the dealing that actually led to the disappearance of the plaintiff's money occurred, if there can be said in all this to be some geographical point, in Nassau. The money was sent from, and some alleged negligent conduct occurred, again if it can be said to be capable of real geographical location, in Switzerland. The electronic processing took place through network facilities, whether on the Internet or otherwise, without meaningful geographical reference points in the new digital world.

10   The plaintiff's preliminary right to choose his jurisdiction is an element to be borne in mind, but in my view is not a factor of powerful significance in this case. It is not here a matter of a plaintiff choosing to litigate 'at home', since he lives in Calgary and air travel must be viewed as a different thing from the old days of having to get on a train to travel for days. This is not a case in which the plaintiff has in a calculated way sought to choose a forum for tactical advantage.

11   The location of prospective witnesses and their importance does not direct the mind to any single place. There are bankers in Geneva. The plaintiff is in Calgary. The Barclays manager of the time in Nassau is now in Malta. Barclays facilities not in Canada and not in Switzerland played their part in money transfer. Some of the defendants who have not defended may well still be in the Bahamas, California, New Jersey and New York. Their evidence might be required, by whatever means, to establish loss and cause. The alleged Ontario corporate defrauder probably is still "here", whatever that may mean, but there is no real evidence that it has any corporate mind here now. Certain local employees of the moving parties' Ontario and Quebec corporate operations are in those provinces, although how significant their testimony will be on an almost tangential claim against them strikes me as open to question, not because they have nothing to say on the point but because it looks as though what they have to say is unchallengeably correct, and in any event irrelevant to the plaintiff's real efforts to make out liability on the part of the Swiss bankers.

12   All counsel agree that the physical location of documents is not a matter of consequence in this case.

13   Without wishing to introduce parochial considerations, there may arguably be certain perceived juridical advantages to everyone in leaving the case where it is. There would be discovery of the parties, with special emphasis on the Nassau manager of Barclays.

14   There is at the very least uncertainty as to how it would be possible to litigate conveniently or at all, the fraud, conspiracy, bankers' negligence and contributory negligence claims in Geneva; certainly not without staggering additional expense to those already embroiled in the litigation here.

15   There is no practical solution to the problem of what to do about the present action going forward in all its parties except the moving parties, without substantial duplication of client, lawyer and judicial effort. There is nothing realistic about letting the plaintiff's claim proceed against Barclays and their ex-manager, and at the same time barring be stayed, but not the crossclaim, the practical result for all would be absurd.

16   It is true that Barclays cannot, simply by attorning to the jurisdiction of the Ontario court, deprive the moving parties of their right to assert contractual obligations and their argument that the litigation has no real connection with Ontario, and, contract aside, has more connection to Switzerland, and certainly more to Nassau, where seemingly no one wants to go. Any action commenced in Nassau against the moving party defendants and some or all of the present defendants would of course be subject to the same attack on the points of contract and forum. That emphasizes the point that it is the whole of the litigation that must, in justice to all parties, be considered.

17   I am going to dismiss this motion, because I think that it would be wrong simply to apply the contractual choice sensible and practical forum for disposition of all aspects of the matter, whether or not one uses such emotive words as "clear" and "massive". This is not a case of forum shopping. There is no valid suggestion that the moving parties are thus deprived of any substantive or procedural rights or that, travel to Toronto from Geneva aside, they are unjustly plaintiff is without resources to take care of costs and disbursements. The action is case-managed and can therefore move expeditiously and in an organized manner to a proper determination, which I am sure is what all the parties, probably even those who have not defended, desire.

18   This motion was reasonably and legitimately brought and submitted to the Court. Costs will be to the cause. If counsel wish costs to be fixed I am prepared to undertake that task, but only if they are fairly close to agreement, failing which they may be assessed, if required, in due course.

QUESTIONS

1. What justification is there for the moving party defendant's assertion that the law of Switzerland should apply to this litigation, and that the courts in Geneva have exclusive jurisdiction to deal with the litigation?

2. What factors are there that connect this dispute with Ontario?

3. Why did the court in Ontario decide to exercise jurisdiction in this matter?

4. Do you think that the circumstances of this case are significantly different from those in the Rudder v. Microsoft case? Is the court justified in refusing to give effect to the choice of forum clause?

chapter thirty-four

Electronic Commerce

Peinet Inc. v. O'Brien
(c.o.b. Island Services Network (ISN))

[1995] PEIJ No. 68, 130 Nfld&PEIR 313, 40 CPC (3d) 58, 61 CPR (3d) 334

Prince Edward Island Supreme Court - Trial Division

Judgment: May 8, 1995.

This case illustrates that users of domain names can be vulnerable to legal action if they violate intellectual property rights belonging to others. With the rapid pace of technological development, one must be careful both to protect business names and goodwill and not to infringe on the ownership rights of others. This case also shows the difficulty that judges can have in keeping abreast of new technologies and how those technologies fit into the traditional framework of protection given to intellectual property rights.

MacDONALD C.J.: The plaintiff seeks an interlocutory injunction preventing the defendants from using the name PEI.NET or any similar name or address which may be confused by the public with the corporate name of the plaintiff. The action is one of "passing off". Throughout this decision I shall refer to the two named defendants as "the defendant".

Facts

The parties are in agreement on most of the facts. The plaintiff was incorporated on July 30, 1993. It provides network services to its clients including access to Internet. Internet is a world-wide computer network. In order to gain access to Internet, it is necessary to obtain a 'feed' from a national distributor such as CA Net in Canada or some other national access provider. The plaintiff is a member of CA Net. All subscribers to Internet obtain a 'domain name', which is really an electronics address. CA Net provides domain names to its customers using the following format: name. province.ca. This would mean the regional internet provider in Nova Scotia would have the name: nsnet.ns.ca. The plaintiff as the regional Internet provider in Prince Edward Island was given the name: peinet.pe.ca.

After becoming incorporated, the plaintiff alleges it took extensive steps to develop public awareness of itself. The defendant, Kevin O'Brien, was one of the plaintiff's employees. He remained with the plaintiff until October, 1994 when he was dismissed. Mr. O'Brien then formed his own business as an Internet provider under the name Island Services Network. He was assigned the domain name pei.net from a United States provider. In the affidavit of James Hill, President of the plaintiff, it is stated the defendant was assigned the domain name PEI.NET using upper case letters. The destination is stated to be important according to the defendant.

The plaintiff states that the defendant has communicated to his clients, potential clients, other internet users and the public generally that he can be reached at PEI.NET. The plaintiff refers to an article of January 21,1995 in the local newspaper The Guardian. In that article, describing the defendant's efforts at starting up a new company, the following sentence appeared: "O'Brien can be contacted at 892-4476 or at the e-mail address info@pei.net."

Mr. O'Brien states that when he was interviewed by The Guardian he gave the above address, however, it never was used by him. Further, he points out that in response to the plaintiff's concern he went to the newspaper and had a correction inserted in the publication of January 27, 1995, as follows:

Clearing the Record Island Services Network can be reached at the e-mail address info @ isn.net on the Internet. A January 21 news story about the new Internet provider gave an incorrect e-mail address.

The plaintiff also refers, in support of its allegation that the defendant was using its domain name, PEI.NET, to a letter to the plaintiff from the defendant on January 5, 1995. The defendant, at the bottom of the letter, gave the address as:

Box 988 Cornwall, Consult pei.net (after Jan. 9th)

Mr. O'Brien states that this was his only indiscretion. The defendant states he took all measures possible after being informed of the plaintiff's concern not to use the offending domain name of the plaintiff.

As stated, the plaintiff alleges the defendant listed the name PEI.NET on Internet. However, the defendant states the listing used lower case letters and would not have been confused with the plaintiff who used upper case letters. The defendant said the concern of the plaintiff that he would receive business destined for the plaintiff through the e-mail service is unfounded and there would have been no confusion.

Finally, the plaintiff refers to the correspondence between the parties' attorneys. On January 5, 1995 the plaintiff's attorney wrote to the defendant demanding that he cease using the domain name PEI.NET. This letter was extremely confrontational and undoubtedly got matters off on the wrong footing. It was followed up by a letter from the defendant's attorney on January 9th in which it was stated the defendant was using the domain name 'isn.net' but without prejudice to its right to use the domain name 'pei.net' in the future. This was followed by a further letter on January 10, from the plaintiff's lawyer demanding that the defendant 'de-list' the name PEI.NET from Internet.

Undoubtedly, there was some confusion by the plaintiff as to the domain name being used by the defendant as the plaintiff kept referring to upper case letters while the defendant stated the name was registered in lower case letters. The final correspondence was from the defendant's attorney on January 13, when he stated the defendant would not de-list because the domain name was assigned to him by the Internet network and was governed by the conventions of Internet.

The defendant, in referring to his efforts to satisfy the plaintiff, filed an affidavit from Peter Richards, Managing Editor of the Buzz magazine. Mr. Richards states that on January 8th his company was contacted to change the name pei.net to isn.net in advertising for Island Services Network. The defendant also filed an affidavit from Curtis Duckworth, of Graphic Communications Inc., who states he prepared communication materials for the defendant containing the name pei.net when Internet addresses were being used. However, he states that "about January 5th" this was suspended and about two weeks later Island Services Network requested the name pei.net be changed to isn.net on all communication material.

A further affidavit filed by the defendant is from Peter Rukavina who stated his company, Digital Island, assisted Island Services Network in registering the domain name isn.net with Internet on January 6, 1995. He stated that after January 6, no technical reference to the domain name pei.net existed in Island Services Network Internet host computer. Finally, the defendant filed a fax from the InterNIC Domain Register, Duane Stone, who states he was contacted on January 6, 1995 and asked to register that day the name ISN.NET, which he did, despite their usual time being two to three weeks to change a listing. The correspondence from Mr. Stone used upper case letters further adding to the confusion.

The plaintiff asks for an injunction restraining the defendant from using the domain name of PEI.NET. The plaintiff uses upper case letters. There is no evidence that the defendant used such a domain name, rather the name pei.net was used. The plaintiff also states that the defendant by using the domain name PEI.NET confused the public as to the identity of the plaintiff and defendant, however, it is to be noted that the plaintiff's name is PEINET INC. and the plaintiff does not use a period to separate PEI and NET.

The defendant states that anyone using the internet network would not confuse the plaintiff and the defendant. The defendant states anyone intending to contact the plaintiff using its domain name would not be able to contact the defendant and vice versa. The plaintiff did not answer that allegation.

The whole area of the use of the internet network and its conventions is new to the Court. I find that the plaintiff has only made superficial submissions without explaining the Internet system. The plaintiff merely filed a short affidavit of its president, which leaves much to be desired insofar as an explanation of Internet is concerned. The plaintiff's president did not give viva voce evidence to further expand on his affidavit. The defendant, Kevin O'Brien, did give direct evidence. He raised sufficient concerns to cast doubt on the plaintiff's case. It must be remembered that the burden is upon the plaintiff to prove its case.

Even if the plaintiff had proven that the defendant's use of the domain name pei.net was an infringement of the plaintiff's use of the name PEINET Inc., I am of the opinion that the plaintiff has not established all of the elements of a passing-off action. The Supreme Court of Canada in *Ciba-Giggy Canada Ltd. v. Apoten Inc.* [1992] 3 S.C.R. 120, 95 D.L.R. (4th) 385 has recently stated that the three components of a passing off action are; (1) the existence of goodwill; (2) deception of the public due to a misrepresentation; and (3) actual or potential damage to the plaintiff.

The plaintiff has failed to establish that the defendants had misrepresented the public. I do not consider the limited use the defendants had of pei.net to be sufficient to meet the component of deception of the public due to misrepresentation. It must be remembered that the defendants did not operate or use the plaintiff's company name of PEINET. Basically all the defendants did was, for a very short period of time, use a "telephone" number that was the same as the plaintiff's name. This use of the same name consisted of a reference to it in a newspaper article, not an advertisement, and a listing on Internet, also for a very short period of time.

The misrepresentation must lead or likely lead the public to believe that the goods or services offered by the defendant are the goods and services of the plaintiff. That has not been established.

The plaintiff has shown no actual damage loss. Neither will there be a potential loss to the plaintiff as the defendant has agreed to delist the domain name pei.net from its Internet server.

Neither am I satisfied that the plaintiff has established himself in business under its trade name for such a reasonable time and to such a reasonable extent that it has acquired a reputation under that trade name that would prevent the defendants from using a similar name: Remedies in Tort, Klar, Linden, Cherniak, Kryworuk, pp. 19-21.

In the circumstances I would dismiss the application. There shall be no order for costs.

QUESTIONS

1. What has to be proved to succeed in an action for passing off?
2. Why did the court decide that passing off had not been proved here?
3. What is the effect of an interlocutory injunction?
4. What should a business do to protect its business name?

Saskatoon Star Phoenix Group Inc. v. Noton

[2001] S.J. No. 275, 2001 SKQB 153, 2001 12 CPR 9 (4th) 4, 2001 206 SaskR 106, [2001] 9 WWR 63,

2001 5 CPC (5th) 345

Saskatchewan Court of Queen's Bench

March 28, 2001.

In the following case, the plaintiff is applying for permanent injunctive relief (among other remedies) in an action for "passing off". Again, the case involves alleged misuse of domain names.

1   **LAING J**.:— The plaintiff requests an assessment of damages and an order for permanent injunctive relief with respect to its claim of "passing off" brought against the defendant, which claim has now been noted for default. The defendant was served with notice of this hearing, but did not appear. The facts supporting the claim are set out in affidavit material submitted at the time an interlocutory injunction was granted against the defendant, and additional affidavit material filed for this hearing.

Facts

2   The plaintiff carries on the business of publishing The StarPhoenix, a Saskatoon daily newspaper. The newspaper is the largest daily in Saskatchewan and is widely distributed throughout the province. The name StarPhoenix has been associated with the paper for decades.

3   The plaintiff maintains an internet website with the domain name and address "www.thestarphoenix.com". The main page of the website contains the current day's lead news stories from The StarPhoenix along with advertising paid for by the plaintiff's customers. This main page is the first page that members of the public see when they search for The StarPhoenix on the Internet.

4   Sometime between July and November 2000, the defendant created an Internet website with the domain name and address "http: saskatoonstarphoenix.com" (hereinafter referred to as the "Noton StarPhoenix site). The defendant set up the main page of the Noton StarPhoenix site to look exactly the same as the plaintiff's main page except:

(a)   He substituted his own advertising for the plaintiff's top banner advertising;

(b)   The bottom of his page states "Noton Inc. now offers FREE Internet Access & FREE Website Hosting CLICK HERE";

> (c)   His page contains a scrolling message in the bottom bar of the browser that "saskatoonstarphoenix.com is designed, hosted and marketed by Noton Inc."

A member of the public who is viewing the Noton StarPhoenix site does not see all of the advertising placed by the plaintiff for viewing on its site, and instead, sees advertising placed by the defendant.

5   The Noton StarPhoenix site was set up to be located by members of the public when they conducted an internet search for the plaintiff's site by establishing "metatags" (which are used as key words to locate search results) for the website that contained repeated variations of "StarPhoenix", "Saskatoon StarPhoenix", "newspaper", and combinations of the same. In the case of a member of the public who is looking for the plaintiff's website in relation to The StarPhoenix, that person is likely to enter as search words exactly the words that the defendant has established as his metatags as set out above.

6   The plaintiff asserts and it is accepted, that in choosing the domain name he did, and in using the metatags he has chosen, the defendant was trying to attract members of the public who were looking for the plaintiff's website.

7   The defendant also maintains a website for "Noton Inc." At that site the defendant advertises the sale of domain names. Included among the domain names he offers for sale are:

> (a)   http://thestarphoenix.com
>
> (b)   http://starphoenix.com

He also maintains a website for "http://shoppingonlinemadeeasy.com". On this website listed under "courtesy links" is "The StarPhoenix". When a person clicks on this courtesy link, he or she is taken to the Noton StarPhoenix site.

8   In October 2000 an employee of The StarPhoenix became aware the defendant had created the Noton StarPhoenix site. He telephoned the defendant and requested that he discontinue his StarPhoenix website and cease offering the domain names, including the name StarPhoenix, for sale. The defendant refused. On November 3, 2000 counsel for the plaintiff hand delivered a letter to the defendant which brought to his attention the concerns of The StarPhoenix. This letter states in part as follows:

> Through your use of domain names including thestarpheonix.com, starpheonix.com and saskatoonstarphoenix.com you have:
>
> 1.   Appropriated copyrighted information of my client;
>
> 2.   Appropriated the trade name and business name of my client;
>
> 3.   Damaged my client's reputation and ability to conduct its normal business through association of my client's name and copyrighted information with your name, advertising and banners; and
>
> 4.   Passed yourself off to the public as my client.

In so doing you are in breach of copyright, you are in breach of my client's trade name rights, you are in breach of my client's business name rights, you are guilty of damage to my client's reputation, you are guilty of damage to my client's business and you are guilty of the statutory and common law tort of passing off.

9   The defendant's response to the foregoing letter was to telephone the lawyer, and advise him that he would continue to use the site. However, he did offer to sell the "StarPhoenix" domain names to the plaintiff and indicated this was the sole reason for his having registered the domain names in the first place; namely, to sell them back to the persons who would have a business interest in retaining their name on the Web.

10   As a result of the foregoing response, the plaintiff applied for an interlocutory injunction pending trial which this court granted on December 21, 2000. The day after the issuance of the interlocutory injunction he was interviewed by a StarPhoenix reporter as part of a larger article on "Cybersquatting" as the domain name game has come to be called. Quotes from the article, which the reporter swears in an affidavit are accurate include:

> Our pitch is that it's a basic responsibility to their users to take this name back. We'll continue marketing off it until someone buys it.

> You should cover all your bases on the Internet.

> We do a lot of quick flips. We register a name, it's a really good name, and instead of charging $50,000 we'll say $100 is our minimum bid and we'll sell it for $500. . . .

> We want to have a constant flow. If the Saskatchewan government sat down with us, we'd sell the name [governmentofsaskatchewan.com] for $250. We price our things so that people are actually interested.

11   The plaintiff tendered two e-mails received by it from persons complaining about the Noton StarPhoenix site. One e-mail dated November 28, 2000 states:

> Your recent alliance with Shop Shopping has made viewing your site a waste of my time as it takes far too long. While I have enjoyed catching up with news from Saskatoon I have decided I will look elsewhere.

A second one dated December 8, 2000 states:

> Being a former Saskatoonian (I now live in Vancouver), I like to check up on the events happening back home. However i [sic] am quite annoyed now that I have to go through a big commercial link to get there. Is there another way? If not i [sic] will probably delete this bookmark.

The Law of Passing Off

12   There is no need to review the law of "passing off" in any detail. The Supreme Court of Canada in *Ciba-Geigy Canada Ltd. v. Apotex Inc.,* [1992] 3 S.C.R. 120 reviewed the law in this area including the English Court of Appeal decision in *Reckitt & Colman Products Ltd. v. Borden Inc.,* [1990] 1 All E.R. 873, and concluded:

> The three necessary components of a passing-off action are thus: the existence of goodwill, deception of the public due to a misrepresentation and actual or potential damage to the plaintiff.

13   The plaintiff has established that it is the owner of the goodwill associated with the name StarPhoenix. It has also established that certain members of the public were deceived into believing that the Noton StarPhoenix site was the plaintiff's site. With respect to actual or potential damage the plaintiff admits that it cannot point to any direct pecuniary loss as a result of the defendant's activities in the form of can-

celled subscriptions or lost advertising revenue, but does claim actual and potential loss of reputation for being unable to control its own website and advertising. The plaintiff relies on the English House of Lords decision in *Draper v. Trist et al.,* [1939] 3 All E.R. 513 to point out that when "passing off" has been established, damage will be presumed. In this decision Goddard L.J. at p. 526 stated in part:

> . . .The law assumes, or presumes, that, if the goodwill of a man's business has been interfered with by the passing-off of goods, damage results therefrom. He need not wait to show that damage has resulted. He can bring his action as soon as he can prove the passing-off, because it is one of the class of cases in which the law presumes that the plaintiff has suffered damage. It is in fact, I think, in the same category in this respect as is an action for libel. We know that for written defamation a plaintiff need prove no damage. He proves his defamation. So it is with a trader. The law has always been particularly tender to the reputation and goodwill of traders. If a trader is slandered in the way of his business, an action lies without proof of damage. That does not mean to say that the plaintiff cannot give evidence showing that he has suffered damage in fact. The more he can show that he has suffered damage in fact, the larger the damages he can recover. The more the defendant can show that he has suffered no damage in fact, the less he will recover.

The plaintiff has established all three necessary components in the affidavit material filed.

Damages

14   The plaintiff asks for an award of damages for loss of goodwill and reputation, punitive damages, and costs on a solicitor and client basis.

General Damages for Non-pecuniary Loss

15   Goddard L.J. in *Draper v. Trist,* supra, made the point at p. 527 that where the law presumes damage to the plaintiff, it is for the jury to determine what is fair and proper compensation to the plaintiff, without being limited to questions of what in truth are special damages (namely actual proven monetary loss). He rejected the argument that where a passing off has been established that the plaintiff is limited to nominal damages unless that plaintiff can prove actual monetary loss. He went on to point out that:

> . . .once one has established passing off, there is injury to goodwill, and this court or the jury must assess, by the best means they can, what is a fair and temperate sum to give to the plaintiff for that injury. . .

16   This point was more recently made by MacKinnon J. in *Canwest Telephone Co. Inc. et al. v. Canwest Commercial Phone Centre Ltd. et al.* (1986), 8 C.P.R. (3d) 360 (B.C.S.C.) where at p. 365 he noted that the relief ordinarily sought in a passing off action is injunctive, but nevertheless damages are also to be assessed by considering the particular circumstances of the case and deciding on a proper and a reasonable amount.

17   The following factors are relevant to the assessment of general damages in this matter:

(a)   The plaintiff filed material indicating the defendant had registered his Noton StarPhoenix site July 25, 2000. It is not clear when the defendant's website actually went into operation. As noted earlier an interlocutory injunction was issued by this court on December 21, 2000, which the defendant obeyed.

(b)   The plaintiff only learned of the defendant's activities with respect to his website at the end of October 2000. The defendant declined the plaintiff's request of November 3, 2000 to cease misrepresenting its website and carried on for the next month and a half until the injunction issued.

(c)   The nature of the damage to the plaintiff's goodwill and reputation consisted largely of inconvenience to users of it's website. The advertising content substituted by the defendant on his website was not offensive, and would not in itself have hurt the plaintiff's reputation or goodwill.

In the end result, considering the short period of time the passing off occurred, and what I perceive to be minimal damage to the plaintiff's goodwill and reputation, I conclude a general damage award of $5,000.00 is appropriate.

Punitive Damages

18   Plaintiff's counsel suggests this is an appropriate case for punitive damages on the basis the defendant:

1.   Profited from his "passing off" activity out of proportion to the plaintiff's loss;

2.   Deliberately continued the activity after being advised by the plaintiff it considered it unlawful;

3.   A deterrent element was required to prevent the defendant and/or others persisting in this type of activity.

In the end result, I do not consider this an appropriate case for punitive damages.

19   What emerges from the newspaper interview with the defendant, is that he is 22 years old, and he obtained the idea to register domain names approximately one year ago while travelling in Europe with a friend. Up until the interim injunction was issued he considered domain names a commodity which anyone could register and thereafter sell back to any person who wished to use such registered name. Newspaper articles indicate he was not alone in this belief. One such article indicates Celine Dion recently obtained a United Nations World Intellectual Property Organization Panel ruling restoring to her the right to use her name as a domain name. There was very little, if any, precedent to guide would be entrepreneurs of domain names prior to this and other recent decisions.

20   The defendant's use of the plaintiff's website material to pass off his Noton StarPhoenix site as that of the plaintiff's is in a different category than his registration and sale of domain names. It is difficult to imagine that he thought this activity was legal, and yet, tied in as it was to his overall scheme of selling back registered domain names this activity was not "so malicious, oppressive and high handed that it offended this court's sense of decency" (per Cory J. in *Hill v. Church of Scientology of Toronto,*

[1995] 2 S.C.R. 1130 at p. 1208). Punitive damages may be appropriate in the future if, after several decisions such as this, the defendant or others persist in the activity.

Injunctive Relief

21   The plaintiff is entitled to an order restraining and enjoining the defendant from:

(a)   Using the internet domain names:
http://saskatoonstarphoenix.com
http://thestarpheonix.com
http://starpheonix.com

(b)   Using the name "Star Phoenix" or any variation thereof.

(c)   Directing public attention to his internet websites in such a way as to cause or be likely to cause the public to think the defendant's website is the plaintiff's website.

22   The plaintiff also requests that the defendant be ordered to transfer to the plaintiff registration of the three domain sites referred to above. Its point is that without such an order the defendant would be free to sell the names to a third party whose use of the names would be beyond the control of the plaintiff. Given the fact the defendant admits that he is in the business of selling domain names, there is merit to this request. Therefore, it is ordered that the defendant transfer to the plaintiff registration of the three domain site names referred to above within 30 days.

Costs

23   Plaintiff's counsel in this matter requests costs on a solicitor-client basis. His point is that this was deliberate conduct on the part of the defendant after he was warned that his activity was regarded as unlawful by the plaintiff, and the plaintiff should be indemnified for the costs of the legal proceedings required to prevent the defendant from continuing the unlawful activity. Counsel for the plaintiff indicates his client has incurred costs in excess of $10,000.00 with respect to these proceedings.

24   Awards of solicitor-client costs following litigation are not the norm. The civil litigation system operates largely on a party and party cost basis as set out in the tariff to the Rules of Court. The rationale for limiting the costs available to the successful party in civil litigation, is that cost should not be so onerous as to stifle novel actions or defences which have contributed to the growth of the common law. As noted per McLachlin J. in *Young v. Young,* [1993] 8 W.W.R. 513 (S.C.C.) at p. 541:

> . . . Solicitor-client costs are generally awarded only where there has been reprehensible, scandalous or outrageous conduct on the part of one of the parties. . . .

The conduct referred to may arise in the circumstances that lead up to the litigation, or in the manner in which the litigation is conducted.

25   In *Garcia v. Crestbrook Forest Industries Ltd.* (1995), 119 D.L.R. (4th) 740 at p. 745, Lambert J.A. concluded the word reprehensible was a word of wide meaning and encompassed not only scandalous or outrageous conduct, but also encompassed milder forms of misconduct deserving of reproof or rebuke. This definition was applied by this court in *Bailey v. Registered Nurses' Assn.* (Saskatchewan), [1996] 7 W.W.R. 751.

26   In this case, the activity of the defendant that is deserving of reproof or rebuke is his unwillingness to investigate his legal position after he was warned the plaintiff regarded his activities as unlawful, and thereafter putting the plaintiff to the expense of legal proceedings to shut down this activity. He did not offer a defence to the proceedings, and indeed it is not obvious that a defence was available. Yet the defendant would not desist. In these circumstances it is reasonable that the plaintiff should receive something more than party and party costs, and it is reasonable that the defendant have brought home to him that he cannot with impunity cause other people to incur legal expense to shut down his unlawful activity, as opposed to voluntarily ceasing the same. In the end result I consider it reasonable to award costs to the plaintiff in the amount of $7,500.00.

27   Judgment accordingly.

QUESTIONS

1. What factors did the court rely on to find that the elements of an action for "passing off" had been proved?
2. Why did the court decline to award punitive damages to the plaintiff?
3. What was the most significant remedy that the court awarded?
4. Why did the court award the plaintiff costs beyond those that would be awarded on a party-and-party basis?

Braintech, Inc. v. Kostiuk

[1999] BCCA 169, [1999] BCJ No. 622, 171 DLR (4th) 46, [1999] 9 WWR 133, 120 BCAC 1, 63 BCLR (3d) 156.

British Columbia Court of Appeal; application for leave to appeal to the Supreme Court of Canada dismissed with cost (without reasons) [1999] SCCA No. 236.

March 18, 1999.

Present: Goldie, Donald and Newbury JJA.

Traditional legal ideas about what factors must be present to establish jurisdiction for a court to hear a legal dispute have to be expanded to accommodate increasing commercial use of the Internet. This case illustrates a situation where a court was unwilling to extend jurisdiction to include any location where objectionable material might be accessible on a computer screen.

The judgment of the Court was delivered by **Goldie JA.** The following is a summary of his judgment.

Braintech, Inc. brought legal action in the District Court of Harris County in the State of Texas claiming that Kostiuk defamed it and disparaged its business by transmission and publication in Texas of untruths. The court awarded Braintech a judgment in the amount of $300,000 US. Braintech then sought to enforce the judgment in British Columbia. Kostiuk defended, saying that the court in Texas did not have jurisdiction in the matter, and that he had not been personally served with any process in the Texas proceeding.

Braintech, Inc. was a developmental stage company with corporate offices located in Vancouver, British Columbia. It had research and development facilities located in Austin, Texas. Braintech was involved in the design and development of advanced recognition systems, but did not produce or sell systems. It said it was a publicly held company whose stock was bought and sold via OTC Bulletin Board trading. The OTC exchange was not in Canada. Kostiuk was alleged to have transmitted and published defamatory information about Braintech, Inc. on an Internet bulletin board called the "Silicon Investor". Kostiuk was not a resident of Texas and had no place of business there.

Under the Texas Civil Practice and Remedies Code section 17.042, a nonresident is considered as doing business in Texas if the nonresident:

"1) contracts by mail or otherwise with a Texas resident and either party is to perform the contract in whole or in part in this state;

2) commits a tort in whole or in part in this state; or

3) recruits Texas residents, directly or through an intermediary located in this state, for employment inside or outside this state."

Under section 17.044 b) *"the secretary of state is an agent for service of process on a nonresident who engages in business in this state, but does not maintain a regular place of business in this state or a designated agent for service of process, in any proceeding that arises out of the business done in this state and to which the nonresident is a party."* Under section 17.045 *"if the secretary of state is served with duplicate copies of process for a nonresident, he shall require a statement of the name and address of the nonresident's home or home office and shall immediately mail a copy of the process to the nonresident by registered or certified mail."* Braintech claimed that Kostiuk had committed a tort in Texas and served the secretary of state with the proceedings against him.

A copy of the proceedings was sent to Kostiuk at an incorrect address by registered mail. No response to the registered letter was received by the Secretary of State. Braintech filed an amended petition about three months after the original had been filed. Braintech attempted personal service of the amended petition and the process server swore an affidavit that Kostiuk had been personally served, but Kostiuk said that he did not receive the amended petition. The trial judge found in favour of Braintech saying that according to the rules in the Texas Practice and Civil Remedies Code, service had been validly effected.

Speaking for the British Columbia Court of Appeal, Mr. Justice Goldie questioned whether the trial judge's finding as to the validity of service by Texas rules was correct. He said, however, that it was unnecessary to decide the issue, because one must ask first whether the court in Texas had jurisdiction in the dispute - was there a real and substantial connection between Texas and the subject-matter of the action?

The judge pointed out that Kostiuk was not the operator of Silicon Investor, and that the bulletin board was "passive" in posting information that was accessible only to those with the means of access to it who utilized those means. The real and substantial connection relied upon was based on the alleged publication in Texas of libel that affected the interests of resident present and potential investors. Braintech had offered no proof that anyone in Texas had brought the defamatory material to an actual computer screen in Texas or read it at all, or that Kostiuk had a commercial purpose that utilized the Internet highway to enter any particular jurisdiction. Kotiuk's passive use of an out of state electronic bulletin did not constitute a real and substantial presence within Texas, and the court in Texas was not justified in exercising jurisdiction in the dispute.

The Court of Appeal allowed the appeal, set aside the judgment below and dismissed the action.

QUESTIONS

1. What facts would Braintech have had to prove to show that the court in Texas had jurisdiction in this dispute?

2. Assume the British Columbia Court of Appeal had decided that the court in Texas did have jurisdiction to decide the dispute. Do you think that Kostiuk was properly served with proceedings according to the rules in the Texas Civil Practice and Remedies Code?

3. Assume that the British Columbia Court of Appeal had decided that the court in Texas did have jurisdiction to decide this dispute. Would the Court have found that service of the proceedings was invalid because it did not follow the rules for service of proceedings in British Columbia?